How the Chin

Also by Rongxing Guo

CHINA'S POLITICAL

CROSS-BORDER RES

CROSS-CULTURAL

CULTURAL INFLU

INTERCULTURAL

TERRITORIAL DIS

THE LAND AND N
(4 VOLS)

How the Chinese Economy Works

Third Revised Edition

Rongxing Guo

palgrave
macmillan

First edition published 1999
Second edition published 2007
Third edition published 2009 by
PALGRAVE MACMILLAN

Palgrave Macmillan in the UK is an imprint of Macmillan Publishers Limited,
registered in England, company number 785998, of Houndmills, Basingstoke,
Hampshire RG21 6XS.

Palgrave Macmillan in the US is a division of St Martin's Press LLC,
175 Fifth Avenue, New York, NY 10010.

Palgrave Macmillan is the global academic imprint of the above companies
and has companies and representatives throughout the world.

Palgrave® and Macmillan® are registered trademarks in the United States,
the United Kingdom, Europe and other countries.

ISBN 978–0–230–58100–5   hardback

This book is printed on paper suitable for recycling and made from fully
managed and sustained forest sources. Logging, pulping and manufacturing
processes are expected to conform to the environmental regulations of the
country of origin.

A catalogue record for this book is available from the British Library.

A catalog record for this book is available from the Library of Congress.

10 9 8 7 6 5 4 3 2 1
18 17 16 15 14 13 12 11 10 09

Printed and bound in Great Britain by
CPI Antony Rowe, Chippenham and Eastbourne

To my wife, Yuhui, and my son, Changlei,
whose personal experiences enrich my
knowledge about the working of
the Chinese economy at
the micro-level

Contents

List of Boxes

List of Figures

List of Tables

List of Abbreviations

BECZ	trans-province border economic cooperative zone
CCP	Chinese Communist Party
CCPCC	Chinese Communist Party Central Committee
CEPA	closer economic partnership arrangement
COE	collectively-owned enterprise
CPE	centrally planned economy
CPPCC	Chinese People's Political Consultative Congress
FDI	foreign direct investment
FIE	foreign (including Taiwan, Hong Kong and Macau) invested enterprise
FYP	five-year plan
GDP	gross domestic product
GHG	greenhouse gas
GNP	gross national product
GVAO	gross value of agricultural output
GVIAO	gross value of industrial and agricultural output
GVIO	gross value of industrial output
GVSP	gross value of social product
HRS	household responsibility system
MPS	material product system
NBS	National Bureau of Statistics of China
NIE	newly industrialized economy
NMP	net material product
NPC	National People's Congress
NPL	non-performing loan
PCS	people's commune system
PPP	purchasing power parity
PRC	People's Republic of China
PSE	private, shareholding or other enterprise
RMB	renminbi, Chinese currency
SAR	special administrative region
SARS	severe acute respiratory syndrome
SEZ	special economic zone
SNA	system of national accounts

SOE	state-owned enterprise
SPC	State Planning Commission
SSB	State Statistical Bureau
TVE	township and village enterprise
WHO	World Health Organization
WTO	World Trade Organization

Foreword

The world is watching the miraculous development of the Chinese economy with a mixture of emotions: envy, hope, concern. Even a country such as India, which is experiencing its own miracle, can still cast a jealous eye at the success of the Chinese economy. Other less fortunate countries are looking to China for lessons to guide and accelerate their own development. And still others worry that China's emergence will squeeze them out of markets for their exports or their sources of energy.

The economics profession has devoted much time and effort to understanding what drives the growth of economies. Much of this research has employed cross-country regressions. Useful though such research may be, it can never provide a full understanding of the growth process in economies as *sui generis* and complex as that of China. Careful case studies employing appropriate empirical techniques offer the prospect of a much richer and deeper appreciation of the details of the growth process and of the interactions between key factors. The potential of such studies is increased several-fold when the research is undertaken by investigators with detailed local knowledge and a personal understanding of the economy being investigated. For these reasons, the Global Development Network has promoted case studies undertaken by local authors as a vital means of providing a fuller understanding of the complex process of growth. I am therefore especially pleased to write a foreword for this volume, a volume that provides such an excellent example of this approach applied to perhaps the most important growth experience in recent history.

The volume's author, Rongxing Guo, has drawn on his extensive knowledge of the Chinese economy to update and expand the 1998 edition of his book *How the Chinese Economy Works*. The coverage and content illustrate the value of in-depth case studies. Guo Rongxing examines the functioning of the economy in both the pre-reform and the post-reform periods; he explores the operation of the economy at the national and the provincial level; he investigates the exploitation of and development of natural and human resources; he analyzes the institutional evolution of the economy; and he reports on the economic and social outcomes. The richness of the material and the clarity of the analysis will perhaps make the envious countries even more so; they will certainly provide valuable information for those hoping to learn from the Chinese experience; and they will provide a firmer basis for assessing the concerns of those competing in output and input markets.

The preceding words are the foreword I wrote to the second edition of Rongxing Guo's book. I concluded by saying: "On the evidence of this contribution, one can look forward to the third edition of this volume with great anticipation." Well, the third edition is here and my expectations have been fully realized. In addition to a totally new chapter and revisions of many other chapters, Rongxing Guo has incorporated more case studies, some of which are based on his previous field inspections and micro-level surveys of small rural areas and state-owned firms. These case studies will, I am sure, prove to be very useful to researchers and students alike with an interest in the workings of the Chinese economy and make an already valuable contribution even more so.

Lyn Squire
Washington, DC
September 2008

Preface

This book is intended to provide information and explanations of the operational mechanisms of the Chinese economy during the pre- and post-reform periods and through national, regional, and local dimensions. It examines the driving forces – both exogenous and endogenous – for, and how they have influenced China's economic development for the period since the People's Republic of China (PRC) was founded in 1949, especially since 1978, when China took the decision to transform its economy from a centrally planned system to a market-oriented one. In the *How the Chinese Economy Works*, a multi-regional comparison of the Chinese economy is conducted in terms of natural and human resources, institutional evolution, and social and economic performances; and there is some clarification of the positive and negative consequences of the Chinese economic transformation.

This book was first published in the "Studies on the Chinese Economy" series in 1999. The first edition of this book was the outcome of teaching notes used at Korea University (1994), Peking University (1996), the University of Trier (1997) and the Beijing Graduate School of CUMT (1998–99). In this enlarged edition, a more complete, up-to-date set of data and information on the Chinese economy has been collected and, where appropriate, reconstructed. Specifically, in this revised edition, Chapter 6 is completely new, Chapters 1, 2, 3, 5, 8, and 10 have been subjected to significant revision and all of the other chapters are updated with new data and narratives. In addition, a number of boxed examples and chapter-end case studies are provided in this third edition.

Indeed, writing a book incorporating all of the details about how the Chinese economy works is never an easy job, since the Chinese economy *per se* is on a larger scale and perhaps more complex than any other economy in the world. This job is especially difficult for me – a native Chinese who was born in China's poorest rural area and grew during the most difficult period in recent Chinese history (here, I would like to dedicate this book to the memory of my mother (Hè Yùhuā, 1927–2005) who cared for her children with all her heart during the most difficult period of the Chinese economy). I did not receive a world-class education; and my English was taught in China and, of course, only with Chinese characteristics. Although some of the writing style has been corrected or polished throughout the three editions, some grammatical or stylistic shortcomings must remain. Nevertheless, it is still gratifying to note that, through reading a book written down by "Chinese-style" English one could have an easy understanding of how the Chinese economy has worked through the so-called socialist market system with Chinese characteristics.

Over the course of recent decades, the Chinese economy has worked, and is expected to continue working in the years to come, through a path or approach that is to some extent similar to the one that I have applied to the writing of this book – grammatically or stylistically. At the meantime, I am quite satisfactory, as I have felt that my working experience in China, including the entire writing process of all the three editions of the *How the Chinese Economy Works*, and myself as well have been becoming to some extent an inherent part of the Chinese economy.

How to use this book

In this third revised edition, I add, for the first time, chapter-end case studies, some of which are based upon my previous field inspections and micro-level surveys in China. They are, therefore, very useful for researchers and students attempting to study Chinese economics and for ordinary readers who wish to keep a close watch on China and the Chinese economy in particular. Among the subjects included in the selected chapter-end case studies are the following:

- Why the Yellow river is important.
- Who owns Lake Weishan?
- Age, gender, education and earnings.
- System dynamics – a feedback model.
- Games between radicals and conservatives.
- A tale of two companies in transition.
- Similar initial conditions, varied results.
- Fighting for rainfalls?
- Cultural influences on foreign trade.
- Overseas Chinese economics.

In each chapter one or two boxed examples are inserted where appropriate. It is hoped that this will be illuminating for readers from different academic backgrounds who are seeking to gain more knowledge about the ways in which the Chinese economy has been working.

In this third revised edition, a few ancient Chinese fables, some of which have become popular idioms (*chengyu* – a 'must-know' in the Chinese language), are selected as epigraphs. For tutors' and readers' convenience, I provide each idiom in pinyin form, followed by its Chinese characters, as follows:

- *Yi lin wei he* (以邻为壑) – Chapter 2
- *Bai nian yu ren* (百年育人) – section 3.3 of Chapter 3
- *Hui yi ji bing* (讳医忌病) – Chapter 4
- *Bing ru gao huang* (病入膏肓) – section 4.7 of Chapter 4
- *Han dan xue bu* (邯郸学步) – Chapter 5
- *Bian que zhi yan* (扁鹊之言) – section 5.5 of Chapter 5
- *Zi xiang mao dun* (自相矛盾) – Chapter 6
- *Zheng ren mai lv* (郑人买履) – Chapter 7
- *Lu ren zi yue* (鲁人之越) – Chapter 8
- *Ya miao zhu zhang* (揠苗助长) – Chapter 9
- *Dong shi xiao pin* (东施效颦) – Chapter 10
- *Jie ze er yu* (竭泽而渔) – section 10.5 of Chapter 10
- *Jing di zhi wa* (井底之蛙) – Chapter 11
- *Nan yuan bei zhe* (南辕北辙) – Chapter 12
- *Yu bang xiang zheng* (鹬蚌相争); *Yu weng de li* (渔翁得利) – section 12.4 of Chapter 12

In addition, the following notes may help readers to have a clear and concrete understanding of the entire text:

- The geographical scope of the Chinese economy covers only mainland China, although Hong Kong, Macau, and Taiwan are mentioned in a number of the chapters.
- Chinese names are customarily written in the order of family name (which is in the single syllable in most cases) followed by given name.
- Chinese names and geographic terms in mainland China are written in China's official (pinyin) form, while those outside mainland China are in the conventional form.
- Unless stated otherwise, the statistical data used in this book are from China Statistical Yearbooks (NBS, all issues).
- For the sake of convenience, specific autonomous regions and municipalities directly under the central government will be referred to alongside provinces by a single name.

Acknowledgments

The completion of this book has been facilitated by various factors. The grants from the National Science Foundation of China (1994; 1998), the National Social Science Foundation of China (1992), the Ministry of Coal Industry of China (1998), the Chinese Academy of Social Sciences (CASS, 2003), the East Asian Development Network (EADN, 2002; 2006) and the Global Development Network (GDN, 2004) and the Award for Outstanding Research on Development (GDN and Government of Japan, 2007) make it possible for me to conduct a series of field inspections in China and to collect some specific micro-level data, both of which have contributed to the writing of this book. I have also benefited from the valuable comments received from Professor Zhao Renwei (CASS). During my visits to South Korea and Germany, I benefited from many discussions with Professors Eui-Gak Hwang (Korea University) and Thomas Heberer (University of Trier). I am very grateful to Mr T.M. Farmiloe (former Publishing Director of Macmillan) and Ms Amanda Hamilton (Economics Publisher, Palgrave) for helpful suggestions on the first two editions of this book.

Many individuals and organizations have contributed to the publication of the third edition of this book. Some micro-level findings used in this book are based on the field inspections and surveys that I conducted jointly with Professor Hu Xuwei, Professor Zhao Renwei (who has also kindly granted me to use the figure in Box 5.2), Professor Li Shi, Mr Zhang Yong, Mr Guo Liqing (who also assisted me in drawing Figure 2.5), Mr Zhao Gongzheng, Mr Xing Youqiang, Ms Xie Yanhong and Ms Wang Xiaoping. I have also benefited from research assistance by Ms Wang Huayan. Furthermore, the following organizations and agencies sponsored and provided generous help in carrying out the above activities:

- Chuangda Company, Zichuan District, Shandong Province
- Development and Research Center of the State Council, Beijing
- Government of Peixian County, Jiangsu Province
- Government of Weishan County, Shandong Province
- Guangzheng Company, Zichuan District, Shandong Province
- Jinggezhang Coalmine, Tangshan City, Hebei Province
- Kailuan Group Corporation, Tangshan City, Hebei Province
- Linnanchang Coalmine, Yutian County, Hebei Province
- State Development and Reform Commission, Beijing
- Xuzhou Municipal Government, Jiangsu Province
- Zibo Mining Group, Zibo City, Shandong Province

This book also includes some previously published materials. Specifically, section 2.7 of Chapter 2 is based upon Chapter 10 of my monograph (*Cross-Border Resource Management*, Amsterdam and Boston: Elsevier, 2006, pp. 197–226); section 6.6 of Chapter 6 is based on an article published in Chinese by the *Management World* (guanli shijie) with Li Shi and Xing Youqiang (2003, pp. No. 4, pp. 103–11); and sections 11.4 and 11.6 of Chapter 11 are based on an article published by the *Asian Economic Journal* (2007, vol. 21, pp. 100–21). Thanks go to the co-authors of and the copyright owners of the above publications for their kind permission to using these materials in this edition.

Many valuable comments and suggestions on part of or the whole manuscript were received from the following individuals: Professor José María Fanelli (University of Buenos Aires, Argentina), Dr Gary Mcmahon (World Bank), Ms Isher Ahluwalia (Indian Council for Research on International Economic Relations), Professor Richard Cooper (Harvard University), Professor Amara Pongsapich (Chulalongkorn University, Thailand), Professor Leong Liew (Griffin University, Australia), Professor Shigeyuki Abe (Doshisha University, Japan), Dr Chalongphob Sussangkarn (EADN Coordinator), Dr Chia Siow Yue (Singapore Institute for International Affairs), Dr Josef T. Yap (Philippines Institute for Development Studies), Professor Zhang Yunling (CASS, China), Professor Hiro Lee (Asian Economic Journal, Japan), Dr Jun Li (University of Essex, UK), and a number of anonymous reviewers.

The final appearance of this book has benefited from helpful discussions with Mr Lyn Squire, Founder and First President of the GDN, who also generously wrote a foreword for this edition. Among the Palgrave staff contributing to the publication of this book, Miss Taiba Batool (Commissioning Editor of Economics) kept in regular communications with me when the draft was prepared. I am also grateful to Nick Brock for editing this book.

Guo Rong Xing
Beiqijia town, Beijing

Key Terms

Centrally Planned Economy (CPE) – It is based upon the supposition that 'society' (in practice, the planning agencies, under the authority of the political leadership) knows or can discover what is needed, and can issue orders incorporating these needs, while allocating the required means of production so that the needs are economically met.

Chinese Communist Party Central Committee (CCPCC) – This has been virtually the most important power body in China. Located on the Zhongnan Sea in central Beijing, Political Bureau (PB) is the standing organ of the CCPCC. The PB's members and its more powerful, standing members can be frequently found on the evening news of China's official media, including the CCTV.

Chinese People's Political Consultative Congress (CPPCC) – Under the leadership of the CCPCC, the CPPCC consists of representatives of the CCP, several democratic parties, democrats with no party affiliations, various people's organizations and ethnic groups, and other specially invited individuals. The primary functions of the CPPCC are to conduct political consultations and democratic supervisions, and to discuss and manage state affairs.

Comparative Advantage – A comparative advantage prevails for products which have the lowest opportunity cost of production. According to the law of comparative advantage, a country or region should specialize in the production of those commodities for which it has a comparative advantage.

Dual-Pricing System – Under this system, price was subject to market regulations developed in parallel with a controlled market in which price was kept almost unchanged at an officially fixed level. Because the price was higher in the market-regulated track than in the state-controlled track, supply in the free market grew rapidly, so its share in total output rose steadily. Meanwhile, the planned price was able to rise incrementally until it approached the market price when the gap between supply and demand narrowed.

Economies of Scale – The percentage increase in output exceeds the percentage increase in all inputs. Equivalently, average cost falls as output expands.

Gini Coefficient – This is prominently used as a measure of the degree of inequality in income or owned assets such as land or financial wealth. It is defined as a ratio with values ranging from 0 (perfect equality – every household or person is the same) to 1 (perfect inequality – one household or person owns everything).

Gradualism – This term is used to describe the belief that change ought to be modified in small, discrete increments rather than abrupt changes. Without considering the cost of implementation, a 'big bang' (or shock therapy) reform may have an advantage over a gradual one. However, reversing the full reform sometimes costs more than reversing a single partial or gradual reform measure.

Greenhouse Gases (GHGs) – These include such pollutants as carbon dioxide, methane and chlorofluorocarbons, among others. The GHGs are believed to have contributed to climate modification by absorbing long-wave (infrared) radiation, thereby trapping heat which would otherwise radiate into space.

Great Leap Forward (GLF) – During the period from 1958 to 1960, large quantities of materials and labor were diverted toward heavy industry in China. This resulted in serious imbalances between accumulation and consumption and between heavy industry on the one hand and agriculture and light industry on the other. During the early stages of the GLF, the harvest were poor despite high yields in the rural areas. Consequently, from 1959 onwards, agricultural production dropped spectacularly, leading to a three-year famine.

Household Responsibility System (HRS) – Under this system, each household may be able to sign a contract with the local government to obtain a certain amount of arable land and production equipment depending on the number of rural population in this family and have a production quota. As long as the household completes its quota of products to the state, it can decide freely what to produce and how to sell.

Kuznets Curve – Also called the "inverted-U" hypothesis in which economic development is accompanied at first by an increase in income disparities (or inequalities) and later by a decrease.

Market Economy – An economic system in which resource allocation decisions are guided by prices resulting from the voluntary production and purchasing decisions by private consumers and producers.

National People's Congress (NPC) – It is the supreme legislative organ of China. The NPC's representatives, coming from different regions and sectors, meet regularly in the Great Hall of the People in Beijing to discuss state affairs, to approve those whom are recommended by the CCPCC as central government officials, and to issue laws and regulations.

People's Commune System (PCS) – Under this system, land was owned collectively and the output was distributed to each household according to the work points (*gongfen*). The state purchased a major share of the grain output and distributed it to the non-agricultural population through government agencies. The PCS generally has been known to provide disincentives for the farmers to work harder.

Rent-Seeking Behavior – The use of resources in lobbying and other activities directed at securing increased profits through protective regulation or legislation.

Special Economic Zone (SEZ) – In 1980, Shenzhen next to Hong Kong, Zhuhai next to Macau, and Santou were designed as SEZs and were permitted to exercise "special policies and flexible measures" in foreign economic affairs. At the same time, Xiamen in Southeast Fujian province, which was close to Taiwan, also became a SEZ.

Map

Provincial divisions of China

If you understand others you have intelligence;
知人者智 (zhi ren zhe zhi)

If you understand yourself you are illuminated.
自知者明 (zi zhi zhe ming)

If you overcome others you have strength;
胜人者有力 (sheng ren zhe you li)

If you overcome yourself you are powerful.
自胜者强 (zi sheng zhe qiang)

– (Daode Jing, 33: 1–4)

1
A Brief History of China

Originally proliferated by the Tao,
　(*dao sheng yi*)
One gives birth to Two in opposition.
　(*yi sheng er*)
The Two begets Three in triangle under which
　(*er sheng san*)
everything in the world is ready to be created.
　(*san sheng wanwu*)

– Laozi (*c.*600 BC)

1.1　The origins of the nation

Shaped as a rooster, and situated in East Asia, China has a 14,500 km coastline along the East China Sea, the Korean Bay, the Yellow Sea and the South China Sea. It has a total length of approximately 22,140 km land boundaries with North Korea, Russia and Mongolia in the northeast and north, Kazakhstan, Kyrgyzstan, Tajikistan, Afghanistan and Pakistan in the west, India and Nepal in the southwest, and Myanmar, Laos and Vietnam in the south. Over the course of thousands of years of history, there have been many legendary stories about this huge nation, as well as about its people, culture and history.

The geography of the Chinese nation has shaped its distinctive culture and philosophy. The Yellow (Huang) river – which originates at the foot of the Kunlun mountains in the west and flows over 5,000 kilometers eastward to the Pacific Ocean – has been generally regarded as the cradle of the Chinese nation. It was along the banks of the river that the Chinese civilization first flowered. The shift from Neolithic to Bronze Age culture marks the transition from prehistory to the beginnings of recorded history in China. In the prehistoric period, the progenitors of the Chinese people were scattered in small tribes over the middle reaches of the Yellow river. The present-day Chinese see themselves as the descendants of the Hua-Xia people. The Hua people, who first settled around Mount Hua near the middle reaches of the Yellow river valley, together with the Xia people, who established themselves near the Xia river (the upper course of the Han river, a tributary of the Yangtze river), were referred to as the Hua-Xia people. Both of these areas were located in the central southern region of Shaanxi province. Toward the end of the Neolithic period, these tribes were already using a primitive form of writing, and had developed a system to measure time and count numbers. They had also developed a variety of articles for daily use, including clothing, houses, weapons, pottery and money.

According to mythology, the Chinese nation begins with Pangu, the creator of the universe. However, Chinese culture began to develop with the emergence of emperor Yan (Yandi) and emperor Huang (Huangdi) around 2300 BC. For this reason the Chinese today refer to themselves as the *yanhuang zisun* (the descendants of emperors Yan and Huang). During the period of the reign of emperors Yan and Huang and their successors, people were taught to observe "five basic relationships," including "good relations between sovereign and minister, father and son, husband and wife, brothers and friends." This code of conduct, which was later developed systematically by Confucius (551–475 BC) and his disciples, established an ethical philosophy which has influenced Chinese society for the past two thousand years.

From the twenty-first to the second century BC, three ancient dynasties – Xia, Shang and Zhou – were established in the Yellow river valley. The Xia dynasty, founded by the great Yu and his son, Qi, lasted until 1766 BC. At the very least, the Xia dynasty marked an evolutionary stage between the late Neolithic cultures and the characteristic Chinese urban civilization of the Shang dynasty. During this period, the territorial boundaries of the Chinese nation began to take shape. The country was divided into nine administrative prefectures and a system of land taxes was established.

The Shang dynasty lasted from 1766 BC to 1046 BC. The Shang dynasty (which was also called the Yin dynasty in its later stages) was founded by a rebel leader, Tang, who overthrew the last of the Xia rulers. Its civilization was based on agriculture, augmented by hunting and animal husbandry. Two important events of the period were the development of a writing system, as revealed in archaic Chinese inscriptions found on tortoise shells and flat cattle bones (commonly called oracle bones), and the use of bronze metallurgy. A number of ceremonial bronze vessels with inscriptions date from the Shang period; the workmanship on the bronzes attests to a high level of civilization. For example, in the ruins of the city of Anyang (located at northern Henan province), the last capital of the Shang dynasty, archaeologists have unearthed over 150,000 pieces of oracle bones and other relics of the dynasty, suggesting that China experienced relative stability and prosperity in that period.

In a war with the 28th ruler of the Shang dynasty, the allied forces, under the command of King Wu, defeated the Shang army, leading to the foundation of a new dynasty named Zhou. The power of the rulers in the Zhou dynasty was based on "Zhongfa" – a system of inheritance and ancestral worship at a time when polygamy was the customary practice among the royalty and nobility.[1] In this way, a huge structure was built up, radiating from a central hub through endless feudal and in-feudal sytems. Particularly noteworthy is that in the dynasty education was widespread with a national university in the capital and various grades of schools named. Scholars and intellectuals were held in high esteem and art and learning flourished as never before.

The Chinese name *zhongguo* (or "China" as called in the Western Hemisphere) derives from the term "center under heaven," a term that was first coined by King Wu of the Zhou dynasty (see Box 1.1). The king's intention was to move the Zhou capital from Haojing in western China to Luoyi (now known as Luoyang) in central China in order to maintain more effective control over the entire nation. During the second half of the Zhou dynasty (also known as the "Spring and Autumn and War-ring States" period), a new group of regional rulers sought to obtain the services of talented individuals who could help to increase their political influence. The result was an unprecedented development of independent thinking and of original philosophies. The most celebrated philosophers of this period were Laozi, Confucius, Zhuangzi, Mencius, Mozi, Hanfei and Xunzi. These individuals became the leading sprits of the Taoist, Confucian, Mohist and Legalist schools of thought.

1.2   Rise and fall of the empire

In 221 BC, China was unified by Ying Zheng (also called Qin Shihuang), the first emperor of the Qin dynasty. The most important contribution of the Qin dynasty was the foundation of a completely new social and political order under a strict system of rewards and punishment favored by a group of scholars known as Legalists. In place of feudalism, the country was reorganized into 36 prefectures and a number of counties.

Box 1.1 Hezun

Hezun is a wine vessel made in the early period of the Zhou dynasty (1046–221 BC). With a height of 38.8 cm, top-opening diameter of 28.8 cm and a weight of 14.6 kg, Hezun is named after "He," the owner of the vessel.

Unearthed in the Fall of 1963 on the level of the Jiacun village, Baoji city, Shaanxi province, Hezun is now in the collection of the City Museum of Baoji. There is an inscription of 122 Chinese characters on the inside at the bottom. The main idea is: In 1039 BC King Cheng of the Zhou dynasty (reign 1043–1007 BC) was offering a sacrifice to his father (King Wu of the Zhou), saying: "Once capturing Luoyi [today's  Luoyang at central China's Henan province, the major city of the Shang dynasty], King Wu notified his liegemen that 'it will, as the center under heaven, become a place in which I can govern the whole nation'." The remaining characters of the inscription tell that King Cheng taught a young man, named He, of the King's family a lesson on how the former Kings of the Zhou dynasty reigned the people.

The inscription in Hezun has been regarded as the earliest literal record for the name "China" ("zhongguo" or "center under heaven").

Under this prefecture-county administration, all authority was vested in the central government. For the first time in history, China's written language, currency, and weights and measures were all unified and standardized. In order to consolidate and strengthen his imperial rule, the emperor Qin Shihuang undertook large-scale construction projects, including national roadways, waterways and a great wall that was 5,000 kilometers long. At its greatest extent, the Great Wall reaches from eastern Liaoning to northwestern Gansu. These activities required enormous levies of manpower and resources, not to mention repressive measures. After the conquest of the "barbarians" in the south, the Chinese territory was extended to the shores of the South China Sea. In spite of many political and military achievements, the multicultural development was monopolized in the Qin dynasty. Excessive trust was placed in the efficacy of the Legalist method, while the books on Confucianism and other schools of thought were burned in order to keep the people in a state of ignorance. Even worse, those intellectuals and scholars who criticized the government were either executed or forced to work as slave labor. Due to its cruel and despotic rule, the Qin dynasty was to be overthrown less than twenty years after its triumph. The imperial system initiated during the Qin dynasty, however, set a pattern that was to be repeated over the next two millennia.

Five years later, Liu Bang reunited China and established a long-lived dynasty, the Han (206 BC–AD 220). Strong military forces made it possible for the Han dynasty to expand China's territories to the Western Dominion in today's Xinjiang and Central Asia and also to Taiwan island in the East China Sea. The Han dynasty was a glorious age in Chinese history. The political institutions of the Qin and the Han dynasties were typical of all the dynasties that were to follow. The nine-chapter legal code drawn up in the early days of the Han served as a model for all later versions of Chinese codes. The political and military might of the Han dynasty was so impressive that since this time the Chinese have referred to themselves as the "Han" people. Under the Han rulers Confucianism was given special emphasis and those doing research on Confucian studies were given priority for public positions. Emperor Wudi (reign 140–87 BC) listed the Confucian classics as subjects of study for his ministers, and appointed well-read scholars to positions of authority labeled *Boshi* (doctor). Confucianism thus gained official sanction over competing philosophical schools and became the core of Chinese culture. The Han period also produced China's most famous historian, Sima Qian (145–87 BC), whose *Shiji* (historical records) provides a detailed chronicle from the time of a legendary Huang emperor to the period of Emperor Wudi of the Han. This period was also marked by a series of technological advances, including two of the great Chinese inventions, paper and porcelain.

At the end of the Eastern Han period (AD 25–220)[2] political corruption and social chaos, together with widespread civil disturbances and royal throne usurpation, led eventually to the creation of three independent kingdoms – the Wei (AD 220–265) in the north, the Shu (AD 221–263) in the southwest, and the Wu (AD 222–280) in the southeast. China remained divided until AD 265 when the Jin dynasty was founded in Luoyang in central China. The Jin was not as militarily strong as the non-Han counterparts in the north, which encouraged the southwards move of its capital to where is now called Nanjing (southern capital). Large-scale migration from the north to the south led to the Yangtze river valley becoming more prosperous than before, and the economic and cultural center therefore shifted gradually to the southeast of the country. This transfer of the capital coincided with China's political fragmentation into a succession of dynasties that lasted from AD 420 to 589. In the Yellow river valley, the non-Han peoples lived with the indigenous Han people, forming a more diverse and dynamic Chinese nation than ever before. Despite the political disunity of the times, there were notable technological advances, including the invention of gunpowder and the wheelbarrow. During this period, Buddhism achieved an increasing popularity in both northern and southern China.

China was reunified during the Sui dynasty (AD 581–618). The Sui is famous for its construction of the Grand Canal which linked the Yellow river and the Huai and Yangtze rivers in order to secure improved communication between the south and the north of the country. In terms of human costs only the Great Wall – which was constructed during the Qin dynasty – is comparable with the Canal. Like the Qin, the Sui was also a short-lived dynasty, which was succeeded by a powerful dynasty, the Tang (AD 618–907). The Tang period was the golden age of literature and art. A government system supported by a large class of Confucian literati selected through a system of civil service examinations was perfected under Tang rule. This competitive procedure was designed to draw the best talents into government. But perhaps an even greater consideration for the Tang rulers, aware that imperial dependence on powerful aristocratic families and warlords would have destabilizing consequences, was to create a body of career officials that had no autonomous territorial or functional power base. As it turned out, these scholar-officials acquired considerable status within their local communities, family ties, and shared values that connected them to the imperial court. From the Tang times until the closing days of the Qing empire in AD 1911, scholar-officials functioned often as intermediaries between the grassroots level and the government.

By the middle of the eighth century, Tang power had ebbed. Domestic economic instability and military defeat in AD 751 by Arabs at Talas, in Central Asia, marked the beginning of five centuries of steady military decline for the Chinese empire. Misrule, court intrigues, economic exploitation, and popular rebellions weakened the empire, making it possible for northern invaders to terminate the dynasty in AD 907. The next half-century saw the gradual fragmentation of China into five dynasties and ten kingdoms.

In AD 960, China was reunited once again. The founders of the Song dynasty built an effective centralized bureaucracy staffed with civilian scholar-officials. Regional military governors and their supporters were replaced by centrally appointed officials. This system of civilian rule led to a greater concentration of power in the hands of the emperor and his palace bureaucracy than had been achieved in the previous dynasties. Unlike the Tang dynasty, the Song dynasty (AD 960–1279) was militarily confronted by powerful enemies from the north. The conflict between the Song and the Liao (a non-Han dynasty in northern China from AD 907 to 1125) lasted for more than a century before another non-Han dynasty, the Jin (AD 1115–1234), first defeated the Liao and then in 1127 took control of the Song's capital, Kaifeng, and captured two Song emperors as hostages. With northern China falling into the hands of the Jin, the Song capital moved from the Yellow river valley to Lin'an (today's Hangzhou). As a result, the economic and cultural centers shifted from the central to the southeastern areas of China. Despite its military weakness, the Song dynasty contributed a great deal to the civilization of the world. Many Chinese inventions, including the compass, gunpowder and movable-type printing, were introduced to the West during this period. Culturally, the Song also refined many of the developments of previous centuries. The Neo-Confucian philosophers found certain purity in the originality of the ancient classical texts of Confucianism. The most influential of these philosophers was Zhu Xi (AD 1130–1200), whose synthesis of Confucian thought and Buddhist, Taoist, and other ideas became the official imperial ideology from late Song times to the late nineteenth century. Neo-Confucian doctrines also came to play a dominant role in the intellectual life of Korea, Vietnam, and Japan.

In AD 1279 the Mongol cavalry, under the leadership of Genghis Khan, controled the entire Chinese territory. The 88-year-long Yuan dynasty was an extraordinary one. Under Mongol rule, China once again expanded its borders. During the strongest period of the Yuan dynasty, China's territory even extended as far as the eastern part of Europe. The Mongols' extensive West Asian and European contacts led to a substantial degree of cultural exchange. This led to the development of rich cultural diversities. Western musical instruments were introduced and helped to enrich the Chinese performing arts. From this period dates the conversion to Islam, by Muslims from Central Asia, of growing numbers of Chinese in the northwest and southwest. Nestorianism and Roman Catholicism also enjoyed a period of toleration. Tibetan Buddhism (Lamaism) flourished, although native Taoism endured Mongol persecutions. Confucian governmental practices and examinations based on the Classics, which had fallen into disuse in north China during the period of disunity, were reinstated by the Mongols in the hope of maintaining order over Han society. Certain key Chinese innovations, such as printing techniques, porcelain production, playing cards, and medical literature, were introduced in Europe, while the production of thin glass and cloisonné became increasingly popular in China. European people were also enthralled by the account given by Venetian Marco Polo of his trip to "Cambaluc," the Great Khan's capital (now Beijing), and of the ways of life he encountered there.

In internal affairs, however, the Mongolian caste system – in which the majority of the Han people were seen as inferior to non-Han peoples – was not ideal. Widespread famines, resulting from natural disasters, political corruption, and misgovernment, eventually resulted in a successful anti-Mongol revolution led by Zhu Yuanzhang, who founded the Han-based dynasty, the Ming (AD 1368–1644) in Nanjing. In 1421, the Ming dynasty moved its seat to Beijing, after defeating the nomadic tribes of the northern part of the Great Wall. In Southeast Asia the Chinese armies reconquered Annam, as northern Vietnam was then known, and they also repelled the Mongols, while the Chinese fleet sailed the China seas and the Indian Ocean, venturing even as far as the east coast of Africa. The maritime Asian nations sent envoys with tribute for the Chinese emperor. The maritime expeditions stopped suddenly after 1433, probably as the result of the great expense of large-scale expeditions at a time of preoccupation with securing northern borders against the threat from the Mongols. Pressure from the powerful Neo-Confucian bureaucracy led to a revival of a society that was centered on agriculture. Internally, the Grand Canal was expanded to its farthest limits and proved to be a stimulus to domestic trade. The stability of the Ming dynasty, which suffered no major disruptions of the population (then around 100 million), economy, arts, society and politics, promoted a belief among the Chinese that they had achieved the most satisfactory civilization on earth and that nothing foreign was either needed or welcome. As the Ming dynasty declined, China's last, also the last minority-based dynasty, the Qing (AD 1644–1911), was set up by the Manchus, who rose to power in Manchuria (today's northeast part of China).

Compared with the Mongols, the period of Manchu rule over China can be viewed as successful. At the height of the Qing dynasty, the Manchus utilized the best minds and richest human resources of the nation, regardless of race. Although the Manchus were not Han Chinese and were subjected to strong resistance, especially in the south, they had assimilated a great deal of the Han-Chinese culture before conquering China Proper. Realizing that in order to dominate the empire they would have to do things in the Chinese manner, the Manchus retained many institutions of Ming and earlier Chinese derivation. Furthermore, the Han-based political ideologies and cultural traditions of the Chinese were adopted by the Manchus, resulting in virtually total cultural assimilation of the Manchus by the Han Chinese. After the subduing of China Proper, the Manchus conquered Outer Mongolia (now the Mongolian People's Republic) in the late seventeenth century. In the eighteenth century they gained control of Central Asia as far as the Pamir Mountains and established a protectorate over Tibet. The Qing thus became the first dynasty to eliminate successfully all danger to China Proper from across its land borders. Under the rule of the Manchu dynasty the empire grew once again; during this period Taiwan, the last outpost of anti-Manchu resistance, was incorporated into China for the first time. In addition, the Qing emperors received tribute from many neighboring states.

The 1840s marked a turning point in Chinese history. In the early nineteenth century Britain was smuggling large quantities of opium into China, causing a substantial outflow of Chinese silver and grave economic disruption. In an effort to protect its opium trade, in 1840 Britain initiated the First Opium War. The war ended in 1842, after the Qing court signed the Treaty of Nanjing with Britain, bartering away China's national sovereignty. Subsequently, China declined into a semi-colonial and semi-feudal country. After the Opium War, Britain and other Western powers, including Belgium, the Netherlands, Prussia, Spain, Portugal, the USA and France, seized "concessions" and divided China into "spheres of influence." The second half of the nineteenth century saw the many peasant leaders and national heroes. The Revolution of 1911, led by Dr Sun Yatsen, is of great significance in modern Chinese history, since with the founding of the Republic of China (ROC) it discarded the feudal monarchical system that had ruled China for more than 2,000 years. In the following decades, however, the Chinese nation was on the edge of bankruptcy.[3]

1.3   China in the new millennium

Following the collapse of the socialist system in 1990, old institutions that had provided society with a certain degree of economical and social stability have been overturned rapidly and new market-oriented fundamentals were slow to spread in the economic environment of the former Soviet Union. Whereas by the late 1990s many elements of a market-based formal framework had been established, the implementation was often weak. The enforcement of new laws and regulations has been constrained by the presence of old informal institutions – strong bureaucracy, a low level of respect for law, informal networking and other social factors, which were historically rooted in the behavior of Soviet society. As a result, the speed and sequencing of the economic reforms, which were important at the beginning of the transition, seems to be less important than the necessity of institutional transformation.

During the past century, China's economic development had been interrupted on a number of separate occasions. The Chinese economy was nearly bankrupt at the end of the Civil War in the late 1940s, and was seriously damaged by both the Great Leap Forward (1958–60), and the Cultural Revolution (1966–76) movements. However, since the late 1970s when the Chinese government began the gradual transformation of its Stalinesque centrally planned system, the Chinese economy has grown extremely rapidly. In the reform era since 1978, China has been one of the world's fastest-growing economies. Between 1978 and 2008, China's real GDP has grown at an average annual rate of almost 10 percent.

Using nominal exchange rates, China's 2005 GDP was about half that of Japan and only one-quarter that found in the USA. However, nominal exchange rates underestimate the size of the Chinese economy because Chinese prices are much lower than those found in developed countries. If the purchasing power parity (PPP) rate had been used, China's 2005 GDP would have been much higher than its recorded figure. Furthermore, many scholars and international observers believe that, using the PPP measurements, China could have already surpassed the USA as the world's largest economy, although China's per capita GDP would still be quite low. While the PPP estimates are subject to some margin of error, the Chinese economy certainly has the potential to rival that of the USA in size as a result of the enormous Chinese population.

To date, the Chinese model has been generally regarded as having achieved the most successful transformation of all of the former Soviet-type economies in terms of the improvement of economic performance, with China achieving vigorous economic growth since the implementation of market-oriented reform in the late 1970s. The remarkable performance has been accompanied and facilitated by, *inter alia*, historic, geographic, social, and cultural factors. However, it should also be noted that China still lags behind many market-based, industrialized economies. It is only the huge population that causes the Chinese economy to rank at the bottom of the world's lower-middle-income economies in terms of the per capita measure. The per capita income of China has still been much lower than that of the USA, Japan and other newly industrialized economies (NIEs).

While China's over-centralized planning system was largely responsible for its poor socioeconomic performance, there were also historical,

social, and cultural factors that hindered its socioeconomic development. Indeed, it is not easy to develop a market-system framework
within a short period of time in China – a huge country utilizing the
centrally planned system for nearly 30 years and that was, in particular,
deeply influenced by long periods of feudalism but rarely by economic
democracy.

1.4   Summary

Starting with a brief history of China, focusing on the various factors
that could have shaped China's existing political, economic, and cultural
characteristics, this chapter investigates the causes and consequences of
China's periodic changes of feudal dynasties as well as their political,
economic and cultural implications to the Chinese economy in the new
millennium.

Over recent decades, the Chinese economy has experienced dramatic
changes and a more rapid development than many other transitional
centrally planned economies (CPEs). This was the result of a combination of both internal and external circumstances. In these first few years
of the twenty-first century, we can see that China is scheduled to develop
its economy along its own distinctive lines. At the same time, China's
current situation poses many significant challenges to the Chinese economy. Many inherent problems in relation to economic development still
persist. If the Chinese government does not address these properly, its
efforts, based on the successful introduction of Chinese-style reforms,
will inevitably be jeopardized.

More than two thousand years ago, Confucius use to instruct his pupils
through the telling of this autobiographical story:

> Since the age of 15, I have devoted myself to learning; since 30, I have
> been well established; since 40, I have understood many things and
> have no longer been confused; since 50, I have known my heaven-
> sent duty; since 60, I have been able to distinguish right and wrong in
> other people's words; and 70, I have been able to do what I intended
> freely without breaking the rules.

Hopefully, with the approach of the 60th anniversary of the PRC, the
CCP leaders will finally be emerging from their past confused age and
know where to go and what to do next, in terms of both economic and
political terms.

1.5 Case study: Why the Yellow river is important

When we consider the world's four great ancient civilizations (the Mesopotamian, the Egyptian, the Indus, and the Chinese), it can be seen that all of them are closely associated with rivers. It is no accident that the "cradles" of these great civilizations are centered on riversides or river valleys. The Sumerians were based along the Euphrates and the Tigris rivers and their tributaries. For the past thousands of years and even in modern times, Egyptians' lives have revolved around the Nile. Roots of the ancient Indus civilization were based on the Indus and the Chinese centered their culture on the Yellow river.

The geographical characteristics of river systems heavily influenced the ancient civilizations that grew there. Since these ancient civilizations were dependent on agriculture, it is clear that abundant fresh water would be of critical importance. In addition, since large amounts of manpower are needed in order to make a river work well, there will be an increasing sedentism, high population density as well as the need to establish a centralized administrative role along the river valley. Furthermore, with regard to the utilization of the water resource of a river valley, upstream dwellers usually have geographic advantages over downstream dwellers. As a result, "social stratification and ranking" and "armed military force" can be easily built among the upstream and the downstream dwellers. All of these are very important signals to the birth of an ancient civilization. Furthermore, men living within river valleys have a more urgent need to develop various scientific methods and technological tools in order to survive than those living in the other places.

The development of the ancient Chinese civilization along the valley of the Yellow river provides strong evidence to support the hypothesis that civilization originates from flood. China has had a particularly long and terrible history of flooding. More than five thousand kilometers long, the Yellow river begins high above sea level in the Western mountain area and ends at the Yellow Sea. Westerners have dubbed it "China's Sorrow," because over many thousands of years it has killed more people than any other river in the world. Much of the problem stems from the high silt content of the river. Millions of tons of yellow mud choke the channel, causing the river to overflow and change its course. Water is held in by dikes of ever-increasing height. In its lower reaches, the riverbed has actually become 20 meters higher than the level of the surrounding countryside.

During the course of Chinese history, attempts to control the Yellow river have been categorized by different strategic approaches. One strategy is the active control of the river: to confine it within a narrow channel through the use of a system of high levees. More often than not, Chinese scholars have seen the close confinement of the river as a "Confucian" solution of discipline and order imposed upon nature: this contrasts with the "Taoist" solution of allowing the river a more "natural" course within lighter constraints. In either case, however, river engineering represented a tremendous interference with any "natural" regime: and the contrasting solutions were more accurately characterized as being opposites of engineering than philosophical approaches. Certainly, these phenomena are the defining results of the differing living conditions on which the two religious founders were based (see Table 1.1). Specifically, the Confucians, including Confucius and Mencius, all of whom lived along the lower reaches of the Yellow river, had either suffered more seriously from river floods, or been more deeply impressed by such flood-related stories as told by their elders, than Laozi, the founder of Taoism. For example, the following story is included in the analects of Mencius (372–289 BC):

Table 1.1 Confucianism versus Taoism: some basic facts

	Confucianism	Taoism
Founder's name	Kongzi (Confucius)	Laozi (Lao Tzu)
Founder's year of birth	551 BC	c. 600 BC
Founder's place of birth/living	Qufu – lower reaches of Yellow river	Luyi/Luoyi[a] – middle and upper reaches of Yellow river
How the founder suffered from river flood	Very serious	Not serious
Overall goal	Find peaceful and harmonious place of life	No overall goal
Rule of behavior	Follow a certain relationship between people	Follow the life according to the Tao
Attitude toward flood control	Narrow channel by high levees	Wider flood plain between lower levees

Note: [a]Laozi spent most of his career first at Luoyi (capital of the Eastern Zhou dynasty) and later at the mountain areas in western China.

In the time of Emperor Yao [about the 22nd century BC], the waters, flowing out of their channels, inundated the Central Kingdom. Snakes and dragons occupied it, and the people had no place in which they could settle themselves. In the low grounds they made nests for themselves on the trees or raised platforms, and in the high grounds they made caves. It is said in the Book of History, "The waters in their wild course warned me." Those "waters in their wild course" were the waters of the great inundation. Emperor Shun dispatched Yu to reduce the waters to order. Yu dug open their obstructed channels, and conducted them to the sea. He drove away the snakes and dragons, and forced them into the grassy marshes. On this, the waters pursued their course through the country, even the waters of the Jiang, the Huai, the He and the Han, and the dangers and obstructions which they had occasioned were removed. The birds and beasts which had injured the people also disappeared, and after this men found the plains available for them.[4]

Subject to differing living conditions within the valley of the Yellow river, the Confucian and Taoist schools each has its unique view on basic beliefs, overall goals, the goals of individual behavior, the view of life, the rule of behavior and views about society. The overall goal of Confucianism is to find a peaceful and harmonious place in life, whereas that of Taoism has no overall aim. The Taoists simply have to follow the life according to the Tao, but the Confucians follow a certain behavior and seek to be in harmony with nature. The Confucians believe that you should be improved by education and the development of your character and that you need to understand the complicated relationships with your family members, with the government and with the society as a whole, while the Tao believed that the life you lived with the Tao was good and that following the ways of society was bad.

Indeed, the Yellow river is the most important dummy to explain the differences between the Chinese culture and the other cultures in the rest of the world. The changes of the river's course have been spectacular, and the river mouth has sometimes changed catastrophically by hundreds of kilometers. It has had dozens of major and numerous minor changes in course during the past thousands of years, each leading to enormous human casualties but also property losses. All of these features have influenced the lifestyles of the Chinese people, especially of those with close proximity to the Yellow river. For example, after having compared the architectures of the Yellow river valley and of southeast provinces (such as Guangdong and Fujian), we can see that the houses and other buildings of the Yellow river valley, especially at the lower reaches of the Yellow river, are much simpler and, of course, less firm in structure, with the use of fewer expensive materials. Since the majority of the Han population living in the southeast provinces are descended from those who immigrated from the Yellow river valley, only geographical features can explain this difference. People living in the Yellow river valley must have frequently abandoned their homes in order to escape from the unruly, disastrous floodwaters.

The Yellow river can provide us with more details about Chinese society. For example, the difficulties in securing sufficient food within the valley of the Yellow river, probably a result of the frequent natural disasters, have built the economical foundations for Chinese cuisine. In contrast to the Westerners, the Chinese have a much smaller percentage of fat and meat as the main ingredient in their daily diet. This reminds me instantly of the hypothesis that it is the shortage of food in quantity and category that drove the Chinese to develop many cooking methods (including braising, boiling, braising with soy sauce, roasting, baking, grilling, scalding, deep-frying, steaming, drying, and salt-preserving) in order to *make* their food more delicious. In addition, the scarcity of food has resulted in a distinctive eating habit (that is, dishes are placed in the center of a table so that everybody can share the meal) in ancient China. More often than not, all of the above conditions have also contributed to the development of a collectivist-style culture in China.

2
Spatial and Administrative Divisions

Baigui [a minister of the state of Wei in today's Henan province during the Warring States period] said, "My management of the waters is superior to that of Yu." Mencius replied, "You are wrong, Sir. Yu's regulation of the waters was according to the natural laws of water. He therefore made the four seas their receptacle, while you make the neighboring states their receptacle. Water flowing out of its channels is called an inundation. The inundating waters are disastrous to the neighboring states, and what a benevolent man detests. You are wrong, my dear Sir!"

– *Analects of Mencius* (Gaozi II)

2.1 Administrative divisions

During ancient times, the Chinese nation was generally regarded as being divided into nine states (or prefectures). More often than not, China, now called *zhongguo* (center under heaven or central state) in pinyin form, had an alternative name, *jiuzhou* (nine states). However, there have been a number of different viewpoints as to the precise classification of these nine states. For example, according to *Yugong* (the geographical records of the tribute to the Yu), a book which was probably written in the Xia dynasty (*c.*1988–1766 BC),[1] the nine states are Jizhou (in the northern side of the Yellow river), Yanzhou (in the eastern side of the Yellow river), Qingzhou (in the Shandong peninsula), Yangzhou (in the southeast), Jingzhou (in the south), Yuzhou (in the southern side of the Yellow river), Yongzhou (in the near west), Liangzhou (in the far west) and Xuzhou (in the east, between the northern Jiangsu and southeast Shandong provinces). In another book entitled *Lvshi Chunqiu* (historical records compiled by Lv Buwei), these states include Jizhou,

Yanzhou, Qingzhou, Yangzhou, Jingzhou, Yuzhou, Yongzhou, Youzhou (in the northeast) and Bingzhou (in the north).

Since the foundation of the feudal system, China's provincial administrations have been named as, *inter alia*, *jun* in the Qin dynasty (221–206 BC), *junguo* in the Western Han dynasty (206 BC–AD 25), *zhou* in the Eastern Han (AD 25–220) and the Wei (AD 220–265), the Jin (AD 266–420) and the North and South (AD 420–589) dynasties, *dao*^{2} in the Tang dynasty (AD 618–907), *lu* in North and South Song (AD 960–1279) and the Jin (AD 1115–1235) dynasties, *zhongshu-xingsheng* in the Yuan dynasty (AD 1279–1368), *xingsheng* in the Ming (AD 1368–1644) and the Qing (AD 1644–1911) dynasties, and *sheng* thereafter. Notice that the Chinese character *sheng* originally refers to the term "ministry", which is still being used in Japan and Korea. *Zhongshu-xingsheng* and *xingsheng* (the latter has evolved to the term *sheng* in contemporary Chinese language) refer to the "ministerial representative agencies of central government to provinces".

At present, China's territorial-administrative hierarchy has three different types of provincial-level units: *sheng* (province), *zhizhiqu* (autonomous regions) and *zhixiashi* (municipalities directly under the central government) (see Table 2.1). In the Chinese state administration "autonomous" refers to self-government by a large and single (but not necessarily majority) ethnic minority in any given unit within the territorial hierarchy. Autonomous regions are provincial-level units of state administration where the presence of an ethnic minority is officially recognized. They have the name of the specific ethnic minority incorporated in their title, as, for example, in the Guangxi Zhuang autonomous region, where Guangxi is the geographic name of the region and Zhuang is the name of a nationality. Municipalities are large cities, directly subordinate to the CCPCC and the State Council.

It should be noted that the three kinds of provincial administrations (*sheng, zizhiqu* and *zhixiashi*) have different functions. More often than not, top *zhixiashi* leaders have been appointed as members of the Political Bureau of the CCPCC, something which has only happened to a small number of *sheng* and *zizhiqu* leaders. The autonomous regions (*zizhiqu*) are only established in areas where the ethnic minorities constitute the majority of the population. Compared to other forms of provincial administrations, the *zizhiqu* is, at least in form, the most politically and culturally autonomous of the three kinds of provincial administrations.^{3}

While the formation of most provinces had taken place well before the foundation of the PRC, in recent decades a few of the others were either incorporated with their neighboring provinces or divided

Table 2.1   China's current provincial conditions

Province	Capital city	Political form	Population (million persons)	Land Area (000 km^2)
Anhui	Hefei	S	63.3	130.0
Beijing	Beijing	ZXS	13.8	16.8
Chongqing	Chongqing	ZXS	31.0	82.4
Fujian	Fuzhou	S	34.4	120.0
Gansu	Lanzhou	S	25.8	390.0
Guangdong	Guangzhou	S	77.8	180.0
Guangxi	Liuzhou	ZZQ	47.9	230.0
Guizhou	Guiyang	S	38.0	170.0
Hainan	Haikou	S	8.0	34.0
Hebei	Shijiazhuang	S	67.0	190.0
Heilongjiang	Harbin	S	38.1	460.0
Henan	Zhengzhou	S	95.6	160.0
Hubei	Wuhan	S	59.8	180.0
Hunan	Changsha	S	66.0	210.0
Inner Mongolia	Huhehaot	ZZQ	23.8	1,100.0
Jiangsu	Nanjing	S	73.6	100.0
Jiangxi	Nanchang	S	41.9	160.0
Jilin	Changchun	S	26.9	180.0
Liaoning	Shenyang	S	41.9	150.0
Ningxia	Yinchuan	ZZQ	5.6	66.0
Qinghai	Xi'ning	S	5.2	720.0
Shaanxi	Xi'an	S	36.6	190.0
Shandong	Ji'nan	S	90.4	150.0
Shanghai	Shanghai	ZXS	16.1	5.8
Shanxi	Taiyuan	S	32.7	150.0
Sichuan	Chengdu	S	86.4	477.6
Tianjin	Tianjin	ZXS	10.0	11.0
Tibet	Lasha	ZZQ	2.6	1200.0
Xinjiang	Wurumuqi	ZZQ	18.8	1600.0
Yunnan	Kunming	S	42.9	380.0
Zhejiang	Hanzhou	S	46.1	100.0

Notes: (1) S (sheng) = province; ZZQ (zizhiqu) = autonomous region; ZXS (zhixiashi) = municipality directly under the central government. (2) Hong Kong, Macau and Taiwan are not included.

into new provinces. For example, in 1954, Pingyuan province, which included the marginal administrative areas of the present Hebei, Shanxi, Shandong and Henan provinces, was abolished. In 1988, Hainan island, Guangdong province, was established as a new province; and, in 1997, Chongqing city and its surrounding areas, all of which had belonged to Sichuan province, became a province-level municipality under the direct control of the central government. In addition, during the history of the

PRC, some provincially marginal areas have been administratively transposed between the neighboring provinces. For example, in 1953, Xuzhou administrative region, Shandong province, was placed under the administration of Jiangsu province; and, in 1955, Yutai county was transferred from Anhui to Jiangsu provinces. It is worth noting that some territorial readjustments have placed interprovincial relations on an unstable foundation.[4]

At present, there are three classes of administrative divisions in China – the first-class administrative divisions (including provinces, autonomous regions, and municipalities directly under the central government), the second-class administrative divisions (including prefectures, autonomous prefectures, municipalities and other prefecture-level administrative divisions), and the third-class administrative divisions (including counties, autonomous counties and other county-level administrative divisions). An organizational pattern involving more classes of administrative divisions has been generally known to have a lower level of administrative efficiency. Recently, some provinces have been granted permission by the central government to practise a two-class pattern of administrative divisions (that is, to eliminate the second-class administrative divisions) in order to increase spatial economic efficiency. However, this administrative reform has encountered difficulties in dealing with large provinces. For example, in Henan or Shandong province there are more than 100 counties and county-level administrative divisions. Without the participation of the prefecture-level administrations, it would be very difficult, if not impossible, for a provincial governor to exert any direct effective influence on all of these county magistrates concurrently.

Most of China's provinces, autonomous regions, and municipalities that are under the direct control of the central government (in what follows, unless stated otherwise, we will use the term "province" to denote all the three kinds of administrative divisions), which are the average size and scale of a European country in population and land area, are considerable political and economic systems in their own right. These large provincial administrations, although they have some comparative advantages over the small ones in some circumstances, have been known to lack spatial administrative efficiency (see Box 2.1).

Given China's huge size and enormous population, establishing new provincial administrations (including provinces or other provincial-level units) in the border areas of some adjacent, large provinces seems to serve two positive functions. The first concerns the increase of the efficiency of spatial administration over the marginal, adjacent areas by transferring

Box 2.1   Cost–benefit analysis of large administrations

Generally, the sources of benefits for large administrations may be grouped into two categories: (i) The large administrations can make relatively efficient use of their fixed cost and hence gain considerable advantages over small administrations. (ii) Marketing in a larger economy has many benefits, but the main economies of scale from marketing include the bulk purchases and distribution potentialities.

A number of advantages can lead to larger administrations experiencing risk-bearing economies. The underlying factor is that large administrations frequently engage in a range of diverse activities, so that a fall in the return from any one unit of economy does not threaten the stability of the whole economy.

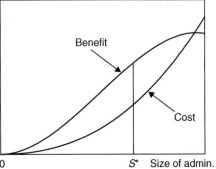

While increases in size frequently confer advantages on an administration, there is a limit to the gains from growth in many cases. In other words, there is an optimal level of capacity, and increases in size beyond this level will lead to a loss of economies of size and manifest themselves in rising average cost. Without doubt, the increasing complexity of managing a large administration is the major source of administrative inefficiencies when its size grows beyond a certain level, and management of diverse socioeconomic affairs and risks become increasingly difficult.

the multitude of administrative systems into a unitary administrative structure; and the second relates to the realization of increased economies of scale for provincial administration by separating the marginal areas out of the over-sized provinces.

Over recent decades, the total number of China's provincial administrations has increased: from 29 in the mid-1950s to 30 in 1988 and 31 in 1997. But economic geographers and regional scientists still believe that the introduction of smaller provinces may help to improve the spatial efficiency of the Chinese economy.[5]

2.2 Great regions

When the PRC was founded on October 1 1949, the Chinese economy was managed through six great administrative regions (North, Northeast, East, Central South, Southwest and Northwest). With the exception of the North region, which was under the administration of the central government, the other five great regions also had their own governmental bodies in charge of areas such as agriculture and forestry, industry, public finance, and trade. In 1954, the six great administrative regions were abolished and, three years before their final reorganization in 1961, seven cooperative commissions were established in North, Northeast, East, Central, South, Southwest and Northwest regions. The six great regional administrations were destroyed during the period of the Cultural Revolution (1966–76). In 1970 the Chinese economy was spatially organized via ten economic cooperative zones (namely Southwest, Northwest, Center, South, East, Northeast, North, Shandong, Fujian and Jiangxi, and Xinjiang). It is generally believed that this arrangement was based on the centrally planned system and reflected the state's efforts to meet the desperate need for regional self-sufficiency at the high point of the Cold War era (Yang, 1993, p. 248).

From 1981 to 1985, and guided by the State Council (1980b), six economic zones were organized in the Northeast, North, East, Central South, Southwest and Northwest regions. Notice that Shandong was excluded from this list of six economic zones; Guangxi was included in both Central South and Southwest economic zones; and eastern Inner Mongolia was included in both the North and Northeast economic zones. In 1992, when the Chinese government decided to develop a market-oriented economy, the State Planning Commission (SPC) was authorized to map out the development plans for the following economic regions (*People's Daily*, 1992, p. 1):

- Yangtze delta (Jiangsu, Zhejiang and Shanghai).
- Bohai Sea rim (Beijing, Tianjin, Hebei, Shandong, Shanxi, central Inner Mongolia and Liaoning).
- Southeast Coastal area (Guangdong, Fujian and Hainan).
- Northeast area (Liaoning, Jilin, Helongjiang and eastern Inner Mogolia).
- Southwest area (Sichuan, Guizhou, Yunnan, Tibet and Guangxi).
- Central area (Henan, Anhui, Hubei, Hunan and Jiangxi).
- Northwest area (Shaanxi, Gansu, Ningxia, Qinghai, Xinjiang and western Inner Mongolia).

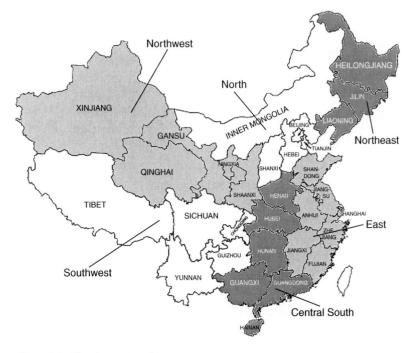

Figure 2.1   The six great regions

Since the early 1980s, China's official statistical authorities (such as the State Statistical Bureau (SSB) or, as it is now called, the National Bureau for Statistics (NBS)) and other statistical departments and divisions under ministries or administrations) have used six great regions (as shown in Figure 2.1):

- North (including Beijing, Tianjin, Hebei, Shanxi and Inner Mongolia, with 16.3 percent of the land area).
- Northeast (including Liaoning, Jilin and Heilongjiang, with 8.2 percent of the land area).
- East (including Shanghai, Jiangsu, Zhejiang, Anhui, Fujian, Jiangxi and Shandong, with 8.3 percent of the land area).
- Central South (including Henan, Hubei, Hunan, Guangdong, Guangxi and Hainan, with 10.6 percent of the land area).
- Southwest (including Sichuan, Chongqing, Guizhou, Yunnan and Tibet, with 24.6 percent of the land area).

- Northwest (including Shaanxi, Gansu, Qinghai, Ningxia and Xinjiang, with 32.0 percent of the land area).

This method of dividing the country into six great regions has been applied in many scholarly research works.[6]

2.3 Geographical belts

The 12 provinces surrounded by the Yellow, East China and South China Seas are classified as the coastal area, while the remaining provinces are regarded as the inland area (see Figure 2.2). Generally, the coastal area is more developed than the inland area, as a result of its proximity to the market economies along the western shore of the Pacific Ocean as well as the fact that it was the region that experienced the earlierst introduction of economic reform and opening up to the outside world. There have been different definitions of the coastal and inland areas. For example, Mao (1956, p. 286) treats Anhui and eastern Henan provinces as a part of the coastal area according to the principle of geographical proximity to the coastal area, while the State Council (1993) classifies the two coastal provinces of Guangxi and Hainan into the inland area according to the principle of economic similarity.

Even though China's economic divergence has not been as large within the inland area as it has between the inland and coastal areas, there are still some plausible reasons to explain why the inland area needs to be further divided into smaller geographical units. As the western part of the inland area has less-developed social and economic infrastructures than the eastern part, China's inland area can be further divided into two sections – the Central belt, which is next to the coastal area (here it is referred to as the Eastern belt), and the Western belt.

The Eastern, Central and Western belts first appeared in the proposal for national economic and social development in the seventh Five-Year Plan (FYP) (1986–90), which was adopted in April 1986 by the National People's Congress (NPC). In this document, the government advocated that: "The development of the eastern coastal belt shall be further accelerated and, at the same time, the construction of energy and raw material industries shall be focused on the Central belt, while the preparatory works for the further development of the Western belt shall be actively conducted."[7] Since this time, the three-belt definition has been used widely in government policy documents as well as in the literature (see, for example, Yao and Zhang, 2001a, b; Brun *et al.*, 2002; and Wu, 2004).

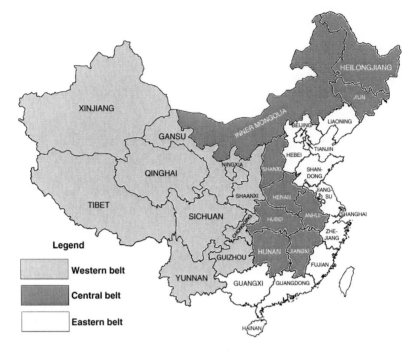

Figure 2.2   The Eastern, Central and Western belts

The Eastern, Central and Western belts (shown in Figure 2.2) have their component provinces, as follows:

- Eastern belt (including Liaoning, Hebei, Beijing, Tianjin, Shandong, Jiangsu, Shanghai, Zhejiang, Fujian, Guangdong, Hainan and Guangxi, with 13.5 percent of the land area).
- Central belt (including Shanxi, Jilin, Heilongjiang, Anhui, Henan, Hubei, Hunan, Jiangxi and Inner Mongolia, with 29.8 percent of the land area).
- Western belt (including Sichuan, Chongqing, Guizhou, Yunnan, Shaanxi, Gansu, Qinghai, Tibet, Ningxia and Xinjiang, with 56.7 percent of the land area).

The above definition has been applied in many government documents and much of the scholarly literature.[8] It should be noted that the government's definition changed slightly after 1999, when the southern province of Guangxi, which was originally part of the Eastern (coastal) belt, was reallocated to the Western belt and Inner Mongolia, originally part of the Central belt, was reallocated to the Western belt. In addition, there have been other different definitions on the tripartite division of the Chinese economy. For instance, Guangxi, a coastal province along the Gulf of Tonkin, is included in the Western belt by Yang (1989, pp. 90–6), Gu (1995, pp. 45–51) and Chen (1994, p. 57). In Gu's analysis, moreover, Jilin and Heilongjiang, two inland provinces in Northeast China, are included in the Eastern belt.

2.4 Southern and Northern parts

The introduction of the concept of the "North" and "South" of China in this book seems to be necessary for the bi-regional comparison of the Chinese economy. From the south to the north, the landmass of China is characterized by dramatic geographical, geological and hydrogeological diversities. Its land surface ascends from north to south in four distinct climate zones: the arid zone, the semi-arid zone, the semi-humid zone and the humid zone.

In addition to the natural and climatic diversities, social and cultural conditions also differ between northern and southern China. Without good reason, the Chinese are usually identified as Northerners and Southerners in terms of their birthplaces and, occasionally, the homes of their parents or relatives when they are introduced to one another. While it is not quite clear when the saying "South China raises intelligent scholars while marshals mainly come from the North" was first aired and whether or not it can be used to spatially characterize China's ethnic nature, many conflicts and wars in Chinese history did take place in the Northern part.

The first major Han-Chinese migration from the northern to the southern part of the Yangtze river took place during the Wei (AD 220–265), the Jin (AD 265–420) and the South and North (AD 420–589) dynasties, and was accelerated during the Five Dynasties and Ten States period (AD 907–960) when China's northern part became the nation's battlefield. Large-scale Han-Chinese migration was promoted later by frequent wars between the Chinese and the Liao, Jin, Mongol and other non-Han minorities in the North Song (AD 960–1126) and the South Song (AD 1127–1279) dynasties. In the wars with their far northern enemies, the Han-Chinese first lost their northern part after the late North Song dynasty. Naturally, the frequent wars greatly accelerated the emigration of northern intellectuals to the Southern part of the country.

In research, the geographic definition of the Southern and Northern parts may differ slightly. For example, the Qinling range and the Huaihe river are traditionally used to divide the South and North, while the Yangtze river is sometimes known as the boundary of northern and southern China. The only difference between the two definitions lies in the fact that the Qinling range and the Huaihe river are located in Shaanxi, Henan, Anhui and Jiangsu provinces, while the Yangtze river runs through Sichuan, Chongqing, Hubei, Anhui, Jiangsu and Shanghai provinces.

In most cases, nevertheless, there are an approximately equal number of provinces in each of the Northern and Southern parts, shown in Figure 2.3:

- Northern part (including Beijing, Tianjin, Hebei, Shanxi, Inner Mongolia, Liaoning, Jilin, Heilongjiang, Shaanxi, Gansu, Qinghai, Ningxia, Xinjiang, Shandong and Henan, with 59.8 percent of the land area).
- Southern belt (including Shanghai, Jiangsu, Zhejiang, Anhui, Fujian, Jiangxi, Sichuan, Chongqing, Guizhou, Yunnan, Tibet, Hubei, Hunan, Guangdong, Guangxi and Hainan, with 40.2 percent of the land area).

2.5   Ethno-cultural areas

China is not a culturally and ethnically homogeneous country. In addition to the Han majority, 55 other non-Han ethnic minorities also exist in China (see Appendix 1 at the end of the volume). In 1947 China's first, and ethnically based, autonomous region, Inner Mongolia, was established at the provincial level by the CCP. Then, after the foundation of the People's Republic of China in 1949, the Chinese government began to introduce a system of regional autonomy for other non-Han ethnic areas. For example, Xinjiang Uygur autonomous region was established in October 1955; Guangxi Zhuang autonomous region in March 1958; Ningxia Hui autonomous region in October 1958; and Tibet autonomous region in September 1965.

In most cases, the name of an ethnic autonomous area consists of the name of the place, the name of the ethnic group and the character indicating the administrative status, in that order. Take the Ningxia Hui autonomous region as an example: "Ningxia" is the name of the place, "Hui" is the name of the ethnic group and "region" indicates the level of

Figure 2.3 The Northern and Southern parts

administration. By the end of 2005, China's non-Han ethnic administrative areas included: (1) five autonomous regions (as mentioned above); (2) 30 autonomous prefectures (APs) in nine provincial administrations including:

- Gansu province: Gannan Tibetan AP; Linxia Hui AP.
- Guizou province: Qiandongnan Miao-Dong AP; Qiannan Buyi-Miao AP; Qianxi'nan Buyi-Miao AP.
- Hubei province: Enshi Tujia-Miao AP.
- Hunan province: Xiangxi Tujia-Miao AP.
- Jilin province: Yanbian Korean AP.
- Qinghai province: Yushu Tibetan AP; Hainan Tibetan AP; Huangnan Tibetan AP; Haibei Tibetan AP; Guoluo Tibetan AP; Haixi Mongolian-Tibetan AP.
- Sichuan province: Ganzi Tibetan AP; Liangshan Yi AP; A'ba Tibetan-Qiang AP.

Figure 2.4   The ethno-culture areas

- Xinjiang Uygur autonomous region: Bayin'guole Mongolian AP; Bo'ertala Mongolian AP; Kezilesu Kirgiz AP; Changji Hui AP; Yili Kazak AP.
- Yunnan province: Xishuangbanna Dai AP; Dehong Dai-Jingpo AP; Nujiang Lisu; Dali Bai AP; Diqing Tibetan AP; Honghe Hani-Yi AP; Wenshan Zhuang-Miao AP; Chuxiong Yi AP.

and (3) 120 county-level autonomous administrations in 18 provincial administrations (see Figure 2.4).[9]

Communities of one ethnic group may establish, according to their respective sizes, different autonomous administrations. If we take the Hui ethnic group as an example, this includes: (i) a provincial administration, called Ningxia Hui autonomous region; (ii) a sub-provincial administration, called the Linxia Hui autonomous prefecture of Gansu province; and (iii) a sub-prefecture administration, called the Mengcun Hui autonomous county of Hebei province. In places where different ethnic groups live, each autonomous administration can be established based on either one ethnic group (such as Tibet autonomous region; Liangshan Yi autonomous prefecture of Sichuan province; and Jingning She autonomous county of Zhejiang province); or two or more ethnic groups (such as Haixi Mongolian-Tibetan autonomous prefecture of Qinghai province; and Jishishan Bao'nan-Dongxiang-Salar autonomous county of Gansu province). If a minority ethnic group lives in an autonomous area of a bigger ethnic group, the former may establish their own subordinate autonomous areas. For example, Yili Kazak autonomous prefecture and Yanqi Hui autonomous county are both to be found in the Xinjiang Uygur autonomous region.

Organizationally, China's non-Han ethnic administrative areas are oriented in a multi-ethnic manner. For example, in addition to deputies from the ethnic group or groups exercising regional autonomy in the area concerned, the people's congresses of the autonomous areas also include an appropriate number of members from other ethnic groups who live in that autonomous area. Among the chairman or vice-chairmen of the standing committee of the people's congress of an autonomous area there shall be one or more citizens of the ethnic group or groups exercising regional autonomy in the area concerned. The head of an autonomous region, autonomous prefecture or autonomous county alike shall be a citizen of the ethnic group exercising regional autonomy in the area concerned. Other members of the people's governments of the autonomous areas shall include an appropriate number of members of the ethnic group exercising regional autonomy alongside members of other ethnic minorities. The functionaries of the working departments subsidiary to the organs of self-government shall be composed in a similar fashion.

2.6 Summary

In any discussion of the Chinese economy, at least two important points must be noted: first, China's vast territorial size and the diversity of physical environments and natural resource endowments have inevitably resulted in considerable regional economic differences; secondly, China has a population of more than 1.3 billion, comprised of 56 ethnic groups. It is geographically divided into 31 provincial administrations, each of which would have been equivalent to a medium-sized country. Furthermore, all of the provinces are independent from each other in terms of developing local fiscal, tax, labor and trade policies and economic development plans which have, *ceteris paribus*, resulted in differing levels of regional economic performances in China.

In short, the Chinese economy is one of the most complicated and diversified spatial systems to be found anywhere in the world. The only feasible approach one can adopt is, therefore, to divide it into smaller geographic elements through which one can gain a better insight into the spatial mechanisms and regional characteristics. In this chapter, we have divided the Chinese economy into: (1) provincial administrations; (2) great regions; (3) geographical belts; (4) southern and northern parts; and (5) ethno-cultural areas. It is common for the method of spatial division of the Chinese economy to differ, depending upon the analytical purposes.

2.7　Case study: Who owns Lake Weishan?[10]

Lake Weishan is located on the border of Shandong and Jiangsu provinces in East China, mid-way between Shanghai and Beijing. It is composed of four connected sub-lakes: Dushan, Nanyang, Zhaoyang and Weishan. As the largest freshwater reservoir in northern China (with an area of 1,260 square kilometers), Lake Weishan receives water from 53 rivers in a broad catchment area spread across 32 counties and cities of four provinces (Jiangsu, Shandong, Henan, and Anhui). The maximum capacity of the lake is 4.73 billion cubic meters.[11] For centuries, Lake Weishan has been an important storage area for freshwater, but it also assists in the prevention of flooding, the development of water-related industries, as the route for local shipping, and the source of water for agricultural and industrial production. It remains vital to the daily life of the residents of 14 cities and counties (districts) in Jiangsu and Shandong provinces. High-quality coal resources have also been discovered beneath the lake. These are seen as extremely important by the economic policy makers at both central and provincial level government in China.

Prior to 1953, most of Lake Weishan was part of the Xuzhou Administrative Region, and under the jurisdiction of Shandong province. 90 percent of the southern part of Lake Weishan was shared by two counties (Peixian and Tongshan); and the eastern part of the lake was part of the Seventh District of Peixian county, with Xiazhen township being the administrative center of the district, which comprised eight towns and more than 100 villages. In 1953, Xuzhou Administrative Region was transferred from Shandong to Jiangsu province. During the process of territorial readjustment, Shandong province submitted a proposal that, for the sake of the unified administration and the public security of the entire lake area, the sub-lakes of Zhaoyang and Weishan, together with some villages in Tongshan county (all of which had been under the jurisdiction of Jiangsu province), should comprise a new county (Weishan) and be placed under the administration of Shandong province.[12]

The interprovincial border established at that time followed the principles set by the Central Government: Shandong's Weishan county was to be separated from Jiangsu's Peixian and Tongshan counties by the border between the lake's waterline and lakeside land, with the exception of a few villages located outside the lakeside land. These villages were set as border markers between the two provinces. The State Administrative Council, the former State Council, approved this proposal on August 22 1953 (zhengzhengbuzi [53] official letter, No. 136). The newly established county of Weishan was entitled to administer 267 villages and four towns.[13] In March 1956, the counties of Fushan and Xuecheng were also placed under the administration of Weishan county. However, between May and September of the same year, some villages were transferred from Weishan county to Xuzhou municipality of Jiangsu province and others were transferred from Yixian, Jiaxiang and Jining counties of Shandong province to Weishan county. In early 1984, another 14 villages from Peixian county in Jiangsu province were transferred to Weishan county in Shandong province.

As a result of the administrative readjustments outlined above, the county of Weishan now contains 565 administrative villages and five neighborhood committees, covering a total geographical area of 1,780 square kilometers (this includes 514 square kilometers of lake). As of 2001, Weishan county had a total population of 682,000. The majority are Han Chinese, but 25 other ethnic minorities, including Hui (Muslims), Miao, Mongol, Zhuang, Manchu, Korean, Yi and Hani, are also resident in Weishan.[14]

During the twentieth century, the Lake Weishan area has experienced a number of drastic changes in provincial administration. This has placed the Shandong–Jiangsu interprovincial relation on an unstable foundation. The 1953 border readjustment scheme created many problems. The fact that changes in natural conditions could result in either a rise (during the rainy season) or a fall (during the dry season) of the water level in Lake Weishan, which would in turn either reduce or increase the size of lake and lakeshore land, was not taken into consideration. Naturally, such fluctuations would cause frequent changes in the location of the interprovincial border-line which followed the decision that: "Wherever water reaches is under Shandong's jurisdiction; but the land is regarded as Jiangsu's territory."

In addition, it was clearly assumed in the 1953 border delimitation scheme that the whole area of the lake should be under the exclusive administration of Weishan county in Shandong province. Jiangsu residents living along the lakeside were permitted to continue conducting their lake-related businesses, such as fishing in the lake and farming in the lakeside land.

During the first years of this arrangement, when Shandong province exercised its governance over the entire area, Jiangsu province did not fully realize the lake's crucial importance to the agricultural and industrial economy of the region, nor was there sufficient recognition of the area's importance to the people's livelihood. It was only when Jiangsu province attempted to build an iron-ore mine in Liguo at the southern side of Lake Weishan, in an area near the provincial borders, that the debate strengthened. The mining proposal was impeded in 1956 and this stimulated the Jiangsu administrators to demand the return of 35 villages which had been transferred to Shandong province in 1953.

The central government in Beijing agreed to Jiangsu's request in principle, but still kept the whole lake under the sole administration of Weishan county.[15] Since that time Jiangsu has increasingly sought to gain strategic recognition of the lake as part of its provincial economy.

In 1958, Shandong province decided to construct a dam, which effectively divided the whole lake into two parts – an upper lake and a lower lake. While the construction of the dam in the middle of the lake was good for the provincial economy of Shandong province it was not beneficial to the economy of Jiangsu province. Jiangsu had no administrative jurisdiction over Lake Weishan, and could neither change Shandong's construction scheme nor exercise any control over water rights. Not only did the dam result in 90 percent of the lake's water reserves being contained on the Shandong side of the border, but it also submerged 210,000 mu [one mu is approximately equal to 667 square meters] of arable land on the Jiangsu side. Even worse, it made the farmers of Peixian district completely unable to irrigate their crops during a drought or to drain their waterlogged fields after heavy rain.[16]

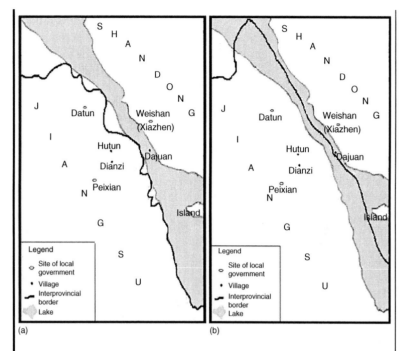

Figure 2.5 The differently defined borders between Shandong and Jiangsu provinces (a) Based on the map drawn by the government of Weishan county, published by Xi'an Map Press, Xi'an, Shaanxi province, 1995. (b) Based on the map drawn by the government of Peixian county, published by China Map Press, Beijing, 1995

The central government made great efforts to resolve the Lake Weishan disputes and these attempts can be traced through three documents issued by the Chinese Communist Party Central Committee and the State Council in 1984. The three documents, which transferred disputed areas and villages from Jiangsu to Shandong, provide a large part of the present administrative picture of the Shandong–Jiangsu border area issues (see Figure 2.5a).

However, the Shandong and Jiangsu provincial governments have each chosen to interpret the three central documents in a different manner. The result has been uncertainty over the interprovincial border and a lack of resolution of what is a fundamental border demarcation issue. Over the course of the following years, the Shandong administrators emphasized an exact implementation of the three central documents, insisting that Lake

Weishan should be under the sole administration of Weishan county. However, the Jiangsu administrators argued that the decisions made by the central government were unfair.[17] Jiangsu suggested that the use of the widely recognized principle on water-area delimitation that "shared lakes are divided along the deepest line" (see Figure 2.5b). Both provinces found that there were far too many differences between them to enable them to reach an agreement.[18]

The argument about the ownership of Lake Weishan continued, as did the border conflict between the provinces. In the period between the founding of the People's Republic of China in 1949 and the year 2000 there have been nearly 400 cases of cross-border conflicts in the region, with nearly 400 people being either killed or seriously wounded. The figures include the following: 16 people died and 24 people were disabled in Peixian county; four people died in Weishan county; and there were numerous casualties in Tongshan and Fengxian counties of Jiangsu province.[19] The main causes for these causalities came from fights between the cultivators of the lakeside land and fishermen operating other lake-related business, as well as workers involved in the construction of various water conservancy, public security, construction of communication equipment programs, and the collectors of fees and taxes for the use of lake-related resources.

The border disputes between Shandong and Jiangsu provinces have had a serious effect on social solidarity and public security in the Lake Weishan area. In addition, owing to the lack of appropriate coordination between all stakeholders concerned, natural and environmental resources have been either over-exploited or destroyed. The border disputes have damaged the ecological sustainability of the lake and caused a substantial amount of environmental degradation. During our field inspections, we found that five major rivers, the Chengguo, Xiaoni, Peiyan, Zhengji and the Sulu, have been the major sources of pollution. Freshwater fish and important limnobiological plants were no longer present around the mouths of these rivers. Water pollution has not only endangered the local fishery and the collection of limnological plants; it has also affected the daily lives and health of the nearby residents. According to a survey conducted by a correspondent of the Qilu Evening News, the frequency of cancer-causing illnesses and tumors has been much higher in the lake region than in the nearby inland areas. Reported health events related to liver diseases, diarrhea and birth defects have also been much more frequent in the polluted area than in the non-polluted area. For example, the following case was reported in the newspaper:

> Located at the mouth of Chengguo River, Shadi village, Liuzhuang township in Weishan county, has a population of 1,000 persons and an area of over 20,000 mu of shoaly land. Due to the lack of arable land (with a per capita area of only 0.013 mu), most of the residents were used to taking reeds, lotus-roots and other lake-related resources. Fishing and fishery cultivation have been their major sources of living. During recent years, as industrial and living waste water discharged from Tengzhou city into Lake Weishan via Chengguo River has increased, water sources on which the residents have depended for their living have been seriously polluted. Consequently, fish stocks have been extinguished, and limnological plants have died. Even worse, the health conditions of the residents living in the region have been seriously affected. Since 1988, 26 young residents have died from diseases caused by, as diagnosed by hospitals at county or higher levels, the drinking of the polluted well water.[20]

Usually, armed disputes in the Lake Weishan area were resolved by the relevant local authorities. However, there have been a few extremely serious examples. These have been resolved by higher-level authorities. It was told that the self-resolved cases have not been documented[21] but that from the 1960s to the mid-1980s, there were six jointly resolved cases for the armed fights in 1961, 1967, 1973, 1980, 1981, and 1984. The resolution of the conflicts required participation by officials from both provinces and the related counties. However, since most of the resolutions were not mediated by the central government, they did not resolve the fundamental problems underlying the disputes. Each side, Shandong and Jiangsu, only emphasized their own interests. As a result, only some minor border-related problems were resolved.

During the field research carried out in the Lake Weishan area, we noted that local officials doubted about the fairness of the central government's final decisions in relation to the resolution of the Lake Weishan disputes. Their most serious concern was that those key central government officials who had provincial ties to either Shandong or Jiangsu were inclined to make resolutions in favor of one side or the other. According to our talks with the local officials from Peixian county, the final decision made by the central government concerning the resolution of the Weishan lake disputes was seen as unfair by Jiangsu provincial authorities since the top decision makers, Wan Li and Tian Jiyun – both of whom held the position of vice premier of the State Council during the 1980s – had been born in Shandong province. Jiangsu officials complained that the speech given by Mr Wan Li had set the scene for the final resolution of the disputes in 1983. For example, Wan Li pointed out: "In order to find a thorough resolution to this problem, the State Council has made a fairly definite decision. After having taken into account of all gains and losses, it seems better to put all disputed villages under the administration of Shandong province."[22]

In our meetings with the local officials in Peixian county, the Jiangsu side stated that since some key central officials were natives of Shandong province, Jiangsu province had been placed at a disadvantage. By contrast, there was also a growing fear from the Shandong side that the resolution of the local disputes had favored Jiangsu province since, during the 1990s, more key central government officials came from southern China. For example, with regard to their victory in the resolution of the interprovincial taxation disputes, the Jiangsu officers admitted in an internal, confidential, report that they had done "hard and meticulous works."[23] The key issues that were not included in the final resolution were: (1) the legality of the ownership transfer of Shandong's underground resources to Jiangsu province; and (2) the entitlement by Shandong province to levy taxes and fees on the exploitation of resources underlying its territory.[24]

The Shandong–Jiangsu border disputes have resulted in a long history of human suffering and environmental damage. Such a situation can rarely be found in any other disputed interprovincial border areas in mainland China. The border disputes have been fought over lakeside land, submerged resources, drainage and irrigation projects, water conservancy projects, the communication infrastructure and public security. The disputes have received urgent attention from many ministries and even the State Council and the CCP's Central Committee. For decades, the border conflicts have peaked during periods of seasonal calamity. It has been recognized that: "A great drought occurred in the lake for every eight or nine years; this 'drought' has usually lasted for three years and during this period conflicts have reached their highest levels."[25]

The interprovincial conflicts have wasted energy and resources at all levels of provincial and local government. This has impeded the economic and social development of the lake area as a whole. In Weishan county, the position of magistrate deputy has been established principally for the purpose of dealing with border conflicts and related matters; at the same time in Peixian county, an office has been established to take charge of the lakeside land cultivation and border-related affairs. Given the difficulties in the current administrative arrangements, is there an alternative to the present situation of continual interprovincial border disputes?

3
Human and Cultural Contexts

> Zigong asked what was needed for government. Confucius said, "Sufficient food, excellent armaments, and people's trust in the government." Zigong asked, "Suppose you were forced to get rid of one of the three, which one would you get rid of first?" "Armaments," said Confucius. Zigong went on asking, "Which one would you get rid of if you were to get rid of one of the remaining two?" Confucius answered, "The food. Although man will die of hunger without food, man has been destined to die since time immemorial. But if people lose their trust in the government then the state has lost its basis."
>
> – *Analects of Confucius* (12: 7)

3.1 Population

At the beginning of the twenty-first century, China's population has risen above 1.3 billion, accounting for more than 20 percent of the global total; it is nine times higher that of Japan, five times that of the USA, and three times that of the entire European Union. The dynamic mechanism of population growth has been substantially influenced by China's population policies. When the PRC was founded in 1949, the population of mainland China was about 450 million. Since then China has experienced two major peaks of population growth. From 1949 to 1958, when the Great Leap Forward movement was launched, the birth rate was as high as 3 to 4 percent while, in contrast, the death rate decreased significantly. This dramatic growth in population was largely encouraged by the government in line with Mao Zedong's thought "the more population, the easier are the things to be done." China's population began to grow rapidly once again after the famine period (1959–61), during which

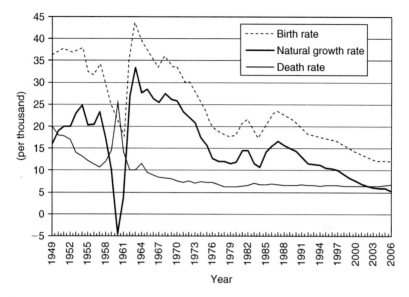

Figure 3.1 Birth, death and natural growth rates

many people died from starvation.[1] The birth rate peaked at 4.3 percent in 1963 and then decreased gradually but still stood at more than 2 percent until the early 1970s when the government realized the importance of population control (see Figure 3.1).

Unfortunately, by this time it was too late for China to control its population, which has continued to grow at a rate of more than 10 million per annum. According to UN population predictions, in the coming decades, China will continue to be the world's most populous nation before being overtaken by India in the 2030s (see Table 3.1).

The Chinese government's promotion of its "sea of manpower" approach led simultaneously to the development of a number of population problems. During recent decades, when the population densities of some developed countries has either stayed constant or decreased gradually, China's population density has increased sharply from 40 persons per square kilometer of land area in 1949 up to 130 persons per square kilometer of land area at the end of the 1990s – a figure which is more than three times that of the world as a whole. In fact, China's population density is not particularly high when compared with South Korea (443 persons per km²), Japan (329 persons per km²), India (290 persons per km²), the UK (237 persons per km²) and Germany (226 persons per km²).

Table 3.1   Population forecasts for selective countries (million persons)

Country	2000	2025	2050
China	1270	1476	1437
India	1046	1391	1747
USA	289	349	420
Indonesia	211	271	297
Brazil	174	229	260
Russia	147	129	109
Pakistan	144	229	295
Bangladesh	139	190	231
Japan	127	119	95
Nigeria	125	205	282

Source: UNPD (2007).

However, because much of China's territory consists of mountains, desert and other uninhabitable lands, the number of persons per square kilometer of the *inhabitable* land area is much larger than the nominal population density in China. For instance, the population densities of many provinces in East China are more than 400 persons per square kilometer of land area (see Figure 3.2) much higher than that of most of the most populous nations in the world.

Today, when considering the poor living conditions in the countryside and the unemployment problem in the urban areas, one cannot help but remember the ridiculous debate about whether or not population growth should be subjected to effective controls. Stimulated by the idea that population equals production, some people believed blindly in the link "more people → more labor force → more production → faster economic development", which led eventually to China's problem of over-population.[2]

In fact, faced by the grim reality of population growth, in his later years even Mao Zedong acknowledged the increasing pressure of over-population on the Chinese economy, when he began to puzzle about his earlier prediction that "Of all things in the world, people are the most precious. … Even if China's population multiplies many times, she is fully capable of finding a solution" (Mao, 1949, pp. 453–4). In the early 1970s, the Chinese government had to implement a birth control policy that aimed to encourage late marriages, prolong the time period between births and reduce the number of children in each family. In 1978, the encouragement of birth control made its first official appearance in Article 53 of the PRC Constitution. Following the implementation of

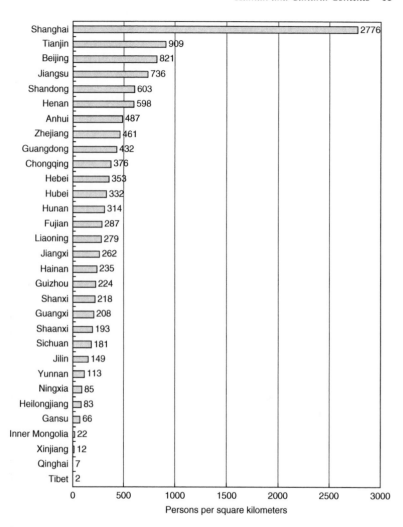

Figure 3.2   China's population density, by province

a population control policy, the First National Conference on Birth Control (NCBC) was held in Beijing in 1979. The conference requested "that one couple has only one child and at most two children but with a three year interval. Those couples who do not plan to have a second child will be rewarded and those who have a third child will receive economic punishment."

Since the 1970s, and especially since the early 1980s, China has effectively controlled its population trends through the introduction of a series of strict measures. The rate of population growth rate declined dramatically – from 3 percent in the 1960s to less than 1 percent by the end of the 1990s. Obviously, without this reduction, China's population would have increased by more than 20 million (that is, $(0.03 - 0.01) \times 1$ billion) per annum. In other words, as a result of China's population control efforts, every two or three years the increase in population has been reduced by an amount equal to the size a medium-sized nation such as the UK or France. Furthermore, the reduction of population growth also increased China's per capita GNP by more than 2.0 percent (that is, $1/(1 - (0.03 - 0.01)) - 1$). Despite these successes, some problems still remain.

First, China's population control policy has generated a gender imbalance. In the poorest and most remote rural areas, the traditional discrimination against women has remained very strong. Because there is very little social security in those rural areas, sons offer the best hope for parents who are still earning their living by physical labor. This provides a strong incentive for people to have more than one child until they have son(s). Partly as a result of the birth control policy and partly because of the increasing burden of having an additional child (girl), the inhumane practices of foeticide and infanticide can be occasionally found, especially in rural areas where men generally have a higher social position than women. China's national birth gender proportion (i.e., male to female) is much higher than that found in the developed nations. According to a sampling survey conducted on October 1 1995, the birth gender proportions for population at the ages of 0, 1, 2, 3, 4 years were 116.57:100, 121.08:100, 121.26:100, 119.17:100 and 115.01:100, respectively (SSB, 1996, p. 72). If only the rural area is taken into account, the birth gender difference would, of course, be much larger.

Secondly, a lower birth rate will result eventually in a higher proportion of aged people. This is already a social problem in the advanced nations and, sooner or later, it will also affect Chinese society. Thanks to the government's efforts in raising the social position of women[3] and the strict domicile system for urban citizens, China's "one-child" policy has been successfully implemented in the urban areas since the early 1980s. At present, it is very common in urban China for a couple to have only one child. However, the policy is to rigidly transform China's urban family pattern into a reverse pyramid over the coming decades. In China in 1953, the ratio of the population aged 65 or over was only 4.4 percent. This ratio was reduced further to 3.6 percent in 1964, but rose again to 4.9 percent in 1982, 5.6 percent in 1990 and 7.0 percent in 2000 (NBS, 2002). The population age composition also differs from region to region. In 1982, Shanghai became the first province where the percentage of the population aged 65 years or over exceeded 7 percent of the total – a criterion that is generally seen as characterizing an aged society. At the end of the 1990s, a number of other provinces also shared this classification: Beijing, Tianjin, Jiangsu, Zhejiang, Shandong, Guangdong, Liaoning, Sichuan and so on. According to Du (1994, p. 88), the proportion of the aged population in China will increase steadily to 8.1 percent in 2010, 10.9 percent in 2020, 14.7 percent in 2030, 19.8 percent in 2040, and 20.9 percent in 2050.

Thirdly, patterns of population growth show considerable differences between the rural and urban areas of China. In some poor rural areas, where labor productivity is to a large extent physically determined, parents have strong incentives to have large numbers of children. By contrast, in urban and other relatively well-off areas, parents who receive higher education and have lifetime social welfare usually have to make a trade-off between having more children and improving their living standards and quality of life. Faced with cramped living conditions and the high cost of education, as well as severe competition for university entrance, urban parents have little incentive to have a second child, not to mention the fact that those who illegally raise more than one child would not receive the subsidies from the government and could be fired from their current posts. As an only child is, in general, better protected by its family than one with siblings, those children born in urban areas usually receive better care and education than those born in rural areas. In brief, the fact that the rural poor have more children than the urban and well-educated people will reduce the overall educational level of the Chinese population.

As a result of the diverse regional natural and geographical conditions, the population of China is unevenly distributed. Generally, population density is higher in the Eastern belt than in the Central belt, while the Central belt has a higher density than the Western belt. The most populous provinces are Shanghai (2,776 persons per km^2), Tianjin (909 persons per km^2), Beijing (821 persons per km^2), Jiangsu (736 persons per km^2), Shandong (603 persons per km^2) and Henan (598 persons per km^2). On the other hand, however, Tibet, Qinghai, Xinjiang and Inner Mongolia have only 2, 7, 12 and 22 persons for each square kilometer of the land area, respectively (see Figure 3.2).

3.2   Labor force

The size of the labor force in a country can be defined as follows: the population in the productive age group multiplied by the labor force participation rate. In turn, the labor force participation rate can be calculated as the ratio of the labor force to the population at or above a certain age. The international standard for the productive age is defined as 15 years or over. In a market economy, labor force demand is positively related to gross production output. When labor supply exceeds labor demand, unemployment occurs. According to China's official definition, the registered unemployment rate in urban areas refers to the ratio of the number of the registered unemployed persons to the sum of the number of employed persons and the registered unemployed persons. The registered unemployed persons in urban areas are defined as: persons who are registered as permanent residents in the urban areas engaged in non-agricultural activities, aged within the range of laboring age (for male, 16 years or older but younger than 50 years; for female, 16 years or older but younger than 45 years), capable of work, unemployed but wishing to be employed and registered with the local employment service agencies.

Table 3.2 gives a cross-national comparison of the economically active population, a term defined by economists as "all men or women who simply work for the production of economic goods and services during a specific period." It is noticeable that China had an incredibly high level of per capita annual labor input (947 hours), compared with the African nations (608 hours) and the Western nations (709 hours). The high labor input of China may help us to understand, at least in part, its levels of rapid economic growth over the course of recent decades.

Table 3.2   Characteristics of human capital, China and the rest of the world

Item	Africa	China	Western nations	World
Proportion of female labor (%)[a]	38.1	37.3	42.5	36.2
Ratio of employment to population (%)[a]	39.3	44.0	44.5	40.5
Per capita labor input (in hours)[a]	608	947	709	736
Gross enrolment ratios[b]	53	99	104	86
(1) Male	58	100	104	89
(2) Female	50	98	105	82

Notes: [a]: Calculated by the author based on Maddison (1996, Table J-1). [b]: Gross enrolment in primary education (UNESCO, 1999).

Table 3.3 Comparison of human development index (HDI), 2003

Nations	HDI	Chinese provinces	HDI
Norway	0.96		
Hong Kong	0.92	Shanghai	0.91
South Korea	0.90	Beijing	0.88
Argentina	0.86	Tianjin	0.86
Mexico	0.81	Guangdong, Liaoning, Zhejiang, Jiangsu	0.81–0.82
Brazil, Malaysia, Colombia	0.79	Heilongjiang, Fujian	0.79
Thailand	0.78	Shandong, Hebei, Jilin	0.77–0.78
Philippines	0.76	Hainan, Xinjiang, Hubei, Shanxi, Hunan, Chongqing	0.75–0.76
China 2003	**0.75**		
Turkey	0.75	Henan, Inner Mongolia	0.74
China in 1999	*0.72*	Jiangxi, Guangxi, Shaanxi, Sichuan, Anhui	0.73
Indonesia, Vietnam	0.70	Ningxia	0.71
		Qinghai, Gansu	0.68
		Yunnan	0.66
China in 1990	*0.63*	Guizhou	0.64
India	0.60		
Myanmar	0.58	Tibet	0.59
China in 1980	*0.56*		
Pakistan	0.53		

Sources: UNDP and CDRF (2005) and UNDP (2005, pp. 219–23). Cited from Naughton (2007, p. 226).

A human development index (HDI) has been computed by the United Nations Development Program (UNDP) for a number of countries. This is simply the average of indices for life expectancy, literacy and school enrollment, and price-adjusted PPP GDP per capita. Table 3.3 shows that: (i) internationally, China's HDI has improved significantly since 1980; and (ii) domestically, there is significant variation among China's provinces. For example, we can see that Shanghai's HDI is comparable to that of Hong Kong or South Korea; and several coastal provinces have, like Mexico, inched into the high HDI category. However, several western provinces, such as Gansu, Yunnan and Tibet, are below Indonesia and Vietnam.

3.3 Education

If you plan for a year, sow a seed; if for ten years, plant a tree; if for a hundred years, teach the people. You will reap a single harvest by sowing a seed once and ten harvests by planting a tree; while you will reap a hundred harvests by teaching the people.

– Guanzhong (?–645 BC)

Education was highly regarded by Guangzhong – a famous primary minister in the state of Qi during the Spring and Autumn period (771–475 BC). For more than one thousand years, and as a result of the Confucian influences, people in China have placed a substantial value on education. At present, most Chinese parents still believe it to be a glorious thing for their children to achieve the highest school degrees.

However, for the majority of the past one hundred years, the development of education in China has not been particularly successful. In 1964, when the second national population census was conducted, 56.76 percent of the total population aged 16 years of age and above were classified as being either illiterate or semi-literate. Thereafter, the illiterate and semi-literate rate decreased considerably, but it was still estimated at 31.88 percent and 20.61 percent in the third and fourth national population census in 1982 and 1990, respectively (SSB, 1996, p. 71).

According to UNESCO (1995, tab. 1.3), in 1990 the literacy rates for China were 87 percent for males and 68 percent for females, which were higher than of the corresponding figures for India (62 percent and 34 percent), Pakistan (47 percent and 21 percent) and many other low-income countries, while being lower than those of Indonesia (88 percent and 75 percent), the Philippines (90 percent and 89 percent), Thailand (95 percent and 91 percent), Malaysia (86 percent and 70 percent) and many other low- and upper-middle income countries, and much lower than those found in Japan, the USA, Germany and other high-income countries. China's moderately high illiteracy rate has been determined by both historic and institutional factors. Before 1949, China's education was very backward and had been seriously damaged by the long-lasting wars. For instance, more than 60 percent of people born in the 1930s and more than 70 percent of people born in the 1920s were either illiterate or semi-literate. During the two peaks of population growth in the 1950s and the 1960s, neither the government nor their families were capable of providing an adequate educational opportunity for each child.

The period of the Cultural Revolution (1966–76) saw a substantial revision of China's education system which had formerly, to a large extent, been grounded in the principles of Confucianism. The length of primary school education was reduced from six years to five years; and that of junior and senior middle schools was cut by one year in each instance. In addition, the textbooks were heavily revised and simplified. Even worse, the status of schoolteachers, who had been highly regarded in traditional Chinese society, became subject to political discrimination. At the same time, the destruction of the higher education system was even more severe because universities were closed during between 1966 and 1970 and operated in line with political rather than academic considerations between 1971 and 1976. The Cultural Revolution resulted in a severe shortage of scientists and engineers, which has already had a negative effect on China's socioeconomic development.

China's educational system began to return to a more normal path as soon as the Cultural Revolution came to an end. In 1977 there was a resumption of the national entrance examinations for higher learning institutes. One year later, the Chinese government made the first recognition, during the First National Conference on Science and Technology (NCST), that "science and technology is a productive force" and began to treat intellectuals as "a branch of the working class." Since this declaration education has been the subject of much state attention. In 1995, the Chinese government decided to implement a nine-year compulsory education system (that is, six years of primary school followed by three years of junior middle school), with the aim of achieving universal access to junior middle school within six years in urban and coastal areas and within ten years in the other parts of the country.

Particularly worthy of praise is the fact that the primary and junior-middle education has achieved substantial progress in recent years, with the enrollment rates increased to nearly 100 percent in the early years of the twenty-first century. At this time China's higher learning institutions (including three- and four-year colleges), which were only able to absorb a small proportion of graduates from senior-middle schools before the 1990s and an even smaller proportion of them before the 1980s (data are not shown in Figure 3.3) have provided opportunities to more than two-thirds of senior-middle school graduates. However, problems still remain in senior-middle school education. For instance, almost one-third of graduates from junior middle schools have not been able to enter senior middle schools in the 2000s (see Figure 3.3).

In 1978, China's expenditure on public education accounted for 2.07 percent of its GNP. In later years, this ratio tended to rise gradually, reaching 2.69 percent in 1986, before dropping back to 2.08 percent in 1995. From 1995 to 2002, the ratio increased considerably to a level of near 3.5 percent; however, it has dropped back again since that time (see Figure 3.4). A regression based on the data on China's educational expenditure and national income from the 1980s and the early 1990s reveals

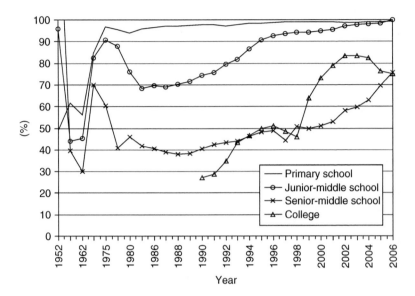

Figure 3.3   Enrolment ratios of various educational institutions
Notes: (1) the proportion of graduates of junior middle schools entering senior middle schools was higher than 100% in the early 1950s as the students graduated from junior middle schools were less than the students enrolled in senior middle schools; (2) graduates of junior middle school include vocational schools; (3) "college" includes three- and four-year colleges.

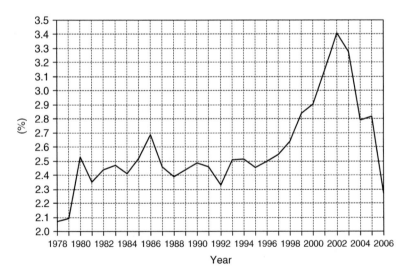

Figure 3.4   Government expenditure on education as a percentage of GNP

that at a time when the per capita national income grew from 250 yuan to 1,000 yuan, the ratio of educational expenditure to national income fell from 6.3 percent to 2.8 percent (Hsueh, 1994b, pp. 80–1). Obviously, the empirical estimate is inconsistent with the hypothesis that there exists a positive correlation between the income level and the ratio of educational expenditure to GNP, as estimated by Chenery and Syrquin (1975, p. 20).[4]

Even though the two estimates are based on different statistical definitions, it can still be seen that China's expenditure on education lagged behind its levels of economic growth, at least during the 1980s and the early 1990s. In China, expenditure on public education as a percentage of GNP China is ahead of only a few of the poorer nations such as Nigeria (0.5 percent, 1992), but still lags far behind that of the world as a whole (5.1 percent, 1993) and many other nations such as Canada (7.6 percent, 1992), Hungary (7.0 percent, 1992), Bulgaria (5.9 percent, 1992), Portugal (6.1 percent, 1990), USA (5.3 percent, 1990) and Japan (4.7 percent, 1991) (UNESCO, 1995, table 4.1).

China's education is unevenly provided across the provinces. Usually, the mean value of education is much higher in the eastern coastal areas (such as Beijing and Shanghai) than in the western inland provinces (such as Qinghai and Tibet). However, the mean values of education in years are more even in the urban areas, the reasons for which may be twofold. First, the central government attempts to equalize educational opportunities across provinces: the richer provinces tend to receive less and the poor provinces more central government funding for education. Secondly, the assignment of college graduates to employment is carried out on a national basis. The government gives preferential treatment to the poor provinces by assigning graduates from colleges in rich provinces to work in poor provinces (Knight and Li, 1993, p. 300).

Modern science developed in Europe. The characteristic of Western culture is reflected in the making of bold hypotheses followed by a meticulous search for evidence. The basis of this approach to science is the experiment. The experiment can not only verify the soundness of the hypothesis; it can also improve or debunk it. It is as a result of these cultural traits that Westerners are more accustomed to making bold hypotheses. As a result, many important and revolutionary discoveries were made. The disadvantage of this is that some of these new ideas and hypotheses may not have solid foundations, but this fault is a minor one where creativity is concerned. The traditional Eastern system emphasizes building a solid foundation, and then constructing basic knowledge step by step. However, it is evident that the Eastern tradition places too much emphasis on foundations. The insistence on rote learning reduced the initiative to make bold hypotheses about new situations and new problems (Pan, 2006).

There is a difference in the understanding and definition of manpower and creativity between China and the Western nations. Creativity is the driving force behind the development of technology, economy, arts and culture as a whole. As a result, it is a multi-level and complex process that covers all fields. Although Asian traditions are conservative in comparison, and the social climate and ideological make-up of the West are more liberal, each of them can make valid contributions toward the nurturing of creativity. Western culture lays an emphasis on the contributions of individuals. There may perhaps be some particular historical or religious reasons, but the mainstay of Western culture is individualism. This trait is manifested in the adulation of individual heroes in Western culture. The individuals' heroic exploits and contributions are prized above collective effort. The advantage of this is that it can spur people on to greater heights. The flaw is that it results in the development of self-centered individualism, which has an indirect influence on creativity (Pan, 2006). Creativity is a multi-level and complex process, involving many different factors. At a certain level, creativity requires the coordination of all sides, and the Eastern culture, which lays emphasis on collectivities, can play a positive role in bringing this about.

3.4   Cultural context

As well as being used to describe the content of libraries, museums, and moral and religious codes of conduct, the world "culture" is used commonly to describe many other aspects of social life. As such, "culture" is the living sum of symbols, meanings, habits, values, institutions, behaviors, and social artifacts which characterize a distinctive and identified human population group. It confers upon individuals an identity as members of some visible community; standards for relating to the environment, for identifying fellow members and strangers; and for distinguishing between what is important and what is unimportant to them (Goulet, 1980, p. 2). While others usually suggest more complicated compositions for a culture, in this chapter we will only discuss three elements – ethnicity, language, and religion. Of course, our discussion of these cultural elements is not definitive and perhaps would not satisfy anthropologists. Nevertheless, our consideration is due to the concerns that: (i) "ethnicity" provides a genetic basis in which socioeconomic behaviors between similar and differing groups of people can be differentiated easily; (ii) "language" is an effective tool of communication; and (iii) "religion" can provide the insights into the characteristics of culture.

For the majority of the Christian era the members of the ethnic majority in China have traditionally been referred to as the Han race. This may well be because of the relatively long period of social, political, economic and military consolidation and stability enjoyed by the Chinese nation during the perid of the Han dynasty (206 BC–AD 220). The term "Han", however, does not offer a full account of the cultural and ethnic origins of the Chinese people. It was, instead, an inclusive name for the various tribes that lived together on the Central China Plains well before the time of Christ. The trend over the ages was for many ethnic groups living adjacent to the Hua-Xia people to be assimilated at different times and to different degrees into what the Chinese have termed ultimately the Han culture. The original ethnic stock for this amalgam seems to have primarily included the Hua-Xia, Eastern Yi, Chu-Wu and Baiyue groups. Other non-Han peoples were assimilated into the Han culture at different points in China's history.[5]

While the Han majority can be found throughout the country, China's ethnic minorities are scattered over vast areas of China (see Appendix 1 for details). Historically, the total number of ethnic groups has never been fixed precisely. For example, in 1953, only 42 ethnic peoples were identified, while the number increased to 54 in 1964 and 56 in 1982. Geographically, most ethnic minorities are concentrated on the western inland areas, such as Hui in Ningxia, Ugyur in Xinjiang, Mongols in Inner Mongolia and Qinghai and Tibetans in Tibet and the surrounding areas. However, the ethnic Zhuang form the majority in Guangxi Zhuang autonomous region in the southern coastal area.

During their histories, many ethnic groups have also established diversified their own economic and cultural backgrounds. For example, the names of some ethnic groups can reveal certain information about their particular economic and cultural conditions, with a number of these highlighting a group's characteristic occupation. For example, in the language of Lahu people, "Lahu" means "roasting tiger-meat on fire", from which it can be understood that the Lahu people used to live by hunting. This can also be witnessed by their neighbors in Southwest China, the Dai and Hani, who called themselves Mushe ("the hunters"). There is a small ethnic group entitled the "Oroqen" (a word which has two meanings: "people who herd tamed deer" and "people who live on the mountains") living in the Greater and Lesser Xing'an Mountains in Northeast China. Another ethnic group, also living in Northeast China, call themselves the Daur (meaning "cultivator"), indicating that the Daur people engaged in agriculture during ancient times.

Since the dawning of China's Neolithic period, agriculture has been the economic mainstay of the Han people. In the embryonic stages of its ethnic development, the Han group lived primarily along the banks of China's major rivers. The area along the Yellow river, characterized by a semi-arid climate, with loose, fertile soil, was suitable for the growing of millet; while the tropical and semi-tropical climate of the areas along the Pearl and Yangtze rivers was good for rice production. Thus millet and rice could be said to be the staple crops that defined early Han culture. While the Han culture continued to develop, commerce, industry, education and government service were also viable livelihoods, as, for example, in the case of the transportation of food, clothing and jewelry between the large walled cities and smaller, more remote towns. The non-Han minorities, such as the Tibetans, in western China, on the other hand, have traditionally had a mixed nomadic economy. The minority peoples in northeast China rely on either fishing and hunting or nomadism, while the Mongols have been mainly nomadic. The other minorities, such as the Uygurs in Xinjiang, have historically engaged in either agriculture or nomadism, but have supplemented their incomes through commerce.

China's linguistic system is understood in terms of its lexicon, grammar, syntax, phonetics and so on. Chinese, the language spoke by the Han people – China's official language, which belongs to the Sino-Tibetan language family – is the most commonly used language in China and one of the most common languages in the world. Written Chinese emerged in its embryonic form of carved symbols approximately 6,000 years ago. The Chinese characters used today evolved from those used in bone and tortoise shell inscriptions more than 3,000 years ago and the bronze inscriptions produced soon after. Drawn figures were gradually reduced to patterned strokes, pictographs were reduced to symbols, the complicated became simplified. Earlier pictographs and ideographs were joined by pictophonetic characters. Chinese is monosyllablic. The vast majority of Chinese characters used today are composed of an ideogramatic portion on the left and the phonetic on the right.[6]

In addition to Chinese, a number of other languages are also used regionally and locally in China (see Appendix 1 at the end of the volume). Specifically, 23 of these languages have taken written forms. Five linguistic systems are represented: 29 languages, including Zhuang, Dai, Tibetan, Yi, Miao and Yao, are within the Han-Tibetan language family; 17 languages, including Uygur, Kazak, Mongolian and Korean, are within the Altaian language family; three languages, the Va, Deang and Blang, are within the South Asian language family; and Gaoshan is an Austronesian language. The Jing language has yet to be classified typologically. The main non-Han Chinese languages used in China are: Zhuang (spoken) in most parts of Guangxi and some parts of Guangdong, Yunnan and Guizhou; Ugyur (spoken and written) in Xinjiang and some parts of Qinghai; Tibetan (spoken and written) in Tibet and the surrounding areas; Mongolian (spoken and written) in Inner Mongolia, Qinghai and the surrounding areas; Yi (spoken) in some parts of Sichuan, Yunnan, Guizhou and Guangxi provinces; and English (spoken and written) in Hong Kong, and so on.

Although the Mandarin is standardized nationwide as *putonghua*, each region speaks its own local version, usually reflecting influence from the native dialect of the area (see Box 3.1). The main unifying force of China's many diverse dialects is the shared written system. It is generally believed that the unified Chinese characters used by people speaking different dialects make it possible for the central government to maintain control effectively over a vast size of territory. However, achieving mastery of the many thousands of Chinese characters is a very long and time-consuming process. This, as argued by Maddison (1996, p. 54), strengthened Chinese ethnocentrism, encouraged self-satisfaction, and inhibited the intellectuals' deviance or curiosities. On the other hand, Fairbank (1980, p. 41) notes that written Chinese is not a wide open door through which the mass peasants gain access to truth and knowledge; rather, all too often it is the stumbling block for their progresses.

Religion has been defined as "belief in the existence of a supernatural ruling power, the creator and controller of the universe, who has given to man a spiritual nature which continues to exist after the death of the body" (Oxford Advanced Learner's Dictionary, 1974, 3rd edn, p. 712). The main religions in China are Confucianism, Buddhism, Taoism, Islam, Catholicism, Protestantism, along with shamanism, Orthodox Christianity and the Naxi people's Dongba religion. The native religions are Confucianism, Buddhism, Taoism, shamanism and animism, while Buddhism was imported from India and evolved later into a Chinese-style religion. The section below discusses the features of some of these religions.

Founded by Kongzi or Confucius (551–479 BC), Confucianism was reputed to have served as the basis of the traditional Chinese culture. *Lunyu* (Analects of Confucius) records the saying and deeds of Confucius

---

Box 3.1   Chinese dialects

Chinese dialects are spoken in three-quarters of the country by two-thirds of the population. Generally, these dialects can be classified into six groups: Xiang, Gan, Kejia, Wu, Min, and Cantonese (Yue). These dialects have the following features:

- The Xiang dialect (in the Hunan area) and the Gan dialect (in the Jiangxi area) each have six tones, including the entering tone. In some areas such as Changsha and Nanchang, these dialects do not distinguish between the constants *l*- and *n*-.
- The Kejia dialect, whose speakers are found mostly in Guangdong, Taiwan, and other scattered areas in Southeast Asia, also has six tones.
- There is a great deal of variation among the Wu dialects, mostly spoken in Shanghai, Jiangsu, and Zhejiang provinces. The Suzhou dialect of Jiangsu province, representing the northern Wu, has seven tones; the Wenzhou dialect of Zhejiang province, treated as the southern Wu, has eight tones; and Shanghai dialect has five tones.
- The Min dialects are spoken widely in Fujian, Taiwan, Hainan and many areas of Southeast Asia, including Singapore and the Philippines. The Min group includes Northern and Southern Min. While the Northern Min is represented by Fuzhou, the Southern Min dialect, which has seven tones, is mostly spoken in eastern Fujian and most parts of the Taiwan area. Southern and Northern Min dialects are for the most part mutually unintelligible.
- Cantonese (Yue), with a total of nine tones, which is more than any other dialect, is the main dialect of Guangdong, Hong Kong, Macau and many overseas Chinese communities.

Sources: Chao (1970) and Ramsey (1989).

---

and his disciples. It covers a wide range of subjects, ranging from politics, philosophy, literature and art to education and moral cultivation. With only 12,000 characters, it is terse but comprehensive, rich yet profound; as the major classic of Confucianism as well as the most authoritative text, it has influenced Chinese society for over two thousand years. Its ideas have set down such firm roots in China that all Chinese – both Han and non-Han ethnicities – have been more or less influenced by it. Since the Han dynasty, every ruler has had to pay at least some heed to this, and people also expected their ruler to act accordingly. Confucian philosophy concerning the relationship between politics and morality serves as the basis of the Confucian school's emphasis on moral education. This can be found in the Analects of Confucius: "Regulated by the edicts and punishments, the people will know only how to stay away out of trouble, but will not have a sense of shame. Guided by virtues and the rites, they will not only have a sense of shame, but also know how to correct their mistakes of their own accord." This idea also represented the distinguishing feature of the Oriental culture realm under the influence of Confucianism.

Taoism originated from sorcery, the pursuit of immortality and other supernatural beliefs that were present in ancient China. Taoists look to the philosopher Laozi (or Lao Tzu, born in about 600 BC) as their great leader, and take his work *The Classic of the Way and Its Power* ("Daode Jing" or "Tao Te Ching") as their canon. Mystifying the philosophical concept of "Dao" or "Tao" (the way, or path), they posit that man could become one with the "Dao" through self-cultivation and can thereby achieve immortality. As an escape from Confucianism, Taoism has been promoted by a group of scholars working against the ritualism and detailed prescriptions of Classical texts. It has also denoted the common people's belief in certain traditional super-institutions. Applying the idea of balance in all things, Taoism argues that human moral ideas are the reflection of human depravity, that the idea of filial piety springs from the fact of impiety, that the Confucian statement of the rules of propriety is really a reflection of the world's moral disorder. Later, Taoism has developed via two directions. The first one, represented by Zhuangzi (*c.*369–295 BC), resulted in so-called nihilism. The second one, with the Tao as the basis of proprieties and laws, led to the founding of the Legalist school.

Through the entire course of Chinese history, Chinese culture has been reconstructed as the result of external influences. Among the first, and the most important is the importation of Buddhism from India in the first century BC. At the heart of Buddhism there are Four Noble Truths: (1) existence is suffering; (2) suffering has a cause, namely craving and attachment; (3) there is a cessation of suffering, which is Nirvana; and (4) there is a path to the cessation of suffering, which includes the Noble Eightfold Path – that is, right view, right intention, right speech, right action, right livelihood, right effort, right mindfulness, and right concentration. Nirvana is the ultimate goal of Buddhism. It represents the extinction of all cravings and the final release from suffering. To the extent that such ideal reflects the thinking of the mass of people, a Buddhist society's values would be considered antithetical to goals such as acquisition, achievement, or affluence. Buddhism became increasingly popular after the fourth century AD and has now been both a Chinese religion and an important part of Chinese culture. Tibetan Buddhism, or Lamaism as it is sometimes called, is founded primarily in Tibet and Mongolia. One of the tenets of Buddhism is that life is painful and that it is not limited to the mortal span with which we are familiar.

In the mid-seventh century, Muslim Arab and Persian merchants came overland through Central Asia to northwest China and by sea to Guangdong and other southeastern ports, bringing with them the Islamic faith. Christian belief was first introduced to China approximately one thousand years ago. During the Ming (AD 1368–1644) and the Qing (1644–1911) dynasties, a large number of Christian missionaries began to arrive in China. They brought not only their religion but also new concepts of science and technology. Today, China is a country which displays considerable religious diversity. Apart from the Protestants and Roman Catholics, who are scattered across the nation, most of the other religious followers in China have either a geographical or ethnic orientation. Most Han people traditionally engage in folk religious practices, usually mixed with elements from Confucianism, Taoism and Buddhism. The Hui, Uygur, Kazak, Kirgiz, Tatar, Ozbek, Tajik, Dongxiang, Salar and Bonan people, mostly in the area of Northwest China, adhere to Islamic culture. The Tibetans, Mongols, Lhoba, Moinba, Tu and Yugur follow a creed of Tibetan Buddhism (also known as Lamaism); by contrast, the Blang and Deang in Southwest China favor Theravada Buddhism. The minorities of Southwest China such as the Dai tend to be adherents of the Hinayana school of Buddhism. Some minorities in Jilin and Heilongjinag provinces subscribe to shamanism, while other ethnic groups living in the valleys of the southwestern mountain ranges embrace animist beliefs.

For most of the past thousands of years, Confucianism has had a substantial influence on China's political culture. The ethical beliefs of Confucianism have remained consistently within the bounds of a set of orthodox principles governing interpersonal relationships in China. They have been applied officially to all strata of society: loyalty, filial piety, benevolence, righteousness, love, faith, harmony and peace. As a result, China has developed a different culture in respect of economic development than is found in the rest of the world, in response to its own particular environment and social conditions (see Box 3.2). For instance, in contrast to other peoples, the Chinese pay heed to their own spiritual interests (including the richness of spiritual life and harmonization of feeling) more than the material ones. This characteristic results largely from the Confucian philosophy which emphasizes "faithfulness", "kindheartedness", "trustworthiness", "ritualism", "peace" and so on. All of these have influenced Chinese economic life and structure, which eventually results in China's economic culture.

Box 3.2 Chinese characteristics

More than one hundred years ago, Arthur H. Smith, who had served as the Missionary of the American Board for 22 years in China, wrote a book entitled *Chinese Characteristics*. The book was first published in Shanghai by an English newspaper in 1890. The second edition of the book was published in London in 1892. The third, fourth, and fifth revised editions were published in New York, London, Edinburgh, and London in 1894, 1895, and 1900, respectively. Based on the rural Chinese life during the late nineteenth century, Smith presented an interesting description of Chinese characteristics. To make comparisons easier, we classify all the chapters in Smith's (1972) book into three types, as follows:

Positive	Negative	Neutral
Economy	Disregard of time	Face
Industry	Disregard of accuracy	Flexible inflexibility
Politeness	Talent for misunder-	Absence of nerves
Physical vitality	standing	Indifference to
Patience and	Talent for indirection	comfort and
perseverance	Intellectual turbidity	convenience
Benevolence	Contempt for	Content and
Mutual responsibility	foreigners	cheerfulness
and respect for law	Absence of public	Filial piety
Polytheism, pantheism,	spirits	
and atheism	Conservation	
	Absence of sympathy	
	Social typhoons	
	Mutual suspicion	
	Absence of sincerity	

3.5   Summary

Historical evidence suggests that from the sixteenth century the Western countries gradually pulled ahead of the rest of the world.[7] Northern Italy and Flanders played the leading role from the sixteenth to the seventeenth century, the Netherlands from then until the end of the eighteenth century, the UK and Germany in the nineteenth, and the USA since that time. The main institutional characteristics of Western society that have favored its development can be broadly summarized as follows: (1) the recognition of human capacity to transform the forces of nature through rational investigation and experiment; and (2) the ending of feudal constraints on the free purchase and sale of property, followed by a whole series of developments which gave scope for successful entrepreneurship (Maddison, 1996, p. 50).

A huge population does not represent an advantage in human resources for economic development, particularly for a country that has been transformed from an agricultural society that has used mainly traditional methods of production to an industrial society that requires not only advanced sciences and technologies but also a qualified workforce. A well-educated and law-abiding population that possesses a strong work ethic is the *sine qua non* of modern economic growth. At present, the development of its educational system is a particularly pressing matter for China – a country with a high proportion of illiteracy and whose educational system had been seriously destroyed in the Cultural Revolution period (1966–76). At the same time, ways must be found to raise the technical and professional level of the workers already in employment.

Creativity and innovation have been the most fundamental elements in promoting, either directly or indirectly, economic development and social change. In China, there were great thinkers such as Confucius, Mencius, Laozi and Zhuangzi. But these achievements go back the periods of the Spring and Autumn (770–476 BC) and the Warring States (475–221 BC), and there has not been a similar breakthrough within the past 1,000 years. Throughout its history, Chinese culture has two obvious historical traits. One is that it had a very long period of feudalism. The second trait is that the Imperial Examination (*keju*) system was too rigid and deeply entrenched. The feudal period in Europe was, by contrast, shorter and was followed by over 200 years (from the fourteenth to the sixteenth century AD) of the Renaissance, a revolutionary movement in intellectual thought and inventiveness spurred on by the call to revive the arts of classical Greece. The Enlightenment and the Industrial Revolution that followed caused a tumultuous transformation in Europe.

Shaking off its feudal shackles, Europe created a brave new world for itself. Under such circumstances, Europe produced many new creations and inventions in the realms of art, science, music, architecture and so on. Over the course of the past 200 years, the United States has attracted many high caliber immigrants and provided very favorable conditions for creativity and inventiveness, making it the world's only present-day superpower.

Chinese culture is perhaps the most sophisticated in East Asia. Its religious heritage, which aims to achieve a harmonious balance between Confucianism, Buddhism and Taoism, worked particularly well over a very long period of time. It is probably for this very reason that the Chinese remained intoxicated by past prosperity and still proudly regarded China as the *zhongguo* (center under heaven) of the world, even when it was beginning to lag far behind the Western nations. This kind of ethnocentrism and self-satisfaction eventually made China a typical autarkic society. The following were blamed for China's backwardness: the attachment to the family becomes nepotism; the importance of interpersonal relationships rather than formal legality becomes cronyism; consensus becomes the greasing of wheels and political corruption; conservatism and respect for authority become rigidity and an inability to innovate; much-vaunted educational achievements become rote learning and a refusal to question those in authority; and so on.

3.6 Case study: Age, gender, education and earnings

J and L are two state-owned mining firms that belong to the Kailuan Group Corporation.[8] Firm J is located near Jinggezhuang village, northeast Tangshan city, Hebei province. It was established in 1958 and went into operation in 1979, with a production capacity of 1.2 million tons per year. Following some technological readjustments in 1981, it has risen to more than 1.7 million tons per year since this time. About 100 km from Tianjin city and 72 km from Tangshan city, Firm L is located at Linnanchang town, southwest Yutian county, Hebei province. The firm was originally established by Tianjin municipal government in April 1970 and was transferred to Kailuan Group in April 1978. In November 1985 the firm went into operation, with a production capacity of 0.6 million tons per year, down from 1.2 million tons per year in the first year.

At the end of 2000, there were 5,605 and 2,926 staff in Firms J and L, respectively. In our surveys, we only collected the data on

617 (for Firm J) and 554 (for Firm L) staff (see Table 3.4). In general,
Firm J's average educational level (in length of years) is 11.83, which
is higher than Firm L's 8.10. Restricted by bad working environment
in underground mines, China's retirement ages are officially defined
as of 45 years for underground miners and of 60 years (for males) and
55 years (for females) in other industrial sectors. In Firms J and L, the
average ages are 35.98 and 35.26 years, respectively. These figures are
less than the average age (39.64) of China's state-owned enterprises
as a whole in the mid-1990s (Zhao, 1999, p. 455).

Since Firms J and L were established during the 1970s and the
1980s, their organizational behaviors in production and business
activities have reflected, to a certain extent, the outcome of a centrally
planned system. Moreover, economic performances differed between
these two firms. For example, in 1999 Firm J produced 1.794 million
tons of raw coal with a gross profit of 14.28 million yuan; however,

Table 3.4   About the samples (October 2000): Firms J and L

		Firm J	Firm L
Total samples (persons)		617	554
As % of total staff		11.01	18.93
Proportion of female staff (%)		5.51	4.51
Proportion of CCP members (%)		16.86	2.53
Proportion of ethnic minorities (%)[a]		0.72	1.06
Proportion of underground miners (%)		68.07	65.88
Composition by education[b]	Average length of education (years)[c]	11.88	8.10
	Primary school (%)	0.00	5.60
	Junior high school (%)	2.43	53.43
	Senior high school (%)	17.50	8.30
	Technical school (%)	11.67	0.18
	College (3 or 4 years)	15.56	0.00
Composition by age group	Average age (years)	35.98	35.26[d]
	20 years or younger (%)	3.57	0.00
	21–30 years (%)	27.23	28.80
	31–40 years (%)	35.98	47.73
	41–50 years (%)	29.66	21.60
	51 years or older (%)	3.57	1.87

Notes: [a] The samples are 556 (for Firm J) and 76 (for Firm L). [b] The samples are 291
(for Firm J) and 376 (for Firm L), representing 47.16% and 678.7% of the total samples,
respectively. [c] Based on the length of years for the stage of each education: 5 for primary
school, 8 for junior high school, 11 for senior high school, 12 for technical school, 14
for 3-year college and 15 for 4-year college. [d] The samples are 375.
Source: Author's survey in 2001.

Firm L only produced 0.600 million tons of raw coal, recording a deficit of 4.20 million yuan.

Table 3.5 compares the two firms' average wage levels between various groups of staff. Generally speaking, in Firms J and L the basic wages are not so different as the bonuses and the subsidies. But in both firms the levels of total wages are significantly different between male and female staff. This is quite easily understood, since female workers only engaged in those jobs with low work intensities and with, accordingly, relatively low levels of compensation.[9] In addition, since most, if not all, high-ranking staff were also CCP members, whereas very few low-ranking staff were, the wage levels differed significantly between CCP and non-CCP members.

Although Han ethnic staff accounted for the majority of the employees, some non-Han ethnic minorities (such as the Hui, Mongol, and Manchu) were also employed in both Firms J and L. According to the Chinese constitution, every employee should be treated fairly and paid equally if they carried out the same jobs, no matter which ethnic groups they belong to. Nevertheless, we found two ethnically related items in the list of wages in both firms:

- "Penalty on the birth of a second child": since the non-Han ethnic minorities are permitted a more flexible birth-control policy than Han ethnic couples, this item applies more frequently to the Han ethnic staff.
- "Subsidy to the Hui ethnic staff": since Muslims do not eat pork, which is a common food in Chinese cafeterias, they may use this subsidy to prepare their own food by themselves.

Generally, wage levels vary with respect to age. According to Machin (1996, p. 52, Table 4), the ratio of wage levels of Ages 40–49 to 21–24 was 1.36 in the UK in 1990, and that of Ages 45–49 to 20–24 was 2.14 in the USA in 1990. In our surveys, the ratios of wage levels of 40–49 to 21–24 were 1.58 for Firm J (which is higher than the UK's) and 1.29 for Firm L (which is lower than the UK's), and those of Ages 45–49 to 20–24 were 1.59 for Firm J and 1.28 for Firm L (which is much lower than the figure for the USA). From Table 3.5, we can also find that the level of monthly wages was the highest for the group with Ages >50 in Firm J (1,466.72 yuan), while it was the highest for the group with Ages 41–50 in Firm L (1,209.36 yuan).

Table 3.5 Average wages by groups of workers (yuan/person, October 2000): Firms J and L

By group of workers		Basic wage		Bonus		Subsidy		Total wage	
		Firm J	Firm L	Firm J	Firm L	Firm J	Firm L	Firm J	Firm L
All samples		612.02	502.13	363.50	318.82	256.66	151.05	1232.18	972.00
Gender	Male	618.48	506.65	364.95	330.26	260.61	153.77	1244.04	990.68
	Female	501.38	406.36	338.52	76.92	188.76	93.40	1028.67	576.68
Political status	CCP membership	752.78	549.79	636.15	403.50	218.11	175.36	1607.05	1128.64
	Non-CCP	583.49	500.89	308.22	316.63	264.47	150.42	1156.18	967.94
Ethnicity	Han ethnic	624.63	530.42	378.59	398.11	257.10	183.97	1260.33	1112.49
	Non-Han ethnic	567.67	532.75	265.28	424.50	212.07	193.00	1045.02	1150.25
Occupation	Underground miner	602.83	533.68	303.48	401.03	280.81	186.24	1187.12	1120.94
	Office worker	631.63	441.20	491.44	160.07	205.16	83.10	1328.23	684.36
Education	College	729.36	NA	582.52	NA	211.20	NA	1523.08	NA
	Technical school	571.56	565.00	435.67	1386.00	212.09	221.00	1219.32	2172.00
	Senior high school	488.88	522.96	280.55	429.63	244.22	186.93	1013.65	1139.52
	Junior high school	597.98	522.46	257.60	388.99	241.59	183.97	1097.17	1095.42
	Primary	627.85	615.16	315.41	416.45	284.70	181.58	1227.96	1213.19
	Others[a]	627.85	443.56	315.41	152.39	284.70	82.09	1227.96	678.03
Age group	20 years or younger	430.19		131.32		243.16		804.67	
	21–30 years	467.12	476.79	287.24	361.44	230.59	188.37	984.94	1026.59
	31–40 years	613.88	528.36	410.31	407.75	257.32	185.63	1281.52	1121.75
	41–50 years	739.18	599.12	401.22	431.74	282.08	178.49	1422.48	1209.36
	50 years or older	823.94	617.14	391.80	299.00	250.98	141.43	1466.72	1057.57

Note: [a] including illiterate and unidentified staff.

Table 3.5 also shows that, in the case of both firms, staff with higher levels of education usually received higher wages. However, some exceptions do exist in Firm J in which the average level of wages of the "Senior high school" staff (1,013.65 yuan) was lower than that of the "Junior high school" staff (1,097.17 yuan) and even lower than that of the "Primary school" staff (1,227.96 yuan).[10] Theoretically, in firms the levels of wages are decided by many factors through very complicated patterns which are either linear, non-linear, random, or even fuzzy. According to Kotlikoff and Gokhale (1992), the compensations of office workers and marketing staff follow the following patterns with respect to age: (i) For office workers, the level of compensation is lower than that of labor productivity before the age of 50 years and is higher than that of labor productivity thereafter. (ii) For marketing staff, the level of compensation is higher than that of labor productivity near the age of retirement and lower than that of labor productivity thereafter. In fact, as Prendergast (1999) points out, since most workers have been employed under the condition that "performances are achieved not individually but collectively", the determinants of wage levels are very complicated.

It should be noted that firms with different types of production techniques have different requirements in respect of the educational and professional backgrounds for their staff. All of these will decide the distributions of earnings in different firms. In addition, the mechanism of earnings distribution for unskilled workers with unlimited supply is also different from that for skilled workers with limited supply. In order to understand and compare the determinants of earnings distributions in Firms J and L, let us use the data collected in our surveys to estimate the wage functions with respect to various explanatory variables, including age, age-squared, gender, CCP membership, ethnicity, position, and education (as both continuous and dummy variables).

From Table 3.6, we may find that the estimated coefficients on some explanatory variables are statistically significant, while others are not. In both cases, these exist differences between Firms J and L. For example, the estimated coefficients on "Age" and "Age-squared" show that the wage level (in natural log form) rises with the increase of age before the ages of 27.5 (that is, $0.033 \div (0.0006 \times 2)$) years (for Firm J) and of 25.0 (that is, $0.025 \div (0.0005 \times 2)$) years (for Firm L) and decreases with age thereafter. In addition, the estimated results of the two firms have the following differences: (i) the coefficients

Table 3.6 Determinants of wages: Firms J and L

Explanatory variable	"Education" as dummies		"Education" as a continuous variable	
	Firm J	Firm L	Firm J	Firm L
Constant	6.357 (63.462)[a]	6.054 (75.303)[a]	5.963 (35.298)[a]	6.317 (22.823)[a]
Age	0.033 (5.410)[a]	0.025 (3.486)[a]	0.033 (4.177)[a]	0.026 (2.655)[a]
Age-squared	−0.0006 (−3.293)[a]	−0.0005 (−2.089)[b]	−0.0006 (−2.432)[a]	−0.0006 (−1.704)[c]
Male	0.100 (1.541)	0.157 (2.400)[a]	0.086 (1.349)	0.073 (0.329)
CCP membership	0.264 (4.770)[a]	−0.029 (−0.352)	0.250 (4.486)[a]	−0.023 (−0.261)
Han-ethnic	0.082 (1.583)	−0.094 (−0.741)	0.048 (0.694)	−0.080 (−0.489)
Underground miner	0.193 (2.976)[a]	0.343 (3.858)[a]	0.188 (3.339)[a]	0.370 (3.166)[a]
Education			0.044 (3.246)[a]	0.010 (0.836)
College	0.190 (2.480)[a]			
Technical school	0.102 (1.400)	1.002 (3.022)[a]		
Senior high school	0.000 (0.005)	0.314 (2.172)[b]		
Junior high school	0.011 (0.109)	0.296 (2.147)[b]		
Primary school		0.290 (1.943)[b]		
R^2	0.290	0.414	0.426	0.083
F	24.611	38.293	29.593	4.747
Samples	617	554	291	376

Notes: (1) Based on ordinary least squares (OLS) regressions, with the natural log of monthly wages as the dependent variable. (2) Figures and figures within parentheses are estimated coefficients and their t-statistic values, respectively. (3) [a], [b] and [c] denote statistically significant at the 1%, 5% and 10% levels, respectively.

on "Male", "Han ethnic", "Technical school", "Senior high school" and "Junior high school" are not significantly estimated in Firm J; (ii) the coefficients on "CCP member", "Han ethnic" and "Education in years" are not significantly estimated in Firm L. The estimated coefficients on "Underground miner", which are statistically significant in both firms, show that the underground miners' wages are 21.29 percent (i.e., $\exp(0.193) - 1$) and 40.92 percent (i.e., $\exp(0.343) - 1$) higher than those of the other staff in Firms J and L, respectively.

During the 1980s and the early 1990s, there was an unusual phenomenon in terms of the distribution of earnings in China, which is called "nao ti daogua": this indicates that physical labors are paid more than technical ones (Zhao, 1990). Since the mid-1990s, however, that situation has been changed significantly (Liu, 1998; and Lai, 1999, p. 452). Table 3.6 shows that in Firms J and L the coefficients on higher education dummies are always larger than those on lower education ones. The estimated coefficient on education in years, also called "ratio of return to education" by labor economists, is 0.0436 for Firm J. Obviously, this coefficient is larger than that for urban and rural China (0.038 and 0.020, respectively) in 1988 (Li and Li, 1994, p. 445) and of state-owned enterprises and collectively owned enterprises (0.042 and 0.032, respectively) in 1996, but smaller than that of foreign invested enterprises (0.0791) in 1996 (Zhao, 2001).

By contrast, Firm L's ratio of return to education is not only smaller than that of Firm J, but is also insignificantly estimated in statistics. Does this phenomenon result from the fact that Firm L's production technologies are more backward than and its economic performances are much poorer than Firm J's? We leave this question for future research.

4
Political Economic Systems in Transition

Bianque stood looking at Duke Huang of Cai for a while and spoke, "Your Majesty is suffering from an ailment, which now remains in between the skin and the muscles. But it may get worse without treatment." "I am not at all indisposed," replied the Duke complacently. When Bianque left, the Duke remarked, "It is the medical man's usual practice to pass a healthy person as a sick man in order to show his brilliance." Ten days later, when Bianque saw the Duke, he pointed out: "The ailment has developed into the muscles. It will go from bad to worse if no treatment is conducted." To this the ruler showed a greater displeasure than before. Another ten days went by. On seeing the Duke again, Bianque warned him that the illness had gone into the stomach and the intestines and that unless an immediate treatment be given, it would go on worsening. Again the Duke looked angrier. After a third ten days, when Bianque saw the Duke, he simply turned round and went away... (*to be continued*)[1]

– Hanfeizi (*c*.280–233 BC)

4.1 Plan and market

In traditional socialist countries, economic development is realized mainly through a plan worked out by the central planning authorities. The plan, however, is a mental construct which may or may not correctly reflect the objective requirements of economic development. If the plan is correct, economic development is smooth; if it is incorrect, not only is it of no help – it may even lead to stagnation and decline. Obviously this has been proven in China's economic sphere, especially during the pre-reform period.

During the early 1950s, the transformation of private ownership of the means of production into public ownership and the establishment of a powerful socialist sector paved an effective way for planned development of the national economy. During the first FYP period (1953–57), much attention was paid to industrial construction, especially in heavy industry. At the same time, the socialist transformation of agriculture, handicrafts, and capitalist industry and commerce was effectively carried out. In line with these goals, 156 key projects and other items were arranged with the guidance of the Soviet Union. The first FYP was generally known by the PRC's central planners and economists to be very successful because all scheduled targets were fully met.[2]

Facing the economic difficulties during the late 1950s and the early 1960s, the CCPCC and the State Council advanced a policy entitled "readjustment, consolidation, filling-out, and raising standards" (*tiaozheng, gonggu, chongshi, tigao*). The production targets for heavy industry were reduced and investment in capital construction was cut back. The accumulation rate, which had risen to as high as 39.9 percent in 1960, was adjusted sharply downwards, reaching only 10.4 percent by 1962. The enterprises with high production costs and large losses were closed or switched to other products. With the adjustments, the economy rapidly returned to normal. From 1962 to 1965, the GVIO was growing at an annual rate of 17.9 percent, GVAO at 11.1 percent, and national income at 14.5 percent (Liu, 1982, p. 31).

In contrast to the first FYP and the readjustment period (1963–65), the years 1958–60 provided a typical case of errors in planning, resulting in serious economic imbalances. During this period, the Great Leap Forward movement was effectively launched by the establishment of a series of high targets within a given period, most of which, however, were incapable of being fulfilled due to the limitation of resources and production capacities. To accomplish its ambitious target for an overnight entrance to the "communist heaven", large quantities of raw materials and labor were diverted toward heavy industry while, in contrast, the development of agriculture and light industry received less attention. This situation lasted until 1960, when the serious imbalances between accumulation and consumption and between heavy industry on one hand and agriculture and light industry on the other hand, suddenly became very apparent. Despite this profound lesson, similar problems arose again thereafter.[3]

Since a socialist economy is rigorously directed by state planning, as soon as errors occur in the plan, this will have an effect on every economic activity. China bore witness to this point by its experience and lessons. Theoretically, it is essential to make a "perfect" plan for the healthy operation of the economy. However, it is almost impossible for the state planners to accurately manage a balance between social production and social needs and efficiently distribute the scarce resources even with the use of the sophisticated computers. In fact, because of information constraints and asymmetries the central planners could never obtain complete and accurate information on economic activities from which to formulate plans. Furthermore, the centrally planned system also generated a number of other problems. For example, as wages were fixed workers had no incentive to work after they had reached the factory's output quota. Any extra production might have led to the increase of the following year's quota while the level of salaries would remain unchanged. Factory managers and government planners frequently bargained over work targets, funds and material supplies allocated to the factory. Usually, government agencies allocated less than managers requested so managers would, in turn, request more than they needed; when bargaining over the production, the managers, however, proposed a smaller quota than they were able to finish, and so they were usually ordered to fulfill a larger quota than requested.[4]

China's decentralization of its mandatory planning system and the introduction of market mechanisms which began in 1978 first focused on a gradual transition from the people's commune system (PCS) to the household responsibility system (HRS) under which farmers were free to decide what and how to produce in their contracted farmlands and, having fulfilled the state's production quotas, were permitted both to sell the excess of their produce on the free market and also to pursue some non-agricultural activities. In 1984, when urban reform was implemented, China aimed to regulate industrial production through the operation of market forces. In a similar manner to the system adopted in the agricultural sctor, after fulfilling their output quotas, enterprises could make profits by selling their excess products at free or floating prices. It is worthwhile noting that the above efforts resulted inevitably in dual prices for commodities during the transition period and had both positive and negative effects (this will be discussed in detail in the next chapter).

China's economic reform has followed a double-track system in which the reform was implemented first in the area of agricultural products and thereafter spread slowly to consumer goods and intermediate goods. In each case, a free market in which the price was subject to the market regulations developed in parallel with a controlled market in which the price was kept almost unchanged at an officially fixed level. Because the price was higher in the market-regulated track than in the state-controlled track, the free market supply grew rapidly, and its share of total output rose steadily. Meanwhile, the planned price was able to rise incrementally until it approached the market price when there was a narrowing of the gap between supply and demand. The dual-pricing system provided opportunities for people who had access to state-controlled goods and materials to make large profits by buying them at an artificially fixed low price and reselling them at a market-based price, which often led to unequal competition as well as official corruption. The result was that this dual market created various distortions and speculative transactions.

By the end of 1986, the number of key industrial products under the direct control of the State Planning Commission (SPC) has fallen from 120 to 60; accordingly, its share of industrial production fell from 40 percent to 20 percent; the number of commodities and materials distributed by the state (i.e., *tongpei wuzhi*) dropped from 250 to 20 and the number of goods controlled by the Ministry of Commerce (MOC) decreased from 188 to 25; the share of prices which were "free" or "floating" increased to about 65 percent in agriculture and supplementary products, 55 percent of consumer goods and 40 percent of production materials (State Council, 1988a, p. 198). During the 1980s and the early 1990s the double-track system extended across almost every sphere of the Chinese economy, from agriculture, industry, commerce, transportation, post and telecommunications to health care, education, and so on. By the late 1990s, the dual-pricing system had decontrolled more than 90 percent of retail prices and agricultural and intermediate product prices and removed the mandatory plans of a large number of products including fuel and raw materials.

Between regions there are some slight differences in the process toward the decentralization of mandatory planning. Roughly speaking, the Eastern belt is more marketized than the Central belt, while the Western belt is the least marketized. According to Table 4.1, the share of the marketized agricultural products (SMAP) ranged between 20.3 percent (in Qinghai province) and 43.3 percent (in Jilin province) in 1988 and between 60.0 percent (in Henan province) and 98.8 percent (in Guangdong province) in 1994. It is more interesting to note that some developed provinces (such as Shanghai, Beijing and Jiangsu) were not so highly marketized as the poor provinces (such as Anhui, Guangxi and Hainan) in 1988. This probably stems from the fact that China's agricultural reform was carried out first in Anhui and other poor and agriculture-based provinces, whereas Shanghai and Beijing – the centrally administered municipalities with strong industrial bases – lagged behind.

Table 4.1   Agricultural marketization, by province

Province	SMAP (%)		RMP
	1988	1994	1988
Anhui	40.1	81.7	0.822
Beijing	29.6	94.2	1.116
Fujian	32.5	91.0	0.984
Gansu	20.8	85.0	1.119
Guangdong	36.0	98.8	0.887
Guangxi	35.9	81.2	0.940
Guizhou	24.8	NA	1.690
Hainan	34.1	NA	0.887
Hebei	29.3	88.8	0.993
Heilongjiang	29.3	81.2	0.996
Henan	26.4	60.0	1.049
Hubei	27.3	72.7	1.030
Hunan	35.1	79.3	0.970
Inner Mongolia	26.9	NA	0.837
Jiangsu	29.5	77.4	1.015
Jiangxi	31.6	74.7	0.897
Jilin	43.3	85.9	0.957
Liaoning	33.1	90.4	1.042
Ningxia	28.5	81.5	0.961
Qinghai	20.3	77.5	1.215
Shaanxi	31.0	77.2	1.026
Shandong	28.9	73.5	0.953
Shanghai	27.8	91.7	1.024
Shanxi	23.3	80.9	1.005
Tianjin	38.4	N/A	1.020
Tibet	23.0	N/A	1.008
Yunnan	21.5	67.3	1.164
Zhejiang	33.5	76.5	1.004

Notes: SMAP = share of marketized agricultural products; RMP = ratio of market price to state-controlled price; N/A = data not available.
Sources: SSB (1989b, p. 130), Riskin (1994, p. 350) and PYC (1995, p. 19).

Using the data in Table 4.1, we observe that, in 1988, the ratio of market-regulated price to the state-controlled price (RMP) was negatively related to the share of the marketized agricultural products (SMAP) (see Figure 4.1a). This was reasonable and reflected to some extent the government's efforts to stabilize the market, for example, letting the provinces with market-regulated prices close to or lower than the state-controlled one share a higher proportion of the market-oriented reform in the agricultural sector during the earliest period of reform (that is, 1978–88). Between 1988 and 1994, since the government allowed the speed of the

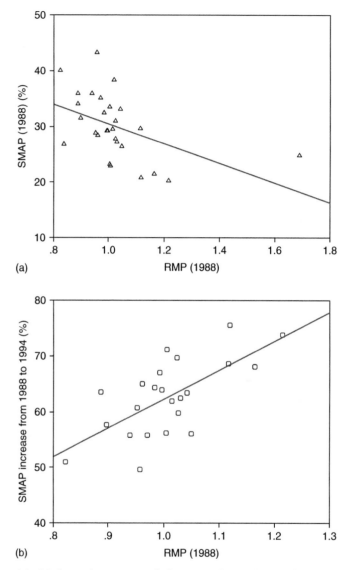

Figure 4.1   Market and state-controlled prices and agricultural reform
Notes: (1) each point in the figures denotes a province; (2) SMAP = share of mar-
ketized agricultural products; (3) RMP = ratio of market to state-controlled prices.
Source: Created by the author based on Table 4.1.

market-oriented agricultural reform to be positively determined by the RMP (see Figure 4.1b), high inflation and other macroeconomic risks occurred accordingly during this period.[5] In other words, had the agricultural reform not followed the spatial pattern shown in Figure 4.1b, the Chinese economy would not have encountered so many difficulties during the late 1980s and the early 1990s.

4.2 Employment

Following the establishment of the new China, the labor market was officially eliminated because according to Marxist theory labor is not a commodity to be bought and sold. From the late 1950s, a system of state allocation for all urban employment was introduced gradually. After 1966, the state became responsible for the allocation of jobs for the entire urban labor force. All labor was allocated either to units owned by the states or to large collectives which were essentially the same as the state-owned units. In the centrally planned system, the labor force was allocated to enterprises by the state and lifetime employment was guaranteed. Wages were also determined by the state in the principle of "distribution according to working performance" (*anlao fenpei*). There is no doubt that this kind of system eliminated the widespread occurrence of unemployment that had usually existed in the "old" China and that exists in all capitalist countries. It also effectively equalized wages and led to a considerable reduction in the gaps between the haves and the have-nots.

This rigid system of job allocation, however, has resulted in some disadvantages. Once people were employed in the state sector, their jobs were secure, regardless of the quality of their work. The system thus became known as the "iron rice bowl" (*tie fanwan*) because of the employment security it implied. Under the equal wage system (labeled "eating from the same pot", or *daguo fan*) human resources were not allocated in an efficient manner. Egalitarianism, a lack of interest in economic outcomes, and a low sense of economic responsibility are among the expressions of this mentality. Employing units could not exercise free choice over who they selected and they also had to provide almost equal pay to workers whose perform might differ widely. This hindered the improvement of labor productivity. Furthermore, the system did not encourage people to develop their talents and enthusiasm fully since they could not choose the work which best suited them (see Box 4.1).

Recognizing the negative effects of this labor system, in the early 1980s the government began to introduce a series of reforms. The earliest efforts included the introduction of a contract system – setting up a production

Box 4.1 Documentary

The College Rd. No. 11
Beijing 1000083
People's Republic of China

Dear Sirs:

On behalf of the Scholars at Risk Network, I am writing to inquire about Dr. Rongxing Guo, who until recently served as professor at the Beijing Graduate School of China University of Mining and Technology ("CUMT").

The Scholars at Risk Network is a non-governmental organization based at the University of Chicago with members at more than 70 universities and colleges in the United States and partners worldwide. Scholars at Risk is dedicated to protecting the human rights of scholars and to raising awareness, understanding of and respect for the principles of academic freedom and its constituent freedoms of thought, opinion, and expression-- freedoms essential to any healthy academic community and civil society generally. In cases such as this one, Scholars at Risk inquires on behalf of an individual scholar.

We received allegations about Dr. Rongxing Guo's employment situation at CUMT, information which alleges an unwillingness to allow him to seek positions at other universities, or to accept offers received from several other prestigious academic institutions in China. We are writing to request your help in clarifying the situation. We would appreciate your responding to our letter and providing whatever information you deem appropriate.

According to the information we received, Dr. Guo had tried to accept an invitation to Peking University in 1996. Shortly thereafter, his wife's employment at CUMT was terminated. We understand she had been working there since 1981. We are also led to believe that in March 2002 Dr. Guo had been offered employment at the Chinese Academy of Sciences, and that CUMT had originally consented to his departure, but later the consent was rescinded. These allegations, if true, raise serious concerns about Dr. Guo's ability to conduct his work and to freely and openly exchange ideas and information with colleagues at other institutions. It is unclear to us at this point, however, whether the allegations are in fact true and, even if true, whether the situation is specific to Dr. Guo or is suggestive of a larger problem effecting many scholars. We therefore respectfully ask for your help in clarifying the situation.

Thank you for your urgent attention to this matter. We look forward to your reply.

Very truly yours,

Robert J. Quinn
Director

HUMAN RIGHTS PROGRAM, THE UNIVERSITY OF CHICAGO, 5828 S. UNIVERSITY AVE., CHICAGO, IL, 60637 USA
TEL: 773-834-4659 * FAX: 773-702-9286 * http://scholarsatrisk.uchicago.edu * E-MAIL: rquinn@uchicago.edu

quota for each employee. Nevertheless, this system was not so successful in the industrial (mainly state-owned) sector as in the agricultural sector as a result of the complicated production processes in the former. In July 1986, the NPC announced four laws concerned with employment.

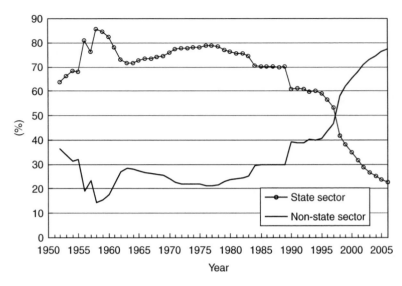

Figure 4.2 Employment shares of the state and non-state sectors in urban areas

According to the laws the governmental allocation of workers and life-time employment were abolished and, simultaneously, a contract system (*hetong zhi*) was introduced. Under the contract system, all employees were hired as contractual workers (*hetong gong*) and the employed terms varied from less than one year to more than five years. Naturally, when the contract expired, either the worker was laid-off or the contract was renewed. Unfortunately, in practice the contract system has not worked better in the state sector than in the non-state sector.

Since the introduction of its reform and its opening up to the outside world, the pattern of employment in China has been undergoing structural changes, along with the decline of the state sector and the expansion of the non-state sector in urban areas (see Figure 4.2). This kind of employment structure was the result of China's institutional transformations. Particularly noteworthy in this respect was China's large-scale privatization or its policy of contracting out the operations of small and poorly performing SOEs or to let them go bankrupt during the late 1990s and the early 2000s (see subsection 5.3.2 of Chapter 5 for a detailed analysis). For example, from 1995 to 2001, there were 45 million laid-off staff (excluding those who were normally retired from their current posts) in the urban state sector, of which about 30–35 million were re-employed, mostly in the non-state sector (Hu, 2002).

It should be noted that this dramatic decline in the share of employment in the state sector must have reflected China's social problems
to some extent, although the Chinese government has made various
efforts to secure the welfare of those workers who were laid off from
the state sector. For example, there were a number of major protests
organized by SOE workers: (i) more than 10,000 retrenched and retired
SOE workers held sit-down protests and demonstrations in April 1997
(Panzhihua city, Sichuan province); (ii) about 100,000 retrenched workers and their relatives protested on the streets against the withdrawal of
housing benefits and the misappropriation of their retirement funds in
June 1997 (Mianyang city, Sichuan province); (iii) 30,000 textile workers protested against the non-payment of wages. They interrupted local
traffic and surrounded the airport on December 3 1997 (Jiamusi city,
Heiliongjiang province); and (iv) 100,000 workers in four cities rioted
during protests against retrenchments, non-payment of wages, official corruption and other grievances during November–December 1997
(Heilongjiang province).[6]

4.3   Production and ownership

Each square of land should be divided into nine plots, the whole containing nine hundred *mu*. The central plot will be the public field and
the eight households, each owing a hundred-*mu* farm, will collabo-
rate in cultivating the public field. Not until the public land has been
properly attended to, may each household attend to its private plot.
This is how the countrymen should be required to learn.

– Mencius (372–289 BC)

4.3.1   Agriculture

After the founding of the PRC, the Chinese government reformed the
ownership of land (*tugai*) and distributed the cultivated land proportionally among farmers. As a result, the farmers' incentives to work increased
significantly. However, the new leadership only took this land reform as
a provisional measure and did not consider it to be proper for a socialist
economy. In the second half of the 1950s, China began to transform its
private ownership of land. By 1958, the people's commune system (PCS)
had been adopted as a universal form of agricultural production throughout mainland China. About 150 million rural households were grouped
into five million production teams which, in turn, were organized
nationwide into 50,000 people's communes (Minami, 1994, p. 77).

Under the PCS, land was owned collectively and the output was distributed to each household according to the work points (*gongfen*). The state purchased a major share of the grain output and distributed it to the non-agricultural population through government agencies. For much of the pre-reform period, the independent accounting unit was the production team. In the Great Leap Forward and the high tide of the Cultural Revolution, the production brigade (usually including several production teams) and even the people's commune (usually including several production brigades) were selected as independent accounting units in some "advanced" areas where peasants were persuaded to pool their resources. Naturally, the PCS generally has been known to provide disincentives for the farmers to work harder.

The PCS lasted for more than 20 years before the Chinese government began to introduce a household-based and production-related responsibility system – the household responsibility system (HRS) – in the early 1980s. Under the HRS each household may be able to sign a contract with the local government to obtain a certain amount of arable land and production equipment depending on the number of rural population in this family. They will also be given a production quota. As long as the household completes its quota of products to the state, it can decide freely what to produce and how to sell. Although land is still owned by the state, the HRS and the PCS are definitely different from each other.

In the rural sector, although the system of collective ownership of land has been retained, farmers' rights and responsibilities are now clearer since the leasing period is long (15 years for the initial stage with an extension of a further 30 years). Before the reform, farmers had to sell to the government all the remaining gains (which was seen as being vital to the large Chinese population at that time) and other important agricultural products at a very low price. Following the reforms, the additional benefit to farmers can be decomposed into two parts (Zhao, 1999, p. 194):

(i) one that arises from "price adjustment" within the planned price framework;
(ii) the other that arises from "price release."

The policy of "price adjustment" entailed the government gradually increasing the planned purchased price and changing the relative price of agricultural goods to manufactured goods. "Price release," which in fact implies alteration of the price mechanism, from planned pricing to market pricing, involved the gradual reduction of the quota that farmers were required to sell to the government. The reduction of the quota enabled farmers to sell part of their products in the market at market prices. The policies behind rural price reform were thereafter introduced as part of many urban sector reforms during the 1980s.

The HRS has been recognized as a success (see subsection 5.2.1 of Chapter 5 for detailed evidence). However, this system has also encountered some problems since the 1990s, especially since the late 1990s. This can be witnessed by the increasingly wider gaps between the rural and urban incomes during the 1990s and the 2000s (see Figure 7.2 in Chapter 7). In brief, there have been two shortcomings for the HRS. First, since the management of agricultural production has been restricted within each household (note that the average size of the Chinese rural household has been reduced substantially as a result of the birth control policy implemented during recent decades), large-scale, mechanically-based modern agriculture cannot be easily realized and, consequently, labor productivity has not been able to rise. Secondly, and as a result of the emigration of rural laborers into urban areas (as will be discussed in subsection 9.2.3 in Chapter 9), a certain amount of arable land has been abandoned.

In order to solve these problems, Chinese policy makers have brought forward two countermeasures: (i) within three years, starting from 2004, agricultural tax, which had been applied since 1958, was abolished; and (ii) a de facto land privatization scheme for rural areas, called *tudi liuzhuan* (land circulation), was proposed in the Third Plenum of the 17th CCPCC in October 2008. The scheme has been termed the third land reform in China, and it is anticiapted that it will be implemented throughout the nation over the course of the coming years.

4.3.2 Industry

Generally, China's industrial organization experienced a period of over-centralization and then a period of decentralization. In much of the pre-reform period, China's industrial organization was implemented via a centrally planned system which offered the advantages of rapid structural transformation through direct and strong government participation and the large-scale mobilization of resources to priority sectors. Such a system enabled the industrial sector to grow at highly creditable rates between 1953 and 1978. The advantages of rapid structural change under a centrally planned system, however, were soon outweighed by the problems of low efficiency, slow technological progress, sectoral imbalances, and sharp annual fluctuations in growth rates.

In general, the state-owned enterprises (SOEs) were established to serve five essential roles in the Chinese economy: (1) in many cases they had led to improved efficiency and increased technological competitiveness; (2) they had generally taken a more socially responsible attitude than the purely private enterprises; (3) they had helped to prevent oligopolistic collusion by refusing to collude; (4) they had helped the government to pursue its regional policy by shifting the investment to the poor west of the country; and (5) they had been used by the government as a means of managing aggregate demand to enable it to operate its counter-cyclical policy. Closely copying the Soviet prototype, the Chinese SOEs followed a "unified supply and unified collection" system in which the state supplied all inputs (such as labor, funds, raw material, power supply, and so on) necessary to execute production targets and claimed all output and financial revenues.[7]

The main substantive difference between the collectively owned enterprises (COEs) and the SOEs lies in the extent of government control that is exerted over the organizations. The SOEs serve, to some extent, as the concrete manifestation of the socialist principle of the public ownership of the means of production by the whole population. Local governments are responsible for the provision of inputs to the COEs within their jurisdiction and conversely have first, if not sole claim to their output and revenues. Usually, the COEs are classified into two parts: urban COEs are directly controlled by local governments and subjected to state plans; rural COEs are fully under the jurisdiction of the township and village government units (this will be discussed in detail in subsection 9.2.2 of Chapter 9).

Obviously, the private, shareholding or other enterprises (PSEs) were the freest to decide on investment, labor, output and pricing and, above all, the most market-oriented. China's PSEs practically disapproved in the period between 1958, when the socialist transformation of national capitalist industry was completed, and 1979 when the Chinese government began to reform its CPE (see Figure 4.3). During the reform era, the PSEs have experienced a recovery during the period 1978–88, a period of consolidation during 1989–91, and a mushrooming since 1992. In China, an individually owned enterprise employing up to eight people is defined as *getihu* (self-employed people or individual working unit), but one with eight or more employees is defined as *shiyingqiye* (privately owned enterprise). According to SICA (1995), the number of *getihu* grew by over 11 times, from 1.828 million in 1981 to 22.390 million in 1995, while that of *shiyingqiye* grew by more than five times, from 91,000 in 1989 to 563,000 in 1995. Notice that the actual number could be larger as some PSEs could have reported under the name of "COEs" in order to evade the "individual income" tax.

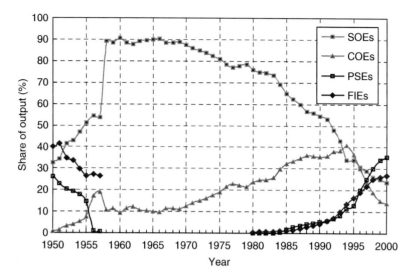

Figure 4.3 Shares of industrial output by ownership
Notes: COE = collectively-owned enterprise; FIE = foreign (Taiwan, Hong Kong and Macau) invested enterprise; PSE = private, shareholding or other enterprise; SOE = state-owned enterprise.

The foreign-invested enterprises (FIEs) mainly comprise joint ventures and wholly foreign-owned enterprises. Like the PSEs, the FIEs have also grown rapidly since the early 1980s, as a result of the dramatic inflows of foreign capital into China. We will discuss this issue in detail in section 11.2 in Chapter 11.

Since 1978, industrial reforms in China have sought to improve the enterprise incentive systems, to utilize indirect economic levers (price, tax, interest rate, credit, banking and the rest) to regulate industrial production, to endow enterprises with greater relative decision-making autonomy and, above all, to compel enterprises to operate according to market regulations. The positive effects of reform on industrial performance are evident from the dramatic industrial growth that was observed during the reform period (see section 9.2 in Chapter 9 for more details). The dynamism of the industrialization may be attributed to a variety of reform measures. One such measure was the shift in sectoral priorities within industry which allowed a greater share of resources to be diverted away from the input- and capital-intensive producer goods industries toward the more efficient and profitable consumer goods industries. Another measure was the lifting of previous restrictions on the development of the non-state sectors and the policy of promoting a diversified ownership structure. This has led to an explosive growth of the non-state sectors which are acting increasingly as the engine of industrial development, particularly since the early 1990s, when China formally tried to transform its economy to a socialist market system. From 1978 to 2000, the shares of industrial output produced by the SOEs, COEs, PSEs, and FIEs changed greatly, with the GVIO growing much slower in the SOEs than in the COEs, PSEs and FIEs. It is particularly noteworthy that the SOEs' share in GVIO first began to rank after the PSEs' and FIEs' in 1997 and 1998, respectively (see Figure 4.3).

The substantial reform of the state industrial organization began in 1984 when the CCPCC and the central government decided to shift the emphasis of reforms from the agricultural sector to the non-agricultural sectors. On May 10 1984, the State Council issued the "Provisional Regulations on the Enlargement of Autonomy of State-owned Industrial Enterprises" which outlines ten specific decision-making powers to be enjoyed by enterprises. The "invigoration" of large and medium-sized SOEs and the application of indirect means to regulate SOEs were adopted as policy in the State Council's governmental report to the Fourth Session of the Sixth NPC on March 25 1986. In December, the "Bankruptcy Law Concerning the State Enterprises" was adopted by the NPC. However, the Bankruptcy Law was not effectively applied until the early 1990s due to fears of unemployment and social instability as China has not a relatively complete social security system.[8]

Following Deng Xiaoping's call for faster economic growth and reform, after 1992 the government began to accelerate and intensify its market-oriented reforms. Industrial reform was focused on the issue of property right reform by granting more autonomy to the SOEs. In June 1992, the State Commission for Restructuring the Economic Systems (SCRES), the State Planning Commission (SPC), the Ministry of Finance (MOF), the People's Bank of China (PBC) and the Production Office of the State Council jointly issued the "Provisional Regulations on Joint-Stock Companies" concerning the formation of shareholding companies. The regulations cover the standardization of joint stock companies, their accounting system, financial management, taxation and auditing, labor and wage systems. This was followed by the State Council's "Regulations on the Transformation of the Operating Mechanisms of State-owned Industrial Enterprises" on July 22 1992, which codified the independent decision-making powers of the SOEs in 14 key areas (including production, investment, labor, marketing, independent profit and loss accounting, assets, mergers, closures, bankruptcy and so on).

Since the formal adoption in 1993 of Deng Xiaoping's theory on the construction of a socialist market economy with Chinese characteristics, there have been rapid and substantial changes in the country's industrial management. One important policy is the importation of the "modern enterprise system" which, in practice, follows the modern Western-style and market-based corporate system. In addition to its critical role in the sustainable improvement of productivity in the industrial sector, industrial reform is also the institutional *sine qua non* in terms of establishing an effectively functioning competitive market system.

The reform on non-performing SOEs was debated once more in the Fifth Plenum of the 14th CCPCC held during September 1995. The outcome was the policy of "grasping the large and releasing the small" (*zhua da fang xiao*). To "grasp the large" (*zhua da*) is to turn a select group of 300 out of a list of 1,000 already successful large enterprises and enterprise groups into world-class businesses. To "release the small" (*fang xiao*) is to privatize or to contract out small SOEs or to let them go bankrupt. This policy allows most small SOEs to be sold off to private individuals and the management of those not sold is contracted out. The majority of the remaining large and medium-sized SOEs are to be turned into corporations with various forms of ownership, ranging from corporations with 100 percent private ownership to those with a mixture of private and state capital and others with 100 percent state capital.[9] The central government, however, will continue to be the only shareholder in companies that produce "special-category" and defense-related products.

State ownership, which had been defined as the classic feature of socialism, was discussed at the 15th CCP National Congress during October 1997. The CCP's final conclusion was that public (*gongyou*), instead of state (*guoyou*), ownership is to be the dominant form of ownership.[10] In addition, it encouraged the development of every other form of ownership, including private ownership. Furthermore, private and individual businesses are not only tolerated but are now considered to be making valuable contributions to the economy. The shift in the CCP's view on ownership is now enshrined in the Chinese constitution, with two amendments to the constitution at the Ninth National NPC held in March 1998. The first amendment was to Article 6 of the constitution, which saw the addition of a clause stating that China is now at its preliminary stage of socialism. This amendment is used to justify having public, instead of state, ownership as the main form of ownership of the means of production. The clause further states that public ownership will develop alongside other forms of ownership. The second constitutional amendment was to Article 21, with the addition of a clause stating that individual, private and other forms of non-public ownership are "important components of a socialist economy" and they "supplement the system of socialist public ownership".

One example of the policy of "grasping the large" is the restructuring of China's oil industry and the four state-owned oil companies – the China National Offshore Oil Corporation (CNOOC), the China National Petroleum Corporation (CNPC), the China Petrochemical Corporation (Sinopec), and the China National Star Petroleum Corporation (CNSPC). In August 1999 CNOOC grouped the shares of all of its subsidiaries into the newly formed China Offshore Oil Corporation (COOC). Three months later, in November 1999, CNPC did likewise and formed China Oil & Gas Stock Co. Ltd. (Petrochina). Sinopec is expected to follow suit. Meanwhile, China National Star Petroleum Corporation (CNSPC), the smallest state-owned oil company, was merged with Sinopec in late November 1999. The aim behind the formation of the new companies and the merger was to reduce the four state oil companies into three state holding companies and to consolidate the shares of their subsidiaries into three companies for overseas listing. As part of the restructuring, the core and non-core businesses of the state oil companies are to be separated, some debt is to be converted to equity and their workforce is to be reduced with state financial help. Adverse stock market reactions toward the end of 1999 led to the postponement of the initial public offering (IPO) of CNOOC in Hong Kong and New York. But despite continuing uncertainties over the potential success of their IPOs, CNOOC, CNPC and Sinopec were pushed ahead with their restructuring plans in 2000 because of China's expected entry into the WTO after its successful negotiation with the USA (Liew, 2000).

4.4   Public finance

To a large extent public finance determines the use of a nation's aggregate resources and, together with monetary and exchange rate policies, it influences the macro balance of payments, the accumulation of foreign debt, the rates of inflation, interest, and so on. However, the degree of impact may differ significantly and depend upon whether the economy is managed under the market-oriented system or under the centrally planned system. Public finance usually plays an important role in promoting balanced development and equilibrium in both wealth accumulation and distribution for a planned economy in which central government collects and directly dispenses much of its budget for society, while the local budget is collected from and used for local administrative organs, factories, enterprises, and welfare facilities. As the market economy is a private-ownership system, the channels of policy influences are much more indirect and mainly through the *laissez-faire* approach.

Since the early 1980s, public finance, as an important component of the Chinese economic system, has undergone a series of reforms in terms of the development of central–local relations.[11] The goals of these reforms were to decentralize the fiscal structure and to strengthen the incentive for local government to collect more revenue for themselves and for the central government to maintain an egalitarian fiscal redistribution among the provinces. Briefly, China's efforts toward this end have experienced different stages, all of which sought to find a rational revenue-raising formula between the central and the local governments. In 1980 the Chinese government began to implement the fiscal system entitled *"huafen shouzhi, fenji baogan"* (divide revenue and expenditure, set up diversified contract system). The main contents of the fiscal reform include:

- Transformation from the traditional system of "having meals in one pot" (*yizhao chifan*) to that of "having meals in different pots" (*fenzhao chifan*); and
- Transformation of financial redistribution from mainly through sectors directly under the central government to mainly through regions.

In the period from 1980 to 1984, the basic structure of the central–local fiscal relations was framed and amended on a number of occasions. In 1980, for example, there were ten provinces (Inner Mongolia, Fujian, Guangdong, Guangxi, Guizhou, Yunnan, Tibet, Qinghai, Ningxia, and Xinjiang) on which the central government taxed a zero marginal rate. Specifically, Guangdong – a coastal province with close proximity to Hong Kong and Macau – was required to pay a lump-sum (LT) tax to the central government; Fujian – another coastal province with close proximity to Taiwan – was able to retain all the revenue it collected plus a lump-sum subsidy (LS) from the central government; the remaining eight poor provinces and ethnic minority-based autonomous regions could retain all of the revenue they collected and, in addition, would be in receipt of a lump-sum but growing subsidy (GS) from the central government. In five provinces (Beijing, Tianjin, Liaoning, Shanghai and Jiangsu), the total revenue collected was to be shared with the central government in fixed proportions (SOR), varying from 12 percent to 90 percent.[12] In the remaining provinces, revenue was shared between the central and local governments in more complicated ways and, as a result of considerable and frequent politicing, negotiating and bargaining with

Table 4.2 Changes of the central–local fiscal relations

Province	1980–81	1982	1983–84	1985	1986–87	1988–90	1991–93
Anhui	DR	SOR	SOR	SOR	SOR	SOR	SOR
Beijing	SOR	SOR	SOR	SOR	SOR	STR	STR
Fujian	LS	LS	LS	LS	LS	LS	LS
Gansu	DR	SOR	DRS	LS	LS	LS	LS
Guangdong	LT	LT	LT	LT	LT	GT	GT
Guangxi	GS	GS	GS	GS	GS	GS	LS
Guizhou	GS	GS	GS	GS	GS	GS	LS
Hainan						GT	LS
Hebei	DR	SOR	SOR	SOR	SOR	STR	STR
Heilongjiang	DRS	DRS	DRS	SOR	LT	LT	LT/STR
Henan	DR	SOR	SOR	SOR	SOR	STR	STR
Hubei	DR	SOR	SOR	SOR	ROR	ROR	LT/SGT
Hunan	DR	SOR	SOR	SOR	SOR	GT	GT
Inner Mongolia	GS	GS	GS	GS	GS	GS	LS
Jiangsu	SOR	SOR	SOR	SOR	SOR	STR	STR
Jiangxi	DRS	DRS	DRS	LS	LS	LS	LS
Jilin	DRS	DRS	DRS	LS	LS	LS	LS
Liaoning	SOR	SOR	SOR	SOR	SOR	STR	STR/SGT
Ningxia	GS	GS	GS	GS	GS	GS	LS
Qinghai	GS	GS	GS	GS	GS	GS	LS
Shaanxi	DR	SOR	SOR	LS	LS	LS	LS
Shandong	DR	SOR	SOR	SOR	SOR	LT	LT/SGT
Shanghai	SOR	SOR	SOR	SOR	SOR	LT	LT
Shanxi	DR	DR	SOR	SOR	SOR	SOR	SOR
Sichuan	DR	SOR	SOR	SOR	ROR	ROR	LS/STR
Tianjin	SOR	SOR	SOR	SOR	SOR	SOR	SOR
Tibet	GS	GS	GS	GS	GS	GS	LS
Xinjiang	GS	GS	GS	GS	GS	GS	LS
Yunnan	GS	GS	GS	GS	GS	GS	LS
Zhejiang	DR	SOR	SOR	SOR	SOR	STR	STR

Note: the definition and formulation of the contents are given in Table 4.3.
Sources: World Bank (1990, p. 89), Oksenberg and Tong (1991, pp. 24–5), Agarwala (1992, p. 68), Wei (1994, p. 298) and Knight and Li (1995).

central government, the fiscal arrangements were amended and the shares of these provinces were generally raised in 1982 and lowered in 1983 in accordance with the central government's revenue requirement (see Table 4.2).

The year 1985 saw the introduction of a fiscal system entitled "*huafen shuizhong, heding shouzhi, fenji baogan*" (divide the categories of tax, verify revenue and expenditure, and set up a diversified contract system). This system, which was to strengthen the method of "having meals

Table 4.3 Definition and formulation of the fiscal policies

Fiscal policy	Definition	Revenue goes to provincial Gov.	Revenue goes to the central Gov.	Marginal tax rate
DR	dividing revenue	$\Sigma\alpha_i C_i$	$\Sigma(1-\alpha_i)C_i$	$\Sigma(1-\alpha_i)C_i/\Sigma C_i$
DRS	dividing revenue and receiving growing subsidy	$\Sigma\alpha_i C_i + S_0(1+r)^t$	$\Sigma(1-\alpha_i)C_i - S_0(1+r)^t$	$\Sigma(1-\alpha_i)C_i/\Sigma C_i$
GS	receiving lump-sum but growing subsidy	$C+S_0(1+r)^t$	$-S_0(1+r)^t$	0
GT	paying lump-sum but growing tax	$C-T_0(1+r)^t$	$T_0(1+r)^t$	0
LS	receiving lump-sum subsidy	$C+S$	$-S$	0
LT	paying lump-sum tax	$C-T$	T	0
ROR	retaining overall revenue	C	0	0
SGT	sharing overall revenue and paying growing tax	$(1+\alpha)C - T_0(1+r)^t$	$-\alpha C + T_0(1+r)^t$	$-\alpha$
SOR	sharing overall revenue	αC	$(1-\alpha)C$	$1-\alpha$
STR	sharing target revenue but retaining residual revenue	$C-(1-\alpha)C_0(1+r)^t$	$(1-\alpha)C_0(1+r)^t$	0

Notes:

C = revenue collected by province (C_0 denotes C at time zero);

C_i = revenue collected by province from source i ($i=1, 2, 3$ denote revenue from source i goes to central government, to provincial government, and is shared between them respectively)

S = lump-sum subsidy from central government (S_0 denotes S at time zero);

T = lump-sum tax to central government (T_0 denotes T at time zero);

r = annual growth rate;

α = fixed share of revenue accruing to province ($0 < \alpha < 1$);

$\alpha_1, \alpha_2, \alpha_3$ (where $\alpha_1 = 0, \alpha_2 = 1, 0 < \alpha_3 < 1$).

in different pots," divided revenue into three parts: centrally fixed revenue, locally fixed revenue, and the revenue shared by the central and local governments. Among other changes of the central–local fiscal relations, Jilin, Jiangxi and Gansu provinces moved from DRS to LS, Shaanxi province from SOR to LS, Heilongjiang province from DRS to SOR in 1985 and LT in 1986, respectively. Simultaneously the favorable fiscal policies were still applied in Guangdong and Fujian provinces and other minority-based autonomous regions, as shown in Table 4.2.

Between 1988 and 1993 a fiscal responsibility system entitled "*chaizheng baogan*" was introduced through two sub-stages: (i) from 1988 to 1990, seven methods were introduced: (1) STR (*shouru dizheng baogan*); (2) SOR (*zhong'e fencheng*); (3) GT (*shangjie'e dizheng baogan*); (4) LT (*ding'e shangjie*); (5) LS (*ding'e buzhu*); (6) GS (*ding'e buzhu, meinian dizheng*); and (7) ROR (*zhong'e baogan*). (ii) from 1991 to 1993, six further methods were introduced: (1) STR: Beijing, Hebei, Liaoning, Jiangsu, Zhejiang, Henan and Shenyang of Liaoning, Harbin of Heilongjiang, Ningbo of Zhejiang, and Chongqing of Sichuan; (2) SOR: Tianjin, Shanxi and Anhui; (3) GT: Guangdong and Hunan; (4) LT: Shanghai, Shandong and Heilongjiang; (5) LS: Jilin, Fujian, Jiangxi, Shaanxi, Gansu, Inner Mongolia, Guangxi, Yunnan, Guizhou, Qinghai, Hainan, Hubei and Sichuan; and (6) SGT (*zhong'e fencheng jia zhengzhang fencheng*): Dalian of Liaoning, Qingdao of Shandong and Wuhan of Hubei.

In conclusion, in the post-reform period the economic incentives facing the provinces appeared to improve over time. In 1980, for example, no fewer than 19 provinces were involved in some form of revenue sharing or division, whereas by 1985 revenue division had ceased and 15 provinces shared their respective revenues. In the 1988 reforms, most of these provinces had been switched to lump-sum taxation or the sharing of target revenues, while only three provinces remained on a revenue-sharing formula. In sum, this account of the fiscal relationship between the central and local governments highlights four problems: first, the non-uniform treatment of provinces appeared neither efficient nor equitable; secondly, the uncertainty associated with changing rules and bargaining had disincentive effects on the revenue collection of the province governments; thirdly, the high marginal tax rates faced by some provinces could be expected to deter revenue collection; finally, the various efforts to reform the centralized fiscal system reduced the central government share of the revenue collected by the provinces (Knight and Li, 1995, p. 5).

Since 1994, China has implemented a so-called "tax-sharing system" (*fenshui zhi*). At this stage, Chinese fiscal policy, through transferring much of the revenue collection function from local to central government, attempted to tackle the principal–agent problem of the revenue-contracting period. The solution was essentially to transpose the principal and agent. Under this system, China's tax revenues have been collected by and shared between central and local governments, as follow:

(i) "Central taxes" (i.e., those that are collected by the central government): these include customs duties; the operations tax paid by the railways, various banks and insurance companies; import-related VAT and consumption tax collected by the customs; consumption tax; and so on.
(ii) "Local taxes" (i.e., those that are collected by local governments): these included operation tax (excluding the part paid by railway, various banks and insurance companies); city and township land use tax; and so on;
(iii) "Shared taxes" (i.e., those that are shared between central and local governments): these include domestic VAT (75 percent for central government); income tax (60 percent for central government); resource tax (except the tax paid by offshore oil enterprises, all the rest goes to local government); stamp tax in the stock market; and so on.

It can be shown that since the early 1980s China's diversified fiscal systems have resulted in differences in central–local relations. During the period 1980–84, which saw implementation of the first stage of fiscal reform, China's share of local revenue to total revenue decreased from 75.5 percent to 59.5 percent; over the course of the same period its share of local expenditure to total expenditure increased from 45.7 percent to 47.5 percent. Over the following years, both of these shares had increased considerably (see Figure 4.4). It can also be seen from Figure 4.4 that since the implementation of the "tax-sharing system" in 1994, China's fiscal transferring mechanism has been reversed from its previous pattern (i.e., the "local-to-central transference" during the 1980s) to the present "central-to-local transference" pattern. As a result, China's central government has become more powerful than it was in the 1980s.

4.5 Banking

Since 1978 banking reforms have played an important role in China's overall efforts to transform a centrally planned economy into a

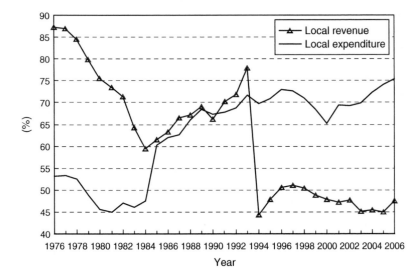

Figure 4.4 China's local revenue and expenditure shares
Notes: (1) 'revenue' excludes borrowing from domestic and abroad, 'expenditure' excludes repayment of the principal and payment of interest, borrowing from domestic and abroad.

market-based economy. Although the banking sector has undergone remarkable changes over the course of this period, deep-seated structural problems of asset quality, capital adequacy and profitability continue to pose considerable challenge. Arguably, the major problem in the present-day Chinese banking sector is the high level of non-performing loans (NPLs) – and the continued lending to loss-making SOEs. Until recently, banking reforms were focused mainly on introducing competition, broadening the channels of financial intermediation and providing a legal framework for bank supervision. In 1995, two notable developments in this respect were introduced: the promulgation of the Central Bank Law that firmly established the PBC as the sole government agent to supervise and regulate the banking sector; and the enactment of the Commercial Banking Law that clearly defined the scope of business for commercial banks.

The 1997 Asian financial crisis accelerated the pace of reform in China's banking system. China quickened the pace of reform in 1998 and seems to be aware of two lessons that can be drawn from the Asian financial crisis. The first lesson is that a sound banking system is crucial for an economy to withstand external shocks. The second lesson from the Japanese banking saga is that delays will only allow NPLs to grow and to erode the levels of bank capital. Under the reforms that began in December 1998, the directors of the regional branches of the PBC would be appointed directly by its headquarters in Beijing without consultations with the provincial governments. Instead of the previous arrangement of a PBC branch being established in each province and SEZ, the regional PBC branches were now located in only nine cities.[13] Furthermore, powers that had previously been delegated to PBC branches to control the volume of credit were concentrated in the central PBC headquarters. Moreover, projects above a certain scale would now have to be approved by central bank headquarters. However, in isolation the above reform effort was not enough for the construction of a healthy banking and financing system, since there had been too many bad loans advanced to the SOEs (something that we will discuss this in greater detail in next section).

The reform of the SOEs was delayed as a result of the 1997 Asian financial crisis.[14] Two years later, in 1999, China introduced a debt–equity swap scheme (*zhai zhuan gu*) which would convert a portion of SOEs' bank debt into equity. China's four largest state-owned commercial banks set up their own state asset management companies – "Cinda" (of the China Construction Bank), "Huarong" (of the Industrial and Commercial Bank of China), "Great Wall" (of the Agricultural Bank of China) and "Oriental" (of the Bank of China) – to deal respectively with their bad loans to selected SOEs that have potential as going business concerns but are burdened by heavy debts. The bad loans are converted into equity and then sold at a discount to investors. The immediate objectives of debt–equity swaps are to improve the balance sheet of the commercial banks and reduce the debt service of the SOEs. In the longer term, it is hoped that investors in these debt–equity swaps would have the managerial and technical expertise to turn the SOEs around permanently. There are strict guidelines specifying conditions that the first enterprises have to fulfill before they are allowed to have their debts converted into equity.

The conditions under which enterprises were chosen include: (1) they must have good marketing records and competitiveness; (2) their technical equipment must be in line with environmental protection; (3) they must have high-quality management and good accounting systems; (4) their leadership must be specialized in business and administration; and (5) they must take "effective reform measures," including plans to "cut the number of employees to increase efficiency." By the end of 1999, 601 non-performing SOEs had been approved by the State Economic and Trade Commission (SETC) to transform their debts (459.6 billion yuan) into equity.

On April 1 2000, China introduced a "real name" banking system under which all of the household bank deposits require a depositor's ID. This is an important step in moving from anonymous banking to real-name banking, an international practice. In reality, this change was concerned not so much with increasing tax revenue, as with reducing political corruption by making the flow of money transparent.

Since the late 1990s, and especially since China joined the WTO in 2001, several measures have been taken to establish a strong prudential framework that encompasses all types of banking and non-bank financial institutions. Specifically, these institutional improvements include:

- Liberalizing interest rates for bank deposits and bank loans; improving indirect policy tools; abolishing directed, political lending).
- Continuing the commercialization process by allowing more competing and accepting a diversified ownership structure; improving the quality of banks' assets through debt destructing and debt transfer; increasing operational efficiency while reducing overstaffing and over branching).
- Screening and rectifying the numbers and the business scope of local trust and investment corporations; modernizing the payment system; supporting new financial products while dealing carefully with associated risks).
- Continuing to develop securities markets by simplifying trading procedures, improving information disclosure procedures, and upgrading the legal framework).
- Strengthening prudential supervision; clarifying and harmonizing operational standards, provision requirements, and accounting rules; developing a new law for closure and bankruptcy of financial institutions).
- Further simplifying the foreign exchange administration; allowing more exchange rate flexibility; starting a gradual removal of capital controls; permitting foreign banks and other financial institutions to enter China, in accordance with the WTO agreement).

However, in the coming years, more banking and financial reforms are still required:

- *Monetary policy* (adopting a fully market-based strategy of demand management; exploiting new channels of monetary transmission; adopting policies of greater independent and accountability).

- *Banking* (finishing the process of cleaning up banks' balance sheets and introducing uniform capital adequacy ratios based on internationally accepted standards; giving up majority state ownership).
- *Financial service* (streamlining the structure of the financial service industry; expanding the supply and improving the quality of products).
- *Direct finance* (liberalizing asset prices and allowing the stock market to reflect borrowers' financial conditions and to execute corporate control).
- *Regulation/supervision* (finishing the process of replacing direct state intervention and state protection with a market-oriented regulatory framework; reconsidering the segmentation of banking, investment, and insurance).
- *External liberalization* (adopting a fully flexible exchange rate regime; continuing the gradual and cautious removal of capital control and ultimately, if preconditions are met, adopting full capital account convertibility; allowing foreign banks and other financial institutions to compete on a level playing field with domestic banks).

4.6 External relations

For a long period after the foundation of the PRC in 1949, the Chinese economy was characterized as a closed economy.[15] In 1979, in order to attract foreign investment, the NPC enacted the "Law of the People's Republic of China Concerning the Joint Ventures with Chinese and Foreign Investment" (NPC, 1979). In the same year, the CCPCC and the State Council decided to grant Guangdong and Fujian provinces "special policies and flexible measures" in foreign economic affairs. On December 26 1979, the People's Congress of Guangdong province approved the provincial government's proposal that a part of Shenzhen (next to Hong Kong), Zhuhai (next to Macau) and Santou be designed as SEZs in which experiments can be undertaken with an market-oriented system with Chinese characteristics. At the same time, Xiamen in Southeast Fujian province (near Taiwan) also became a SEZ with the approval of the NPC. Subsequently, Guangdong and Fujian gained substantial autonomy in developing their regions as the central government granted them authority to pursue reform "one step ahead" (*xian zhou yibu*). As a result, not only did these areas enjoy lower tax rates, but they also gained more authority over economic development. The four cities are below the provincial level, but have independent budget agreements with the central government.[16]

Prior to the early 1980s, the management of foreign economic affairs rested in the hand of one government ministry that maintained an overly rigid control of matters. In the first years of the implementation of China's outward-oriented development strategy, the reform of the foreign economic system was conducted via three aspects. First, under the unified control of the state, there was a closer relationship between production and marketing and between industry and trade, which enabled production units to participate directly in foreign trade. Secondly, the special policies and measures relating to foreign trade were handed to the local governments. A third type of reform was to expand the autonomy of the SOEs to act on their own initiatives and have direct links with foreign traders at meetings arranged by specialized export SOEs.

In 1982, the Ministry of Foreign Trade (MFT) was renamed the Ministry of Foreign Economic Relations and Trade (MFERT). At the same time, trade bureaus were established at the provincial and local levels to manage both foreign trade and FDI. The MFERT and local trade bureaus were, in principle, not allowed to interfere in the management of foreign trade enterprises. Many large SOEs received permission to engage in foreign trade. Local enterprises were also able to establish their own foreign trade companies. In 1988, foreign trade was reformed by a system of contracts under which the separation between ownership (state) and management (enterprise) was maintained and thus foreign trade enterprises were able to operate independently. Despite these reforms, the fundamental structure of central planning and state ownership has not been changed fundamentally, particularly in large and medium-sized SOEs.

Before the 1980s, international trade was in the hands of central government planning, which controlled more than 90 percent of trade by monopolizing the imports and exports of more than 3,000 kinds of commodities. These commodities can be classified into two categories: plan-commanded goods (in which both the value and the volume of trade are strictly controlled) and plan-guided goods (in which only the value of trade is controlled). In 1984, there was a reform of the trade management system, with foreign trade enterprises being given autonomy to deal with international trade. In 1985, the number of goods under these categories was cut to about 100 each. By 1991, almost all exports were deregulated, with only 15 percent controlled by specially appointed trading companies. Imports have also been deregulated. The proportion of plan-commanded imports in the total import volume was reduced from 40 percent in 1985 to 18.5 percent in 1991 (Wan *et al.*, 2004).

In parallel with the gradual acceleration of its economic reforms, China has increasingly amplified its foreign-related legal system, steadily improved its trade and investment environment and enforced the intellectual property rights protection system. With regard to the issue of trade system transparency, China has sorted out and publicized all management documents that used to be deemed confidential. In 1993, the Ministry of Foreign Trade and Economic Cooperation (MFTEC) was established to reform laws and regulations on the management of foreign trade and economic cooperation. Import restrictions were eased still further. By 1994, almost all planning on imports and exports were abolished, with only a few exceptions where extremely important goods were traded by specially appointed trading companies. One year later, by the end of 1995, China had rescinded import licensing and quota controls on 826 tariff lines.

China's foreign exchange system used to be subject to rigid control by the government. Since China began its economic reform in the late 1970s, the foreign exchange system has been subject to a gradual process of liberalization. In the early 1980s, Chinese currency RMB was non-convertible and foreign exchanges were strictly supervised by the state. During this period two exchange rates were in operation: an official rate published by the government and another special one for foreign trade. The intention of the system was to enhance the country's exports and to restrict its imports, for at the time China was suffering from a serious lack of foreign exchange. In 1984, a new policy of retaining exchange was adopted by the government as a result of improvements in China's foreign trade and economy. It allowed domestic enterprises and institutions to retain a part of their foreign currency earnings, compared with the previous one in which these units handed over all of their foreign currency earnings to the state. Although a larger part of foreign exchange was still under the control of the government, the new retaining policy stimulated domestic enterprises to increase their exports, and hence there was a significant improvement in China's foreign trade performance.

On January 1 1994, China established a new unitary and floating exchange-rate system. Although it is based on market supply and demand, this system is still, to a large extent, determined by the government, as the People's Bank of China (PBC), China's central bank, takes the position of the largest demander of foreign exchange and the Bank of China (BOC), which is also owned by the state, is the largest supplier of foreign exchange. Furthermore, the newly established foreign exchange rate system is still officially controlled and the central bank is one of the biggest participants in the market in order to maintain the RMB rate at a reasonable level.

4.7 Summary

The advocates of new institutional economics recognize that a good market economy requires "getting institutions right" (Coase, 1992; North, 1997; Williamson, 1994). This is because institutions in general set the rules to affect the behavior of economic agents in a fundamental way. The institutional economists thus regard the conventional wisdom of transition focusing on stabilization, liberalization, and privatization as inadequate, because it overlooks the important institutional dimension. To them, a set of institutions are critical for sustained growth, including secure private property rights protected by the rule of law, the impartial enforcement of contracts through an independent judiciary, appropriate government regulations to foster market competition, effective corporate governance, transparent financial systems, and so on (Qian, 2002). Standing in marked contrast with the failures of Russia, which was to some extent based on a "blueprint" or "recipe" from Western advisors, has been the enormous success of China, which created its own transition path (Stiglitz, 1999, p. 3).

Many efforts have attempted to probe into the characteristics of the Chinese reform that has been introduced since the late 1970s. For example, Montinola *et al.* (1995) suggest that the system of federalism and the inherent jurisdictional competition places striking limits on this system of patronage and political spoils. As defined by McKinnon (1991a) and Weingast (1995), the Chinese system provides a partial basis for a special kind of federalism called *market-preserving federalism*. Central to the success of market-preserving federalism is the element of political durability that is built into the arrangements, meaning that the decentralization of power is not merely at the discretion of the central political authorities. In an extensive discussion of the topics central to the success of China's economic reforms, Shirk (1994) included the importance of gradualism, the initial role of agrarian reform, and the political mechanisms underpinning reform within the central government. In comparison with other researchers, Shirk placed greater weight on the political organization of local governments and their control over the economy, arguing that local political officials should be viewed as creating systems of patronage and loyalty.

Obviously, experience of the Chinese reform defies conventional explanations. In the late 1950s, the same authoritarian regime was waging a massive campaign under the name of the "Great Leap Forward," which resulted in the loss of a large number of lives. From 1966 to 1976, the same regime was launching a so-called "Great Cultural

Revolution," causing serious cultural and economic damages to this nation. Furthermore, influential theories of the political economy of the former socialist systems emphasizes that unless the one-party (Communist Party) monopoly is abolished, reforms are doomed to fail (Kornai, 1992). Consequently, this will lead to the asking of questions such as: Why has Chinese-style reform worked during the past decades? Can China's market-oriented reform be sustained in the long run? If China's reform had adopted a "Big bang" approach instead of the gradual approach that it has utilized, how would the Chinese economy have performed in the past decades?

China's reform experience has supplied ample and valuable narrative to provide some answers to these questions. But narrative alone cannot give a sufficient answer to the above questions since they relate to events that did not occur and the motivation for *not* behaving in a particular way. Addressing these questions requires an appropriate model for linking what we observe with what we do not observe. A full understanding of China's economic reform cannot be based solely on theories. The narrative matters because from the historical point of view some specific events can yield a multiplicity of equilibria. To be sure, the Chinese reform has been shown to be a complicated process in which a series of endogenous and exogenous factors are interlinked and play differing roles in the institutional changes. Thus, in order to evaluate such issues as what have determined or influenced the Chinese reform process and how well the Chinese reform has performed, we require a theoretical undepinning of any empirical analysis.

Before ending our discussion about China's political economic transformations, let us finish our account of the story told by Hanfeizi at the beginning of this chapter:

> Feeling it strange, the Duke sent a man to ask Bianque for the reason. "Well, an ailment lying in between the skin and the muscles remains on the surface, and so external application with warm water and ointment can cure it," said Bianque, "If it sinks into muscles, acupuncture will do good; if it resides in the stomach and the intestines, a decoction of herbs will take effect. But when the sickness penetrates into the bone marrow, it becomes fatal and nothing can be done about it. Now, as the Duke has come to that last stage, I have nothing to recommend." Five days after that, the Duke felt pains and ordered his men to look for Bianque, but to find that he had fled to the state of Qin. Soon afterwards, the Duke died.

4.8   Case study: System dynamics – a feedback model

In this section, we will present a theoretical model to examine the mechanisms of market reforms under different initial and exogenous (domestic and external) conditions. Frankly speaking, there is no single, well-defined political and institutional framework for carrying out market-oriented reforms. For example, in most cases, a market-oriented reform implies a reduction in the depth and scope of government participation and interference in an economic activity; in other cases, however, government intervention is necessary (see, for example, Williamson, 1995; Rodrik, 1996). To avoid the ambiguity, we consider a highly simplified centrally planned economy (CPE). Specifically, the CPE is characterized by the following assumptions:

I   The reform scheme may be either accelerated or reversed, depending upon the improvement or deterioration of political stability, respectively.

II Political stability is associated with three factors – public satisfaction (as will be defined in Assumption III), social shock resulting from the reform, and external irritation (which is positively related to the extent to which the CPE opens its economy to the outside world).

III Population is treated as constant. Public satisfaction is positively related to the increment of income level.

IV External environment refers to economically marketized and politically democratized economies. The CPE's open-door policy has two effects: economically, it will promote economic growth through foreign trade and FDI inflows; politically, it will affect political stability through external irritation (as defined in Assumption II).

Based upon the above assumptions, we can build a simplified model for reforms in the CPE, as shown in Figure 4.5. According to the principles of system science, social systems, no matter how complicated, are composed of different feedback loops. A positive feedback loop means that the target grows without any limit, while a negative feedback loop will not grow after the achievement of the target.

In order to simulate the dynamic behaviors of the above model, one may use a modeling method that first appeared in Forrester (1959). This method, which was developed on the basis of conceptions in control theory and organization theory, and on the available techniques of computer simulation, can be used to simulate the dynamic behaviors of the CPE under different initial and exogenous conditions. It is a unique tool for dealing with questions about the way in which complex systems behave through time. Before building a system dynamics model, one must identify the correlations between the important factors that could influence the dynamic behaviors of the system of our interest endogenously.

There are two categories for quantification of the causal relations described in the feedback model in Figure 4.5. The first category of causal relations includes those that can be precisely formulated.

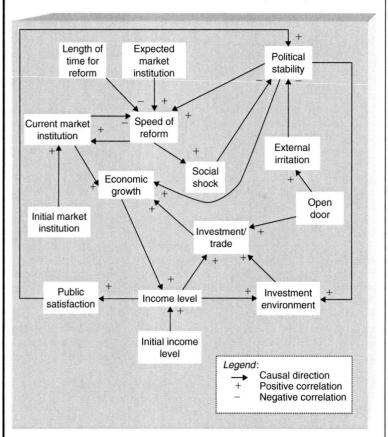

Figure 4.5 A simplified model of economic reforms

The other category of causal relations includes those that can be determined only roughly. The rationale for this simplification relies on the fact that our analysis is not to precisely predict a set of time-series outputs of the macroeconomic indicators, but to show the general tendency of how the performances of the CPE will depend on exogenous variables. There are also some dependent variables that can be more precisely formulated on the basis of the existing literature. However, if this increases the complexity of calculations by involving more explanatory variables, we may simplify their mathematical formulations.

5
Understanding Chinese Economic Reform

There lived a young man in the state of Yan (today's Beijing). He was at a loss as to how to behave all the time. As the days went by, he even began to doubt whether he should walk the way he did, for he felt more and more that his walking gestures were too clumsy and awkward. One day, he learnt that people in Handan walked most gracefully. He could not picture in what way their walking gestures were graceful and, therefore, decided to go there to learn how to walk. As soon as he arrived in Handan, he was dazzled to find that everything was novel. He learnt from the children there how to walk, because he thought the children's walking gestures were lively and pleasing to the eye. He learnt from the old people there how to walk, because he thought the old people's walking gestures were steady. He learnt from the women there how to walk, because he thought the women's walking gestures were beautiful. That being the case with him, in less than half a month he even forgot how to walk. As he had already used up his traveling expenses, he had to crawl back home.

– Zhuangzi (*c*.369–286 BC)

5.1 A brief narrative

From the foundation of the PRC in 1949, the Chinese government had uneasily followed the Soviet Union and adopted a centrally planned economy (CPE). Generally, this kind of planning system has the following problems. First of all, it makes almost all productive enterprises subordinate to administrative organs. To a large extent, this neglects the economic independence of the enterprises and thereby leads to the neglect of their material interests and responsibilities, blunting the levels of initiative and enthusiasm. Secondly, the system involves excessive command planning from above and is overly rigid. So long as the enterprises meet their stipulated targets, they are considered to have performed satisfactorily – regardless of whether or not its products satisfy society's needs.

In the Third Plenum of the 11th CCPCC, held on December 18 1978, Deng Xiaoping and his senior supporters took decisive control of the Chinese Communist Party Central Committee (CCPCC). This ended what has been described as two years of uncertainty and indecisive strategy and policy following the death of Mao Zedong. The Third Plenum of the 11th CCPCC, which was held in December 1978, marked a major turning point in China's reform and development. After a decade of turmoil brought about by the Cultural Revolution (1966–76), the new direction set at this meeting was toward economic development and away from class struggle. The course was laid for the CCP to move the world's most populous nation toward the ambitious targets of the Four Modernizations in the sectors of industry, agriculture, science and technology and national defense.

In brief, the institutional evolution in the Chinese economy since 1978 has followed a gradual path and may be outlined by the six phases listed below:

(1) centrally planned economy (before 1978);
(2) economy regulated mainly by planning and supplementally by market (1978–84);
(3) commodity economy with a plan (1985–87);
(4) combination of planned and market economy (1988–91);
(5) socialist market economy with *state* ownership as the main form (1992–97);
(6) socialist market economy with *public* ownership as the main form (from 1998 onwards).

Guided by the CCPCC (1984), the roles of central planning and market regulation were reversed in the modified system "commodity economy with a plan".[1] Generally, Phase 3 was known to be based loosely on the Hungarian model of market socialism. Nevertheless, the state continued to own the bulk of large and medium-sized enterprises and to regulate the production and pricing of a number of strategic commodities, but the market mechanism was permitted to play an increasing role in the pricing and allocation of goods and services and in the allocation and remuneration of labor in some non-strategic sectors. In the ideological struggles between the radical reformers and the conservatives, there was a new term "socialist commodity economy"[2] from 1988 to 1989, but this was replaced by Phase 4 ("combination of planned and market economy") immediately after the Tian'anmen Square incidents of May–June 1989. Nevertheless, Phase 4 was extremely important insofar as it legitimated the abolition of the traditional mechanisms of the central planning system in favor of the introduction of market regulation.

During the 1980s, China's reform and open-door policy resulted in an increase in economic prosperity, but also led to some political and social instability. This can be witnessed by the CCP's "anti-spiritual pollution" and "anti-bourgeois liberalization" campaigns, which were launched in 1983 and 1987, respectively. This kind of political disequilibria between the CCP conservatives and intellectuals reached its high point in 1989, and, in combination with other factors such as high inflation and official corruption, eventually became a leading cause of students' protests against the CCP and central government during May–June 1989. As soon as the aftermath of the Tian'anmen incident had subsided, there was a shift of power in economic decision making from the reformers to the conservatives. This led to a temporary brake being placed on China's economic reforms and also its rates of economic growth.

At the beginning of the 1990s the socialist camp in Eastern Europe and the former Soviet Union both suffered sudden collapses. China's immediate reaction to the collapse of these communist regimes was a policy of re-centralization, but the CCP soon realized that its legitimacy could be sustained only through economic growth brought about by further reforms. Amid the political deadlock between the reformers and conservatives concerning how to combine the planned and market economic systems, Deng Xiaoping made his now famous southern tour to the province of Guangdong in early 1992. Drawing on regional support for continued reforms, Deng's visit tipped the political balance at the CCPCC and the central government. This resulted in China's official declaration in October 1992 of its intention to build a "socialist market economy," as well as a calling for faster reforms and economic development.

In the early 1990s, some of the policies applied to the coastal SEZs were extended to a list of inland regions and cities along the Yangtze river and, as a result of the normalization of China's diplomatic relations with the former USSR, to the border cities and towns adjacent to Russia and other neighboring countries. Furthermore, many inland cities, which did not qualify for this special treatment, established numerous economic and technological development zones (ETDZs) inside their regions. It is noteworthy that the wide-ranging pro-development reforms during these years led to not only high economic growth but also the two-digit inflationary pressures that occurred in 1993. Facing with an overheating economy, the Chinese government announced a series of banking and financial reforms in 1994, which were aimed at eliminating some of the structural inefficiencies in the financial sector.

China's ambitious agenda geared toward transforming the Chinese economy into a market-oriented one was unveiled as early as 1992, when Deng Xiaoping's Southern Speech[3] eventually had an influence on China's decision makers. On November 14 1993, a formal document entitled "Decision of the CCPCC on Several Issues Concerning the Establishment of a Socialist Market Economic Structure" was finally approved by the Third Plenum of the 14th CCPCC. The aim of the decision was that the government should withdraw from direct involvement in enterprise management. Instead, "Government functions in economic management consist mainly of devising and implementing macroeconomic control policies, appropriate construction of infrastructure facilities and creation of a favorable environment for economic development" (Article 16). The Plenum also declared that "the government shall take significant steps in the reform of taxation, financing, investment and planning systems, and establish a mechanism in which planning, banking and public finance are coordinate and mutually check each other while strengthening the overall coordination of economic operations" (Article 17).

The 15th National Congress of the CCP, held in 1997, witnessed a historic breakthrough in terms of the reform of the ownership structure of the national economy. The three aspects of the adjustment were: (i) to reduce the scope of the state sector and to withdraw state capital from industries that were not considered essential to the national economy; (ii) to seek various forms for materializing public ownership that can generally promote the growth of the productive forces and to develop diverse forms of public ownership; and (iii) to encourage the development of nonpublic sectors of the economy such as the individual business sector and the private sector and to make them important components of a socialist market economy (Wu, 2005, p. 86). In September 2003, when the "Decision on Issues Regarding the Improvement of the Socialist Market Economic System" was adopted by the Third Plenary Session of the 16th CCPCC, this indicated that China's economic, social and political reforms will continue to be advanced comprehensively in the years to come.

China's commitment to the creation of a market-oriented economy has been the central plank of its program of economic reform, and considerable progress toward this end has been achieved since 1978, through the gradual withdrawal of the government from the allocation, pricing, and distribution of goods.[4] To date the reforms introduced have achieved remarkable results. Particularly praiseworthy are the facts that the Chinese-type reforms have avoided the collapse in output character-istic of transitions in other former CPEs and generated unprecedented increases in the level of living standards across the country. Over the course of the past few decades, China has successfully implemented a stable economic reform and opening up to the outside world and, in particular, achieved a faster economic growth than any other socialist or former socialist countries in the world.

5.2 Interest groups and stakeholders

In this section, we allow reform to be determined endogenously. Our task is to find how the interest groups and stakeholders interact with each other throughout the whole of the reform process and also how they have had a decisive influence upon the outcomes of the reform. For the sake of simplicity, we assume that the CCP is the only player (policy maker), and that it can be further divided into different cliques (such as radicals and conservatives) in different reform periods. Interest groups can be defined as collections of individuals who share a specific common interest. It is noteworthy that the various interest groups can overlap. For instance, the same individual can be both an entrepreneur and a university professor. Stakeholders then are members of an interest group whose interests are affected by a particular decision.

The evidence described below will demonstrate how Chinese eco-nomic reform has evolved from the collusion of the CCP radicals and conservatives (during the early stages of reform) to the collusion of all political, economic, and cultural elites (during the later stages of reform) as well as how this evolution has influenced the outcomes of the Chinese reform per se.

5.2.1 Radicals and conservatives in the early reforms

To understand the implications of the incentives for the implementation of a reform in China, we must make a point of the relationship between the CCP radicals and conservatives.[5] Both Deng Xiaoping and his senior supporters in power had been victims of the Cultural Revolution (1966–76) during which Mao criticized them for economic liberalism. The special events of Cultural Revolution meant that – regardless of their liberal or conservative ideology – they must unite or, at the very least, must not challenge each other in mutually tolerable matters during the early period of reform.

One of the initial challenges facing the Chinese leadership was to provide for the creation of a rational and efficient governing system in order to support economic development. In pursuit of that goal, the cult of personality surrounding Mao Zedong was unequivocally condemned and was replaced by a strong emphasis on collective leadership. An example of this new emphasis was the CCP's restoration in February 1980 of its Secretariat, which had been suspended since 1966. The new CCP constitution, adopted in 1982, abolished the post of CCPCC chairman – a powerful post held by Mao Zedong for more than four decades, thereby providing a degree of balance between the CCP radicals and conservatives.

The most striking feature of the Chinese reform during the 1980s was the collusive game between the radicals and the conservatives. In considering a reform strategy, the radicals must take into account not only the benefit from the reform but also the political cost stemming from the possibility of losing their coalition with the conservatives. Since deterrence implies cost, the reform strategy that both players (radicals and conservatives) would find it optimal to cooperate does not equate the marginal economic benefit with the marginal economic cost. Instead, a player's optimal strategy of reform equates the marginal economic cost with the marginal economic and political costs. In other words, it is political cost that creates a wedge between the efficient and optimal strategies of reform.

Although the strategy of pursuing faster reforms maximizes the radicals' gross payoff, it does not maximize its net payoff. The radicals would find it optimal to have a strategy involving slower reform in which the marginal economic gains from cooperation equal the marginal political and economic costs.[6] For example, Li Peng's long-lasting political career as premier is one of the outcomes from the collusion of the radicals and conservatives. In 1987, Li became a member of the Politburo's powerful Standing Committee, and a year later Deng Xiaoping picked Li to succeed Zhao Ziyang as premier after Zhao had become the CCPCC's general secretary. This choice might have been seen as unusual because Li Peng did not appear to share Deng's advocacy of economic reform. However, it illustrated clearly that Deng had to seek compromises with the conservatives.[7] However, this might be an early case of the *Baiping* game (see Box 5.1).

As a matter of fact, during the massive mandatory retirement program which was facilitated by a one-time buyout strategy (this will be discussed

---

Box 5.1 What is *Baiping*?

Since the late 1990s, a new Chinese terminology – *Baiping* – has become popular in mainland China. The term "Baiping" is composed of two Chinese characters – "bai" (to place, to put, to arrange, etc.) and "ping" (flat, uniform, fair, etc.). The original meaning of Baiping is "to put flat; or to arrange uniform." The term had been so informal before the twenty-first century that even the 1999 edition of *Cihai* – the largest and the most influential Chinese dictionary published by Shanghai Cishu Publishing House – did not collect it. Notice that the frequently used Baiping has extended from its original meaning to "to treat fairly", "to compromise", "to tradeoff", "to punish" and so on.

After the death of Deng Xiaoping in 1997, Jiang Zemin must deftly play its various wings against each other. In this scenario, Li Peng, Chairman of the eighth National People's Congress (NPC), was selected to hold the No. 2 post of the Chinese Communist Party Central Committee (CCPCC), higher than that of Zhu Rongji – Premier of the State Council – during the 1998–2003 tenure. This was the first time in the PRC's history that the NPC Chairman held a political rank higher than that of the Premiership. Moreover, a large number of non-Communist party and non-party personages were selected as state leaders with the titles of vice Chairpersons of the NPC and of the Chinese People's Political Consultative Congress (CPPCC) in exchange of their support of the CCP as the permanent ruler of the state. For example, as for the 2003–08 and the 2008–13 tenures, China's state-level leaders have included nine standing members of the CCPCC Politburo (some of whom also held the posts of President, Premier, the NPC and CPPCC Chairmen) and dozens of vice Chairpersons of the NPC and of the CPPCC. The total number has been the highest since the 1980s.

---

in subsection 5.3.1), the outgoing CCP officials were partially compensated, in both economic and political terms. For example, a special name was coined for this kind of retirement, *lixiu* – literally "to leave the post and rest." After *lixiu*, retired officials continued to enjoy all of their former political privileges, such as reading government circulars of the same level of confidentiality. Some served as special counselors for their successors. As economic compensations, they could retain their official cars with chauffeurs and security guards. In addition, officials under *lixiu* received an extra month of wages each year and extra housing that their children and grandchildren were entitled to enjoy after their death (Li, 1998, p. 394). As will be discussed in subsection 5.3.1, without that reform, in which many younger cadres were able to play an important role, the reforms that followed afterwards would have been impossible.

Past reform events show that in China the institutional improvement toward a market-oriented system followed a non-linear pattern. From the late 1970s to the early 1990s, China's reform indicated a recurring pattern of reform and retrenchment identified by a four-stage process: "decentralization immediately followed by disorder, disorder immediately followed by concentralization, concentralization followed by rigidity, and rigidity followed by decentralization," a cycle of "decentralization (*fang*)–disorder–over-centralization (*shou*)–rigidity."[8] As a matter of fact, the *shou-fang* circle represents the dynamic process of the political games between radicals and conservatives. Specifically, the *fang* (decentralization) was initiated by the radicals, while the *shou* (over-centralization) was insisted upon by the conservatives. As a result of their very nature (as stated at the beginning of this section), both radicals and conservatives have compromised with each other's initiatives during the majority of the reform era.

In considering the profitability of more rapid reforms, the conservatives take into account not only the benefits that may result from the reforms but also the political cost stemming from the possibility of them losing their supreme position in society. Since deterrence implies cost, the reform strategy that both players (radicals and conservatives) would find it optimal to cooperate does not equate the marginal economic benefit with the marginal economic cost. Instead, a player's optimal strategy of reforms equates the marginal economic cost with the marginal economic and political costs. In other words, it is political cost that creates a wedge between the efficient and optimal strategies of reforms. Although the efficient strategy of reforms maximizes the radicals' gross payoff, it does not maximize its net payoff. The radicals would find it optimal to conduct slower reforms in which the marginal economic gains from cooperation equal the marginal political and economic costs.[9]

When dealing with the early reforms, it is necessary to mention other stakeholders as well as their attitudes toward reforms. Farmers and urban workers – two groups that benefited from the reform-driven economic growth – did not oppose the CCP, and the reform in particular. Intellectuals, especially those who had received Westernized training and been seriously mistreated during the Cultural Revolution, adopted a more critical stance. They had a strong desire for Western democracy. On the other hand, however, the CCP elites, especially the CCP conservatives, could not accept a totally Western-oriented reform (Kang, 2002). Since the radical reformers had been much less powerful than the CCP conservatives during the period when most CCP seniors were still alive, their attempt at uniting with the intellectual elite failed during the Tian'anmen incident in June 1989.

It seems likely that, as a result of the disappearance of the CCP seniors and the conservatives on the one hand and the emergence of more young and Western-learning officials on the other, the Chinese reform should have become increasingly radical since the mid-1990s. What does the evidence tell us?

5.2.2 Political, economic, and cultural elites in the later reforms

As the initiation and sustainability of a reform requires political, economic, and cultural support, the identification of interest groups and stakeholders of the reform in general, but especially those who are politically (and otherwise) active as allies and opponents of reform, is an important step toward the successful completion of the reform. An important distinction is whether interest groups and stakeholders are organized – in other words, whether they pursue their common interest jointly in a coordinated fashion. It is natural to believe that stakeholders will exert pressure on policy makers. This, however, need not always be the case, as not all stakeholders are organized (Fidrmuc and Noury, 2003). Because organized interest groups are better informed than the citizenry at large, they can provide key personalities (the government officials, legislators) with intelligence of various kinds.

Beginning in the mid-1980s, the bureaucratic reform generated a large surplus of government officials. At the same time, many government agencies began to establish business entities, and bureaucrats became managers of these businesses. As a result, a phenomenon that later came to be known as *xiahai* ("jumping into the ocean"). Since the early 1990s, *xiahai* has been an immensely popular phenomenon among Chinese government officials.[10] By joining the business world, the former bureaucrats obtain much higher economic payoffs as well as a higher degree of personal freedom, despite being exposed to increased economic uncertainty. On the other hand, there is a high demand for those bureaucrats, since in the half-reformed economy many non-state enterprises need their knowledge and skills in order to deal with the remaining government regulations.

Since the 16th National Congress of the CCP, held in Beijing in November 2002, CCP membership has been formally opened to China's business elite. The removal of the clause in the CCP's constitution that officially prohibited private businessmen from becoming party members and serving in the government is intended to bring the CCP constitution into line with the reality of the party's character and social composition as it prepares to accelerate the pace of market reforms. In a rambling opening address to the Congress, Jiang Zemin articulated the class interests of the new Chinese elite. He called for the Beijing regime to persevere in opening up to the capitalist market and declared that the CCP should protect the "legitimate rights and interests" of business-people and property owners (Jiang, 2002). The formal opening of the CCP to different levels of businesspeople in 2002 represented a turning point. The fact that Jiang's "Three Represents" theory formalizes what has already emerged was highlighted by the year 2002 *Forbes* magazine list of China's 100 richest multi-millionaires. One-quarter of those on the list declared that they were CCP members (Chan, 2002). In addition, many Chinese CEOs of private companies or transnational corporations also have connections with the CCP.

Since the mid-1990s, cultural elites (including noted intellectuals, popular entertainers, and ethnic minority-based social elites) have been establishing closer links to the political and economic elites in China.[11] The factors resulting in the collusion of the political and cultural elites might include the following. First, the disappearance of senior CCPCC members has weakened the power of the conservatives since the early 1990s, while the younger political leaders are usually more highly educated than their predecessors. Secondly, after the Tian'anmen incident, radical intellectuals were subjected to serious retaliation, most of them either fleeing the country or disappearing from academic circles. Thirdly, the changing external environment (such as the collapse of the former Soviet Union followed by the unsuccessful "Big bang" reforms introduced in Russia and also the USA transferring from standing against the CCP to against China) helped most, if not all intellectuals to cooperate with the CCP and the government.

Several books have portrayed the post-Tian'anmen period as one of intense political disagreement (see, for example, Fewsmith, 1999; and Lam, 1999). Certainly, this was true until the mid-1990s. Yet disagreements since this time have been expressed increasingly through non-sanctioned means by non-sanctioned actors. The elite battles evident today are based upon illegitimate end-running, rather than legitimate contestation. Thus the politics of contestation – legitimate competition within the structures of the polity properly used by a range of agreed actors – remains absent. The earnestness of contestation in the early reform era has been replaced by the anomie of compliance or the intrigue of crypto-politics in the post-reform era (Gilley, 2004, p. 121).

Among China's rural peasantry and the industrial working class, a seething hostility is building up over official corruption, poverty, the loss of services, unemployment, and the widening income gap between rich and poor. After several years of factional debate within the CCP, a consensus has emerged that the lesson to be drawn from the Tian'anmen events is that the regime must build a solid base among the urban upper and middle classes, while making no democratic concessions to the masses (Chan, 2002). The government believed it could weather the opposition of workers and peasants by keeping them like "scattered sand" – that is, lacking any national organization or coherent political program (Kang, 2002). Commenting on the sentiment of the political establishment, Kang (2002) points out:

> There is a stable alliance between the political, economic and intellectual elite of China. The main consequence is that the elite won't challenge the CCP and the government. The economic elite love money, not democracy. Their vanity will also be satisfied as the CCP has promised them party membership and government positions.

How has the Chinese reform been linked to the collusion of the political, economic and cultural elites? First of all, faced by the example of the failure of the radical reforms in the former USSR, the political elite – no matter how radical they had been during the previous period of reform – has become increasingly pragmatic over time. In essence, they would now be more likely to choose a more gradual/partial (or alternatively, less radical) reform strategy than they had chosen in the 1980s. Secondly, the political, economic, and cultural elites have increasingly become beneficiaries of the existing system that was based upon the past gradual and partial reforms. As a result, there will be less and less incentive for them to see any (radical and thorough) political and economic reforms that could affect their existing benefits. Last but not least, in contrast to the reforms that had been merely decided by the political elite (including both CCP radicals and conservatives) before the mid-1990s (as will be discussed in subsection 5.3.1 in Chapter 5), the reforms that have been decided by the political elite in cooperation with the economic and cultural elites since then have been far more limited in scope (as shown in Figure 5.1).

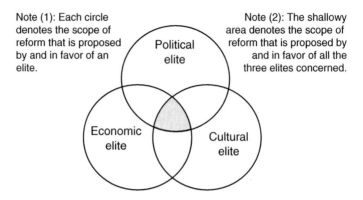

Note (1): Each circle denotes the scope of reform that is proposed by and in favor of an elite.

Note (2): The shallowy area denotes the scope of reform that is proposed by and in favor of all the three elites concerned.

Figure 5.1   Collective actions of the Chinese elites on reforms

5.3   Radical reform: the (un)successful cases

5.3.1   Radical reform: the successful cases

China's agricultural reforms began in September 1980 and had been successfully completed before the end of 1982. The CCP and the Chinese government took only about two years to decollectivize about 700 million farmers across the huge nation, through a method known as HRS. Under the HRS, each household may be able to sign a contract with the local government: it will then obtain a certain amount of arable land, production equipment and a production quota in line with the number of rural population in this family. Once the household fulfills its quota, it can decide freely what to produce and how to sell. Although land is still owned by the state, the incentive for agricultural production has increased significantly. The decollectivization of agriculture, which has been recognized as a radical reform (Sachs and Woo, 1994; and Zhao, 1999, p. 192), has been universally recognized as a success. For example, from 1978 to 1984, grain output increased by 56 percent (Lin, 1992). Even more rapid was the growth in the output of other agricultural commodities (during the pre-reform period, the growth in grain output had been at the expense of these commodities). Over the longer period of reform from 1978 to 2002, gross agricultural output had grown in real terms at an average annual rate of more than 5 percent (NBS, 2003).

The special political and economic features of China determine the driving forces and the outcomes of the reform in agricultural ownership. First, more than 80 percent of China's population still lived in 1978 in rural areas – a backward and autarkical society.[12] Secondly, China's agricultural sector had been dominated by collectivist ownership before the reform – which did not fit a standard socialist model. As a result, the reform of the collective sector (while keeping the state-owned sector unchanged) would not have been regarded by the conservatives as fundamentally affecting China's socialist orthodoxy. Thirdly, and most importantly, the Chinese policy makers – from both reformist and conservative cliques – still had remembered the three-year famine (1959–61) during which millions of farmers died of starvation. They should have recognized that the horrible famine had attributed to, at least partially, China's highly centralized agricultural system, and that if it would occur again, the CCP would lose its power base in China.

Since the initial and external conditions of the agricultural sector were similar to those of the industrial sector (especially those of the small state-owned and collectively owned industrial enterprises), we argue that at least some of the industrial reforms – which had followed a too gradual/partial pace (as will be discussed in subsection 5.4.2 of Chapter 5) – were misguided during the early 1980s. Had the industrial reform followed a more radical approach in terms of speed and scope during the early stage of reform, there would have been more positive economic performances in the industrial sector.

Another successful case relates to the reform of Chinese bureaucracy. The first task undertaken by Deng Xiaoping after he resumed his job was to reform the bureaucratic institutions. Manned by millions of workers, the system was acknowledged officially to be overstaffed and sluggish. There was an intensification of the drive to weed out tens of thousands of aged, inactive, and incompetent personnel. In an even more revolutionary move, the life tenure system for state and party cadres was abolished, and age limits for various offices were established and, on a less restrictive basis, an education requirement for each level of government positions (see Table 5.1 for a summary of the reform). While removing superfluous personnel, the reform leaders stressed the importance of creating a "third echelon" of younger leadership to enter responsible positions and be trained for future authority.

The major and direct consequence of the bureaucratic reform is that many younger and better-educated bureaucrats have replaced the older revolutionary veterans. The new, younger officials were generally more supportive of the government reforms, as well as being more adaptable and more pragmatic. Being better educated in almost all cases, they were also generally more competent than their predecessors (Li, 1998, p. 394). Clearly, the Chinese-style reform of bureaucracy served as a stable political foundation for the implementation of the economic reform during the past decades. Without that reform, in which more younger cadres

Table 5.1   Chinese bureaucratic reform, February 1982 to September 1984

Statistic	Provincial governors	Ministers	City mayors or department chiefs	County sheriffs or division chiefs
Mandatory retirement age (years)	65	65	60	55
Average retirement age (years)				
– Before reform	62	64	58	–
– After reform	55	58	50	<45
Percentage with college degree (%)				
– Before reform	20	37	14	11
– After reform	43	52	44	45
Average tenure (years)				
– Pre-1982	6.43/6.23[a]	6.56	–	–
– Post-1982	3.84/4.05[a]	4.44	–	–

Notes: By 1988, 90% of government officials above the country level were newly appointed after 1982; 60% of those government officials had college degrees. This was a result of retiring 3.4 million revolutionary veterans. [a]Governor/party secretary.
Source: Li (1998, p. 394), which also gives other references.

were able to play an important role, the later reforms would have been impossible.

Although the two reforms outlined above have been regarded as successful, they also had some negative effects. For example, the cooperative medical care system, which had worked quite well before the reform in rural areas, was abandoned as a result of the HRS.[13] The implementation of the policy of "buying-out" the ageing bureaucrats also had some negative effects. An implicit and informal arrangement for most senior officials was that their children were allowed to enter politics in senior positions, which resulted in the birth of the infamous *taizhidang* (party of crown prince) in China. It is worth noting that the rise of the *taizidang* often happened in parallel with political and economic corruption. However, the above problems were not because the reforms were too radical but because they were too mild (especially in the case of bureaucratic reform) and limited in scope (especially in the case of agricultural reform).

5.3.2   Radical reform: the unsuccessful cases

The dual-pricing system, discussed in section 4.1 of Chapter 4, provided opportunities for people who had access to state-controlled goods and materials to make large profits by buying them at an officially fixed low price and reselling them at a market-based price. Consequently, it created various distortions and speculative transactions, which have often led to unequal competition as well as instance of official corruption.

After nearly ten years of reforms and debates over the relative merits of plan and market, a radical price reform was introduced suddenly in June 1998. This was based on the idea that "long pain is not better than short pain", and that market prices should be implemented at once. Theoretically, if price subsidies are a significant cause for deficits and if supply is highly elastic then fiscal stabilization calls for early and speedy price liberalization (Liew *et al.*, 2003). According to this theory, the greater the fiscal deficits (if they are not due to price subsidies) and the value of forced savings and the smaller the supply elasticities, the longer should be the lag between fiscal and monetary stabilization and price liberalization. The macroeconomic environment was not favorable to the implementation of any such radical price reforms: the level of inflation was very high (18.5 percent in 1988) and friction from dual pricing was at its worst (for example, the planned price for steel was 700 yuan per ton while the market price was 1,800 yuan per ton) (Zhao, 1999, p. 195). From 1985 to 1988, the level of price subsidies increased (Jin *et al.*, 2001), as did the resulting fiscal deficit. The supply was constrained as a result of the decreasing marginal return from the early reform in the agricultural sector on the one hand, and the unsuccessful reform in the state-owned industrial sector (as will be discussed in subsection 5.4.2 of Chapter 5) on the other. The implementation of price reform in China under these circumstances was both politically and socially impractical.[14]

Another notable case concerned China's various attempts to achieve radical SOE reform during the late 1980s and the 1990s. This had been delayed on several occasions, owing to serious concerns about the social instability that might result from the reform. The SOE reform is sufficiently extensive to cause large increases in unemployment. In December 1986, the "Bankruptcy Law Concerning the SOEs" was adopted by the NPC. However, the law was not effectively applied until 1994 due to fears of unemployment and social instability, as China had only relatively primitive social security system.

The reform on non-performing SOEs was debated once again in the Fifth Plenum of the 14th CCPCC which was held during September 1995. The outcome was the policy of "grasping the large and releasing the small". To "grasp the large" (*zhuada*) is to turn a select group of 300 out of a list of 1,000 already successful large enterprises and enterprise groups into world-class businesses. To "release the small" (*fangxiao*) is to privatize or to contract out small SOEs or to allow them to go bankrupt. This policy allows most small SOEs to be sold off to private individuals; the management of those not sold is contracted out (Liew, 1999, p. 93). During the first two years, when the government began to release small and non-performing SOEs and to lay off superfluous workers, there was serious resistance to these reforms.

Note that since the mid-1990s the CCP and the central government have been particularly concerned about the increasing number of illegal organizations established to organize protests against the radical SOE reform (see the final paragraph of subsection 4.4.2 for some detailed evidence). This can be found, for example, in Jiang Zemin's speech at the meeting commemorating the twentieth anniversary of the Third Plenum of the Eleventh CCP National Congress (Jiang, 1998, p. 2). In contrast to the Western democratic countries, in which protests against government are a regular occurrence, such protests were unusual in the PRC, especially during the post-reform period. They could easily remind the CCP and central government of the Tian'anmen incident in June 1989. Consequently, they could retard any further efforts to radically reform the SOEs.

We are not able to verify if – or to what extent – the SOE reform, if it had been implemented earlier, could have been more successful. But, arguably, if the substantial ownership reform of the small and rural-based SOEs were introduced in parallel with or immediately following the radical agricultural ownership reform during the early stages (that is, in the late 1970s or the early 1980s), there would have been similar, positive economic performances. The primary reason lies in the fact that the market culture based on private ownership – the main form of ownership before the 1950s – still remained a memory of most middle-aged SOE workers in China in the early 1980s. The critical role that the retired SOE workers played in the dramatic growth of the township and village-based enterprises (McMillan and Naughton, 1992; and World Bank, 1996, p. 51) indicates that the SOEs and the SOE workers could become more productive if the property right and incentive system moved away from the model of state ownership.

5.4   Gradual/partial reform: the (un)successful cases

5.4.1   Gradual/partial reform: the successful cases

The key component of China's gradual/partial reform was the introduction of a dual-track system, which was implemented first in the area of agricultural products, before spreading slowly to consumer goods and intermediate goods. In each case, a free market in which the price was subject to market regulations developed in parallel with a controlled market in which the price was kept almost unchanged at an officially fixed level. Because the price was higher in the market-regulated sector than in the state-controlled sector, the supply in the free market grew rapidly, so that its share of total output rose steadily. Meanwhile, the planned price was able to rise incrementally until it approached the market price when there was a narrowing of the gap between supply and demand. The dual-track system extended through almost every sphere of the Chinese economy, from agriculture, industry, commerce, transportation, post and telecommunications to health care, education and so on during the transition. For example, between 1979 and 1992, the proportion of industrial goods and materials distributed under the central plan system declined from 95 percent to less than 10 percent. There was a parallel reduction in the planned allocation of consumer goods: the number of first-class goods distributed by the state dropped from 65 to 20 and that of the production of materials distributed by the state was reduced from 256 to 19 during the period (Liu, 1995, p. 53).

The smooth implementation of the dual-track system depended on the material compensation of and the spiritual consolation for various losers. For example, although consumers have been able to buy foodstuffs on the free market since 1980, urban food coupons (for the purchase of grain, meat, oil and so on) were only finally removed in the early 1990s. Guangzhou completed the removal of the above coupons in 1992 and spent on average 103 yuan in 1988, 113 yuan in 1990, and 43 yuan in 1992 per urban resident for compensation. Beijing also spent 182 yuan in 1990, 185 yuan in 1991, and 123 yuan in 1994 per head before its removal of the coupons (Qian, 2002). In addition, when the reformists decided to reduce the share of the centrally planned economy during the 1980s, spiritual consolation also applied to the conservatives who had believed strongly that the Chinese economy must be regulated mainly by planning and only supplementally by the market mechanism (see Box 5.2).

In short, a brief review of the gradually declining trend of the plan track throughout the 1980s provides evidence that, *ex post*, there is no "ratcheting up" of the plan. Moreover, recent data reveal that the plan track in the product market has been largely "phased out" in the 1990s, and that this phasing out of the plan track was accompanied in general by explicit compensation. With rapid growth, the plan track becomes, in no time at all, a matter of little consequence to most potential losers, which in turn reduces the cost required for compensating them

Box 5.2 The art of reforming a centrally planned economy

During the 1980s there had been extensive and heated arguments about how plan and market could be appropriately combined in the Chinese economy. While the CCP conservatives strongly believed that the Chinese economy should be regulated mainly by planning and supplementally by market, some economists advocating *laissez-faire* suggested an increasing share of market regulation. In order to resolve this dispute, Chinese reformists invented a term – "guided plan." Compared to "commanded plan" (under which both the price and the quantity of each commodity are strictly controlled by the central government), "guided plan" only relates to those that are under the loose control of the central or local government.

It is interesting to note that the definition of the term "guided plan" is quite fuzzy. In practice, commodities under the "guided plan" scheme can be treated either as part of those regulated by "plan" or as part of those regulated by "market" (see figure below). What the reformists intended to do was to, while not violating the principle of "regulation mainly by planning," move Line B closer to Line A so as to reduce the scope of the "commanded plan" (Zhao, 1998). Even though the conservatives still wanted to move Line B closer to Line C in order to retain a larger portion of purely commanded plan for the Chinese economy, confrontations between the reformists and conservatives were reduced substantially.

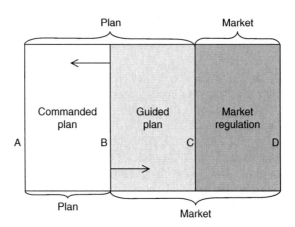

Source: Drawn by Prof. Zhao Renwei.

(Lau *et al.*, 2000, p. 142). In general, the dual-track reform has been regarded as being successful, since it not only avoided the decline of output but also improved the level of efficiency (Wu and Zhao, 1987; and Li, 1997). It must be noted that the dual-track system did not always work well, especially when a large gap existed between market-regulated and officially fixed prices (we will discuss this point later).

Another key initiative of China's gradual reform was the decentralization of authority, that is, transferring economic management and decision making from central government to the provincial and local governments (see Chapter 4 for details). How did the reform work in practice, and to what extent had the provincial governments' fiscal incentives been strengthened as a result of this reform? Jin *et al.* (2001), based on the panel data of 28 provinces between 1982 and 1992, find that the marginal fiscal incentives of provincial governments increased during the reform period between 1982 and 1992, compared with those during the pre-reform period from 1970 to 1979. A comparison of these findings with parallel investigations in Russia is also revealing. Zhuravskaya (2000) examined the fiscal incentives of city governments in the region–city fiscal relationship in post-reform Russia (in which the city is one level below the region, which in turn is one level below the federal government). Using the data from 35 cities for the period 1992–97, she found that increases in a city's own revenue were almost entirely offset by decreases in shared revenues from the region to the city.[15]

China's foreign exchange system used to be controlled strictly by the central government. Yet since China began its economic reform in the late 1970s, the foreign trade system has been liberalized gradually. In the early 1980s, Chinese currency RMB was non-convertible and the foreign exchanges were strictly supervised by the state. Two exchange rates were in operation during that period: an official rate published by the government and another special one for foreign trade. Such a system was aimed to enhance the country's exports and to restrict its imports, for China suffered from a serious lack of foreign exchange at that time. In 1984, as a result of improved performance in foreign trade and the economy as a whole, the government adopted a new policy of exchange retention. This policy allowed domestic enterprises and institutions to retain some of their foreign currency earnings, in contrast to the previous one in which these units turned over all of their foreign currency earnings to the state. Although a larger proportion of foreign exchanges was still under the control of the government, the new retaining policy stimulated domestic enterprises to increase their exports, and hence there was a significant improvement in China's foreign trade performance.

However, this kind of gradual/partial reform, together with other gradual and partial reforms on the external economic sectors, has also faced difficulties, as will be discussed in detail in subsection 5.4.2.

5.4.2   Gradual/partial reform: the unsuccessful cases

The evidence shows that not all gradual/partial reforms have performed well in China. Among the most typical unsuccessful examples were the introduction of the responsibility system and the contract system in the SOEs in 1983 and 1986, respectively. These reforms had some positive impacts on SOEs' performance, but overall they still did not achieve the objective of turning SOEs into efficient enterprises. In brief, there are at least the following problems for this system. First, the operating mechanism of the contract system strengthened the vertical one-to-one bargaining relationship between government and firm. It did not strengthen the competitive horizontal relationship between firms, and therefore was inconsistent with market-oriented reform (Zhao, 1999, p. 196). Secondly, it did not guarantee that the SOEs became independent economic identities. Last but not least, the contract did not solve the long-term behavioral problems of the managers and employees. Their behavior was still driven by short-term motivations, impinging on the interests of the owner, the state, and damaging firms' long-term development (Huang, 1999, p. 103).

In order to develop a full understanding of the characteristics of the Chinese-style reform, one must keep in mind two important facts: first, China's vast territorial size and wide diversity in physical environments have inevitably resulted in great differences in regional economic conditions; secondly, with China's population of 1.3 billion and its 56 distinct ethnic groups, most provinces, which would be equivalent in size to a medium-sized country, are considerable political and economic systems in their own right. The differences between these provinces have long been a defining characteristic of China's politics since in most instances their boundaries have been created more than two thousand years ago (Gottmann, 1973; Goodman, 1997). Furthermore, Chinese culture is not homogeneous across provinces, in terms of ethnic and linguistic groups as well as provincial politics. As a result, the chances of the adoption of a common standard and interprovincial coordination between different groups of people are not likely to be enhanced if there are markedly differing religious beliefs and cultural values.

The Chinese-style decentralization of economic authority (as discussed in subsection 5.4.1) did not always work well, especially during the earliest stages of the reforms. Since the advent of administrative decentralization, China's national economy had become effectively "cel-lularized" into a plethora of semi-autarkic regional enclaves during the 1980s. In order to protect local market and revenue sources, it became common practice in China that provinces restrict imports (exports) from (to) other provinces by levying high, if informal taxes on commodi-ties and by creating non-tariff barriers. Xinjiang autonomous region, for example, effectively banned the import of 48 commodities on the grounds that they would harm its domestic economy. Jilin refused to market beer produced in its neighboring provinces of Heilongjiang and Liaoning. Hunan province prohibited exporting grain to its neighbor, Guangdong province. ... In some provinces, local authorities estab-lished, and provided finance for, a variety of schemes in order to promote the sales of local products. Enterprises from other provinces, however, often had difficulties in finding office spaces, accommodation, or land for their business activities.[16]

Another case is the reform of China's banking system, which is gen-erally recognized to lag well behind China's dramatic moves toward a market economy that are so evident in other sectors. Prior to the commencement of reforms in 1983, the People's Bank of China (PBC), China's central bank, dominated the country's highly centralized finan-cial scene. Not only did it control the money supply; it also managed all banking and savings activities. In effect, before the reforms the PBC was only the accounting department of the Chinese central government. At the end of 1993, the State Council issued a new plan to spur changes in the monetary and financial system that would strengthen the PBC's grip on the macroeconomic environment, create specialized banks to serve priority sectors, and push the other banks towards becoming true commercial banks. The overall objective was to separate monetary pol-icy from normal banking functions and to convert most banks into truly independent financial entities. However, the PBC remains subservient to the finance ministry and thus cannot refuse to finance government expenditures. Branches of the PBC in the provinces and districts are also subject to the dictates of both PBC and local government officials. As a result, it is very difficult for them to refuse loans to local government entities that demand more and more credit (Xu, 1995).

In the late 1990s, the Asian financial crisis served a very useful func-tion: it alerted Chinese leaders to the dangers of operating a weak financial system. Aware of the lessons drawn from the Asian financial crisis, in 1998 China wanted to quicken the pace of banking reform. The major measure was that ¥270 billion (US$33 billion) in special bonds was issued in 1998 in order to recapitalize the state banks. In the following year it created an asset management company (AMC) for each of the big four state banks. The AMCs received ¥400 billion (US$48 billion) in seed capital from the Ministry of Finance (MOF) and issued ¥1 trillion (US$121 billion) worth of MOF-guaranteed bonds. They then used these funds to buy ¥1.4 trillion (US$170 billion) of bad loans from the state banks at face value. But the program has failed to cure the banks' woes, since other relevant financial and economic reforms had not been implemented. Since 1998, the percentage of bad loans on the banks' books has not fallen much, and the AMCs have had limited success in recovering or selling off the bad assets. Meanwhile, corporate governance, transparency and risk management at the state banks have only shown slight improvement (Lo, 2004).

China's gradual/partial open-door policy has serious implications for its legal system and its lack of transparency, and problems of assimilating a non-market economy.[17] For example, there have to be changes to about 220 Chinese laws that are incompatible with WTO rules (Reti, 2001). Furthermore, in accordance with the requirements of the WTO, banks, insurance companies, telecommunications and other service industries of the rest of the world will be allowed to operate in China according to the negotiated timetable. The impact may eventually break up the status of monopoly and state control that have existed in China for around half a century. The new bank reforms starting on December 1 2003, opening the sector further to foreign competition, have still been too mild and limited in scope. Pressing banking and financial reforms are needed in the years to come.

5.5   Whither Chinese-style reform?

> Doctor Bianque went to see King Wu of the state of Qin. The King told the doctor about his poor health and Bianque was ready to give him treatment. The ministers at the King's sides said to him: "Your Majesty, the malady is in front of your ears and below your eyes. Even with treatment it might not be cured and very likely you will lose your hearing and sight." The King passed these messages to Bianque. Bianque was enraged and threw down the stone needle which he used for giving treatment, saying: "Sire, you discuss your illness with one who knows how to effect a cure but you allow those who know nothing about medicine to spoil the whole thing. If the Qin is governed in this way, then a single such mistake on your part is enough to bring down the state."
>
> – Zhanguoce (475–221 BC)

According to the new institutional economics, system, like other production factors required for economic development, is a special kind of scarce resource and should thus be treated properly in economics. The economic system of any nation is the mechanism that brings together natural resources, labor, technology, and the necessary managerial talents. Anticipating and then meeting human needs through the production and distribution of goods and services is the end purpose of every economic system. While the type of economic system applied by a nation is usually decided artificially, it is also to a large extent the result of historical experience, which becomes over time a part of political culture.

Let us consider a reform program consisting of two reform measures that can be carried out either simultaneously or sequentially. Suppose that the economic outcome of the full reform is in most circumstances better than that of each partial reform measure. Without considering the cost of implementation, a big bang reform may have an advantage over a gradual one.[18] However, once reforms are turned back sometimes due to the political and economic uncertainties, the reversal is more costly for the full reform than the partial one, which means that reversing the full reform sometimes costs more than reversing a single partial reform measure.[19] In the previous sections, we have examined various successful and unsuccessful cases of the Chinese-style reform. It should be noted that the judgment of a reform as being "successful" or "unsuccessful" is based on some available data and literature. Frankly speaking, there is no mandatory standard for this definition since each reform – no matter whether not it has been "successful" ("unsuccessful") – has both positive and negative effects on the Chinese economy. In addition, the terms "radical" and "gradual/partial" reforms used in these sections are also defined elastically, since judged by international standards, over the course of the past three decades China's reforms as a whole have been implemented only via a gradual/partial approach.

During the twentieth century the failure of the centrally planned economies (CPEs) to keep pace with their market-oriented counterparts demonstrated quite clearly that planning entire economies at the level of the central government does not offer a productive path to long-term development. Since 1978, economic reforms in China have sought to improve, among other things, enterprise incentive systems with greater relative decision-making autonomy. The dynamism of the Chinese economy may be attributed to a variety of reform measures. One such measure was the lifting of previous restrictions on the development of non-state sectors and the policy of promoting a diversified ownership structure.

This has led to the explosive growth of the non-state sectors that are acting increasingly as the engine of economic development particularly since the early 1990s when China formally tried to transform its economy to a socialist market system.

The economic reforms introduced in many former CPEs followed their domestic political crises (such as the collapse of the Soviet Union in the case of Russia, and the death of Mao Zedong and the fall of the leftist "Gang of Four" in China). However, successful reforms are also promoted by a favorable international environment. Haggard and Webb (1994) have found that international factors influence reform through a number of channels, such as the prospect of trade concessions and agreements, conditionality and ideas brought by external advisers and technocrats trained overseas. The significant role of the open-door policy in market-oriented reform can be witnessed by the Chinese experience. China's application to get access to the GATT/WTO lasted for 16 years – from 1986 to 2002. After each of the long-running negotiations, China's centrally planned system on foreign trade had a gradual reform toward the market-oriented economic system. During the 1990s, almost all major Chinese reforms of the foreign trade system were influenced by the WTO accession negotiations (Chi, 2000).

It is now generally believed that the Chinese outward-oriented development policy was borrowed in part from the experiences of the newly industrialized economies (NIEs) in East Asia. On the one hand, the reformist leaders were also deeply aware that their rivals from the Chinese Civil War across the Taiwan Strait, their compatriots in colonial Hong Kong, and their Cold War enemies in southern Korea were enjoying sustained economic success that raised deeply challenging questions about China's own continuing levels of backwardness (Garnaut, 1999, pp. 2–3). On the other hand, China and the USA saw the former Soviet Union as their common enemy and this led Mao and Nixon to normalize Sino-US relations in 1971, which paved the way for China's re-engagement with the non-communist world. Later the defeat of the US forces in Vietnam meant that the West appeared to be a less threatening place to China's leaders, facilitating China's re-entry into the global economy (Liew *et al.*, 2003).

Essentially, China's economic reform has provided fewer incentives and opportunities for provincial and local governments to make use of the comparative advantages for interregional cooperation in the 1980s than in the 1990s. The following research evidence can witness this phenomenon. Young (2000), based on the pre-1990s data, finds that China's economic reform resulted in a fragmented internal market with

Table 5.2 A comparison of selected reform programs

Strategy	Successful cases[a]	Unsuccessful cases[a]
Gradual/partial approach[b]	Dual-pricing system reform (1979–92); foreign exchange system reform (1984–)	Industrial contract system (1983; 1986); administrative decentralization (1980s–early 1990s); banking reform (1983–)
Radical approach[b]	Agricultural reform (1980–82); bureaucratic reform (1982–84)	Price-release reform (1988–89); SOE ownership reform (1980s; 1990s)

Notes: [a]The judgment of a reform program as being "successful" or "unsuccessful" is based on available data and literature. [b]The terms "radical" and "gradual/partial" are elastically defined, since according to international standard, during the past three decades China's all reform programs as a whole have been implemented via only but a gradual/partial approach.
Source: Defined in sections 5.3 and 5.4 of Chapter 5.

fiefdoms controlled by local officials whose economic and political ties to protect industry resembled those observed in Latin American economies in previous decades. It seems plausible that the endogenous response of actors to the rent-seeking opportunities created by gradualist reform could give rise to new distortions, whose lifespan far exceeds that of the rents which had motivated their initial arrival (Young, 2000). Based on the data from 1988 to 2000, Cai *et al.* (2002), however, argue that the decentralization of authority has already generated comparative advantages for interregional cooperation in the manufacturing sector during the reform period. If both results are correct, the Chinese reform might suggest that "Big bang" tends to be optimal in the early stage of reform and that gradualism tends to be optimal in the late stage of reform.

It is almost certain that the Chinese-style reform (see Table 5.2 for a qualitative comparison of major reform programs) would not be reversed in the foreseen future. This is not only because the Chinese-style reform has become a win–win game for all who are in power, but also because it has meant that the Chinese economy is increasingly dependent on the outside world. Since China's entrance into the WTO in November 2002, external stakeholders (such as international financial organizations and foreign-owned enterprises) have been exerting an increasing influencing on Chinese economic reform. However, the collective actions of these stakeholders on the Chinese reforms are much more complicated than those of Chinese domestic stakeholders. For example, with regard to the reform on the current exchange rate system under which the Chinese currency has been, as generally recognized, devalued, there are two different voices from the outside world. While countries having large trade deficits with China have requested that the level of the Chinese currency should be more freely determined by the market, their overseas enterprises in China have benefited significantly from this currency devaluation through the export of their products to the outside world.

China is now faced by the dilemma of whether to follow the past tune (that is, the gradual and partial strategy) in order to minimize the risk of macroeconomic transition or to go faster in order to satisfy the WTO requirements with the fixed timetable. However, it seems that the Chinese government is not prepared to bear the potential risk of any substantial or radical reforms. One example is the reform of the foreign exchange system. As stated in subsection 5.4.1, China's gradual/partial reform of the foreign exchange system has contributed significantly to its robust foreign trade performance on the one hand and its domestic economic stability on the other. However, since 1994 when a unitary and floating exchange-rate system was established, there has been no substantial reform. Obviously, this system is to a large extent determined by the government; the foreign exchange rate is controlled officially and the central bank is one of the biggest participants in the market.

While China's reform has been driving its economic growth strongly (see Chapters 6 and 7), it has also led to the development of a series of socioeconomic problems. By openly proclaiming itself a party of the "economic elite" that has benefited from its free market agenda, the CCP has been hoping to consolidate a reliable base of support for its continued rule. With its pro-growth polices, its ban on independent trade unions and its low environmental standards, the CCP has created an advantageous atmosphere for the economic elite to make money. Policies so favor the rich and business that China's economic program, in the words of one Western ambassador, resembles "the dream of the American Republican Party."[20]

Indeed, the CCP's "three representatives" theory states clearly that the CCP is no longer the single representative of poor, working-class people; rather, it has also been the representative of the economic and cultural elites in China. A glance at China's past social and economic transformations reveals that the large surge in income inequalities (see Chapter 6 for a detailed analysis) was not the only unwanted result of the Chinese-style reform. The worsening of social and political progress during the 1990s and the 2000s is another example. For example, China's "control of corruption" score was more than 50 in 1996 (see Figure 5.2a) but it dropped to only 30 in 2007 (see Figure 5.2c); between 1996 and 2002 its score in terms of "voice and accountability" was among the lowest of all of the nations considered by the World Bank (see Figure 5.2b) and there is no sign of improvements between 2002 and 2007 (see Figure 5.2c). Without good reason, China's party-state political system lacked the informational and incentive roles of democracy that, working mainly through open public discussion, could be of pivotal importance for the reach of social and public policies.

Since the beginning of its economic reform policies, China has benefited increasingly from global interdependence and the modern world's free flow of goods, capital and people. However, with those benefits have also come the responsibilities of accountability and transparency. China's party-state system has exposed the dearth of political dynamics. The Severe Acute Respiratory Syndrome (SARS) epidemic which spread throughout China in April 2003 exposed some of China's institutional weakness.[21] Yet the greatest impact of the SARS crisis may be on China's antiquated political system. Chinese mismanagement of the outbreak has plainly exposed just how far political reform has lagged behind economic development. Beijing's long concealment of the truth is exposing political faultlines by simultaneously weakening the economy and damaging the government's credibility. The crisis has undermined traditional supporters, aggravating old demographic strains, and emboldening detractors to make more assertive protests against government policy. While the growing pressure from a more demanding public and an increasingly interdependent world has forced China to re-evaluate its political and socioeconomic policies, the extent of any resulting political reform depends upon whether or not the enhanced incentives for accountability and transparency among public officials override the traditional incentives for party and factional loyalty.

In short, for the majority of the past three decades, China's reform has achieved two objectives simultaneously: to improve economic efficiency by unleashing the standard forces of incentives and competition on the one hand; and to make the reform a win–win game and therefore in the interests of those in power on the other (Qian, 2002). And they take into consideration China's specific political and cultural conditions. With its impressive economic achievements, today the Chinese reform is rarely called into question. However, it still remained problematic in social and political perspectives throughout the reform era. Ironically, China's economic growth was obtained at the cost of a retardation of political reforms, not to mention worsening income inequalities as well as other social problems. As China continues to integrate with the world economy and accepts other global values, there are mounting pressures for political reform.

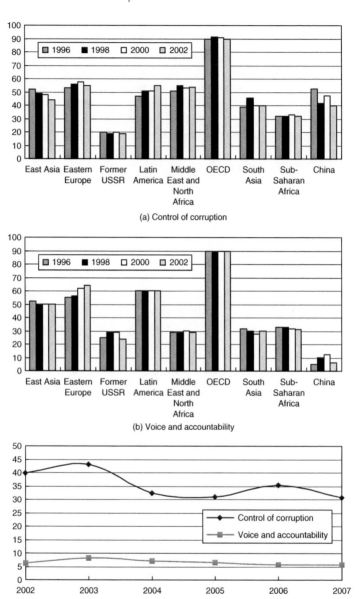

Figure 5.2   Social and political capacities, China and the world
Note: The y-coordinates denote the degrees of "control of corruption" and "voice and accountability", respectively (100 = maximum level; 0 = minimum level).
Source: Created by the author based on Kaufmann *et al.* (2008).

5.6 Summary

The ultimate goal of any economic system is the allocation of scarce resources among competing factions. To accomplish this goal, the economic system must deal explicitly with the supply and demand of goods and services as well as the interaction between the two. The Chinese economy is no exception to this rule. This chapter has explored the elements underpinning the design and implementation of the Chinese economic reform from 1978 onwards. It has provided an explanation for the causes and timing of the major reform programs, as well as for how the success and failure of the reform efforts were associated with the initial conditions and the reform strategies.

The importance of initial conditions and strategies for economic reforms has been noted (Fischer and Gelb, 1991; and De Melo *et al.*, 1997). The question of how such issues affect the final results of economic reforms still remain unresolved, however (Campos and Coricelli, 2002, p. 828). When considering the remarkable differences between the reforms pursued in China and Russia, one must not overlook the initial institutional conditions in each of the countries. Prior to reform, the central planning system in China lasted only a relatively short period of time (that is, from the late 1950s to the late 1970s) compared to that in the former Soviet Union (FSU) (that is, from the early twentieth century to the late 1980s). As a result, the capitalist ideology and market culture still had a strong base in China vis-à-vis the FSU.[22]

The analytical narrative of the political economic events shows that the efficiency of China's reform depended upon: (i) the initial institutional conditions; (ii) the external environment; and (iii) the reform strategy. We argue that a radical reform tends to be more efficient than a gradual/partial one during the early stages (the late 1970s and the early 1980s), while a gradual/partial reform tends to be more efficient than a radical one in the later stages. Finally, we find that between 1978 and 2008 Chinese-style reform has evolved from the collusion of the CCP radicals and conservatives to that of the political, economic and cultural elites, at the cost of sacrificing the benefits of the rest of the people.

In comparison to those introduced in Eastern Europe and the former Soviet Union, the reforms in China have some distinctive characteristics. First, the degree to which the economic system derived from the former Soviet Union has exerted an influence on the Chinese economy varied from sector to sector. The sector that was most affected was the industrialized sector of the national economy, while there was less influence on the disaggregated agricultural sector and small industries. Secondly, the economic reforms in China started at a time when China was regarded as a quasi-militaristic model of communism (Zhao, 1999, p. 186), which was different to the patterns of reforms in Eastern Europe. Thirdly, the economic reform in China preceded political reform.

Except for a few cases in which reform followed an approach similar to that of the "Big bang," most Chinese economic reforms can be identified as being gradualist in nature. To date the Chinese-type reform introduced since 1978 has achieved remarkable results. Particularly praiseworthy are the facts that the Chinese-type reform has avoided the collapse in output that has been characteristic of transitions in other former centrally planned economies and that it has generated unprecedented increases in the level of living standards across the country. Over the course of the past three decades, China has successfully transformed its centrally planned system and has achieved a more rapid economic growth than any of the world's other socialist or former socialist countries. However, China's unusual reform experience might not be generalizable to other transition economies, since it has been shaped by a set of unique initial conditions. A particularly intriguing and understudied factor is the legacy of the Great Famine (1959–61) and of the notorious Cultural Revolution (1966–76), two major events that not only boosted Deng Xiaoping's credibility and authority as a reformer, but also laid a foundation for the smooth implementation of agricultural and bureaucratic reforms.

5.7   Case study: Games between radicals and conservatives

The following two games illustrate both the threat to radical economic reform and the value of the balance rule for precluding this threat. The first game is between three players: the radicals (R), the conservatives (S), and the incumbent bureaucrats (IB). The second game adds a fourth player who may veto the entire set of policies: the backstage ruler (BSR). We assume that BSR holds the balance of political power between the R and S. In addition, uncertainty affects how the players view the reform strategy. To make this circumstance concrete, we assume that uncertainty concerns political stability: the country may experience either normal (political stable) times or a political crisis. Finally, we further assume:

(i) R chooses a radical ("Big bang") reform (labeled as BB) during normal times; it chooses a gradual reform (labeled as GR) during a political crisis.[23]

(ii) When R chooses BB, IB supports S; when R chooses GR, IB supports R during normal times and supports S during a political crisis.

(iii) As defined by their very natures, R and S cannot reach an agreement concerning a reform in any circumstances, but they can compromise in the following ways: S accepts no reform (labeled as NR) when R advocates GR; and it accepts GR when R advocates BB.

(iv) BSR can veto over R's BB (in case of political crisis) and S's NR (during normal times); it instead tolerates all other reforms, no matter who will lead the reforms.

To simplify the decision tree, we assume in both games that the winner implements the policy it advocated. As to the information assumptions: We assume that R must choose in ignorance of the state of political stability while IB knows and, to some extent, decides the state of political stability when it must choose between R and S. The games are a highly stylized representation of post-Mao politics.

Game 1: Reform in the absence of a BSR veto

Understanding the game's implications requires a calculation of the equilibrium outcomes. To begin this step, consider the sequence of choices made by the players. The game represents uncertainty over the society by a non-strategic player, called political status (PS), who has the first move (see Figure 5.3). With probabilities of π and $1 - \pi$, PS chooses normal times and a political crisis, respectively. The move by PS represents a convenient way to express the uncertainty facing the second player, who must choose prior to knowing the state of political stability.

After PS moves, R moves and may advocate either BB or GR. The shadowed area around R's two decision nodes in Figure 5.3 indicates that R does not know the state of political stability at the time of its decision. After taking into account the characteristics of China's political evolutions, we suppose that R must choose in ignorance of the state of political stability, while IB knows and can, as a resultn of its deep influence on Chinese society, decide the state of political stability when it must choose. The outcomes are summarized as follows. If R wins BB, the outcome is A; if it wins GR, the outcome is B if IB and S do not form a coalition and is C if IB and S form a coalition. If S wins, the outcome is "no reform" (D). The preferences of R, IB, S and BSR are given in Table 5.3.

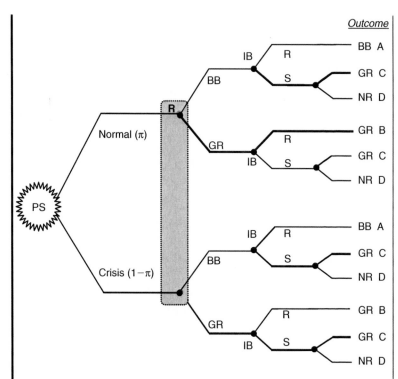

Figure 5.3   Choice of reform without a BSR veto – Game 1

Note: BB = 'big-bang' reform; GR = gradual reform; IB = incumbent bureaucrats; NR = no reform; PS = political status; R = radicals; S = conservatives.

Table 5.3   Players' preference ranking

No.	Radicals (R)		Incumbent bureaucrats (IB)		Conservatives (S)	Backstage ruler (BSR)
	In normal times	In political crisis	In normal times	In political crisis		
1	A	B	B	D	D	B, C
2	B	A	D	C	C	
3	C	C	C	B	B	A, D
4	D	D	A	A	A	

Notes: (1) the reason for R_C to rank C after A is that in a political crisis R losses supporters in both cases it would be more likely to stake a "big bang" reform (A) than to exercise a gradual reform (B); (2) the reason for IB_N to rank D and C after B is that in normal times, a gradual reform means more benefits rather than costs; and (3) since it is difficult to differentiate C from B and D from A, we equally treat B and C and A and D.

The IB's preferences depend upon the state of political stability. During normal times, IB (IB_N) prefers R's gradual reform (B) to S's no reform (D). The four outcomes are ranked as follows: R's gradual reform (B) is preferred to no actions on reforms (D), which are preferred to S's gradual reform (C) and, finally, to R's "Big bang" reform (A). During a political crisis, however, IB (IB_C) prefers S's policies to R's policies, ranking the four outcomes as follows: no reform (D) is preferred to S's gradual reform (C), which are preferred to R's gradual reform (B) and, finally, to R's "Big bang" reform (A). Regardless of the state of political stability, S ranks the outcomes as D, C, B, A, and BSR ranks the outcomes as B(C), A(D).

To determine the outcome of the game, we solve a subgame-perfect equilibrium, requiring that an action be specified for each decision maker at each node of the game. Consider IB's choices in Figure 5.3. During normal times, if R chooses BB, IB will cooperate with S for a gradual reform (C); if R chooses GR, IB will cooperate with R for a gradual reform (B). Although the final outcomes of B and C are the same, the cost of implementing B is lower than that of implementing C, since in C there is an extra risk for reversing BB to GR. As a result, IB prefers the R-advocated gradual reform (B) to the S-advocated gradual reform (C). This leads to the following behavior by IB: during normal times, IB will cooperate with R for a gradual reform (B) if R advocates GR, otherwise IB will cooperate with S for a gradual reform (C); during a political crisis, IB will cooperate with S for a gradual reform (C) if R advocates BB, otherwise IB will cooperate with S for no reform (NR). In both cases, R will lose its power in the country during a political crisis.

IB's behavior sets the stage for R's decisions. R does not know whether there will be a political crisis. Because it does not win regardless of its decision if there is a political crisis, and because it wins during normal times only if it chooses GR, it will choose GR. In this game, S is able to attract IB in normal times if R advocates BB and in a political crisis regardless of R's choices. By contrast, R is often isolated and, without careful treatment, R is in trouble.

Game 2: Reform under a BSR veto

The sequence of action in the second game adds an additional (fifth) move by BSR to the four moves of the first game. BSR may veto the entire set of policies (Figure 5.4), resulting in a payoff of 0 to IB and BSR. If R leads reforms, BSR prefers B to A; if S leads reforms BSR prefers C to D (see Table 5.3).

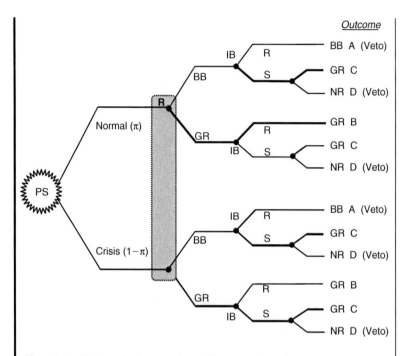

Figure 5.4   Choice of reform under a BSR veto – Game 2
Note: BB = "Big bang" reform; GR = gradual reform; IB = incumbent bureaucrats; NR = no
reform; PS = political status; R = radicals; S = conservatives.

We again solve for the equilibrium by backward induction.
Although this game has 24 end nodes, there are only four possible
outcomes, making it relatively easier for us to solve. In the game's
last move, BSR must choose between the outcome arrived at by the
previous move, or by exercising its veto. Because BSR prefers 0 only
to outcomes A and D, it will exercise its veto only when the previous
moves yield A and D. In all other circumstances, a veto would make
BSR worse off. The following contingent rule for exercising its veto
summarizes BSR's behavior at its 12 decision nodes: BSR's exercises its
veto if and only if R chooses BB during a political crisis and S chooses
NR during normal times. This implies that BSR exercises its veto only
at its first and last decision nodes (numbering the nodes from top to
bottom).

Working backward the next set of decision nodes requires a choice
by S and IB, who take BSR's behavior as given. Consider normal times.
If R advocates BB, it will not receive any support from IB; even worse,

it will lead IB and S to form a coalition, and in addition it will face a veto by BSR since the coalition of IB and S could result in a political crisis. Therefore, R will choose GR instead of BB. If instead R advocates GR, choosing R yields outcome B, whereas choosing S yields outcome C. In both cases, IB prefers R's GR to S's. In a political crisis, IB never supports R, even though the latter chooses a moderate reform strategy (GR). Choosing S yields outcome C if R advocates BB and outcome D if R advocates GR. But since S knows in advance that BSR will veto over outcome D (no reform), choosing S will yield outcome C in both cases.

Next consider R's decision at the first node. Taking IB and BSR's behavior as given, we observe that IB never chooses R during a political crisis, whereas during normal times IB chooses R if R advocates GR. R can never win by advocating BB, but it can win during normal times and if it advocates GR. So R will choose GR as long as the possibility of political stability, π, exceeds zero. In the equilibrium of this game, S will win when the relative frequency of political crisis is high ($\pi < 0.5$). In the face of a BSR veto, both R and S will temper their radical initiatives.

Game 2 demonstrates that the outcome changes when the BSR holds a veto over both R and S. Because the BSR will veto R when R attempts to implement the "Big bang" economic reform policies, IB prefers S to R when R advocates BB. This leads to a change in R's behavior and instead it advocates only GR policy. R's behavior under balance implies that IB prefers S to R during bad times and R to S during good times. Both the radicals and the conservatives could have decided the extent of their cooperation in negotiating a mutually accepted strategy of reforms. At the same time, they could have also initiated a costly confrontation with each other so as to gain supremacy over Chinese society. This situation may be depicted as a repetitive, complete information game (Bates *et al.*, 1998, p. 30).

The analytical framework presented in this section sets out to deal with the characteristics of the set of mutual deterrence (sub-game perfect) equilibria (MDEs).[24] In such equilibria, the confrontation between the radicals and the conservatives does not occur. Concentration on these equilibria is motivated by two considerations. First, the stable and mutually accepted reforms during most, if not all of the 1980s and 1990s indicates that both the radicals and the conservatives were indeed deterred from challenging the other. Secondly, since confrontation is costly, refraining from it was economically efficient. Furthermore, since implementing reforms was efficient, studying whether the need for the Chinese political system to be self-enforcing affected its economy is to examine whether this need constrained cooperation in reaching an MDE with the efficient reform strategy (i.e., the length of time for the reforms to be completed).

Examining whether China's self-enforcing political system reached an MDE with the efficient reform strategy requires an examination of the incentives for the radicals and the conservatives to cooperate with each other. For simplicity, our analysis first examines the MDE for a given set of reform strategies; only then is it extended to allow the reforms to be determined endogenously. This approach reveals the distinct political and economic characteristics of efficient and inefficient MDEs, enabling us to compare the insights gained from the theoretical finding with the historical evidence.

To understand the implications of the incentives for the policy makers to implement reforms, the relations between the radicals and conservatives should be made explicit. For ease of analysis, we assume that: (i) the radicals prefer a "Big bang" to gradual reform; and (ii) the conservatives do not prefer any reforms or at least prefer a gradual to big-bang reform. Since both the radicals and the conservatives can recruit supporters through their contributions to the growth of incomes, the tradeoff between them was inherent in the nature of the political exchange through which reforms were implemented.

Assume that there is a fixed length of time for the reforms to be completed, T^*, that maximizes the (gross) income for the radicals and the conservatives.[25] Hence, if the actual length of time for the reforms is shorter than that length, the income for the radicals is larger than for the conservatives; by contrast, if it is longer than that length, the income for the conservatives is larger than for the radicals.

The analysis can now be extended to examine the reform strategy in acquisition of which both the radicals and the conservatives would find it optimal to cooperate; in other words, to examine the length of time by which to implement the reforms. The analysis addresses the following question: Does the efficient MDE maximize the conservatives' incomes? If the answer to this question is affirmative, it can be concluded (at least from the static point of view) that the need to sustain China's self-enforcing political system did not theoretically entail economic cost. If the answer to this question is negative, however, it can be concluded that, theoretically, the need to sustain China's self-enforcing political system hindered economic efficiency, since the conservatives would not cooperate in achieving the efficient MDE. If this is the case, we can also use the model to identify the exact sources of this inefficiency.

Addressing these questions requires an examination of when an MDE implies an increasing number of supporters. In Condition 1, if there are no reforms, this implies no gains from cooperation. Hence, in the absence of reforms, the conservatives would neither increase the incomes of their own, nor recruit supporters from the society. At the same time, since the reform could increase incomes for all of the sides concerned, the radicals would be able to provoke challenges if they were facing resistance from the conservatives. By contrast, incentives for the conservatives to cooperate with the radicals decrease in Condition 2, since each side only obtained a decreasingly marginal gain.

Let us now come to Condition 3, in order to examine how external policy influences the choice of reform strategies.[26] Why did the open-door policy yield incentives for policy makers to choose the gradual vis-à-vis "Big bang" reforms in China? To understand this case, one must bear in mind the characteristics of the political evolution in China. During the 1980s and 1990s, most of the political elite (especially those conservatives) continued to treat the open-door policy as a measure that was both economically beneficial and politically damaging (we have addressed them in Figure 5.3).

This analysis has been motivated by the quest to identify the possible sources for political order in China and, specifically, by the inability of narrative to resolve two conflicting interpretations of the prevalence of economic reforms during most of the 1980s and 1990s. Our analysis indicates that both reform strategies – gradual/partial and radical – can be correct, depending upon the internal and external environments of the Chinese economy.

6
Economic Growth and Income Distribution

There was a man who was hawking spears and shields. To advertise the firmness of his shields, he shouted, "Look, my shields are very strong. Nothing in the world, no matter how hard and sharp, can penetrate my shields." A moment later, the man put down his shield and picked up a spear. Brandishing the spear, he cried, "Look, my spears are the best under heaven. They are so hard and sharp that they can penetrate everything, no matter how tough and strong it might be." "How about using your own spear to try on your own shield?" someone asked. The man could not make a reply.

– An ancient Chinese fable

6.1   China's growth performance

Over the past few decades, the Chinese economy has experienced a number of dramatic changes. Specifically, China's macroeconomic performance experienced steady growth in the first Five-Year Plan (1953–57), a short leap forward followed by a sudden economic disaster in the period 1958–62, a rapid growth period (1963–65), a chaotic period stemming from the "Cultural Revolution" movement (1966–76), and a fast growth period (1977–) during the post-reform era, with a few exceptions in 1981 and 1989–90 (see Figure 6.1). Particularly praiseworthy in the light of all of these developments is that the economic growth of China has been sustained an average annual rate of about 10 percent since 1978, making it one of the most dynamic economies in the world during the same period. This average growth rate is approximately three times that the average of the developed nations, more than double that of India, whose conditions are similar to those of China, and even higher than

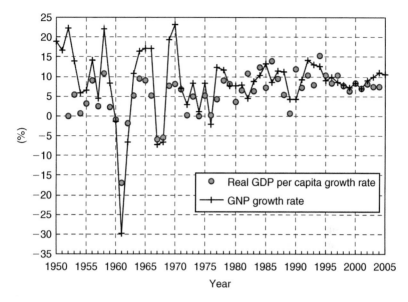

Figure 6.1   China's economic growth rates
Notes: GNP growth rates from 1952 to 1977 are represented by national income growth rates
(SSB, 1996; NBS, 2006); the real GDP per capita growth rates are based on Heston *et al.* (2006).

that of the newly industrialized economies (NIEs) including South Korea, Taiwan, Hong Kong and Singapore.

China's GNP is already one of the largest in the world, ranking behind only the United States, Japan and Germany. Although China's total GNP is large, its per capita GNP is lower than that of South Korea, Malaysia and Thailand, but higher than that of other neighboring nations such as India, Mongolia, North Korea and Vietnam.[1] In addition, according to the classifications of the World Bank, China has just moved from the least developed economy to a lower-middle-income economy by per capita GNP.[2] It should be noted, however, that if it is calculated by the purchasing power parity (PPP) rates, China's economic size would be much larger than that it is as measured by the current exchange rate.

In recent decades there have been many encouraging reports about the performance of the Chinese economy. For example, World Bank (1992) issues a range of evidence explaining why China looks set to become the world's largest economy by the year 2010 and that the Chinese economic area (including mainland China, Taiwan, Hong Kong, Macau and other Chinese alien areas in Southeast Asia) has been one of the world's "growth poles".[3] Segal (1994, p. 44) notes that the current figures on

Chinese GDP might have been misleading because they do not take into account real PPP rates. According to Noland (1994), the Chinese economy is already the second largest in the world if measured in terms of PPP rates instead of standard international prices. What is more important, however, is the trend per se, rather than any specific figure. Generally, even though they differ greatly, the per capita GDPs adjusted by PPP rates are between two and four times that the figures measured by exchange rate. Of course, the optimistic estimations of Chinese GDP have not been widely accepted, because of the incomplete price statistics.[4] Nevertheless, it is unbelievable that the gaps in real living standards between China and the advanced nations are as large as the per capita GNPs in US dollars between them.

Arguably, the size of the Chinese economy may have been underestimated if international statistical standards are applied. For example, according to *Asia-Pacific Economic Times* (1996), China's actual GDP could have been more than 30 percent larger than the current figure, the gap of which is contributed by the following aspects:

(1) Real estate sector (10 percent),
(2) Government, science and technology, education, culture and health care sectors (4 percent),
(3) Self-service within enterprises (3 percent),
(4) Rural construction (2.2 percent) and other rural economic activities (2 percent), and
(5) National defense and underground economic activities[5] (10 percent).

Box 6.1   Underground economics

The size of underground economic activities varies enormously from country to country. Obviously, it is impossible to get precise estimates because, by their very nature, the details have been largely hidden from the authorities. Nevertheless, the following factors determine the size of the underground economy (Sloman, 1991, p. 574):

(1) The level of taxes and regulations. The greater their level, the greater the incentive for people to evade the system and "go underground."
(2) The determination of the authorities to catch up with evaders, and the severity of the punishments for those found out.
(3) The size of the service sector relative to the manufacturing sector. It is harder for the authorities to detect the illicit activities

of motor mechanics, gardeners and window cleaners than the output of cars, bricks and soap.
(4) The proportion of the population that is self-employed. It is much easier for the self-employed to evade taxes than it is for people receiving a wage where taxes are deducted at source.

Table 6.1 Decomposition of Chinese economic growth (%)

	1953–60	1961–78	1979–90	1991–99
Average annual GDP growth rate	9.40	4.70	9.00	10.30
Average annual GDP growth rate (adj.)	6.63	3.31	8.50	8.10
Factor contribution to average annual GDP growth rate (adj.)				
Capital contribution	2.90	2.40	4.85	5.45
Labor contribution	0.84	0.84	0.99	0.48
Human capital contribution	0.58	1.32	1.32	0.40
TFP contribution	2.31	−1.25	1.34	1.77

Notes: GDP = gross domestic product; TFP = total factor productivity.
Source: Wang (2000).

A breakdown of the economic growth in China in the second half of the twentieth century is shown in Table 6.1. Physical capital was always the factor that made the greatest contribution to economic growth. However, the percentage points of the GDP growth rate contributed by physical capital were almost doubled after the launch of the reform in 1978. The gap can be further decomposed into the increase of the savings rate, foreign capital and the more efficient use of money. The contribution of the final one of these factors was the largest but the least mentioned. For example, the ratio of formulated capital to savings increased from about 50 percent for the pre-reform era to more than 60 percent for the reform era. It seems that it is not proper to describe the economic growth of China as being simply "inputs-driven" since considerable efficiency improvement, which cannot be covered by total factor productivity (TFP), is hidden by the growth in input. In addition, the contribution of foreign capital will be 0.6 percentage points if its direct and indirect impacts are considered (Wang, 2000, p. 4).

Table 6.1 also shows that the average annual GDP growth rate contributed by labor input was as high as 0.84 (or about 25 percent of the GDP growth rate) between 1961 and 1978, but was only 0.48 (6 percent of the GDP growth rate) from 1991 to 1999 after the effects of the strict population controls became apparent. As happens in other counties, the contribution of human capital was of little importance, especially from 1953 to 1960 and from 1991 to 1999, but the period from 1961 to 1978 was an exception with a surprisingly high share of 40 percent of the GDP growth rate. It is quite impressive that TFP contributed 1.34 (16 percent of the GDP growth rate) and 1.77 percentage points (22 percent of the GDP growth rate) for the periods of 1979 to 1990 and of 1991 to 1999, respectively. It should be clarified that the TFP covers not only technological innovation, but also management improvement, resource reallocation and even the provision of incentives. For example, the period 1961–78 witnessed negative contribution from the TFP due to the turmoil of the "Cultural Revolution" period (1966–76).

The high rate of capital accumulation has its basis in the liberalization of a labor-surplus economy that has a high savings rate. Investment is highly profitable because the surplus labor prevented the real wage from rising significantly and the large pool of domestic savings prevented a rise in the interest rate. The importance of the latter is seen in that household savings as a proportion of disposable income in China have been higher than those in most developed and developing nations. China's savings rate has been extremely high during the reform period. From 1978 to 1997, the average savings rate was 37.1 percent. By contrast, governmental savings kept falling in both absolute and relative terms. Its share of domestic savings was more than 50 percent in 1978, but fell below zero in the 1990s, showing a reversal from the circumstances of the command economy. From 1978 to 1988, the annual growth rate of private financial savings (including security assets) was more than 30 percent, and a similar increase occurred in the period 1989 to 1998. This rapid increase has been attributed to the following factors: expected uncertainty, income increase, deflation, nominal interest rate, the level of monetization in the economy, capital market development and income inequality (Wu, 2000). Other factors that help to explain the rapid growth of private financial savings in China include corporate savings in private accounts and illegal income.

Another key factor behind China's impressive growth is its integration into the global economy. This factor operates through four channels. First, the access to international markets for labor-intensive manufactured goods accelerated the movement of labor out of low-productivity agriculture into high-productivity industry. Secondly, China could now buy modern technology (some of which were previously denied to China). Thirdly, foreign direct investment (FDI) increased the level of capital stock, transferred new technology, made available global distribution networks, and introduced domestic firms to more efficient management techniques. Fourthly, the competition from international trade forced Chinese enterprises to be more efficient and innovative (Woo, 1998).

6.2 Measuring income inequality

Economic difference (or inequality) has several dimensions. Economists are mostly concerned with the income and consumption dimensions. Several inequality indices include the most widely used index of income inequality. Non-income inequality includes inequality in skills, education, opportunities, happiness, health, wealth and other similar factors. Results from a review of the literature suggest a relationship between inequality in income and non-income dimensions. This indicates that one should account for the interrelationship between the different dimensions in the measurement and analyses of inequalities.

The simplest measurement for economic differences is standard error (SR). SR is a statistical approach by which economic differences are measured in absolute terms, while the other approaches, such as the Gini coefficient, the coefficient of variation (CV), and the weighed coefficient of variation (MCV), may be used to derive the economic differences in relative terms.[6] Usually, the results of economic differences derived from CV and Gini approaches are consistent with each other, while, in some instances, an inconsistency of measurements may be generated by the two approaches. For instance, after having mathematically illustrated the Gini and CV indices through the use of the Lorenz curve, Zhou (1994, pp. 193–200) concludes that when the Gini coefficient changes slightly, it may not be consistent with CV, whereas when the Gini coefficient changes at a relatively large rate, it may be consistent with CV.

In contrast to Gini and CV approaches, generalized entropy (GE) is a family of measures depending on a parameter (c). Users may adjust the value of the parameter to suit their ethical preferences. As described in Shorrocks and Foster (1987, pp. 485–97), the parameter (c) determines the relative sensitivity of distribution: when c is less than two, the corresponding GE is sensitive in the sense that a composite progressive-cum-regressive income transfers of the same magnitude at the upper and lower tails of the income distribution leads to an increase in inequality. In two special cases, i.e., when $c = 0$ and 1, the GE family becomes two versions of Theil's entropy (TE) measure. In the extreme case when $c \to -\infty$, the ranking of the corresponding GE is same as that of Rawls' maximum criterion, i.e., to focus exclusively on the well-being of the worst-off province (Shorrocks, 1980, pp. 613–25).

It must be noted that SR, CV, Gini and MCV approaches can only deal with the measurement of economic differences in terms of a single index. However, it is necessary sometimes for one to conduct a joint analysis of the various disparities according to different indices, particularly when these indices contradict one another. For instance, Nolan and Sender (1992, pp. 1279–303) and Sen (1992, pp. 1305–12) argue that China has paid more attention to economic growth than to education, health care, and other service sectors since the early 1980s. Thus, when evaluating the various inequalities in China, one should take different indices into account.[7]

Although other approaches are also useful in economic analysis (the mathematical description of these approaches will be discussed in section 7.4 in Chapter 7), the Gini coefficient has been most frequently applied by economists worldwide to measure the level of income inequality. Developed by the Italian statistician Corado Gini in 1912, the Gini coefficient is most prominently used as a measure of inequality of income distribution or inequality of wealth distribution. It is defined as a ratio with values between 0 and 1: a low Gini coefficient indicates more equal income or wealth distribution, while a high Gini coefficient implies a more unequal pattern of distribution. In the extreme cases, 0 corresponds to perfect equality (when everyone has exactly the same income) and 1 corresponds to perfect inequality (when one person has all the income, while all remaining people have zero income). Mathematically, the Gini coefficient is defined as a ratio of the areas on the Lorenz curve diagram (see Figure 6.2). If the area between the line of perfect equality and the Lorenz curve is A, and the area under the Lorenz curve is B, then the Gini coefficient is $A/(A+B)$. Since $A+B=0.5$, the Gini coefficient becomes $A/(0.5)=2A=1-2B$. If the Lorenz curve is represented by the function $y = L(x)$, the value of B can be found with integration. As a result, the Gini coefficient becomes

$$\text{Gini} = 1 - 2 \int_0^1 L(x)\mathrm{d}x \qquad (6.1)$$

If an income distribution is represented by a vector of incomes, $x = (x_1, x_2, ..., x_n)$, where x_i indicates the income of the ith individual in a society consisting of n individuals, the Gini coefficient can be computed by the following formula:

$$\text{Gini} = \frac{\sum\sum\sqrt{(x_i - x_j)^2}}{2n^2\bar{x}} \qquad (6.2)$$

where, $\bar{x}$ is the mean for all x.

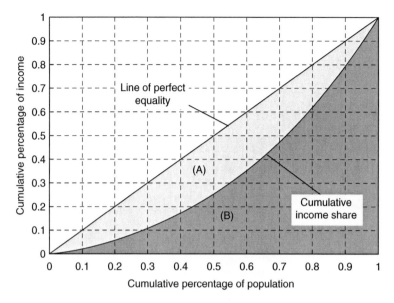

Figure 6.2   The Lorenz curve

While China's reform has been a strong driver of its economic growth, it has also derived a series of socioeconomic problems. Prior to the reform, China was an egalitarian society in terms of income distribution. In the initial stage of the reform, the policy of "letting some people get rich first" (*rang yi bufen ren xian fu qilai*) was adopted in order to overcome egalitarianism in income distribution, to promote efficiency with strong incentives and to ultimately realize common prosperity based on an enlarged pie. But this policy has quickly enlarged income gaps between different groups of people (see Table 6.2). Compared with other countries, China's Gini coefficients have been very high, only being lower than those of a few nations in Latin America and Africa; whereas the latter have been usually treated to have been the most unequal economies in the world.

Nevertheless, there have been two different views with respect to the current situation of income inequality in China. One view supposes that China's Gini coefficients have been underestimated since in most, if not all cases the earnings of the low-income groups were usually overestimated whereas those of the higher-income groups were usually underestimated. For example, in some poor agricultural households a portion of earnings had to be used for productive investment and, as a

Table 6.2   China's income Gini coefficients, selected years

Year	Rural area	Urban area	China as a whole
1952	0.230	0.165	0.255
1979/80	0.310	0.160	0.330
1988	0.338	0.233	0.382
1995	0.381	0.280	0.437
2002	0.366	0.319	0.454
2007	0.370	0.399	0.496

Sources: (1) World Bank (1983, pp. 83 and 92) for 1979/80; (2) Zhao (2001) for 1988 and 1995; (3) Li (2004) for 2002 and (4) www.ahpc.gov.cn for 2007.

result, the earnings that can be used for consumption will be reduced. By contrast, in the urban, high-income group some earnings and welfare payments were not included in the current reckoning of incomes (Ge, 2000). However, there is a different view in respect of this issue: China's current income inequality has been overestimated and, if measured in terms of purchasing power parity (PPP) rates, China's income Gini coefficients should have been reduced considerably. In most cases, the price levels in poor areas are much lower than those in rich areas (see, for example, Box 7.1). Due to various difficulties in securing reliable data, we are not able to provide a convincing answer here and have to leave it for our future's research.

6.3   Inequality: causes and consequences

China has experienced rapid economic growth with a major impact on inequality during recent decades. Using the panel data on Chinese income inequality at the provincial urban level, Xu and Zou (2000) show that the Gini coefficient increased from 0.17 in 1985 to 0.23 in 1995. The periods' average varies in the interval 0.17 and 0.25 by provinces and 0.13 and 0.34 by years of observation. The data are obtained from urban household surveys in each of the 29 provinces and from various provincial statistical yearbooks covering the period 1985–1995 (except years 1987 and 1988). Based upon average incomes for each five percentiles, Xu and Zou compute the Gini coefficients, percentage of income of the bottom, top and third and fourth quintiles and the ratio of top to bottom quintiles for each province. Xu and Zou find that since the beginning of economic reforms in 1978, aggregate output growth has been on average 9.9 percent per year while the average growth in GDP per capita was 8.8 percent during the period 1978–94. The difference can be explained by changes in the population. The growth rates differ by location between 4.8 percent for inland and 14.2 percent for coastal provinces. The correlation between the growth rate and the Gini coefficient is 0.27 and seems to support Kuznet's (1955) inverted U-curve. This contradicts the findings of Alesina and Rodrik (1994) and Persson and Tabellini (1994) who, based on a cross-section of international data, observed a negative association between income growth and inequality. In analyzing the causal mechanism relating to inequality and growth in China, Quah (2002) highlighted that there is no single evidence about such a relation. In addition to inequality, the rate of economic growth is also influenced by many other macroeconomic, technological, political, and institutional factors. Ravallion (1998) suggests that the aggregation can bias tests of whether inequality impedes growth.

Zhao (2001, pp. 35–40) presents a qualitative method to analyze the positive and negative effects of such factors as economic growth and various institutional changes and policy reforms on China's income inequality, which are shown in Table 6.3. It should be noted that some, if not all of these factors have influenced the income inequality jointly and, therefore, it may be difficult to clarify the directions of these influences.

Xu and Zou (2000) considers the role played by output growth, increasing exposure to international trade, urbanization, taxation, government spending, inflation, human capital formation, geography, and the sectoral structure of the economy in determining the changes in income inequality. The relation is specified as:

$$INEQ_{it} = \beta_0 + \beta_{SOE}SOE_{it} + \beta_{INF}INF_{it} + \beta_{DIS}DIS_{it} + \beta_{SCH}SCH_{it}$$
$$+ \beta_{GDP}GDP_{it} + \beta_{TRA}TRA_{it} + \beta_{EXP}EXP_{it}$$
$$+ \beta_{URB}URB_{it} + \Phi_i + \varepsilon_{it} \tag{6.3}$$

where $INEQ_{it}$ is the Gini coefficient or it can alternatively be measured as the (ratio of) quintile income shares Q5/Q1, Q5, Q1, or Q34. Φ_i captures unobserved province-specific effects. The explanatory variables are: the share of state-owned enterprises (*SOE*), the inflation rate (*INF*), the distance of a province's capital to the nearest port by railroad (*DIS*), the share of residents with more than secondary schooling (*SCH*), the GDP growth rate (*GDP*), trade measured as the ratio of value of import and export to GDP (*TRA*), the share of government expenditure as a share of GDP (*EXP*), and the change of urbanization level of a province measured as the growth rate of the share of non-agricultural population

Table 6.3   Determinants of income inequality for the reform era

Item	Inequality within urban or rural areas	Inequality between urban and rural areas
1. Economic growth or development		
Faster growth of urban nonstate-owned economy	+	+
Faster growth of rural nonagricultural economy	+	−
Development of agriculture	?[a]	−
2. Economic reform or institutional changes		
Order changes		
Price reform in rural areas	−	−
Household responsibility system in rural areas	−	−
Internal migration of rural laborers	?[b]	−
Commercialization of urban housing	+	+
Disorder changes		
Rent-seeking activities	+	?
Insider control[c]	+	+
Monopoly	+	+
Corruption	+	+
3. Economic policy and its changes		
Low purchasing price for agricultural products	?	+
Taxation on agricultural products	?	?
Extra-taxational burden peasants	?	+
Personal income tax	−	−
Reduction of urban subsidies		
(a) Per head	+	−
(b) By position	−	−
Transfer of urban residents' benefits to private property		
Access to the WTO	?	+[d]

Notes: (1) Usually, if an item is related to urban (or rural) areas, its effect on inequality is also related to the urban (or rural) areas. (2) "+" denotes increase of inequality; "−" denotes decrease of inequality; "?" denotes difficulty to judge. [a] According to Li *et al.* (1997), although inequality within rural areas had slightly increased from 1979 to 1984, it is hard to attribute this result to the development of agriculture. [b] Generally, internal migration of rural laborers has enlarged income differentials within rural areas as a whole, but it has narrowed the gap in some specific rural areas (Zhao, 2001, p. 38). [c] "Insider control" is described here as a mechanism through which public assets can be appropriated to serve the interests of particular departments, regions, work units and individuals (Massahiko and Qian, 1995, p. 17). [d] Based on Li and Zhai (2000). However, Wei and Wu (2003) conclude with a negative relationship between urban-rural disparity and the trade/GDP ratio.
Source: Zhao (2001, p. 36) except those that are noted otherwise.

in the province (*URB*). The estimated results show that income distribution has been affected by the changing structure of the economy, the role of the state, and increasing levels of urbanization. Inequality and Q5 increased (and Q1 decreased) with reduction of SOE share of output, higher inflation, higher growth rate, and foreign trade. Government spending tends to shift resources from the rich and the poor to the middle class. Provinces furthest from the coast had higher levels of inequality, probably reflecting greater imperfections in their capital markets. Schooling and increasing urbanization did not affect the levels of income inequality. It has not been possible to identify determinants of (unobserved) level differences in inequality across different provinces.

Based on the survey data, Riskin, Zhao, and Li (2001) provide a comprehensive analysis of inequality and poverty in China for the years 1988 and 1995; and Gustafsson, Li, and Sicular (2008) extend this analysis through the year 2002. They observe major changes in the composition of income between the two survey dates. Rural household income, mainly from farming, has declined from 74 percent to 56 percent, while non-farming wages increased from 9 percent to 22 percent, resulting in increasing levels of income inequality. The Gini ratio for rural income grew by 23 percent from 0.34 to 0.42 due to the unequal distribution of faster-growing wage components of rural income. The corresponding increases in inequality in the urban areas were 43 percent in seven years from 0.23 to 0.33. The increasing inequality of distribution of income caused a rise in the level of urban income inequality. The wage share of income grew from 44 percent to 61 percent. Other components of income like income of retirees and housing rental were subject to fast growth as well. Subsidies declined from 20 percent of urban income to 1 percent.

Previous studies have suggested that non-agricultural activities have been the major cause of rural income inequality. The increase in agricultural income was considered to be a key policy measure to reduce rural inequality in China. Cheng (1996), using household data from five grain-producing Chinese regions in 1994, finds that inequality within the grain-producing areas was also very high, with differences in crop income as the major source of inequality. The decomposition of inequality indicates that 61 percent of the income inequality of peasant households is to the result of intra-provincial while the remaining 39 percent is from the interprovincial inequality components.

A substantial literature has analyzed the effects of income inequalities on macroeconomic performances, as reflected in rates of economic growth.[8] Most argue that greater income inequality is actually an impediment to economic growth. A seemingly plausible argument points to the existence of credit market failures such that people are unable to exploit growth-promoting opportunities for investment (see, for example, Benabou, 1996; Aghion *et al.*, 1999; and Barro, 2000). With only limited access to credit, the exploitation of investment opportunities depends upon individuals' levels of assets and incomes. Specifically, poor households tend to forego human capital investments that offer relatively high rates of return. In this case, a distortion-free redistribution of assets and incomes from rich to poor tends to raise the quantity and average productivity of investment. With declining marginal products of capital, the output loss from the market failure will be greater for the poor. So the higher the proportion of poor people there are in the economy the lower the rate of growth (Ravallion, 2001).

A second way in which inequality could affect the future levels of economic growth is through political channels. The degree of inequality could affect the median voter's desired pattern of policies or it could determine individuals' ability to access political markets and participate in costly lobbying. If the mean income in an economy exceeds the median income, then a system of majority voting tends to favor the redistribution of resources from rich to poor.[9] As the median voter's distance from the average capital endowment in the economy increases with the aggregate inequality of wealth, he or she will be led to approve a higher tax rate. This in turn could reduce incentives for productive investment, resulting in lower levels of growth. If this is correct, democratic societies with a more unequal distribution of wealth should be characterized by the exploitation of the rich by the poor – that is, high taxes and, consequently, low investment and growth, whereas undemocratic ones with similar characteristics would not (Deininger and Squire, 1998).

Indeed, the negative effects of income inequality might exist in almost every sphere of human life. But there also exists some evidence that supports the view that income inequality could encourage economic growth – both directly and indirectly. The most intuitive thesis is that a lower degree of inequality would mean a greater amount of redistribution from rich to poor. It is this redistribution that would become an impediment to the creation of incentives for people (especially the poorest and richest groups of them) to work hard (Li and Zou, 1998). There is also a positive view for the effect of inequality on economic growth: if individual savings rates rise with the level of income, then a redistribution of resources from rich to poor tends to lower the aggregate rate of savings in an economy. Through this channel, a rise in income inequality tends to raise the level of investment.[10] In this case, greater inequality would enhance the rate of economic growth. However, there is an argument that inequality may lead to higher fertility rates, which could, in turn, reduce economic growth (Perotti, 1996).

Worsening levels of inequality of wealth and income motivate the poor to engage in crime, riots, and other disruptive activities (see, for example, Hibbs, 1973; Venieris and Gupta, 1986; Gupta, 1990; and Alesina and Perotti, 1996). In a civilized world the existence of millions of starving people is not only unacceptable from an ethical point of view but can hardly be expected to lead to conditions of peace and tranquility. As a consequence, it is believed widely that inequality could become an impediment to economic development. Unfortunately, the existing empirical analyses, using data on the performance of a broad panel of countries, have yielded conflicting results. Perotti (1996) and Benabou (1996), for instance, report an overall tendency for income inequality to generate lower economic growth in cross-country regressions, whereas some panel studies, such as that of Forbes (1997) and Li and Zou (1998), find relationships with the opposite sign. Nevertheless, Deininger and Squire (1998) provide evidence in support of the view that inequality retards economic growth in poor countries but not in richer countries. Using a large bulk of time-series and cross-national data, Barro (2000) also supports this hypothesis.[11] However, other carefully conducted research projects, such as Eichera and Garcia-Penalosab (2001) and Ravallion (2001), provide little evidence that supports the above views.

6.4   Poverty and social security

With regard to the term "poverty", there have been two separate definitions – "broad poverty" and "deep poverty". Specifically, the first one refers to the threshold which is based on the cost of 2,100 kilocalories per person per day with an adjustment for non-food purchases, broadly consistent with the preference of low-income consumers; the second one relates to the threshold, which is defined as 80 percent of the broad poverty threshold (Khan and Riskin, 2001). China experienced rapid economic growth after economic reform, accompanied by increased income levels (see Box 6.2 for a personal case). However, the reduction in poverty is still a challengeable task in China.

Until the mid-1980s, the total number of poor had been reduced; since then, however, it has grown continuously, especially in urban areas. From 1988 to 1995, for example, the incidence of "broad poverty" in the urban area fell by only 2.4 percent – from 8.2 percent to 8.0 percent of the total urban population. Moreover, the urban population itself grew

---

Box 6.2   Xing's happiness index

Before her retirement in 2003, Ms Xing had worked as an ordinary staff at a horticultural company in Changping district, northern Beijing. Now a materfamilias, Ms Xing is counting her "happiness index" based on the pay-notes she collected during the past 30 years:

- During the 1970s, her husband and herself each received a monthly pay of about 60 yuan, which almost was not changed until the early 1980s.
- In 1985, and as a result of the rise of food prices, her monthly wages increased from 60 yuan to 82 yuan, the net increase of which could even cover her family's food expenditure for an entire month.
- In 1993, her monthly pay was 103 yuan, including 30 yuan of subsidy, 20 yuan of *"baogan jiang"* (reward for a task until it is completed), 20 yuan of fee on gloves, 12 yuan of administrative fee, 8 yuan of unemployment fee, among others.
- In 1995, the pay increased to more than 400 yuan, which was really a big surprise to her.
- In 2000, for the first time her monthly pay surpassed 1,000 yuan; during this year, she replaced her color TV set with a new, larger one, upgraded her 10-year-old refrigerator, and installed an air conditioner in her apartment.
- In 2003, Ms Xing retired, with an amount of pension of about 1,200 yuan per month, which kept on increasing in the following years.
- In 2008, her retirement pension, after an increase of over 200 yuan, reached 1,800 yuan per month; though facing an exceptional higher inflation than that during the previous years, Ms Xing was very satisfied with her life.

Source: Ma (2008).

---

rapidly. As a result, the total number of urban broad poor rose by 19.6 percent during the period: that is, from 23.5 million people in 1988 to 28.1 million people in 1995 (Khan *et al.*, 2001, p. 128). This situation persists into the early twenty-first century and some scholars have put the total number of China's urban poor to more than 30 million people.[12]

According to a report undertaken by the Asian Development Bank (2002), China's urban poverty has varied considerably from province to province. Specifically, China's provinces can be classified into five groups by the incidences of "broad poverty" (i.e., <2%, 2–4%, 4–6%, 6–8% and >8%):

(i) <2% (including Beijing, Jiangsu, Zhejiang, and Guangdong)
(ii) 2–4% (including Shanghai, Fujian, Hunan, Guangxi, Yunnan, Anhui, and Jiangxi)
(iii) 4–6% (including Hebei, Hubei, Guizhou, Chongqing, Qinghai, Shandong, and Sichuan)
(iv) 6–8% (including Tianjin, Inner Mongolia, Liaoning, Jillin, Hainan, Xinjaing, Shanxi, Heilongjiang, and Gansu) and
(v) >8% (including Henan, Shaanxi, Ningxia, and Tibet).

A simulation exercise conducted by Khan *et al.* (2001, p. 127) shows that by 1995 this high level of income growth in the urban area would have reduced the broad poverty rate to under 1 percent of the urban population had the distribution of urban income remained unchanged between 1988 and 1995. In other words, had there been no rise in inequality, such a rapid increase in average incomes would have sufficed virtually to eradicate urban poverty. This rise in inequality, however, offset the rise in per capita income and, as a result, the estimated effect on the incidence of poverty ranges from an insignificant improvement to a significant deterioration, depending on the poverty indicator used and the cost of living index chosen to adjust the poverty income threshold.

Before reform, China's social security system had been a "pay-as-you-go" system, in which the funding to the older generation had to come from the contributions of the young generation. In addition, this kind of system was operated by enterprises or organizations (which is commonly called *danwei* in Chinese). The *danwei* form of social security system had at least the following defects (Zhao and Tang, 2002): First, since China's first implementation of a strict family planning policy in the early 1980s, most families, especially those in the urban areas, have had only one child, and the burden of supporting the old generation under a "pay-as-you-go" system was high and, placed an unfair burden on the younger generation. Secondly, workers in newly founded *danwei* would have a lower burden of old workers than those in the previously founded *danwei*. This is unfair on the latter. Thirdly, some *danwei* might become bankrupt. If so, the right of its workers to social security would be threatened. Fourthly, it was very hard for workers to change locations and jobs.

According to the "Decision on Issues Concerning the Establishment of a Socialist Market Economic Structure," which was adopted by the Third Plenum of the Fourteenth Party Congress in November 1993, the aim of the reform of the social security system was to establish the criterion of efficiency as the first priority while considering fairness at the same time and to change the "pay-as-you-go" system to a funding system, which is based upon the contribution of the recipients themselves. In addition, the collection and payment of social security funding will be unified. Administrative management and funding management will be separated.

Improvements in pension insurance were among the most rapid. Currently, it covers all state-owned and other ownership enterprises in urban areas and also some non-public owned enterprises and rural areas. The challenge of this reform comes from the funding of the pensions of older workers, who had received relatively low salaries over the course of their working lives. A large proportion of their salary was channeled into investment and construction while they were promised pensions after they retired. Following the implementation of the funding system, their pension will come from the selling of some state-owned enterprises or assets. The medical care system consists of four parts: compulsory basic medical insurance; supplementary medical insurance freely chosen by enterprises; commercial medical insurance freely chosen by individuals; and a social medical rescuing system. The principle of compulsory basic medical insurance is "low level, wide coverage".

In September 1997, the State Council promulgated a document relating to the safeguarding of minimum living standards for urban inhabitants in China. The criterion of minimum living standards and the entailing fund are the tasks of local governments. However, the majority of people, rural inhabitants, still face a weak social security system, if any exists at all. They have to rely on their own deposits or the support of their relatives and offspring.

6.5 Summary

After the introduction of economic reform China experienced a period of rapid economic growth, accompanied by increased levels of income. Prior to the reform, China was an egalitarian society in terms of income distribution. In the initial stage of the reform, the policy of "letting some people get rich first" was adopted to overcome egalitarianism in income distribution, to promote efficiency with strong incentives and ultimately to realize common prosperity based on an enlarged pie. But this policy has quickly increased income gaps between different groups of people. Compared with other countries, China's Gini coefficients have been very high, only being lower than those of a few of nations in Latin America and Africa.

While China's reform has been a strong driver of its economic growth, it has also caused a series of socioeconomic problems. However, the level of income inequality has also increased dramatically during recent decades and the reduction of poverty is still a considerable challenge in China. China's income inequality can be decomposed further into various components associated with provincial components and their determinants in turn identified. An analysis of within-country regional inequality can reveal the effects of openness, marketization, convergence due to factor mobility, and it may also indicate regional polarization, or disintegration and widening inequality driven by structural differences between regions, issues that will be discussed in Chapter 7. Furthermore, it is important to consider heterogeneity in income inequality in terms of both its level and its development over time, as well as different characteristics of sub-group dimensions (we will discuss this issue in a case study in the next section).

6.6 Case study: A tale of two companies in transition[13]

Located in Shandong province, the Zibo Mining Group (ZBM) is a large conglomerate which has been in operation for more than one hundred years. It has therefore experienced every stage of China's political and economic transformations during the twentieth century. After the 1970s, the ZBM entered into serious recessions; up to 1996, it had operated with deficits for a continuous period of 24 years. At the end of June 2001, the ZBM had a total number of 36,447 registered staff, along with 25,922 retired personnel and 10,198 dependents of deceased members of staff. It had 4.249 billion yuan of fixed assets and 3.325 billion yuan of debts, with a debt/asset ratio of 78.25 percent. During the late twentieth century, the ZBM had for a long time been treated as one of 36 worst performing state-owned enterprises (SOEs) in China.

In September 1995, the State Council put forward a series of guidelines on the reforms of SOEs (see subsection 5.3.2 of Chapter 5 for details). Based on the opinions of the Ministry of Coal Industry (MCI) concerning the reconstructions of SOEs as shareholding and partnership companies (MCI, 1997), the ZBM decided to introduce ownership reforms in its two money-losing subsidiary companies (Guangzheng and Chuangda) in 1997 and the Fall of 1999, respectively. Following the reforms in ownership, both companies were able to make profits in 2001. In September 2001 and March 2002, and requested by the Development Research Center of the State Council and by the State Development and Reform Commission, respectively, we conducted two field surveys of these two companies.[14] Our goals are: (i) to assess how well the ownership reform performed in the SOEs; and (ii) to clarify the relationships between ownership reform, output growth and the distribution of earnings within the SOEs.

Guangzheng company, formerly called the Shigu coalmine, is located at Chawang township, Zichuan district. The coalmine was initially established by the Japanese in 1921, was reconstructed by the ZBM in March 1958 and went into operation on September 29 1960, achieving an annual production capacity of 250,000 tons of raw coal. Restricted by the complicated geological and hydrological conditions, the coalmine produced only a total amount of 8.1 million tons of raw coal between 1960 and 1990. As a result, its operations had been based on the subsidies from the central government, with a highest annual deficit of 13.0 million yuan, before 1996. After ownership reform was finalized in 1997, Guangzheng's staff held about 90 percent of its total shares. By 2001, Guangzheng had been successfully transformed from a single coal producer to one capable of manufacturing dozens of labor- and capital-intensive goods, with a total number of 2,150 registered staff.

Chuangda company, also formerly a coalmine with the name of Hongshan, is located at the town in Luocun, Zichuan district. The coalmine, initially established by the Germans in 1904, was occupied by the Japanese in 1914 after Germany was defeated by Japan in China during World War I. In 1953 the Hongshan coalmine was incorporated with the ZBM. From 1949 to 1990, the coalmine produced 36.27 million tons of raw coal, with a highest output of 2.24 million tons in 1960. As a result of the exhaustion of coal resources, the coalmine was closed in 1996. Facing increasingly worsening performances in coal production, the coalmine experimented with a three-year contract system and between 1987 and 1989 it introduced a series of reforms on wages. This experiment, although not entirely successful, provided some experience for the later reforms in the late 1990s. Following the corporate restructuring (its name was changed from Hongshan coalmine to the Chuangda company) in 1996, the state-ownership was changed to the one entitled shareholding part-nership in 1999, with 90 percent of its total shares being held by the company's staff. As of the end of 2001, the Chuangda company was composed of 15 independent sub-companies and other economic units, with a total number of 1,785 registered staff.

In brief, during the late 1990s and the early 2000s, the Guangzheng and Chuangda companies went through a process of dual transformation – structural change in production and owner-ship reform. How have these transformations influenced the system of earnings distribution and its outcomes within each company? In this research, we collected the samples of 391 and 446 workers from Guangzheng and Chuangda companies, respectively. The principle of the sample collection is that we try to include workers from all age groups, sex, educational backgrounds and positions. In addi-tion, in order to differentiate the performances between the pre- and post-reform period, we include two years: 1997 (representing the pre-reform year) and 2001 (representing the post-reform year). Our data on workers' earnings are as of December. 1997's earnings only include wages, while those for 2001 also include share bonuses.

Between 1997 and 2001, the distributional policies of earn-ings underwent significant changes in both companies. In the Guangzheng company 11 kinds of wage distribution policies were established: these included "contracted wages for fixed posts," "float-ing wages according to profit," "functional wages of posts," "wages taking a percentage of profits," "awards based on the ratios of funds tied up by purchases or sales," "wages taking a percentage of the ratios of payments actually received to total sales," "awards on special con-tributions," "sharing out bonus according to both work performances and shares of capitals," and "fuzzy awards." In the Chuangda com-pany, following reforms in ownership, all time-based wages that had been applied during the pre-reform period were abolished. The piece rate wage system was applied to those employees whose work per-formances are quantifiable; in addition, the yearly-salary system was applied to all office workers and top managers of all economically independent units. In addition, a system of "post-based wages" is applied to all supplementary staff and a system of "wages taking a percentage of profits" is applied to all marketing personnel.

In order to compare the structural changes of wages between Guangzheng and Chuangda, we classify all the items of wages into three groups – basic wage, bonus, and subsidy.

First of all, the total levels of earnings (wages) are not significantly different between Guangzheng and Chuangda in 1997, with Chuangda's being slightly higher than Guangzheng's. But, in 2001, although the total earnings had increased greatly in both companies, differences did exist: Guangzheng's average annual growth rate of earnings was 40 percentage points higher than Chuangda's between 1997 and 2001. More importantly, there were some structural changes. After ownership reforms, workers from both companies received share bonuses in addition to wages. Specifically, in Chuangda the proportion of the share bonuses to the total earnings was about 15 percent; while this proportion was much higher (near 25 percent) in Guangzheng. It is also worth noting that these two companies are different from each other in terms of the structure of wages from 1997 to 2001. For example, in Guangzheng the proportions of basic wages and subsidies were reduced and that bonus as an instrument of incentives is introduced. From Table 6.4, we can see that Guangzheng's proportions of "basic wage" and "subsidy" are 5 and 10 percentage points lower than those of Chuangda, respectively.

Secondly, we also calculated the Gini coefficients of earnings (see Table 6.4) in order to measure the inequality index of earnings. A noticeable fact is that, following ownership reforms, the inequality of total earnings increased considerably. Between 1997 and 2001, Guangzheng's Gini coefficient of total earnings increased from 0.265 up to 0.326 (for samples excluding laid-off workers) or 0.345 (for all samples). Even though Chuangda's samples are not representative of its entire staff in 1997, its data do show great inequalities of earnings in 2001, with a Gini coefficient of 0.276 (for samples excluding laid-off workers) or 0.414 (for all samples). Obviously, the ownership reforms have led to an increasingly big gap of earnings between workers in each company.

The differences of production patterns and internal organizations between the two companies may influence, to a certain extent, the earnings gaps with each company. For example, Guangzheng was still able to reply on its coal production as a stable source of revenue, while Chuangda had to develop other new businesses since its coal resources were already exhausted in 1996. After losing its comparative advantages in coal production, Chuangda faced more challenges than Guangzheng during the period of ownership reforms.

Finally, the Gini coefficients of the share bonus (about 0.60) are much higher than those of the wages in both companies. This

Table 6.4 Level, composition and inequality of earnings per worker, December

	Guangzheng			Chuangda		
	1997	2001		1997	2001	
		All staff	Excl. laid-off staff		All staff	Excl. laid-off staff
Total earnings (yuan)	490.64	723.39	735.54	493.97	528.20	660.63
(%)	(100.0)	(100.0)	(100.0)	(100.0)	(100.0)	(100.0)
Wages (yuan)	490.64	552.07	563.63	493.97	447.14	566.38
(%)	(100.0)	(76.3)	(76.6)	(100.0)	(84.7)	(85.7)
Share bonus	N/A	171.32	171.91	N/A	81.06	94.25
(%)		(23.7)	(23.4)		(15.3)	(14.3)
Of wages						
Basic wage (yuan)	340.36	376.60	384.48	354.90	260.86	330.42
(%)	(69.4)	(52.1)	(52.3)	(71.8)	(49.4)	(50.0)
Bonus (yuan)	N/A	49.89	50.95	N/A	N/A	N/A
(%)		(6.9)	(6.9)			
Subsidy (yuan)	150.28	125.58	128.20	139.07	186.28	235.96
(%)	(30.6)	(17.4)	(17.4)	(28.2)	(35.3)	(35.7)
Earnings inequalities (Gini coefficients)						
Total earnings	0.265	0.345	0.326	0.186	0.414	0.276
Wages	0.265	0.362	0.320	0.186	0.405	0.247
Share bonus	N/A	0.595	0.601	N/A	0.592	0.590
Of wages						
Basic wage	0.355	0.423	0.411	0.247	0.394	0.233
Subsidy	0.524	0.387	0.373	0.419	0.594	0.461
Samples	229	390	382	36	437	345

Notes: (1) monetary values are represented by current prices. From 1997 to 2001, the consumers price index (CPI) decreased by 2 percent (NBS, 2002, p. 296). (2) "N/A" denotes not available. (3) The samples of Chuangda only come from office workers in 1997, which are not comparable to those in 2001.

indicates that a small portion of staff in both companies secured most of the share bonuses. We can thus conclude that the unequal distribution of share bonuses is the major source for the increasing gaps of earnings. Taking Chuangda as an example: the unequal distribution of share bonuses enlarged the Gini coefficient of total earnings by 2.2 percent (for all samples) or 11.7 percent (for samples excluding laid-off workers). On the other hand, the laid-off workers also resulted in the increasing inequalities of earnings. According to our estimates, affected by laid-off workers, between 1997 and 2001 Guangzheng's Gini coefficients of total earnings and of wages rose by 6 percent and 13 percent, respectively. This influence was more obviously in Chuangda. From 1997 to 2001, Chuangda's Gini coefficients of total earnings and of wages increased by 50 percent and 64 percent, respectively.

Past empirical studies have demonstrated that human capital is the most important factor in the determinants of labor compensation. Human capital, embodied in each laborer, is composed of knowledge, skills as well as other capabilities cohered in the body of each laborer. According to Schulz (1961), these capabilities are the major factor contributing to the growth of production. Economic growth replies on the quality of human capital not on the abundance of natural resources. The empirical studies on the earnings of laborers show that, along with the process of marketization of the Chinese economy, human capital's influences on earnings have increased (Li and Li, 1993; Knight and Song, 1993; Lai, 1999; and Gustafsson and Li, 2001). According to Gustafsson and Li (2000), the gender gaps of earnings rose in urban China during the 1990s. It is more noticeable that the increased share of the earnings gaps have stemmed from the society's prejudices and discriminations against women.

The average earnings of different groups of workers (see Table 6.5) show that workers with higher levels of education also experience a more rapid growth in earnings. In Guangzheng, for example, the average earnings of the workers who had graduated from colleges and senior high schools in 2001 are 2.65 and 1.86 times the levels observed in 1997. Chuangda's average earnings of workers graduated from colleges and senior high schools in 2001 are 2.13 and 1.11 times those in 1997. From the perspective of positions, the average earnings of three groups of high- and middle-ranking staff and office workers changed more quickly than those of the other workers. For example, in Guangzheng these three groups' average earnings in 2001 were 1.82, 2.72 and 3.32 times those in 1997; while they were 3.07, 2.31 and 2.02 times those in Chuangda.

It must be noted that the different levels of earnings among various groups of workers, shown in Table 6.5, do not offer a sufficient reflection of the influences of these group variables (such as age, sex, education and position). In fact, some group variables are related to each other. For example, many high-ranking managers are also highly educated; while physical workers are often young; etc. In order to estimate how these explanatory variables have individually contributed to the changes of earnings, let us borrow a simple model that has been widely used by labor economists:

$$\ln(\text{Wage}) = \beta_0 + \beta_1 \text{Experience} + \beta_2 \text{ Experience}^2 + \beta_3 \text{Male}$$
$$+ \beta_4 \text{Education} + \beta_5 \text{Position} \qquad (6.4)$$

Table 6.5 Average earnings by groups of workers (yuan/person, December)

	1997		2001			
	Wages		Wages		Total earnings	
	Guangzheng	Chuangda	Guangzheng	Chuangda	Guangzheng	Chuangda
All staff	490.64	493.07	552.07	447.14	723.39	528.20
Sex						
Male	582.46	533.42	709.67	475.11	933.65	576.55
Female	435.93	404.29	358.03	390.76	501.26	437.13
Education						
College (3 and 4 years)	509.46	562.69	1163.06	857.61	1348.53	1198.52
Senior high or technical school	493.76	442.17	671.03	402.36	916.99	492.77
Junior high school	513.45	530.89	469.07	415.19	637.66	460.38
Primary	484.90	–	533.42	733.65	740.60	787.82
Others	467.75	–	498.05	505.04	560.71	506.25
Age group						
20 year or younger	–	277.90	426.27	–	426.27	24.17
21–30 years	494.85	339.28	584.80	345.76	679.72	389.63
31–40 years	493.48	512.43	511.22	485.55	665.72	582.45
41–50 years	614.23	560.30	660.64	465.48	1018.20	549.90
50 years or older	–	–	572.72	356.36	688.50	429.91
Position						
Physical workers	477.66	515.52	438.46	515.38	581.00	563.99
Technical workers	515.10	–	534.25	433.80	699.17	482.88
Office workers	312.38	348.21	777.17	640.24	1036.71	703.18
Middle-ranking staff	1066.96	457.90	1742.14	754.04	2910.69	1056.02
High-ranking staff	1416.65	885.02	2281.74	1654.73	2575.06	2721.39

In the above model, ln(Wage), the dependent variable, is the natural log of wages.[15] "Experience" and "Experience^2" denote the length of work experience (in working years) and its square. "Male" denotes male workers; and "Education" is represented by the length of education in years (its data are calculated based on *Zichuan Annuals 1990*).

Table 6.6   Determinants of wages, Guangzheng and Chuangda

Explanatory variable	Guangzheng		Chuangda	
	1997	2001	1997	2001
Constant	6.820 (13.93)[a]	5.503 (24.95)[a]	NR	5.898 (18.99)[a]
Experience	−0.116 (−2.52)[a]	0.015 (1.08)		0.030 (1.81)[c]
Experience-squared	0.0037(2.39)[a]	0.00001 (0.03)		−0.0009 (−2.19)[b]
Male	0.138 (1.00)	0.303 (5.27)[a]		0.177 (2.71)[a]
Education	−0.022 (−0.47)	0.0536 (3.06)[a]		−0.0075 (−0.30)
High-ranking staff	1.051 (1.59)[c]	1.151 (5.44)[a]		1.195 (5.25)[a]
Middle-ranking staff	0.747 (2.34)[a]	1.091 (7.75)[a]		0.449 (3.64)[a]
Office workers	−1.184 (−2.82)[a]	−0.015 (−0.12)		0.396 (3.04)[a]
Technical workers	−0.135 (−0.87)	−0.013 (−0.19)		−0.229 (−1.79)[c]
R2	0.186	0.389		0.223
F	3.335	26.55		11.67
Samples	125	322		334

Notes: (1) Based on ordinary least squares (OLS) regressions, with the natural log of monthly wages as the dependent variable. (2) Figures and figures within parentheses are estimated coefficients and their t-statistic values of the explanatory variables, respectively. [a], [b] and [c] denote statistically significant at the 1%, 5% and 10% levels, respectively. "NR" denotes no regression is tested since the samples are not representative of Chuangda's whole staff.

"Position" includes four dummies: "high-ranking staff", "middle-ranking staff", "office workers" and "technical workers". "Physical workers" are treated as a comparison variable and, thus, excluded from regressions.

From the estimated results (shown in Table 6.6), we may find that some explanatory variables are playing differing roles in the determinants of wages from 1997 to 2001. In 1997, for example, the estimated coefficient on "Education" is not statistically significant, indicating that education background was not taken into account in the determination of wages within Guangzheng. Might education variable exert an influence on wages through various position variables? However, our estimated results do not support this hypothesis. Since the estimated coefficients on "Office workers" and "Technical workers" are negative, indicating that, in 1997 the average level of monthly wages of office and technical workers was, ceteris paribus, lower than that of physical workers in Guangzheng. In addition, "Experience", also a factor contributing to human capitals and, of course, to the level of a worker's earnings under a market-oriented system, only had a negative coefficient in 1997. That is to say, a worker's level of wages is negatively related to his or her work experience (represented by working years) at the beginning of employment in Guangzheng. The coefficient on "Male", which is positive, is only statistically insignificant, showing that gender discrimination did not exist in the determination of wages in 1997.

Different from 1997's estimated results, Guangzheng's "Experience", "Experience^2" are insignificantly estimated in 2001, suggesting that, after ownership reform, the level of wages was no longer related to work experience in Guangzheng. This may also indicate that the influences of work experience on labor productivity in traditional, labor-intensive industries are much less than that in other, especially capital-intensive, industries. The estimated coefficient on "Education" (i.e., 0.0536), which is statistically significant, is quite large, especially given that some position variables included in the regression also have positive effects on wages. Note that education's influences on workers' earnings may be partially included in the coefficients on position variables. In other words, if the position variables are not taken into account, the estimated coefficient on "Education" would rise accordingly. Obviously, Guangzheng's coefficient on education is even larger than those estimated in subsection 3.3.6 of Chapter 3 and in other empirical studies, all of the latter have omitted position variables in their regressions.[16] The estimated results also show that the coefficients on the high- and middle-ranking staff in 2001 are not only larger than those on office and technical workers, they are also larger than those in 1997. We can thus conclude that, as a result of ownership reform, high-ranking staff received higher levels of wages. At last, the estimated coefficient on "Male" is 0.303 (which is statistically significant at the 1 percent level), showing that, *ceteris paribus*, male workers' wages were 35.4 percent higher than female workers in 2001. It seems very likely that ownership reform might have resulted in some kind of gender discrimination in Guangzheng.

Compared with those of Guangzheng, Chuangda's estimated results have several differences in 2001. First, its coefficient on "Education" is not statistically significant, indicating that educational background was not emphasized in the determination of wages. Secondly, the estimated coefficient on other explanatory variables are different from those of Guangzheng. For example, the coefficient on "Experience" is positive and statistically significant, with a ratio of return to work experience (in years) of about 3 percent. Although gender difference existed in Chuangda, it is much less than that in Guangzheng in 2001. In addition, the gaps of wages between high- and middle-ranking staff and the technical and physical workers in Chuangda are smaller than those in Guangzheng.

The two cases demonstrated in this section cannot be used to reach a general conclusion; neither can they illustrate the tales of other Chinese SOEs with similar experiences of transitions. But they do show that ownership reform has significantly influenced the distributional patterns of earnings in the two formerly state-owned, now shareholding enterprises.

7
A Multiregional Economic Comparison

> A man from the state of Zheng (in today's Henan province) wanted to buy a pair of shoes. He measured his foot and put the measurement on a chair. When he set out for the market he forgot to bring it along. It was after he had found the pair he wanted that this occurred to him. "I forgot the measurement," he said. He went home to get it but when he returned the market had broken up and he did not get his shoes after all. "Why didn't you try on the shoes with your feet?" someone asked. "I would rather trust the measurement than trust myself," he replied.
>
> – Hanfeizi (*c*.280–233 BC)

7.1 About the statistical data

The lack of high-quality and comparable cross-section data is always the major hurdle in any study of multiregional economic issues, particularly in the centrally planned economies (CPEs). During the pre-reform period, China only published a fragmentary set of data covering such indicators as national income, gross value of social product (GVSP), gross value of agricultural output (GVAO) and gross value of industrial output (GVIO), the reliability of which, however, is uncertain. The recent research environment has been increasingly improved, along with the transformation of the Chinese economy from the centrally planned system to a market-oriented system. Since the early 1980s, an increasingly complete set of data on national regional economic performances have been released, some sources of which are shown in Table 7.1. Regardless of this progress, many problems, however, still exist when one tries to apply the officially published data to conduct a multiregional comparison of the Chinese economy.

Table 7.1   Main sources for China's statistical data

Title	Years	Editor(s)	Publisher
China Statistical Yearbook	1981–99	SSB	CSP
	2000–	NBS	
A Compilation of Historical Statistical	1949–89	SSB (1990)	CSP
Materials of China's Provinces,		Hsueh *et al.*	WVP
Autonomous Regions and Municipalities		(1993)	
Historical Data on China's Gross	1952–95	SSB	NCUFE
Domestic Product			
Almanac of China's Economy	1981–		EMP
China Industrial Economic	1988–	SSB	CSP
Statistical Yearbook			
Price Yearbook of China	1990–	ECPYC	CPP

Notes: NBS = National Bureau of Statistics of China; SSB = State Statistical Bureau; CSP = China Statistics Press; EMP = Economics and Management Press; ECPYC = editing committee of *Price Yearbook of China*; CPP = China Price Press; NCUFE = Press of Northeast China University of Finance and Economics; WVP = Westview Press.

Since the mid-1980s, China has begun to compile national income statistics according to the United Nations' System of National Accounts (SNA).[1] However, many theoretical and practical problems on how to adopt the SNA to Chinese economic accounting still remain unsolved. For instance, the sum of the regional GDPs may not equal the national GDP published by the central government, the reason for which is that the statistical data compiled by the State Statistical Bureau (SSB) or, as it has been renamed, the National Bureau for Statistics (NBS) are derived from the records of the various ministries in charge of their related sectors whereas the regional statistical data are compiled by the regional statistical bureaux.[2]

The compilation of the GDP data left many in China unpersuaded, especially under the dual-pricing system. With the exception of the data on the tertiary sector, the transformation of net material product (NMP) data to the corresponding GDP data were simply devised by the SSB (NBS) and, therefore, some question whether the GDP data may be arrived at by multiplying the NMP by some conversion factors. In fact, since the socialist accounting system does not take into account the output value of the service sector, historical records of this sector were very fragmentary. China has published the GDP indices at constant prices with 1978 being the base year. The GDP data at constant prices are inextricably linked to the real NMP data collected by the old system. Unlike Western countries that derive real GDP using a system of price indices, the basic production units at the lowest level of the statistical reporting system are responsible for computing the real output value based on a catalogue of fixed prices (*bubian jia*) handed down from above. The raw data are then reported to the higher level of the system to be further aggregated. Many analysts argue that problems may arise in this reporting process of the compilation of GDP data.[3]

There is another question: should real or nominal GDP/NMP data be used for a multiregional comparison of the Chinese economy? Ideally, the adjusted GDP/NMP based on the PPP method in the spirit of Wolf (1985) and Summers and Heston (1991, pp. 327–68) should be used in China because of the vast range of natural and social environments and varying price levels and inflation rates across the country. Unfortunately, few such efforts have been made on the measurement of China's regional GDPs using the PPP methodology due to the lack of sufficient and up-to-date information and data. Hsueh (1994a, pp. 22–56) modifies the nominal NMP data of 29 provinces using the 1980s fixed prices of industrial and agricultural products of which Beijing's relative price index is assumed to be 100 in 1981, while the data on national income (NI) of the remaining provinces are converted by their Beijing-based price levels, respectively. Hsueh's attempt to estimate China's NMP, although heroic, is surely controversial and will leave many unpersuaded, particularly when the provinces' industrial structures differ greatly from one another.

Difficulties may arise from the multiregional economic comparison between the pre-reform period, during which China was virtually a CPE, and the post-reform period, during which China has been transforming gradually into a market economy. In market economies, GNP is the total value of all final products and services generated and national income is the total of all incomes received by all factors in production during a defined period of time. In the CPEs, however, the national income accounts record only productive activities carried out in their territories, rather than incomes received by their residents. China's national income accounts during the pre-reform period were virtually based on the MPS, whose most important aggregate is NMP. The NMP comprehensively covers value added in the "material" sectors of production. The sum of the outputs of all separately enumerated production units multiplied by the relevant prices of outputs is called the gross value of social product (GVSP). As GVSP also includes the values of intermediate products which are simply the material costs for consecutive production units, the values of products were often counted more than once. Obviously, the use of the GVSP concept might result in a series of negative effects, particularly when it is used as an indicator to make a multiregional evaluation of the sizes of the economies, as a part of the GVSP is contributed by intermediate products that are never meaningful to social welfare – no matter how large it is. The national income represents the sum of net product (value added) of all separately enumerated branches of the economy during a given period. In terms of value, it is equivalent to the value of the total social product within the time period minus the value of the means of production consumed during that period; in terms of materials, it is equivalent to the total social product (including means of production and means of consumption) within the given period minus the means of production consumed during that period.[4] The national income was only created in China by material production sectors, such as industry, mining, agriculture, forestry, animal husbandry, building construction and service trades that were productive in nature and carried out such activities as assembly, processing, and repairs. However, it ignored the contributions from non-productive labors, particularly in such non-material spheres as banking, insurance, science, education, culture, health, administration, the military, and so on.

In respect of such official publications as do exist, economic data with political implications such as income distribution, inflation, credit rationing, shadow interest rates, the use of foreign capital and military expenditure have been under partial government control, particularly during the 1980s and the early 1990s. Furthermore, the decline in the professional ability and ethical standards of some local officials in charge of the collection and processing of economic data could largely discredit the quality of data. For instance, it is not uncommon for rural industrial enterprises to report nominal output under the rubric of output at constant prices; government cadres and business officers in rural areas whose promotion is partly based on agricultural and industrial growth may falsify the statistical data by enlarging the output valuation.[5] Therefore, some care should be taken in the use of these published time-series data.

7.2 Macroeconomic performance

Since the foundation of the PRC, China has adopted two different systems to measure its national and regional economic performance: the material product system (MPS) and the system of national accounts (SNA). As explained in section 7.1, the concept of NI (national income) deviates from that of GNP *ex facto*, because the former is based on the traditional MPS used by most centrally planned economies (CPEs), while the latter is based on the SNA used by the market economies. Different approaches have been suggested to arrive at an estimate of the GNP/GDP data (see, for example, Marea, 1985, pp. 15–16 and 27–119).

Table 7.2 Various estimates of China's GDP per capita, selected years

Year	NBS (2005)		Equation (7.2) RMB (Y)[b]	WPT[c] PPP ($)	Other sources[d] PPP ($)
	RMB (Y)[a]	US$[a]			
1979	417	268	455	724	1000
1986	956	277	974	1293	2440
1988	1355	364	1406	1489	2472
1990	1634	342	1668	1678	1031; 2140
1991	1879	353	1895	1798	1680
1992	2287	415	2288	1983	1600
1993	2939	510	2753	2131	2120
1994	3923	455		2453	2510

([a]): at current prices. The exchange rates of RMB yuan to the US dollar are shown in Figure 7.1. ([b]): estimated by the author at current prices. ([c]): Penn World Table (PWT) v6.2 (Heston *et al.*, 2006) at constant prices. ([d]): World Bank (1996, p. 21) and Zheng (1996, p. 1).

None of these could be applied to the CPEs with no comprehensive, consistent and up-to-date statistical information on the NMP or physical aggregation data for direct use (Hwang, 1993, p. 108).

The PWT v6.2 (see the fifth column of Table 7.2 for selected years) provides consistently estimated time-series data for China's per capita GDP under constant prices (Heston *et al.*, 2006), but it does not include provincial and regional data. In 1997, China's State Statistical Bureau (SSB) estimated the country's provincial GDP data for the years from 1952 to 1995 (SSB, 1997). However, many shortcomings exist in these officially estimated data (Xu, 2004). As China has adopted the SNA since the mid-1980s while it did not abandon the MPS until 1994, it is possible for us to make a quantitative estimate of their correlations. Based on the data from 1985 to 1993 (SSB, 1989, p. 29; 1994, p. 33; 1996, p. 42; and 1996b, pp. 13 and 15), we may estimate three linear equations between GNP and GVSP (gross value of social product), NI (national income) and GVIO (gross value of industrial output), as the following:

$$GNP = 0.4837GVSP \qquad (1985–93, R^2 = 0.991) \qquad (7.1)$$
$$(78.456)$$
$$GNP = 1.3259NI \qquad (1985–93, R^2 = 0.993) \qquad (7.2)$$
$$(84.587)$$
$$GNP = 0.5799GVIAO \qquad (1985–93, R^2 = 0.967) \qquad (7.3)$$
$$(39.210)$$

By replacing the NI series into Equation 7.2 (as it is the most significantly estimated among the three equations), the GNP derivation is shown in the second column of Table 7.2. It is worth noting that China's NI/GNP ratio $(1/1.3259 \approx 0.7542)$ estimated in Equation 7.2 is less than North Korea's (0.8) estimated by Hwang (1993, p. 118). The causes of the difference between China and North Korea need to be explored in detail. The differences between the estimated GNP per capita (the fourth column of Table 7.2) and the SSB's GNP per capita (the second column of Table 7.2) may be possibly explained by: (1) the estimation errors produced in Equation 7.2; and (2) the official miscalculation arising from the incomplete application of the SNA. If national income had been more accurately stated by SSB than GNP from 1986 to 1993, we may conclude that China's actual GNP had been understated before 1992 and overstated after 1992 by the SSB.[6]

The provinces' national income (NI) statistical data were only reported for the period between 1952 and 1993, while their GDP statistical data have been available since 1978. In order to conduct a consistent multiregional comparison of the Chinese economy across the pre- and post-reform periods, we have to apply the national income data and Equation 7.2 in order to arrive at an estimate of the GDP indicators for the pre-reform period. In addition, during the early period, when the MPS was transferred to the SNA, the GDP data were not reported by a few provinces (including Liaoning in 1978 and 1979, Qinghai in 1979 and 1981–84, Guangxi in 1979, 1981–85 and 1987, and Tibet in 1978–84). As a result, we have to make some approximations of per capita GDP for these provinces according to their national income data and Equation 7.2. Finally, there still exists an obstacle to the multiregional comparison of the Chinese economy: Tibet had not officially reported any statistical data before 1980. The only possible method we can use is to estimate Tibet's per capita GDP by making reference to other provinces with which it shares a number of similarities in terms of economic conditions. In 1980, the per capita national income of Tibet was 266 yuan, approximately 1.127 times that of Yunnan. Based on Yunnan's GDP data and a conversion factor of 1.127, we may obtain Tibet's per capita GDP data for the period from 1952 to 1979. The estimated per capita GDP data for the selected years (1952, 1979, 1990 and 1995) are shown in Table 7.3, from which the provinces that prospered and those that stagnated can be derived:

(1) **1952–1980** (29 provinces):

- 15 provinces (Beijing, Hebei, Shanxi, Liaoning, Jilin, Jiangsu, Zhejiang, Shandong, Henan, Hubei, Sichuan, Yunnan, Tibet, Shaanxi and Qinghai) ranked higher than before;

Table 7.3   Provincial ranks by per capita GDP, selected years

Province	1952[a]	1980	1990	2000
Anhui	22	27	24	24
Beijing	3	2	2	2
Chongqing	NP	NP	NP	19
Fujian	14	20	12	7
Gansu	16	16	27	30
Guangdong	18	18	5	5
Guangxi	27	28	29	29
Guizhou	29	29	30	31
Hainan	NP	NP	15	15
Hebei	9	7	17	11
Heilongjiang	4	5	8	10
Henan	23	21	28	18
Hubei	20	17	13	13
Hunan	21	22	20	17
Inner Mongolia	7	14	18	16
Jiangsu	13	10	7	6
Jiangxi	11	24	23	25
Jilin	8	6	10	14
Liaoning	5	4[a]	4	8
Ningxia	10	19	19	22
Qinghai	15	9	14	20
Shaanxi	24	12	21	27
Shandong	19	13	11	9
Shanghai	1	1	1	1
Shanxi	17	15	16	21
Sichuan	28	26	26	23
Tianjin	2	3	3	3
Tibet	25[b]	23[b]	22	26
Xinjiang	6	11	9	12
Yunnan	26	25	25	28
Zhejiang	12	8	6	4

Notes: (1) Per capita GDP data are measured at current prices; (2) "NP" denotes "not a province for the year". ([a]) Per capita GDP is estimated based on the data of national income (SSB, 1990b) and Equation 7.2 of section 7.2. ([b]) Per capita GDP is estimated by the author based on the Tibet/Yunnan ratio of national incomes (1.127) and Yunnan's GDP data.
Sources: SSB (1986, 1991) and NBS (2001) except for ([a]) and ([b]).

- ten provinces (Tianjin, Inner Mongolia, Heilongjiang, Anhui, Fujian, Jiangxi, Hunan, Guangxi, Ningxia and Xinjiang) ranked lower than before; and
- four provinces (Shanghai, Guangdong, Guizhou and Gansu) remained unchanged.

(2) **1980–1990** (29 provinces, with the exclusion of Hainan):

- ten provinces (Jiangsu, Zhejiang, Anhui, Fujian, Shandong, Hubei, Guangdong, Yunnan, Tibet and Xinjiang) ranked higher than before;
- 11 provinces (Hebei, Shanxi, Inner Mongolia, Jilin, Heilongjiang, Guangxi, Sichuan, Guizhou, Shaanxi, Gansu and Qinghai) ranked lower than before; and
- eight provinces (Beijing, Tianjin, Liaoning, Shanghai, Jiangxi, Henan, Yunnan and Ningxia) remained unchanged.

(3) **1990–2000** (30 provinces, with the exclusion of Chongqing):

- nine provinces (Fujian, Hebei, Henan, Hunan, Inner Mongolia, Jiangsu, Shandong, Sichuan and Zhejiang) ranked higher than before;
- 13 provinces (Gansu, Guizhou, Heilongjiang, Jiangxi, Jilin, Liaoning, Ningxia, Qinghai, Shanxi, Shaanxi, Tibet, Yunnan and Xinjiang) ranked lower than before; and
- eight provinces (Anhui, Beijing, Guangdong, Guangxi, Hianan, Hubei, Shanghai and Tianjin) remained unchanged.

7.3 Real living standards

7.3.1 General situation

The standard of living improved significantly in China during the period of the first Five-Year Plan (FYP), from 1953 to 1957, but suffered a sudden decline thereafter due to the failures of the Great Leap Forward (1958–60). It did not start to improve significantly until the end of the Cultural Revolution (1966–76) during which period people were largely encouraged to be rich in "spirit" but *not* "material". Since the early 1980s, Chinese living standards have improved steadily. Among China's ten FYPs the eighth FYP (1991–95) is the one in which the per capita personal consumption growth rate is the highest for China as a whole, while the sixth FYP (1981–85) is the one in which per capita personal consumption growth rate is at its highest level for the agricultural households. This was not only because of economic growth but also because of continuous reduction in population growth.

If China's per capita personal consumption is measured in terms of US dollars, the figure is still quite small. However, China's commodity

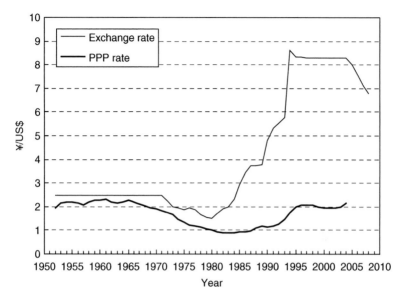

Figure 7.1 China's exchange rates and purchasing power parity (PPP) rates

prices are very low. If measured in terms of purchasing power parity (PPP) instead of exchange rates (as shown in Figure 7.1), the recorded standard of living in China would definitely be higher. For instance, after having calculated personal consumption in China and Japan using exchange rates, Mizoguchi *et al.* (1989, p. 28) find that China's per capita personal consumption expenditure is only 3.1 percent of Japan's. However, when per capita personal consumption expenditure is recomputed using purchasing power, China's figure is 21.5 percent of Japan's when Japan's consumption structure is used for weighting and 15.7 percent when China's consumption structure is used for weighting.

China's data on people's livelihoods (including information such as employment, the disposable income and expenditure of residents, the level of consumption, housing conditions, the quantity of consumer goods owned and so on) have been compiled annually by the SSB (NBS) based on surveys of different samples. Some questions and ambiguities remain when different samples and measurements are chosen. For instance, the SSB (NBS) makes no allowance for the rental value of housing. Furthermore, the SSB coverage of income in kind and subsidies also appears to be much less comprehensive than it is. Moreover,

Khan *et al.* (1993, pp. 34–7) explain in detail why their estimates are different from those of the SSB: the difference in the case of the rural sample is almost certainly due to differences in the definition of income and the method of estimation rather than difference in sampling method or in measurement errors; for the urban area, as the sample is much more weakly related to the SSB sample, the difference between the two estimates could therefore be due in part to differences in sampling and to measurement errors. If we can assume that their calculations are more accurate than those of the SSB, we may thus conclude that the national income under China's macroeconomic accounting was underestimated during the 1980s, which is consistent with the hypothesis advanced in section 7.2.

When comparing China's living standards with those of other countries, one should remember that China has had a very comprehensive social welfare system (even if it is not available to all Chinese citizens), especially during the pre-reform period. Ma and Sun (1981, p. 568), for example, estimate that the total work-related insurance and other types of social welfare expenditure might have been as high as 526.7 yuan per year for each worker, or 81.7 percent of the average wage before 1980. In addition, urban residents also have access to low-cost housing. According to the urban surveys conducted by the SSB, the per capita expenditure for residence in most urban areas is only 32.23 yuan in 1985 and 250.18 yuan in 1995, which accounts for approximately only 4.3 percent and 5.8 percent of the total per capita incomes, respectively, far lower than that of the market economies (SSB, 1986, p. 563 and 1996, p. 282).

One important indicator reflecting real living standards is the measure "life expectancy at birth." In demography, the term "life expectancy at birth" is expressed in terms of the number of years newborn children would live if subject to the mortality risks prevailing for the cross-section of population at the time of their birth. During the 1980s and the 1990s, China's economic growth was faster than the rest of the world. However, its life expectancy did not improve in line with this. Table 7.4 shows that in 1980 five economies in the Asia-Pacific region had a higher level of life expectancy than China. Between 1980 and 2007 China's level of life expectancy rose by 4.88 years, while Australia, Hong Kong, Japan, New Zealand and Singapore, each of which had a higher base level of life expectancy than China, achieved increases of more than six years. During the same period Sri Lanka, which had the same level of life expectancy as China in 1980, had increased its life expectancy by 6.8 years. The infant mortality rate in China was higher than that of the

Table 7.4 Life expectancy and infant mortality rates, selected economies

Country	Life expectancy (years)		Infant mortality rate (%)	
	1980	2007	1980	2007
China	68	72.88	42	21.16
Australia	74	80.62	11	4.51
Hong Kong	74	81.68	11	2.93
Japan	76	82.20	8	2.80
South Korea	67	79.10	26	5.94
Malaysia	67	72.76	30	16.39
New Zealand	73	78.96	13	4.99
Singapore	71	81.80	12	2.30
Sri Lanka	68	74.80	34	19.01
World average	61	65.82	67	42.65

Sources: Wang (2003, p. 55) and CIA (2008).

Asia-Pacific economies during the same period. In addition, after comparing China and an Indian state, Kerala, Sen (2004) points out:

> At the time of economic reforms, when China had a life expectancy of about 67 years or so, the Indian state of Kerala had a similar figure. By now, however, Kerala's life expectancy of 74 years is very considerably above China's 70. Going further, if we look at specific points of vulnerability, the infant mortality rate in China has declined very slowly since the economic reforms, whereas it has continued to fall very sharply in Kerala. While Kerala had roughly the same infant mortality rate as China – 37 per thousand – at the time of the Chinese reforms in 1979, Kerala's present rate, below 14 per thousand, is less than half of China's 30 per thousand (where it has stagnated over the last decade).

7.3.2 Rural–urban disparity

Since the reform, the income differentials between urban and rural China have experienced different patterns. In the early period of the economic reform, which was focused on the introduction of the household responsibility system (HRS) to the agricultural sector, the level of rural income increased very rapidly and the gap between the rural and urban areas narrowed until 1985. Since then, the rural–urban gap has begun to increase again as a result of the diminishing marginal returns of the agricultural

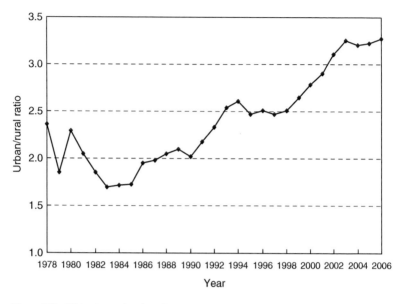

Figure 7.2   China's rural–urban income gaps

sector on one hand and the urban industrial reforms on the other hand. As demonstrated in Figure 7.2, the ratio of urban to rural per capita income fell from 2.36 in 1978 to 1.70 in 1983; it has been above 3.0 since 2000.

Before beginning our in-depth analysis for the causes, there should be clarification of some issues relating to the definition of the rural and urban incomes. The estimates of China's rural and urban incomes conducted by both the SSB and the World Bank are based on the conventional definition of income which excludes several items such as subsidies and payments in kind and undervalues others (production for self-consumption). The understatement of income sources will, of course, artificially decrease both rural and urban true incomes and may miscalculate the income gap between the two. For example, according to Khan *et al.* (1993, p. 34), the difference between the incomes of an average urban household and an average rural household is much higher than the official estimate. The true ratio of urban to rural incomes, for instance, would be 2.42 in 1988 as compared to the ratio of 2.05 estimated by the SSB (1989, p. 719). Li (2004) argues further that, if taking into account the subsidies and other earnings in kind, the actual urban-to-rural ratio of incomes would have been as high as 5–6 times during the early 2000s, which was the largest in the world.

Before the reform, there was a rather uneven distribution of income between the rural and urban areas. In 1957 when the Chinese economy was at its most prosperous, the per capita personal income in urban areas was 3.48 times that found in rural areas (SSB, 1986, pp. 667 and 673). As shown in Figure 7.2, the income gap between the rural and urban areas continued to decrease until 1983, but after 1985 the gap began to widen again and by 1994 the rural–urban inequalities were even greater than during the mid-1960s and 1970s. How can one explain these changes in the relative incomes of the rural and urban populations in China? Zhao (1993, pp. 82–3) argues that China's income differentials between rural and urban areas have been largely the result of government policy. For example, in the pre-reform era, it was the policy to keep agricultural prices low in order to accumulate funds for industrialization. Further, the migration of labor from the low-income countryside to the high-income cities was strictly controlled by the government through a system of registration of urban residents. The consequence of these policies, however, was to aggravate rural–urban inequalities.

7.3.3 A multiregional comparison

Natural and human resources are distributed irregularly in China. Specifically, the Eastern belt is blessed with a mild climate and rich soil, while the Western belt has a vast area and a sparse population. The Northern part is much richer in mineral resources than the Southern part, except for a few non-ferrous metals. In contrast, most of the Southern part, given its favorable climate and terrain, has an agricultural advantage over most of the Northern part (especially the desert North and Northwest regions) and, in particular, dominates most of the nation's rice production. All of the above regional characteristics in the distribution of resources, together with the spatially diversified regional economic development policies that China has pursued during recent decades and other historical and cultural factors, have unevenly decided the spatial structure of the Chinese economy.

The vast size and diversified natural conditions in China have generated many regional differences in terms of climate, geography, soil fertility and other resource endowments, which in turn mean that the living standards vary from region to region. In particular, South and East regions have natural advantages for agriculture over the Northwest region. Minerals and energy resources are much richer in the North than in the South. In other aspects, the eastern coastal area, because of its geographical proximity to market economies, may find it easier to introduce the laissez-faire approach than would be the case for the central and the western inland areas. All of these factors have inevitably resulted in great economic disparities among regions.

A brief look at the composition of personal consumption in China shows that the proportion of total expenditure on food and beverages has dropped in both rural and urban areas since the reform, reflecting Engel's Law (see SSB or NBS, various issues); by contrast, demand for housing, furniture and utensils, clothing, health care, education and others is seen to be more income-elastic, as is suggested by the law. However, economic transformation in China has raised some problems in relation to the application of the law. For instance, when estimating the Engel coefficients with respect to the per capita net incomes, we obtain a significant regression for the rural area and an insignificant regression for the urban area:

$$REC = 69.47 - 5.87 \times 10^{-5} RNI \quad (N = 30, R^2 = 0.48, F = 25.64) \quad (7.4)$$
$$(-5.06)$$
$$UEC = 50.20 + 9.75 \times 10^{-5} UNI \quad (N = 29, R^2 = 0.001, F = 0.02) \quad (7.5)$$
$$(0.15)$$

where *RNI* and *UNI* are the per capita rural and urban net incomes; *REC* and *UEC* are the rural and urban Engel coefficients, the data of which are calculated based on SSB (1996, pp. 288–9, 303 and 305). Equation 7.4 demonstrates a negative correlation between the rural Engel coefficient (*REC*) and per capita net income (*RNI*), which is consistent with Engel's Law. It should be noted that the insignificant and positive correlation between *UEC* and *UNI*, with far smaller t-statistical values in parentheses, R^2 and F-values in Equation 7.5, does not mean that Engel's Law has been disproved by the Chinese urban data; rather, it implies that the Chinese data need to be further clarified in detail. Perhaps the miscalculation of the Engel coefficients for Chinese urban areas might be due to the subsidies from the government which has usually ascribed to the personal consumption in housing and health care.

China's vast landmass, together with an underdeveloped transport system and rigid spatial economic barriers (as will be discussed in Chapter 8.2), differentiates regional purchasing powers. That is, the same level of monetary income may result in different real living standards from region to region. Theoretically, if the price indices and consumption structures are known, the personal consumption expenditure can be

Box 7.1 A spatial guide to go shopping

The following demonstrates the price-tags for some foodstuffs in different provinces in China (as of September 2008):

- 1 kg of chicken costs ¥12.06 in Jiangxi but ¥32.00 in Shanghai;
- 1 kg of fish costs ¥10.04 in Jiangxi but ¥20.10 in Tibet;
- 1 kg of pork costs ¥21.76 in Xinjiang but ¥32.00 in Beijing;
- 1 kg of eggs costs ¥6.8 in Shanghai but ¥10.96 in Hainan;
- 1 kg of milk costs only ¥3.78 in Xinjiang but ¥17.4 in Shanghai;
- 1 kg of apples costs only ¥4.12 in Henan but ¥13.16 in Chongqing;
- 1 kg of oranges costs only ¥3.04 in Henan but ¥7.00 in Qinghai and Tibet;
- 1 kg of bananas costs only ¥2.98 in Jiangxi but ¥7.00 in Chongqing;

Source: China Price Information Network (www.chinaprice.gov.cn).

recomputed for different regions of China based upon purchasing power. Due to the difficulties in collecting comparable regional data, we have to leave this ambitious task. Nevertheless, one is still able to witness the regional differences of purchasing power based on the retail prices of agricultural products at free markets (see Box 7.1).

7.4 Regional economic disparity

One of the most influential theories in regional economics has been the "inverted-U" hypothesis in which economic development is at first accompanied by an increase in regional disparities and then followed by a decrease. The analysis of the convergence hypothesis has a long history that dates back to the work of Kuznets (1955) and the subsequent empirical work of Williamson (1965). At a basic level, this hypothesis is based on a theory in which growth initially occurs in some regions but not in others with the result that interregional disparities widen as growth proceeds. At a later stage, the high-growth regions become saturated and more and more of their industrial activities are shifted to the backward regions, thereby enabling the latter to catch up.

Resulting from the diversified natural and social conditions among the country's different regions, China's regional inequalities have had a long history. It is generally admitted that the Eastern belt has a relatively higher per capita GNP and, of course, higher living standards than the Western belt. It is noticeable that different results have emerged in the estimates of the regional economic inequalities in China. Some researchers believe that China's regional inequalities have definitely increased, reflecting the first stage of the inverted-U hypothesis as well as China's uneven regional development strategy.[7] In contrast, others argue that only the gaps between the Eastern, Central and Western belts have widened in recent years while the interprovincial gaps have been narrowed substantially since the introduction of the economic reform in 1978.[8] Given the use of different data and measurements, it seems that there is no emerging consensus on this issue.

For example, Zhang (1994, p. 300) uses 27 provinces (excluding Qinghai and Tibet) for 1980, 28 provinces (excluding Tibet) for 1981–88 and 28 provinces (excluding Tibet and Hainan, a new province established in 1988) for 1989–90 and obtains an increasing regional inequality in terms of per capita income in rural China. Based on the multiregional data in which three municipalities directly under the central government are incorporated into their neighboring provinces (Beijing and Tianjin into Hebei, Shanghai into Jiangsu) and Tibet and Hainan are excluded from the analysis, Tsui (1993) shows that the level of interprovincial inequality declined from the late 1970s to the mid-1980s and a reversal in the trend preceded the reform era. Jian *et al.* (1996, pp. 1–22) use the data of 28 provinces (Tibet and Hainan are excluded) and obtain a V-shaped pattern for China's multiregional inequalities from 1978 to 1993. Obviously, the regional inequalities will demonstrate differing patterns if different measurements and regionalizations are employed. In addition, great care should be taken when one uses the official data to estimate China's regional inequality index for the pre- and post-reform periods during which different statistical systems were employed.

Let us first of all consider the poorest and richest provinces in China. In 1952, the per capita national income of Shanghai was estimated at 584.15 yuan, which is 10.67 times that of Guizhou (54.77 yuan). In 1979, Shanghai's per capita national income, at constant prices, had risen to 2,860.92 yuan, 27.85 times the figure for Guizhou (102.72 yuan) (SSB, 1990b). Obviously, during the pre-reform period, there was a rapid widening of the economic gap between the richest and poorest provinces. How large is this gap during the post-reform period? Briefly, if we consider per capita GDP the economic gap has experienced two different patterns (see Table 7.3). Shanghai's per capita GDP was 27.88 times of Guizhou's

Table 7.5 Gaps between the top five and bottom five provinces (in per capita GDP, yuan)

GDP per capita	1952	1980	1990	2000	2005
Panel A: All provinces					
Top five (yuan)	397	1766	3833	20129	30528
Bottom five (yuan)	81	176	979	3991	6640
Absolute gap (yuan)	315	1590	2854	16138	23888
Ratio of top five to bottom five	4.87	10.04	3.92	5.04	4.60
Panel B: Excluding Beijing, Shanghai and Tianjin					
Top five (yuan)	226	502	2136	11981	20179
Bottom five (yuan)	81	176	979	3991	6640
Absolute gap (yuan)	144	326	1157	7990	13539
Ratio of top five to bottom five	2.77	2.85	2.18	3.00	3.04

Source: Calculated by the author based on Table 7.2 and NBS (2006).

in 1979 and 7.34 times of Guizhou's in 1990, which implies that the per capita GDP ratio of Shanghai to Guizhou decreased greatly during the above period. From 1990 to 2000, however, the per capita GDP ratio of Shanghai to Guizhou increased once again to 12.6.

A more systematic comparison is presented in Table 7.5. The ratio of per capita GDP for the top five to the bottom five provinces has been in the range of 4.60 in 2005 if all provinces are taken into account. Even if Beijing, Shanghai and Tianjin are excluded, the ratio of the top five to the bottom five provinces is still greater than 3.00. By way of comparison, the ratio of the top five to bottom five states for the United States is 2.46 if Washington DC is included or 1.84 if Washington DC is excluded (Groeneworld *et al.*, 2008, p. 27).

A glance at the year-to-year per capita GDPs of the Eastern, Central and Western belts reveals simply that the regional inequalities have increased significantly, as demonstrated in Figure 7.3. For instance, the per capita GDP in the Eastern belt was 87 percent higher than that in the Western belt in 1978; in 2005, however, it was about 200 percent higher than that in the Western belt.

Until now, we may conclude that there have been very large gaps between the richest and the poorest provinces in China. It is tempting to draw conclusions from Table 7.5 concerning the trend of the disparities

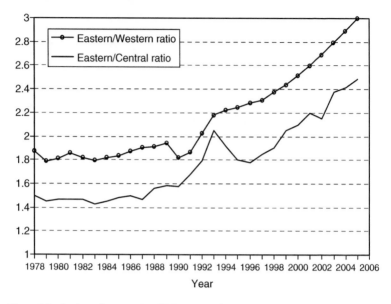

Figure 7.3   Ratios of per capita GDP among three geographical belts

over time. Let us turn to measure China's year-to-year regional inequalities after all provinces are taken into account. Using the provinces' per capita GDP data which have been officially reported and are estimated by the author (based on the method in section 7.2) for the provinces whose GDP data are not reported officially, we may calculate the Gini, CV and MCV coefficients for the years from 1952 to 2000. Since the mathematical formula of the Gini has been given in Chapter 6, the following two formulas demonstrate how the CV and MCV are measured mathematically:

$$CV = \frac{\sqrt{\frac{1}{n}(x_i - \bar{x})^2}}{\bar{x}} \tag{7.6}$$

$$MCV = \frac{\sqrt{\rho_i(x_i - \bar{x})^2}}{\mu} \tag{7.7}$$

Where x_i is the value of the variable of interest for the ith province, there are n provinces; $\bar{x}$ is the sample mean for all $\bar{x}$, ρ_i is a weight for the ith province and μ is the weighted mean of all x using the ρ_i weights.

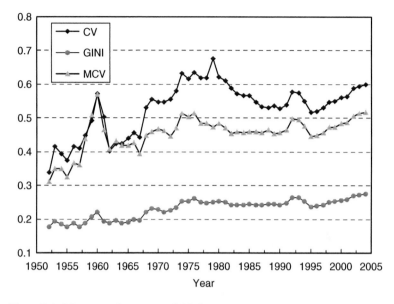

Figure 7.4 Measures of per capita GDP disparities among provinces
Note: 29 provinces are considered from 1952 to 1988 (during which Hainan is included in Guangdong province) while 30 provinces are considered from 1989 to 1997 and 31 provinces from 1998 onwards (since then Chongqing has been separated from Sichuan province).

Generally, regional inequalities (measured by Gini, CV and MCV) have fluctuated frequently over recent decades (see Figure 7.4). With the exception of a few years (including 1954–55, 1957, 1961–62 and 1967), China's regional inequalities increased steadily from the early 1950s to the late 1970s. For instance, the Gini, CV and MCV were 0.178, 0.339 and 0.312 in 1952; by 1980, however, they increased significantly to 0.253, 0.621 and 0.483, respectively. Obviously, during this period China's egalitarian policy did not bring about any economic equalities among the provinces. From the early 1980s to the mid-1990s, with the exception of a few years in the early 1990s, regional inequalities have decreased among the provinces; however, they have increased steadily since this time.

Since the late 1970s, China's experience with trade liberalization and with rapid economic growth in the coastal provinces has given an indication of widening income inequalities among China's regions. Jian *et al.* (1996) examine the tendency toward convergence in real per capita income among the provinces of China during the period 1952–1993. No strong convergence or divergence during the initial phase of central planning (1952–1965) was observed. There is strong evidence of divergence during the period of the "Cultural Revolution" (1965–78) with social planning in favor of richer industrial regions widening the levels of interregional inequality. Regional inequality is equalized with the extent of marketization and openness that began in 1978. Convergence as the result of factor mobility, the flows of labor, capital and technology, increased productivity among the rural regions and convergence within the coastal provinces. A policy to promote the further liberalization of the country's interior will also promote convergence. Variance decomposition of the log of real GDP in each province is obtained. Zhang *et al.* (2001) investigate the time-series properties of per capita income in China's regions during the period 1952 to 1997 and compare the consistency of results with cross-sectional methods. The results based on the Gini coefficient, the ratio of per capita income between regions and the coefficient of variation suggests that eastern and western regions have converged to their own specific steady states over the course of the past 40 years. The regional gap between the east and other regions had widened before the reforms, but the economic reforms have served only to worsen the gap still further.

Demurger *et al.* (2002) examined the growth in GDP per capita for the period 1952–98 and decomposed the location and policy growth rates in the provincial growth regressions in order to quantify the contribution of each factor in the period 1996–99. Their respective contribution varies with the interval of 0–2.8 percent and 1.6–3.5 percent. The highest and lowest rates are associated with the coastal and northwestern provinces, respectively. The authors list a number of policy measures to solve the unbalanced growth and to reduce the regional disparity. The policy measures include: the extension of the deregulation from coastal to include other provinces; the introduction of a registration system to prevent movements from the rural poor to prosperous areas; changes in the policy of the monopoly state bank system to allocate more resources to the western provinces; and improvements in the infrastructure to overcome geographical barriers and also to increase the level of human capital formation.

In China, although commercial activities are subject to a uniform regulatory system set by the central government, provincial and local officials have a large degree of discretion in terms of the enforcement of national legislation. Since the early 2000s, the World Bank, in collaboration with the Chinese Academy of Social Sciences, has conducted a series of annual assessments on the ease of doing business in China. These studies found that the investment climate varies widely across provinces even

Table 7.6 Ease of doing business in China – top and bottom ten provinces

Rank no.	Starting a business	Registering property	Getting credit	Enforcing contracts
1	Zhejiang	Shanghai	Fujian	Guangdong
2	Jiangsu	Guangdong	Jiangsu	Jiangsu
3	Guangdong	Fujian	Guangdong	Zhejiang
4	Shandong	Shandong	Shandong	Shanghai
5	Shanghai	Jiangsu	Shanghai	Shaanxi
6	Beijing	Tianjin	Tianjin	Shandong
7	Fujian	Zhejiang	Beijing	Tianjin
8	Tianjin	Jilin	Zhejiang	Chongqing
9	Liaoning	Chongqing	Hebei	Beijing
10	Jilin	Shaanxi	Heilongjiang	Liaoning
21	Jiangxi	Hebei	Jilin	Heilongjiang
22	Hunan	Yunnan	Qinghai	Xinjiang
23	Qinghai	Hainan	Yunnan	Sichuan
24	Yunnan	Hunan	Jiangxi	Guizhou
25	Shaanxi	Hubei	Guizhou	Jilin
26	Ningxia	Shanxi	Xinjiang	Anhui
27	Anhui	Henan	Ningxia	Hunan
28	Guangxi	Guizhou	Shaanxi	Qinghai
29	Gansu	Gansu	Gansu	Yunnan
30	Guizhou	Guangxi	Guangxi	Gansu

Notes: (1) Each province is represented by its capital city. (2) Hong Kong, Macau, Taiwan and Tibet are excluded from the rankings.
Source: World Bank (2008, pp. 38–9).

though the laws and regulations are fundamentally the same through-out the country. As measured by the four indicators (starting a business, registering property, getting credit – getting and registering collateral, and enforcing contracts) in Table 7.6, the coastal provinces (such as Guangdong, Jiangsu, Shanghai, Zhejiang, Shandong, and Fujian) have the most favorable environments for the conducting of business. The western and central provinces, however, seem to have most challenging business environments. Nevertheless, most provinces measured have at least one indicator which compares favorably with other surveyed provinces.

7.5 Summary

Since economic reform and open-door policies were implemented in the late 1970s, the Chinese economy has demonstrated an increasing asymmetry between different regions. This has resulted in a series of regional economic problems which need to be addressed properly by policy makers. In this chapter, the Chinese economy is analyzed generally and compared via multiregional dimensions. Due to the application of different statistical systems in the pre- and post-reform periods as well as the unavailability of statistical data in some provinces, a complete multiregional comparison of the Chinese economy is extremely difficult and, to some extent, meaningless. Using the best data and the regression approach, section 7.2 tries to estimate a set of time-series data on GDP for all provinces, on which the multiregional comparison of the Chinese economy is based. In section 7.3, efforts of consistent economic comparison are attempted based on the indices of real living standards. Finally, in section 7.4, regional economic disparity indexes are computed for the past decades.

Beginning with a common ideological and historical background, but proceeding with differing paces of economic reform and with different development policies, China has developed its provinces and promoted the welfare of urban and rural people differently. Not surprisingly, over recent decades China's economic reform and open-door policies have disproportionally aided the coastal provinces where per capita GDPs are several times higher than in the poorer inland provinces. When addressing the Chinese economy from a multiregional perspective, at least two issues should be noted.

First, China's rural–urban inequalities are very high compared with other developing countries. For example, in Indonesia the ratio of urban to rural income was 1.66 in 1987. In Bangladesh the highest observed ratio during the 1980s was 1.85, whereas the typical ratio was close to 1.5 (Khan *et al.*, 1993, p. 69). Admittedly, the household surveys on which these estimates are based do not give a full weight to subsidies and incomes in kind. However, in Indonesia and Bangladesh these components are tiny compared to those in China.

Secondly, even though not taking into account its two Special Administrative Regions (Hong Kong and Macau) and Taiwan (an economic comparison of Taiwan, Hong Kong, Macau and mainland China will be conducted in Chapter 12), China still had a per capita GDP ratio of more than 12 for the richest (Shanghai) to the poorest (Guizhou) at the end of 1990s, which is only lower than Indonesia (20.8, 1983), but much higher than many other countries, such as the former Yugoslavia (7.8, 1988), India (3.26, 1980), the Netherlands (2.69, 1988), Italy (2.34, 1988), Canada (2.30, 1988), Spain (2.23, 1988), France (2.15, 1988), West Germany (1.93, 1988), Greece (1.63, 1988), the UK (1.63), South Korea

(1.53, 1985), Japan (1.47, 1981), the USA (1.43, 1983) and Australia (1.13, 1978).[9]

How large will China's regional inequalities be and how will they eventually affect the Chinese economy and society? We are watching with open eyes.

7.6 Case study: Similar initial conditions, varied results

The process of choosing different regional development strategies is always followed by the comparison of results. During the 1980s and 1990s, this kind of scenario occurred in many similar prefectures just across the provincial borders in China: these pairings included Xiangfan (Hubei province) and Nanyang (Henan province); Shangrao (Jiangxi province) and Quzhou (Zhejiang province); and Shaoguan (Guangdong province) and Chenzhou (Hunan province). Below is the example of two twin prefectures, but stories of this type can be replicated in many other cross-province areas.

Shaoguan and Chenzhou are similar in terms of natural and geographic features and resource endowments; but they have experienced very different economic transitions. For example, after the first adoption of reforms in Guangdong in 1980, many commodity prices in Shaoguan rose above the levels of those in Chenzhou since the reforms had not been carried out in Hunan province. As a result, resources were attracted to Shaoguan from Chenzhou. The Chenzhou government set up tax offices on the border in an attempt to stop this outflow. These attempts did not bring prosperity to Chenzhou; rather, they led to an increase in the levels of underground and "illegal" cross-border trading.

Shaoguan had possessed a relatively higher degree of "autonomy" in terms of public finance, credit and banking, trade, price, labor and wage system, while Chenzhou's transition had lagged behind. For example, when Guangdong's provincial government began to implement a new fiscal policy entitled *"dizheng baogan"* (fix the increased rate of the revenue turned over to the state), Hunan province continued to follow a policy of *"zhong'e fencheng"* (proportionally share the total revenue) policy to Chenzhou. Apparently, the latter lacked the incentive for local government to accumulate its wealth. In addition, Shaoguan had a more elastic tax system than Chenzhou. For example, in Shaoguan the ore mining business was only taxed at a rate of 3 percent, but that in Chenzhou the total rate of taxes and fees for the same business was as high as 20 percent (Li, 1988, pp. 338–9). The unequal policies have produced many differences between the two sides of the provincial border. In the 1950s, the two neighbors had developed at almost the same rate of growth. Both of them had 580 million yuan of gross value of industrial and agricultural output (GVIAO) coincidently in 1958 and with little significant difference in the 1960s and 1970s. During the 1980s, the economic performances of these two areas had become increasingly divergent: Shaoguan had 918 million yuan of GVIAO higher than Chenzhou in 1980. But by 1987, the GVIAO gap had reached 2,213 million yuan.[10]

When people in Chenzhou compared themselves with their neighbors in Shaoguan, they found that, although both had begun with similar initial economic conditions, Shaoguan had benefited significantly from economic reform policies. People in Chenzhou urged that they should follow the reforms that had been implemented in Shaoguan. In 1988, Chenzhou was allowed to adopt some reform measures. This enabled Chenzhou to enjoy the benefits of opening markets to Shaoguan. The prefecture government withdrew all its tax offices along the border with Guangdong. Soon the adjacent areas between Chenzhou and Shaoguan were experiencing an economic boom and interregional trade reached record levels. Importantly, the Chenzhou government obtained far higher tax revenues from these businesses than had they had ever received from border tax offices.

8
Spatial Economics and Development Strategy

A man of the state of Lu (in today's southern Shandong province) was skilled in weaving hemp sandals and his wife was good at weaving fine white silk. The couple were thinking of moving out to the state of Yue (in today's Zhejiang province). 'You will be in dire straits,' he was told. 'Why?' asked the man of the Lu. 'Hemp sandals are for walking but people of the Yue walk barefoot. White silk is for making hats but people of the Yue go about bareheaded. If you go to a place where your skills are utterly useless, how can you hope to do well?'

– Hanfeizi (280–233 BC)

8.1 Comparative advantage index

A glance at modern Chinese history reveals that China's economic development has been concentrated in three geographical areas: the Bohai Sea rim (BSR) area, the Pearl river delta (PRD) area, and the Yangtze river delta (YRD). In terms of physical environment, the three areas are mutually complementary. For example, most of the BSR area (including Beijing, Tianjin, the coastal Hebei, and the peninsulas of Shandong and Liaodong) belongs to the semi-arid zone, while the PRD area (including Guangdong, and northern Hainan, Hong Kong and Macau)[1] is classified as tropical. Nevertheless, the YRD area (including Shanghai, Zhejiang, and southern Jiangsu) has a semi-tropical temperature. Culturally, the three areas are dominated by the ethnic Han community. But there also exist some differences. For example, although written Chinese is used widely throughout the country, people in the BSR area speak Mandarin, while those in the PRD and YRD areas use Cantonese and Wu as their native spoken languages, respectively. Daily food is also cooked differently in the three areas.

It is evident that mutually complementary conditions exist in these three areas. In general, the BSR area has advantages in terms of agricultural products, energy, industrial materials, some high-tech products and education. However, this area possesses obsolete equipment; lacks management experience for small and medium-sized enterprises; and has a shortage of capital. This PRD area neighbors Hong Kong and Macau and so has the advantages of accessing international markets and attracting foreign direct investment (FDI). Most overseas Chinese, many of whom were sources of FDI in China during the early 1980s and the 1990s, originated from this area. It is also the area which was the first to open its doors to the outside world. For example, among the original four special economic zones (SEZs), three (Shenzhen, Zhuhai and Shantou) were established in this area. With favorable conditions for international trade, the PRD area has the freest market; and considerable management experience for small and medium-sized enterprises. The disadvantages of the area are, among others, the less-developed education sector, and a shortage of industrial materials, especially energy and some mineral resources. The YRD area has advantages in terms of education, management experience for large modern industrial bases, and rural industrial enterprises. A lack of industrial resources, especially minerals and energy, is one of the many disadvantages in this area. Table 8.1 sorts out the advantageous and disadvantageous industrial sectors for the three areas.

There exist many multiregional differences in terms of natural and social resources, industrial structure and economic development in China. For example, Shanxi (the western part of Mount Taihang) province has abundant coal resources but poor mineral, petroleum and agricultural resources; except for petroleum, non-metal and agricultural resources, metals and coal resources are relatively poor in the province of Shandong (the eastern part of Mount Taihang); Hebei (the northern part of the Yellow river) province has a surplus supply of metals and coal resources but lacks petroleum and non-metals; Henan (the southern part of the Yellow river) province has rich coal, metal and agricultural resources but low non-metals.

To have a better understanding of the multiregional comparative advantages in China, let us introduce a quantitative index (Q_{ij}), which is formulated as follows:

$$Q_{ij} = \frac{x_{ij} / \sum_i x_{ij}}{\sum_j x_{ij} / \sum_i \sum_j x_{ij}} \tag{8.1}$$

Table 8.1 Comparative advantages of China's three economic engines

Area	Advantageous industrial sectors	Disadvantageous industrial sectors
Bohai Sea rim (BSR)	Petroleum and natural gas extraction; coal mining and preparation; nonferrous metals mining and preparation; ferrous metals mining and preparation; petroleum processing and coking	Logging and transport of timber and bamboo; cultural, educational and sport articles manufacturing; chemical fibers; electric and telecommunication equipment manufacturing; instruments, meters and other measuring equipment manufacturing
Pearl river delta (PRD)	Logging and transport of timber and bamboo; running water production and supply; electric and telecommunication equipment manufacturing; leather, furs and manufactured goods manufacturing; timber processing, bamboo, cane, palm fiber and straw products	Petroleum and natural gas extraction; smelting and pressing of ferrous metals; coal mining and preparation; gas production and supply; universal machine manufacturing
Yangtze river delta (YRD)	Chemical fibers; textile manufacturing; instruments, meters and other measuring equipment manufacturing; smelting and processing of nonferrous metals; universal machine manufacturing	Logging and transport of timber and bamboo; petroleum and natural gas extraction; ferrous metals mining and preparation; nonferrous metals mining and preparation; coal mining and preparation

Note: Bohai Sea rim = Beijing, Tianjin, coastal Hebei and Shandong and Liaodong peninsulas; Pearl river delta = Guangdong and northern Hainan (Hong Kong and Macau are excluded); Yangtze river delta = Shanghai, Zhejiang and southern Jiangsu.

where x_{ij} is the output value of the ith sector ($i = 1$, 2, ..., and 6, representing "coal," "petroleum," "metal," "non-metal," "timber," and "food") in the jth province ($j = 1$, 2, ..., and 30, representing China's provinces). Specifically, China's provinces can be classified into three groups according to the values of Q_{ij} (shown in Table 8.2):

(1) when $Q_{ij} > 1$, it means that supply exceeds demand in the ith sector of the jth province;
(2) when $Q_{ij} < 1$, it means that supply is less than demand in the ith sector of the jth province; and
(3) when $Q_{ij} = 1$, it means that supply and demand are in equilibrium in the ith sector of the jth province.

Table 8.2 Interprovincial comparative advantage indexes (Q_{ij}), by industrial sector

Province	Coal	Petroleum	Metal	Non-metal	Timber	Food
Anhui	1.42	0.00	0.93	1.61	0.18	1.34
Beijing	0.63	0.00	0.44	0.62	0.00	1.90
Fujian	0.43	0.00	0.33	1.55	6.23	1.45
Gansu	0.75	2.22	1.01	0.92	0.83	0.46
Guangdong	0.21	0.16	0.82	1.58	0.14	1.78
Guangxi	0.32	0.00	2.58	1.16	0.34	1.59
Guizhou	2.63	0.00	1.30	0.97	1.94	0.76
Hainan	0.04	0.00	3.58	0.83	0.54	1.59
Hebei	1.51	1.30	2.05	0.75	0.00	0.57
Heilongjiang	0.58	2.79	0.12	0.16	3.12	0.32
Henan	1.57	0.94	1.24	0.37	0.00	0.91
Hubei	0.23	0.71	0.66	2.45	0.17	1.37
Hunan	1.21	0.00	2.53	1.44	0.43	1.19
Inner Mongolia	1.48	0.38	1.33	0.95	5.60	0.78
Jiangsu	0.79	0.14	0.16	1.62	0.00	1.66
Jiangxi	1.08	0.00	3.43	1.36	1.38	1.05
Jilin	0.79	0.95	0.56	0.54	6.50	0.88
Liaoning	1.03	1.51	1.18	0.99	0.00	0.75
Ningxia	3.70	0.42	0.05	0.25	0.00	0.52
Qinghai	0.26	2.70	1.13	1.37	0.09	0.37
Shaanxi	1.22	0.58	3.47	0.64	0.67	0.82
Shandong	0.90	1.13	0.97	1.22	0.00	1.01
Shanghai	0.00	0.00	0.01	0.07	0.04	2.31
Shanxi	4.70	0.00	0.89	0.25	0.03	0.20
Sichuan	1.10	0.61	0.43	1.35	1.74	1.16
Tianjin	0.01	2.05	0.02	0.56	0.00	1.12
Tibet	0.03	0.00	5.05	1.88	10.7	0.53
Xinjiang	0.35	3.11	0.44	0.26	0.21	0.37
Yunnan	0.71	0.40	3.24	0.66	1.83	1.09
Zhejiang	0.21	0.00	0.62	2.21	0.01	1.82

Source: Calculated by the author based on Equation (8.1) and SSB (1996b, pp. 118–36).

Generally, China's resource demand and supply may be classified into four different geographical zones which are labeled as follows: (1) $S_L D_L$ (low supply, low demand), (2) $S_H D_L$ (high supply, low demand), (3) $S_H D_H$ (high supply, high demand), and (4) $S_L D_H$ (low supply, high demand). Obviously, Zones $S_L D_L$ and $S_H D_H$ can reach their respective optimum equilibrium point of social welfare even under the condition that inter-zone trade is not available, as their resource supplies can meet their

Box 8.1 Spatial optimum with resource allocation

In the figure below, S_0S illustrates a society's resource supply possibility curve of Zone S_LD_H, W_0W_0' denotes the Zone's social preference curve and OS_0 and OS denote the maximum possibilities of resource supplies of Zones S_HD_L and S_LD_H, respectively. Consider the availability of the inter-zone trade and the absence of the resource supplies from other external sources, the optimum allocation of resource between Zones S_HD_L and S_LD_H will be at point E_0 where S_0S and W_0W_0' meet. When a trade embargo rises from Zone S_HD_L, the S_0S curve shifts to the left to, say, S_1S. As a result, Zone S_LD_H will have to end up with more supply of local resources and less social welfare consumption. In this case, the optimum equilibrium will occur at point E_1, which is lower than E_0, indicating a lower social welfare level upon the introduction of trade barriers between Zones S_HD_L and S_LD_H. It must be noted that, the more Zone S_LD_H is committed to the importing of resources in a world of resource constraints, the less is its social welfare consumption, since higher risks and more extra costs will result from resource imports.

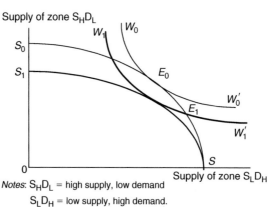

Notes: S_HD_L = high supply, low demand
S_LD_H = low supply, high demand.

resource demands. However, under the disequilibrated supply–demand conditions, neither Zone S_LD_H nor Zone S_HD_L can optimize its social welfare. As a matter of fact, as these two zones' resource supply–demand structures are complementary with each other, the optimization of their social welfare can benefit greatly from their inter-zone trade, more specifically, from the import from Zone S_HD_L to Zone S_LD_H, or the export to Zone S_LD_H from Zone S_HD_L. The trade-off between Zones S_HD_L and S_LD_H can be further explained by Box 8.1.

There have been two potentially contradictory metaphors pervading contemporary commentary on the nature and trajectory of the Chinese political economy. First, there is the more benign metaphor of the "nationalization" of economic activities, which presents a picture of an environment in which economic agents, in particular multiregional firms, are increasingly indifferent to political boundaries, competing in the "national market" and satisfying the demands of consumers whose tastes are increasingly homogeneous across borders. Secondly, there is the view of the national economy as being increasingly defined by different "regional blocs" which are marked by high levels of intra-regional interdependence but which compete at the national level.

In principle, spatial economic separation may effectively be reduced to a minimum level within a sovereign country by the central government. As a result of the diversified natural, geographical environments and the heterogeneous social and cultural conditions in China, however, the Chinese economy has been spatially separated by a series of natural and artificial barriers. This kind of spatial separation became particularly serious during the period when the centrally planned system was transformed into a decentralized administrative system. Let us look briefly at this spatial separation and its negative effects on the Chinese economy through a consideration of three aspects – geographical, administrative and cultural.

8.2 Spatial economic separation

8.2.1 Geographical barriers

In terms of its topography and physical environment, China is one of the most complex countries in the world. Glancing at the map of China, one may find that many administrative regions, especially provinces, have natural geographical barriers such as mountains, rivers, lakes, and so on. This kind of geographical separation between adjacent provinces could have a serious effect on regional economic development if the interprovincial transport and communication linkages are established inefficiently. After checking the highway networks of ten provinces (Beijing, Shanghai, Tianjin, Hebei, Shanxi, Liaoning, Gansu, Qinghai, Inner Mongolia and Ningxia) in the *China Atlas* published in 1983, for example, Guo (1993, p. 119) estimates that, of the 453 highways in the peripheral areas, around 60 percent were transprovincially connected, whereas about 40 percent did not reach their respective province's border.

Obviously, the fragmentary nature of the highway networks has exacerbated the inconveniences for every sphere of the local inhabitants' lives and has had a particularly adverse effect on the Chinese economy.[2]

Many provinces, autonomous regions, and municipalities directly under the central government have been informally demarcated in China. As a result, cross-border relations between the relevant provinces have never been easily coordinated and, sometimes, could become a destabilizing source for social stability and economic development, even though the regulations concerning the resolution of border disputes have been issued and revised by the State Council (1981, 1988b). After 1986, the Ministry of Civil Affairs (MCA) conducted a series of field surveys on the provinces of Xinjiang, Inner Mongolia, Ningxia, Gansu, Shaanxi, Qinghai, Jilin, Hebei and Shandong in order to provide legal, formal, geographical boundaries for those provinces. Many problems, however, still remained unresolved. For example, after having compared the locally mapped borders, Zhang (1990, p. 8) points out that among China's 66 cross-province border lines (totaling about 52,000 km), 59 cross-province borders have been the subject of controversy and 54 cross-province borders, amounting to around 9,500 km, have been disputed by the relevant local governments.

Moreover, there is another geographical characteristic in the Chinese economy: many provinces' borders are naturally marked by mountains, rivers and lakes which bless the border regions with abundant natural and environmental resources. Given the cross-border *imbroglios* between the provinces, the sustainable exploitation and utilization of natural resources (such as energy, metals, forests, fishery and so on) as well as environmental protection in the border regions will undoubtedly pose problems and disputes for both central and local governments in China. Non-cooperative cross-border relations between provinces could eventually become a source of disturbance to economic development. Even worse, some interprovincial disputes led to armed conflicts and seriously affected the social security and economic sustainability in border regions regardless of the regulations concerning the resolution of border disputes between administrative regions issued by the State Council (1981, 1988b).

For example, of China's 66 interprovincial borderlines, 65 are disputed and have even been published, according to their own preferences, by the provincial-level authorities in their official maps and documents (Zhang, 1990, p. 8). According to the statistics released by the Ministry of Civil Affairs, of the 52,000 km of interprovincial borders in the People's Republic of China, only 5 percent are legally fixed; 77 percent are regarded as informal (or customary borderlines); and about 18 percent (about 9,500 km) remain the subject of active disputes.[3] According to the various sources, there were more than 800 cases of cross-border disputes in 333 of the 849 interprovincial border counties of almost all provinces.[4] In defiance of the State Council (1981, 1988b) regulations concerning the resolution of interprovincial border disputes, many disputes were the subject of armed fights between different groups of people. This has seriously affected the social security and sustainability of economic development in those cross-border areas.

8.2.2   Administrative barriers

One of the key initiatives of China's economic reform that began in the late 1970s was the promotion of decentralization in economic operations, i.e., transferring economic management and decision making from central government to provincial and local governments. For example, retail trade, which used to be under the control of local government, is now determined by collectively and individually owned enterprises. Decentralization and the introduction of market forces together imply that the centers of economic power are moving away from central government to the localities. Since the advent of administrative decentralization, China's national economy had become effectively "cellularized" into a plethora of semi-autarkic regional enclaves. Below we will analyze this in detail.

According to the principle of comparative advantage, the uneven distribution of natural resources and industrial structure among different provinces enhances the mutual complementarities of the Chinese economy. However, to a certain extent, administrative separation had formed a rigid self-reliant agricultural and industrial system for each province and had a serious effect on cross-border economic relations, particularly during the high tide of administrative decentralization stemming from economic reform. In order to protect local market and revenue sources, it became very common in China for some provinces to restrict import (export) from (to) other provinces by levying high, if informal taxes and by creating non-tariff barriers on commodities ranging from tobacco to clothing, alcohol, washing machines, TV sets, refrigerators and even automobiles whose production is seen as important to their provincially "domestic" economies. Xinjiang autonomous region, for example, effectively banned the import of 48 commodities on the grounds that they would harm its local economy. In similar moves, Jilin refused to market beer produced in the neighboring provinces of Heilongjiang and Liaoning and Hunan province prohibited the export of grain to the adjacent Guangdong province ... In some provinces, local authorities established, and provided finance for, a variety of schemes that promoted the sale of local products. Enterprises from other provinces, however, often have difficulties in finding office spaces, accommodation or land for their business activities. These protectionist measures, which were often in violation of central directives, were enforced through a patchwork system of roadblocks, cargo seizures, *ad hoc* taxes, commercial surcharges and licensing fees, and in a number of well-publicized cases, highway robbery across the interprovincial borders.[5] Moreover, this unfair competition between provinces could be fierce in the "battlegrounds" of their border regions and there were numerous tales of "trade embargoes" or "commodity wars" between provinces over, among other items, rice, wool, tobacco, soy beans and mineral products.[6]

Experience and lessons from advanced countries have shown that the success of a nation in promoting its economic development depends to a large extent on a complete legislative structure and effective instrumental incentives of its own. China's efforts to this end have achieved much progress, but some detailed work still remains to be done. In fact, China's "commodity wars" between provinces stemmed from the fact that China does not have any constitutional clauses to specifically prohibit barriers against interprovincial commerce, even though the relevant regulations and laws have been issued time and again by the State Council (1980a, 1982, 1986 and 1990) and NPC (1993). More often than not, the state's orders were not accorded the priority status of a self-contained law, but took the form of less formal circulars, or were included as minor elements of larger pieces of portmanteau legislation (Young and Ho, 1993, pp. 9–13).

8.2.3 Cultural barriers

Cultural differences have had a decisive influence on economic and marketing decisions. Although not the only tool in building trusting relationships, doors usually open more quickly when knocked on by someone who shares a familiar culture. The differences between intra- and inter-cultural behaviors have four main aspects: (1) feelings of superiority (and occasionally inferiority) toward people who are perceived as being very different; (2) fear of and lack of trust in such people; (3) communication difficulties resulting from differences in language and accepted civil behavior; (4) lack of familiarity with the assumptions, motivations, such as relationships and social practices of other people (Huntington, 1996, p. 129).

In addition to the Han-Chinese, which account for more than 90 percent of the nation's total population, there are 55 minority groups in mainland China.[7] As early as 1952, the Chinese government issued the Program for the Implementation of Regional Ethnic Autonomy of the People's Republic of China, which included provisions for the establishment of ethnic autonomous areas and the composition of organs of self-government, as well as the right of self-government for such organs. The first National People's Congress (NPC), convened in 1954, included the system of regional autonomy for ethnic minorities in the Constitution of the People's Republic of China. On May 31 1984, on the basis of summarizing the experience of practicing regional autonomy for non-Han ethnic minorities, the second session of the Sixth NPC adopted the "Law on Regional Ethnic Autonomy." This law, which was further amended in 2001, has been the basic legal document for implementing the system of regional autonomy for ethnic minorities. It defines the relationship between the central government and the ethnic autonomous regions, as well as the relationship between different ethnic groups in ethnic autonomous regions.

Geographically, the Han majority are dominant in the Eastern and Central belts with the only exception being Guangxi, which is a Zhuang autonomous region. The other minority-dominated autonomous regions include Ningxia (Hui minority-based) and Xinjiang (Ugyur minority-based) in the Northwest region, Inner Mongolia (Mongolian minority-based) in the North region, Tibet (Tibetan minority-based) in the Southwest region, and so on. In addition, there are also dozens of minority-based sub-provincial administrations (such as autonomous prefectures and prefecture-level municipalities) and even more minority-based autonomous counties and county-level municipalities under the administrations of the above autonomous regions and other provinces in China.

Most of China's provinces, autonomous regions, and municipalities directly under the central government, which are the average size and scale of a European country in terms of both population and land area, are considerable political and economic systems in their own right. The differences between these provinces have long been a defining characteristic of China's politics since in most cases their boundaries were created more than some two thousand years ago. Besides, Chinese culture is not homogeneous across provinces, in terms of ethnic and linguistic groups (see Table 8.3).

More importantly, there are various religiously based areas in China. For example, people in Tibet and its adjacent autonomous areas in

Table 8.3 China's ethnic and linguistic differences, by province

Province	Main ethnic groups	Main languages
Anhui	Han, Hui, She	Mandarin
Beijing	Han, Hui, Man	Mandarin
Chongqing	Han, Yi	Mandarin
Fujian	Han, She, Hui	Min, Kejia
Gansu	Han, Hui, Tibetan	Mandarin, Mongolian
Guangdong	Han, Yao, Zhuang	Cantonese (Yue), Kejia, Miao-Yao
Guangxi	Zhuang, Han, Yao	Chinese dialects, Dai
Guizhou	Han, Miao, Buyi	Chinese dialects, Dai
Hainan	Han, Li, Miao	Chinese dialects, Kejia, Dai
Hebei	Han, Hui, Man	Mandarin
Heilongjiang	Han, Man, Korean	Mandarin
Henan	Han, Hui, Mongol	Mandarin
Hubei	Han, Tujia, Hui	Chinese dialects
Hunan	Han, Tujia, Miao	Xiang (Chinese dialects), Miao-Yao
Inner Mongolia	Mongol, Han	Mongolian, Mandarin
Jiangsu	Han, Hui, Man	Chinese dialects, Mandarin, Wu
Jiangxi	Han, Hui, Miao	Gan (Chinese dialects)
Jilin	Han, Korean, Man	Mandarin
Liaoning	Han, Man, Mongol	Mandarin
Ningxia	Hui, Han, Man	Mandarin
Qinghai	Han, Tibetan, Hui	Tibetan, Mongolian
Shaanxi	Han, Hui, Man	Mandarin
Shandong	Han, Hui, Man	Mandarin
Shanghai	Han	Wu
Shanxi	Han, Hui, Mongol	Mandarin
Sichuan	Han, Yi, Tibetan	Mandarin, Tibetan
Tianjin	Han, Hui, Korean	Mandarin
Tibet	Tibetan, Han, Menba	Tibetan
Xinjiang	Uighur, Han, Kazak	Turkish dialects, Mongolian
Yunnan	Han, Yi, Bai	Mandarin, Tibetan
Zhejiang	Han, She, Hui	Chinese dialects, Wu

Southwest China usually adhere to Tibetan Buddhism, while most minorities in Northwest China have Islamic roots. The Han-Chinese, representing the majority of Chinese population in the Central and Eastern belts, are traditionally in favor of a mix of Buddhism, Confucianism, and Taoism, with a few other minority faiths. Naturally, it is unlikely that people with markedly differing attitudes as well as different cultural values would emphasize the adoption of a common standard and socioeconomic coordination. Apart from abstract questions of justice, this circumstance would not lead itself to an agreement between the cultural regimes concerned.

8.3   China's search for spatial integration

Although rooted in a single culture, the Chinese economic area is politically separated. Hong Kong (until 1997) and Macau (until 1999) were two colonial territories ruled by the United Kingdom and Portugal, respectively. Long before their return to China under the principle of "one country, two systems," these two capitalist economies had set up close and efficient economic links with their communist rival on the mainland. Traditionally, mainland China supplied most of Hong Kong's food and fresh water, and Hong Kong served as China's main port. After 1978 the links between the two economies were extended to production, investment, provision of services and financial relations (Dodsworth and Mihaljek, 1997). Regardless of the political and military tensions between Taiwan and the mainland of China, bilateral trade and economic exchanges across the Taiwan Strait have grown dramatically, as have tourism, technological and labor cooperation. It seems extraordinary that economic ties of this kind could have been sustained between two such politically distrustful and hostile economies.

However, the large size of the Chinese nation does impose some negative influences on its economy, especially in its huge and backward inland areas. Since the advent of the administrative decentralization in the early 1980s, China's national economy had become effectively "cellularized" into a plethora of semi-autarkic regional enclaves. Public finance, as an important component of the Chinese economic system, has undergone a series of reforms on central–local relations. The main goals of these reforms were to decentralize the fiscal structure and to strengthen the incentive for local governments to collect more revenue for themselves. While economic decentralization has been a major factor in China's current economic success, it also had negative impacts on interprovincial relations. For example, in order to protect local market and revenue sources, it became common in China for some provinces to restrict imports (exports) from (to) other provinces by levying high, if informal, taxes and by creating non-tariff barriers on commodities whose production is seen as important to their provincially "domestic" economies (Shen and Dai, 1990, pp. 1–13; and Li, 1993, pp. 23–36). Moreover, this unfair competition between provinces has created fierce economic "battlegrounds" in border areas and there have been numerous examples of "trade embargoes" or "commodity wars" between provinces over, amongst other items, rice, wool, tobacco, soy beans and mineral products.[8]

Most of China's provinces, autonomous regions, and municipalities that are under the direct control of the central government are on a size and scale equivalent to a European country in terms of both population and land area, meaning that they are considerable political and economic systems in their own right. The differences between these provinces have long been a defining characteristic of China's politics. In most cases their boundaries were created more than two thousand years ago (Gottmann, 1973). In addition, Chinese culture is not homogeneous across provinces. There is a broad range of ethnic and linguistic groups as well as religious adherents in the nation. The holding of markedly differing religious beliefs and values implies that the chances of the adoption of a common standard between different groups of people are not likely to be enhanced. Consequently, China's great diversity in terms of physical geography, resource endowment, political economy, and ethnical identity has given rise to many difficulties in interprovincial administration.

Since the late 1970s, the Chinese government has recognized the importance of transprovincial trade and economic cooperation and attempted to tear down its internal trade and economic barriers. In 1979 the CCPCC and the State Council implemented a new spatial development strategy entitled "evading weakness, exerting advantages, protecting competitiveness, and promoting unification." This strategy first attempted to replace the traditional economic method by which the Chinese economy was constructed into several self-supported regional systems. On October 20 1984, the Third Plenum of the 12th CCPCC claimed that "All administrative divisions should open up to each other, the barriers between economically developed and lagging regions, between coastal, inland and frontier regions, between urban and rural areas, and between different sectors and enterprises should be removed for economic unification according to the principle of evading weakness, mutual complementarity and joint development" (CCPCC, 1984). Generally, it is believed that multiregional economic cooperation was promoted substantially during the above period. Between 1981 and 1985, more than 30 regional economic and technological cooperative organizations were established in China.

China's spatial economic integration drive was promoted further by the "Regulations on Some Issues Concerning the Further Promotion of Horizontal Economic Unification" promulgated by the State Council in 1986. According to CASS (1992, pp. 561–7), central and local governments have established more than 100 multiregional economic cooperative zones. Generally, China's multiregional economic cooperative zones are voluntarily established and jointly administered by adjacent local governments. Many of them also have liaison officers and convene regular (annual) meetings co-chaired by the participating sides. The main tasks of the meetings include:

- discuss the key issues related to all sides concerned, such as the regional economic development strategy, regional economic structure, and so on;
- coordinate the policies and measures concerning the promotion of regional economic development;
- develop bilateral and multilateral economic cooperation; and
- study reconstruction and unification in the fields of production, circulation, science and technology;
- implement the specific coordination between all sides concerned.

According to their objectives and functions, the multiregional economic cooperative zones can be classified into seven categories:

- synthesized economic cooperative zones;
- resource-exploiting cooperative zones;
- open economic zones;
- municipal economic cooperative zones;
- municipal economic cooperative networks;
- cooperative zones for economically lagging areas; and
- sectoral economic cooperative zones.

In addition, these economic cooperative zones can be classified into three general categories in terms of administrative level:

- first-class economic cooperative zones, each of which is usually composed of two or more provincial administrations;
- second-class economic cooperative zones (trans-province border economic cooperative zones (BECZs)), each of which is composed of two or more adjacent prefectures, municipalities or counties under different provincial administrations; and
- third-class economic cooperative zones, each of which is composed of two or more adjacent prefectures, municipalities, or counties within a single provincial administration.

Of the economic cooperative zones listed above, the BECZs are worthy of further note, because of their special geographic locations and multidimensional administrative structures. In 1983 the BECZs were

Table 8.4 Average per capita national income by type of border region

Geographical type	2-provincial border counties		3-provincial border counties	
	non-BECZ	BECZ	non-BECZ	BECZ
Plain area	489.79	942.40	391.61	467.69
Mountain area	460.07	566.96	NA	623.01
All	473.79	686.42	391.61	584.18

Note: BECZ = transprovincial border economic cooperation zone.
Source: Guo (1991, tab. 15).

new entries to the regional economic sphere. By the end of 1989, the total number of these BECZs had increased dramatically to 41.[9] The proliferation of BECZs has provided an efficient channel for provincially peripheral areas to develop cross-border economic ties and cooperation. From Table 8.4, we see that the average per capita national income is always higher in BECZs than in other border areas. Specifically, the per capita national income was only 473.79 yuan and 391.61 yuan in 2- and 3-province border counties (an *i*-province border county is one which is bordered by *i* provinces), respectively, given the relative lack of trans-province border economic cooperation; following trans-province border economic cooperation, however, the per capita national income in the 2- and 3-province border counties increased by 44.88 percent and 49.17 percent, to 686.42 yuan and 584.18 yuan, respectively.

8.4   Regional development strategy

After three years of recovery (1950–52), the PRC government began to construct its economy through a centrally planned approach. In order to overcome effectively the disequilibrated industrial distribution between the coastal and inland areas, the government shifted the investment from the coastal area to the inland area. During the period 1953–78, the basic construction funded by the state was divided as follows: 35.7 percent in the coastal area and 55.2 percent in the inland area (see Table 8.5). As a result, industrial production grew unevenly between the coastal and inland areas. From 1952 to 1978, the inland area's share of gross value of industrial output (GVIO) increased from 31.8 percent to 40.2 percent, while the coastal area's share of GVIO accordingly decreased from 68.2 percent to 59.8 percent (Liu, 1994, p. 3). After 1978, when the Chinese government began to realize the importance of

Table 8.5　Spatial distribution of investment between coastal and inland areas

Period	Coastal (%)	Inland (%)	Coastal/inland
1953–57 (1st FYP)	36.9	46.8	0.788
1958–62 (2nd FYP)	38.4	56.0	0.686
1963–65	34.9	58.3	0.599
1966–70 (3rd FYP)	26.9	64.7	0.416
1971–75 (4th FYP)	35.5	54.4	0.653
1976–80 (5th FYP)	42.2	50.0	0.844
1981–85 (6th FYP)	47.7	46.5	1.026
1986–90 (7th FYP)	51.7	39.9	1.296
1953–78 (pre-reform)	35.7	55.2	0.647
1979–90 (post-reform)	49.9	43.2	1.155
1953–90	45.0	46.8	0.962

Note: total investment of coastal and inland areas are less than 100.00% due to the exclusion of the spatially "unidentified" investment which includes (1) the trans-provincial investment in railway, post and telecommunication, electric power, etc.; (2) the unified purchase of airplanes, ships, vehicles, etc.; (3) the investment in national defense.
Sources: (1) SSB (1991, 1992) and (2) Li and Fan (1994, p. 65).

reforming its centrally planned system and paying more attention to efficiency than regional equality, capital investment was concentrated in the coastal area. Between 1979 and 1990, the coastal area accounted for 49.9 percent of the nation's capital investment, while the inland area's share decreased accordingly to 43.2 percent, as demonstrated in Table 8.5.

Since the late 1970s, China has adopted an uneven spatial development strategy, encouraging a portion of regions to go one step further to get rich.[10] This included differing development preferences among different regions and during different periods. To date, the most successful regional development strategy is the so-called "Coastal Area Development Strategy". This strategy, which will be discussed in detail in Chapter 11, has benefited significantly from China's open-door policy. The final, major outcome of this strategy, a familiar development, has been the dramatic growth of foreign direct investment and foreign trade, which have been substantial drivers of the Chinese economy – and of the coastal area in particular. The additional outcome of this strategy is the increasing economic disparity between China's coastal and western areas in recent decades.

In the middle of 1999 the members of the CCPCC, headed by Jiang Zemin, started to talk publicly about the introduction of changes to China's regional development policy. For just over twenty years, ever since the establishment of Mao's principles of equal development and regional self-sufficiency – encapsulated in the description of "The whole country a chessboard" (*quanguo yipan qi*) – had been set aside, a more differentiated approach to regional development policy had privileged the eastern and coastal economies of the People's Republic of China. Without abandoning the regional development policy of the previous twenty years, the new policy initiative has placed greater emphasis on the development of the interior.

While the policy to develop "West China" has clearly been introduced from the top down, and under the leadership of a dedicated office of the State Council, the wider political environment is very different from that of the "Third Front Strategy" (see section 9.1 in Chapter 9). Not only has the project been discussed more openly, but there has been greater lower-level involvement in its development. Even at the planning stage, provinces such as Shaanxi, Sichuan and Chongqing were centrally involved. A West China Development Research Institute was established in Xi'an as a cooperative project of the central government's Ministry of Science and Technology, the Shaanxi Province Committee of the CCP, the Science Commission of the Shaanxi Provincial People's Government and Northwest University in order to provide advice on strategy and policy.

One challenge facing China in the era of globalization is to prevent its uneven growth pattern. In order to narrow the gap with the prosperous coastal area, the CCPCC propagated a campaign called the "Western Region Development Strategy" (*xibu da kaifa*), which constitutes a cornerstone of the 10th Five-Year Plan (2001–2005) and is intended to foster the future development of the inland regions. The stated goals were to bring about social and economic development of the interior and western regions of China. In November 1999, the State Council appointed the newly formed "State Council Leading Group for Western Region Development" to define a new policy. The "Office" was established in January 2003 to deal with day-to-day business. The main goals of the Western Region Development Strategy set out by the central government are as follows:

- To promote the development of the Western and Central regions.
- To eliminate regional disparities gradually.
- To consolidate the unity of ethnic groups.
- To ensure border security and social stability.
- To promote social progress.

It is anticipated that the strategy will initiate a number of programs and projects to stimulate domestic demand, expand the market, and maintain sustained, rapid and healthy development of the national economy. The main tasks are as follows: (i) to construct the infrastructure: water conservancy, communications, energy, telecommunication, and urban infrastructure; (ii) to improve the environment: to convert cultivated land back into forestry and pasture, to protect natural forests, recover and increase the vegetation of forestry and pasture, to reduce water loss and soil erosion, and to develop agriculture with local characteristics: processing industry and by-products. Rural poverty alleviation is also on the agenda. Enterprises are called to be active players in restructuring and upgrading traditional industries, to take advantage of military industries concentrated in the Western region, and to develop high-tech industries in fields such as biology, engineering, aerospace, renewable energy, new materials, electronic information processing, and advanced manufacturing.[11]

In 2002 a new spatial initiative entitled the "Resurgence of the Old Industrial Base in the Northeast Region" was announced. As is suggested by the name of the policy, its purpose was to address the increasing obsolescence of the industrial base of the three provinces of Jilin, Heilongjiang, and Liaoning in the Northeast region. This region, formerly called Manchuria, had been relatively more industrialized than other Chinese regions at the beginning of the People's Republic. The main reasons for this are twofold: the first is that much of its industrial capacity was preserved after the Japanese were defeated at the end of World War II; and the second relates to China's close ties with the former USSR during the 1950s, which had put most of their cooperative, industrial projects within the Northeast region. Since the early 1960s, however, as a result of the worsening relations between China and the former USSR, the Northeast region had become a first-front area reflecting the fact that China needed to prepare for the high probability of war against the USSR (see Chapter 9 for details).

Since the 1980s, the Chinese economy have benefited substantially from both reform and its open-door policy. However, the Northeast region has lagged behind other regions (especially the southeast and coastal provinces) during this period. In order to implement a regional coordinated development during the entire Tenth Five-Year Plan (2000–2005), the State Council spent 100 billion yuan in the Northeast region as part of its proposal to upgrade industry and to provide greater incentives for modernization. This interpretation of both the "Western Region Development Strategy" and the "Resurgence of the Old Industrial Base in the Northeast Region" provides another point of contrast with the Third Front strategy that was implemented during the pre-reform period.

Inevitably because the Third Front strategy was less openly announced and more tightly focused with a highly specific policy goal (defense in the event of invasion) the projects implemented in the twenty-first century have been considerably more contested in its formulation and may also be in its implementation.

8.5 Summary

In theory, multiregional economic cooperation and trade must be mutually beneficial to all of the provinces concerned, given the complementarity in natural resource endowments as well as other economic attributes. However, in China the costs arising from the transactions between provinces cannot be underestimated. Among the factors that hinder attempts at coordination are the differing sub-administrative systems of Chinese provinces and their specific internal social and cultural conditions. Thus, the extent of progress in economic cooperation between the provinces must depend upon the extent to which the related sides pragmatically reorganize and respond to the economic and non-economic benefits and costs involved. If the Chinese economy falls under the jurisdiction of a single political authority, the economic relationship between its internal locations and sectors may be regulated easily by means of unified economic policies and the inefficiencies of allocation of production factors can, therefore, be eliminated. But as the Chinese economy is administered by different regional authorities, this problem cannot be solved so easily.

The experiences and lessons from both developed and developing countries in the postwar period have demonstrated that the success of a nation in promoting its economic development depends, to a large extent, on a complete legal system and effective management and supervision mechanisms of its own. China's efforts to this end have achieved some progress, but some large-scale changes are still needed. In fact, the "commodity wars" between provinces and autonomous regions derived from the fact that China has no constitutional clauses which specifically prohibit restraints on interprovincial commerce, even though the central government has been increasingly concerned and many regulations and laws relating to the protection of multiregional cooperation and the removal of local economic blockades have been issued by the State Council (1980a, 1982, 1986 and 1990) and the NPC (1993).

Despite the mutually complementary conditions between many of its different regions, the Chinese economy has been internally affected by various geographic, institutional and cultural barriers that exist between provincial administrations. Following a theoretical analysis of the spatial efficiency of authoritarianism, this chapter studies the possibilities and conditions under which the Chinese economy can (or cannot) be optimized spatially. In this chapter, we have also analyzed the economic impacts of China's sub-political borders. The result shows that the multiregional complementarities have not been utilized fully and that because of this existing cross-border separation the Chinese economy cannot be spatially optimized. As a practical measure to overcome the interregional barriers and to provide a "bridge" for spatial economic integration, since the early 1980s China has established different forms and levels of multiregional economic cooperative zones. The particular focus of the final part of this chapter has also examined China's various efforts in the search for spatial economic integration.

8.6   Case study: Fighting for rainfalls?

On an overcast day in the western vicinity of Beijing, you will hear the booming sound of anti-aircraft guns from the mountainside of Xiangshan Hills Park. Please don't be startled. That was neither an air raid drill, nor in preparation for a coming war. Rather, it was the sound of Beijing meteorologists shooting canisters of silver iodide into the gathering clouds. The Beijing municipal government has instructed the meteorological workers to shoot at any clouds that could increase the levels of rainfall over the drought-stricken city. In addition to Beijing, other major cities such as Tianjin have also called in soldiers to scan the sky for signs of clouds.

China's first man-made precipitation enhancement was conducted in 1958. It has now become the world's largest cloud seeder, using an array of methods to disperse chemicals into cloud layers in order to make rain. Between 1995 and 2003, China spent a total of US$266 million on rainmaking technology in 23 provinces, autonomous regions, and municipalities, with some 35,000 people working in the field. In 2003 alone, China spent about US$50 million to disperse chemicals into clouds through the use of 30 airplanes, 3,800 rockets, and 6,900 high artillery shells (CMB, 2004). In addition, numerous aircrafts, old anti-aircraft guns, balloons and even mountaintop dispersal devices have been employed by provincial and local meteorological bureaus and rainmaking authorities (note that by law private companies are not entitled to conduct rainmaking activities in China) to fire chemicals into the clouds.

This man-made precipitation has also been part of the efforts of local meteorological authorities to establish a long-term mechanism aimed at minimizing the losses caused by bad weather such as prolonged heatwaves or heavy fogs. China experiences almost all of the water-related problems faced by countries across the world. China's rapid economic growth, industrialization, and urbanization have outpaced infrastructural investment and management capacity, and have created widespread problems of water scarcity. The degradation of groundwater resources and the deterioration of groundwater quality have become striking environmental problems in many Chinese cities. In the areas of the North China Plain, where about half of China's wheat and corn is grown as well as plenteous peach orchards, drought is an ever-looming threat.

Scientific rainmaking or precipitation enhancement began in 1946 when the American scientists Vincent Schaefer and Bernard Vonnegu at General Electric (GE), following up on some laboratory observations, "seeded" a cloud with dry ice and then watched snow fall from its base. Until recent times it was thought that rain might be induced by explosions, updrafts from fires, or by giving the atmosphere a negative charge. Research showed that rain forms in warm clouds when larger drops of condensed water grow at the expense of smaller ones until they become large enough to fall; furthermore, in cold clouds super-cooled water below $-15°C$ freezes into ice crystals that act as nuclei for snow (Battan, 1962).[12] It was also important to determine what kinds of clouds were suitable for seeding. It was found that, for reasons that were not very well understood, there were important differences between clouds formed over land and over sea, with many more but much smaller droplets in continental clouds. Since larger droplets are needed if rain is to form, this meant that continental clouds were much less likely than maritime ones to be a good source of rain, a discovery of considerable significance to would-be Australian rainmakers. The temperature of the upper levels of the cloud was found to be another critical factor. In the case of both cumulus and stratiform clouds, provided this temperature was lower than $-7°C$, seeding would inevitably be followed by precipitation within 20–25 minutes (Ryan and King, 1997, p. 21).

The factors controlling the distribution of rainfall over the earth's surface include the belts of converging-ascending airflow, air temperature, moisture-bearing winds, ocean currents, the distance from the coast, and the presence of mountain ranges. Ascending air is cooled by expansion, which results in the formation of clouds and the production of rain. Conversely, in the broad belts of descending air are found the great desert regions of the earth, descending air being warmed by compression and, consequently, absorbing rather than releasing moisture. If the temperature is low, the air has a small moisture capacity and is able to produce little precipitation. When winds blow over the ocean, especially over areas of warm water (where the evaporation of moisture into the air is active) toward a given coastal area, that area receives more rainfall than a similar area where the winds blow from the interior toward the oceans. Areas near the sea receive more rain than inland regions, since the winds constantly lose moisture and may be quite dry by the time they reach the interior.

The production of rain by artificial means is now generally disregarded by many Western countries, although it is probable that rainmaking hastens or increases rainfall from clouds suitable for natural rainfall. The existing rainmaking techniques have been only moderately successful. Without clouds, there can be no rainfall. So rainmaking activities cannot be relied upon in cases of drought. On the other hand, it should be noted that some clouds would almost certainly result in rainfall, regardless of the artificial seeding. To judge the viability of a rainmaking program, it is important to establish that seeding made a difference – that is, it results in rain from clouds that would not otherwise have yielded it naturally. It was difficult to determine whether fluctuations in rainfall that occur at the time of cloud-seeding were produced by seeding or would have occurred naturally. Besides, the over-seeding can sometimes dissipate a cloud. Researches conducted in China showed that even the best efforts of China's rainmakers produce an increase in rainfall of only 10–15 percent (CMB, 2002). In addition, the vagaries of nature, such as wind direction and velocity, mean the effect of cloud-seeding on any given locality is difficult to predict.

In China, when rare clouds appear over this often-parched region, it has been common practice for workers at the local weather bureau to roll out anti-aircraft guns and blast away at the sky. The exploding shells contain fine particles of silver iodide, which scatter through the moisture-laden clouds. Provincial, county and municipal governments in almost all of the country's 32 provinces, autonomous regions, and municipalities have set up weather modification bureaus assigned to regularly bombard the heavens with chemicals in the hopes of squeezing out more rainfall for demanding farmers and thirsty city dwellers.

With persistent drought still plaguing China, some neighboring regions have begun to squabble about clouds. The most hotly debated topic is around the issue of upwind neighbors unfairly intercepting clouds for seeding, and as a result depriving downwind areas of rainfall. Given the severity of water shortages in northern China, such sensitivity is unsurprising. In a large part of central and northern China, the annual rainfall has decreased significantly in the past two decades, while the level of population has soared. Rivers run dry at certain times of year. A typical case of the accusation of "rain theft" arose in central China's Henan province, after a heavy rainstorm in mid-2004.

Between July 9 and 11, 2004, a moisture-laden cloud drifted northeast across the sky of Nanyang in southern Henan province. This was very good news for all of the northeastern administrative areas (including Pingdingshan, Zhumadian, Luohe and Xuchang cities and Zhoukou prefecture), since most of these areas were experiencing serious droughts during that period. In order to obtain a larger share of rainfall for themselves, the five cities and prefectures competed, using thousands of rocket shells and old anti-aircraft guns to shoot canisters of chemicals into the cloud. The final result of the rainmaking was significant but uneven in geographical distribution: the largest rainfall occurred in Pingdingshan and Xuchang cities (each recording a rainfall of 100 mm or more); while Zhoukou prefecture, with the same input as the other four cities, had only a 27 mm rainfall in its urban area and a paltry 7 mm in the rural area where the need of rainfall was the most urgent (Liu, 2004).

Zhoukou officials complained to a provincial newspaper *Dahe Bao* (Big River News) and to the national Xinhua news agency that the neighboring cities had milked the cloud system nearly dry even before it arrived in their area. Municipal officials later demanded legislation to regulate how to divvy up the clouds (*China Daily*, 2004). Meteorologists in Zhoukou were accusing their counterparts in Pingdingshan of overusing natural resources by intercepting clouds that would have been likely to drift on to other places – such as Zhoukou. "Some places have abused rainwater resources", said a Zhoukou expert who asked not to be named. Zhoukou's meteorological officials stated that the Pingdingshan Weather Modification Office had repeatedly seeded clouds that, if nature had been allowed to follow its course, would have scudded along to other places – such as Zhoukou – before delivering their rainfall.

The Pingdingshan office responded. "We didn't grab the clouds away from other cities," declared the office director, who gave his name only as Wang. "What we are doing is quite a scientific thing. And we reported our cloud-seeding schedule to the provincial government. I believe other cities also did so," Wang said in a telephone interview with the *Washington Post* correspondent, Edward Cody. "The water vapor resource is not like water resources in a river, which could be intercepted from points upstream. Or it is not like a cake – if I have a bite, others get only a smaller piece. Besides, clouds change while floating in the sky, so it is quite complicated."[13]

Over the next two decades, China's economy is expected to grow at a higher rate than the global average. This rapid economic growth, along with continued increases in population, will place an increasing stress on China's natural resource base, especially in relation to the availability of fresh water. Over the next few decades sustainable growth depends in part upon how China deals properly with issues and policies relating to water resources. The demands of intensive farming and burgeoning industrial development, as well as waste and pollution, add to the area's problem of low rainfall. In 2001, China consumed four times as much water for each unit of GDP than the world average (NBS, 2002). China has the opportunity to increase its available water supplies through careful management. Initiatives to encourage the more efficient use of existing water supplies are already underway in some areas. The difficulties will be for national and local governments to craft policies and rules within China's complex cultural and legal-administrative system that provide incentives for users to increase the efficiency of water use, and for polluters to clean up the water they use and return clean water to stream flows (Crook and Diao, 2000, p. 28).

Facing this projected increasing shortage of water supplies, China is experimenting with various precipitation enhancement technologies: as we have shown earlier, airplanes, rocket shells, and old anti-aircraft guns are used to shoot canisters of chemicals such as silver iodide, liquid nitrogen and calcium chloride into the sky in order to build up moisture in the clouds and increase the levels of rainfall. Better water management can increase the available water supply. China abhors open feuding between government bodies. But China's increasingly acute water shortage is causing tempers to fray.

Based on the historical climate data, some Chinese and western scientists predicted at an international conference held in Beijing in May 2002, that eastern and central China (the location, for instance, of those regional rivalries in rainmaking in Henan province discussed in the earlier section) would experience a hotter and drier climate from 2001 till 2030, by which time the available water will decrease by 20 percent (Sun *et al.*, 2002).

Indeed, the rational and optimal utilization of cloud resources among the neighboring administrative areas is becoming an increasingly pressing legal and institutional problem that must be solved appropriately by the Chinese authorities at both central and local levels. To date, China, like most other countries, has not had any laws and administrative regulations dealing with cloud resources or the rational application of manmade precipitation enhancement. However, if this disordered competition in rainmaking continues to exist among the neighboring administrative areas, perhaps some day in the future, the anti-aircraft guns and missiles that are currently used to shoot clouds to make rainfall might be turned to more militaristic purposes.

9
Industrialization and Technological Progress

> A man of the state of Song was worried about his seedlings growing too slowly. He pulled up the seedlings one by one and came home exhausted, saying to his family 'I am tired out today because I have helped the seedlings to grow'. Hearing this, his son hurried to the fields and found that all the seedlings had shrivelled up. There are very few in the world who will refrain from helping the seedlings grow. But there are some who think it useless to give any help and give up. They are those who do not weed the fields. Whereas there are others who want the shoots to grow quickly by pulling them upward. In their case, not only is it of no help, it actually does harm.
>
> – Mencius (372–289 BC)

9.1 China's industrialization efforts

Before the foundation of the PRC in 1949 China had been a typical agrarian society, with more than 90 percent of its population living in rural areas. Thereafter, the Chinese government abandoned the old political and economic systems through the socialist transformation of the capitalist industry and commerce. Between 1949 and 1956, some 123,000 capitalist enterprises were transformed into 87,900 industrial units under joint state–private ownership and, at the same time, many small workshops run by individual laborers were reorganized as collectives (Liao, 1982, p. 130).

During the early period of the PRC, the development of modern and comprehensive industry had always been given the highest priority. With the direct involvement of central and local government, the targets of the first Five-Year Plan (FYP), from 1953 to 1957, were fully completed.

Among the pre-reform FYPs, the first FYP (1953–57) has been generally known to be most successful, because many key macroeconomic issues, such as the relationship between industry and agriculture and the setting of an appropriate rate of accumulation, were properly handled in this FYP. However, some economic problems in relation to over-centralized administration and non-economic methods of management that have been reformed since the late 1970s had their origins in that period.

The time of the first FYP saw national income increased annually by an average of 8.9 percent and the annual growth rate of gross value of industrial output (GVIO) was 18.0 percent (see Table 9.1). As the first FYP was nearing its completion, Mao Zedong pointed out at an expanded meeting of the Political Bureau of the CCPCC held on 25 April 1956: "The emphasis in our country's construction is on heavy industry. The production of the means of production must be given priority, that's settled. But it definitely does not follow that the production of the means of subsistence, especially grain, can be neglected" (Mao, 1956, p. 285). In the subsequent years, however, the construction of heavy industry was overheated.

Guided by Mao's general line of building socialism with "greater, faster, better and more economical results" (*duo kuai hao sheng*), the Great Leap Forward (GLF) movement was launched by the Chinese government, who called for a doubling of output within one year (Mao, 1957, p. 491). For example, in 1958, the target for steel production was raised from the planned output of 6.3 million tons to 10.7 million tons (Liu, 1982, p. 32). Obviously, the achievement of this target was impossible because of the limitations of production capacity and resource bases. Nevertheless, the fulfillment of the quota was stubbornly insisted upon and consequently tens of millions of people had to be mobilized for steel production. The scale of capital construction grew dramatically so that the rate of accumulation suddenly rose from 24.9 percent in 1957 to 33.9 percent in 1958 (SSB, 1990b).

Stimulated by the arbitrary directions given by the central authorities, many heavy industrial enterprises were set up during the GLF period (1958–60), with no consideration being given to their sources of raw materials or their technological requirements. The quality was low and many unwanted and unusable goods were produced, resulting in great losses. Even worse, as large quantities of materials and labor were diverted toward the development of heavy industries, the development of agriculture and light industry received accordingly less attention. Millions of peasants abandoned farming to dig for ore and fell trees in order to make steel using indigenous methods. This situation lasted until 1960,

Table 9.1 Major economic indicators during the pre-reform period

Item	1950–52	1953–57	1958–62	1963–65	1966–70	1971–75	1976	1977	1978
1 Annual growth rate (%)									
1.1 National income	19.3	8.9	-3.1	14.5	8.4	5.6	-2.7	7.8	12.3
1.2 gross value of agricultural output (GVAO)	14.1	4.5	-4.3	11.1	3.9	4.0	2.5	1.7	9.0
1.3 gross value of industrial output (GVIO)	34.8	18.0	3.8	17.9	11.7	9.1	1.3	14.3	13.5
(1) heavy industry	48.8	25.4	6.6	14.9	14.7	10.2	0.5	14.3	15.6
(2) light industry	29.0	12.9	1.1	21.2	8.4	7.7	2.4	14.3	10.8
2 Accumulation/national income (%)		24.2	30.8	22.7	26.3	33.0	30.9	32.3	36.5
3 National income/investment ratio (%)		35.0	1.0	57.0	26.0	16.0	-10.0	26.0	34.0
4 Distribution of capital construction									
4.1 Agriculture (%)		7.8	12.3	18.8	11.8	11.3			
4.2 Light industry (%)		5.9	5.2	3.9	4.0	5.4			
4.3 Heavy industry (%)		46.5	56.1	49.8	57.4	54.8			

Sources: Liang (1982, p. 63, tab. 4); Dong (1982, pp. 88–9, tab. 9).

resulting in serious imbalances between accumulation and consumption and also between, on the one hand, heavy industry and agriculture and, on the other, light industry. In the rural areas, however, the harvest was poor despite the high yields. Consequently, from 1959 onwards, there was a spectacular fall in the levels of agricultural production. The gross value of agricultural output (GVAO) in 1961 was 26.3 percent below that in 1958; compared with the preceding year, industrial production dropped by an incredible 38.2 percent in 1961 and then again by 16.6 percent in 1962. The productivity of industrial labor was 5.4 percent lower in 1962 than in 1957, while the level of national income declined by 14.4 percent over the same period (Liang, 1982, p. 60). Although natural disasters and the deterioration of Sino-Soviet ties played some role in these setbacks, the major cause should be ascribed to China's overheated industrial policy.

In the following years, attempts were made to achieve economic readjustment in order to correct some of the previous errors. Factories were closed, suspended, merged, or switched to other lines of production. The construction of some large plants was either cancelled or delayed. Many industrial workers were redeployed to the countryside (*xiafang*). During the readjustment period (1963–65), some sound progress towards industrial construction was made. The launching of the Cultural Revolution in 1966 and the ten years of social chaos that followed, however, disrupted this process. Similar errors of blind and subjective leadership of industrialization were committed. Many large-scale industrial enterprises were constructed which lacked adequate sources of raw materials and gave no consideration to either the availability of transport and social needs.

From the early 1960s to the late 1970s, China undertook a spatial division of its economy into three fronts according to the principle of "preparing for wars":

- The eastern (coastal) provinces were defined as the first line because of their proximity to the capitalist world;
- A number of inland provinces (such as Sichuan, Guizhou, Shaanxi, Gansu, Qinghai, Ningxia, Yunnan, the western parts of Hubei, Hunan, Henan, Shanxi and Hebei, the northern part of Guangdong, and the northwest part of Guangxi) – most of which are covered by mountains – were treated as the third-front;
- The remaining provinces were treated as the second-front.

During the Cultural Revolution period (1966–76), the development of the third-front area was given priority in the Chinese process of industrialization as it was believed that World War III would occur very

Box 9.1   World dynamics: a pessimist viewpoint

In the early 1970s, and based on system dynamics – a technique rooted in conceptions from control theory, organization theory, and on the available techniques of computer simulation – developed by Jay W. Forrester, a MIT research team constructed a computer model to simulate likely future outcomes of the world economy. The most prominent feature of system dynamics is the use of feedback loops to explain behavior. It is a unique tool for dealing with questions about the way complex systems behave through time. The standard model run assumes no major change in the physical, economic, or social relationships that have historically governed the development of the world system. All variables included in the model follow historical values from 1900 to 1970. One end result of this ambitious study was originally published in 1972 under the title *The Limits to Growth* (Meadows *et al.*, 1972) and subsequently updated and revised in 1992 under the tile *Beyond the Limits* (Meadows *et al.*, 1992).

Three main conclusions were reached by this study. The first suggests that within a time span of less than 100 years, society will run out of the nonrenewable resources on which the world's industrial base depends. When the resources have been depleted, a precipitous collapse of the economic system will result, manifested in massive unemployment, decreased food production, and a decline in population. The characteristic behavior of the system is collapse. The second conclusion of this study is that piecemeal approaches to resolving the individual problems will not be successful. As its final conclusion, the study suggests that overshoots and collapse can be avoided only by an immediate limit on population and pollution, as well as a cessation of economic growth. Thus, according to this study, one way or the other, growth will cease eventually. Still, the authors conclude that it is possible to avoid the collapse if we make the right choices now.

soon and that the first-front area could inevitably become the battlefield. As a result of the government's involvement, the third-line area's share of China's capital investment increased sharply from 30.60 percent in the first FYP (1953–57) to 52.70 percent in the third FYP (1966–70) and the per capita GVIO increased from 22.04 yuan in 1952 to 373.97 yuan in 1983, while the coastal area increased from 93.77 yuan to 871.3 yuan

Table 9.2 Industrial outputs of the third-front area as percentage of China (%)

Item	1952	1965	1978
Gross value of industrial output (GVIO)	17.9	22.3	25.7
Steel	13.9	19.4	27.9
Coal	33.0	40.9	47.6
Electricity	10.5	25.2	33.5
Machine tools	2.2	15.7	27.3
Car	–	–	12.1
Tractor	–	77.4	30.6
Cement	14.1	13.6	37.0
Clothing	15.9	27.9	30.7
Paper	7.1	14.5	23.0
Cigarette	28.6	34.5	42.0

Source: Liu (1983).

during the same period (Jao and Leung, 1986, pp. 3, 6). Promoted by the third-front development strategy, many large and key enterprises (principally in the military, aeronautical, electronic and other high-tech industries), universities, and research institutions were transferred from the coastal (urban) area (the first-line) to the mountainous, remote, and, usually, rural inland area (the third-front).[1]

The third-front area development policy rapidly industrialized some areas of China's inland provinces (see Table 9.2) and provided a template for developing countries to avoid the "polarization" between rich and poor areas. Between 1953 and 1978, the annual GVIO growth rates of Shaanxi, Qinghai, Shanxi, Guizhou and Sichuan provinces reached 20.1 percent, 16.3 percent, 12.0 percent, 11.2 percent and 11.8 percent, respectively, which were much higher than those of the coastal provinces (Hu *et al.*, 1995, p. 5). However, this has not been identified as a successful approach to the modernization of the Chinese economy as a whole. This can be demonstrated by the fact that the average annual capital output coefficient (that is, output/investment ratio) of the third-front area was only 0.256, far less than that of the coastal area (0.973) during the period 1953–79 (Liu, 1984, p. 270). In addition, Yang (1989, p. 76) estimates that there would have been a net increase of 1,434 billion yuan GVIO (in other words, approximately 45 percent of China's total GVIO in 1975), had the investment been distributed in the coastal area rather than the third-front area during that period.

Following the death of Mao Zedong in September 1976, the Chinese government once again tried to accelerate the rate of economic development by setting targets that were much higher than any possible maximum capabilities. These impetuous and unrealistic plans began in 1978 and resembled, in many ways, those of the Great Leap Forward that had begun two decades earlier. Proposals were made enthusiastically by the post-Mao leadership to produce 400 million tons of grain, 60 million tons of steel, 250 million tons of oil, and to develop 120 large and medium-sized projects, including ten major oilfields, ten major steel plants and ten major coal mines, and to import large amounts of modern equipment and technology by the end of the Sixth FYP (1981–85).[2] It was not until the Third Plenum of the 11th CCPCC in December 1978 that the Chinese government began to shift the main focus of its national task from the "class struggle" to the realization of socialist economic construction, calling on the entire people to strive to achieve the four modernization – of industry, agriculture, national defense and science and technology – at the end of the twentieth century. However, many economic problems had been cyclically generated by the previous political struggles and could not be solved immediately. In late 1979, China decided to call a temporary halt to industrial expansion and carried out a policy entitled "readjustment, reform, consolidation and improvement" (*tiaozheng, gaige, gonggu, tigao*) in order to tackle properly the existing structural imbalances of the Chinese economy. This policy lasted for three years and many industrialization programs did not start to work until 1984.

During the pre-reform period, China's industrialization was implemented mainly through a system of central planning. Direct and strong government participation and large-scale mobilization of resources to priority sectors enabled the industrial sector to grow at an average rate of over 10 percent annually (with a few exceptions in 1961–62, 1967–68 and 1974), resulting in a dramatic increase of its share in national income from 19.5 percent in 1953 to 49.4 percent in 1978 (see Table 9.1 and Figure 9.1). The shares of agricultural, light and heavy industrial outputs in GVIAO changed structurally from 56.9 percent, 27.8 percent and 15.3 percent in 1952 to 24.6 percent, 35.4 percent and 40.0 percent, respectively, in 1980 (Liang, 1982, p. 56, tab. 3). The advantages of rapid industrial expansion from a centrally planned mechanism, however, were soon outweighed by the problems of low levels of efficiency, an unbalanced industrial structure dominated by heavy industry, sluggish technological progress, sectoral imbalances, and sharp annual fluctuations in growth rates. In addition, the self-reliant and inward-looking

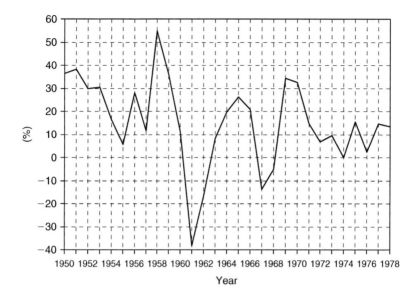

Figure 9.1 Industrial growth during the pre-reform period

policies that had been implemented by the Chinese government for most of the pre-reform period were bore responsibility for these poor industrial performances.

9.2 Post-reform industrialization

9.2.1 General background

"Industry" can be defined as the material production sector which engages in the extraction of natural resources and the processing and reprocessing of natural resources and agricultural products. With regard to the division between light and heavy industry, definitions vary from country to country. According to China's official definition (SSB, 1996, p. 405), "light" refers to an industry that produces consumer goods and tools. This comprises two categories: (1) using farm products as raw materials; and (2) using non-farm products as raw materials. Heavy industry refers to general products used by other manufacturers. According to the purpose of production or use of products, heavy industry is divisble into three separate branches: (1) the extraction of petroleum, coal, metal, and non-metal ores and timber felling; (2) smelting and processing of metals, coke making and coke chemistry, chemical materials and building materials such as cement, plywood, and power, petroleum and coal processing; and (3) machine-building industry which equips sectors of the national economy, metal structure industry and cement works, industry producing the means of agricultural production, and the chemical fertilizers and pesticides industry.

Between the early 1950s and the end of the Cultural Revolution, China devoted much of its energy to heavy industrialization at the expense of agriculture and light and service sectors (see the last rows of Table 9.1). Since the early 1980s, the Chinese government has effectively shifted the emphasis away from heavy industry to industries that have a more direct connection with people's lives. This is a correct approach for China to undertake not only because those industries can meet people's demands but also because they are *labor-intensive* and therefore more appropriate for the conditions prevailing in China – a country which benefits from a cheap and abundant labor supply.

Since the end of the Cultural Revolution, industrial fluctuations have been reduced significantly. At the beginning of the economic reform, the industrial output increased annually by over 10 percent, but this declined to a meager 5 percent in 1981. The industrial growth rate rose by over 20 percent in 1985, followed again by less than 10 percent during 1989–90 as a result of the conservative and tight monetary policy employed by the government. Since the early 1990s, China's industrial output has achieved the longest and fastest growth in the post-reform period (see Figure 9.2).

Economic development, a final result of industrialization, also determines the industrial structure of a country. Increases in per capita income usually lead to increased consumption, which in turn shifts the industrial structure away from agriculture toward manufacturing and service sectors. This also determines the distribution of the labor force among the industries. Between 1952 and 2000, China's sectoral employment shares had changed from more than 80 percent to about 50 percent for primary industry, and from less than 10 percent to more than 20 percent for both secondary and tertiary industries (shown in Figure 9.3). Regardless of the increasing move toward secondary and tertiary industries, Chinese employment has still been dominated by primary industries, especially in the western provinces (such as Tibet, Yunnan, Guizhou, Guangxi), with the exception of a few provinces whose employment is dominated by secondary industries (for example, Shanghai, Tianjin, and Liaoning) and tertiary industries (such as Beijing) in the coastal area.

Since the early 1980s, there has been a fundamental change in the investment system, characterized mainly by decentralization and

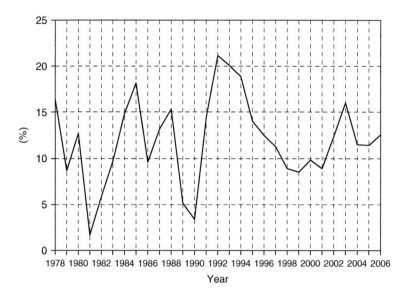

Figure 9.2 Industrial growth during the post-reform period

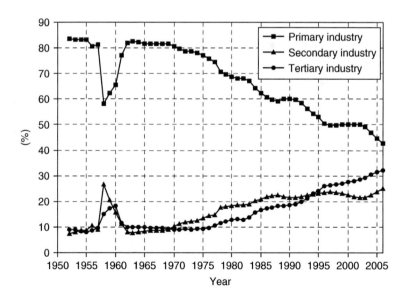

Figure 9.3 Employment by type of industry

regional autonomy. In respect of decentralization, the responsibilities are shared proportionally between central and local governments: (1) projects which are closely related to the overall structure of the national economy, such as key energy, raw material industry bases, transprovincial communication and transportation networks, key mechanical, electronic, and other high-tech development projects, key agricultural bases as well as the national defense industry, are still financially controlled by the state; (2) the primary industrial and local projects, such as agriculture, forestry and wood, local energy, raw material industries, regional communication and transportation networks, mechanical and light industries, science and technology, education, culture, public health, urban public infrastructure and services and so on, are mainly invested and managed by local government. In the case of regional autonomy, the quotas of industrial construction and technological remolding items that needed to be approved by the State Planning Commission (SPC) were increased: from 30 million yuan or more to 50 million yuan or more for energy, communication, and raw materials industries; and from 10 million yuan or more to 30 million yuan or more for light and other industries. Production construction items beyond the above limits and non-productive construction items are to be determined by the provinces themselves (Yang, 1993, p. 179).

9.2.2   Rural industrialization

In the early 1950s, almost 90 percent of the Chinese population lived in the countryside and earned their living from the land. During the period up to the end of the 1990s, this proportion decreased gradually to two-thirds, although the total rural population increased during the same period. It is inevitable that the situation of a rapidly increasing rural population combined with limited cultivable land will generate a large rural labor surplus, particularly given the increased productivity that has resulted from the introduction of advanced technologies.

In 1978, more than 80 percent of the population in China still lived in rural areas. Over the following years, the rural population as a percentage of the total population in China experienced a substantial reduction as a result of industrial expansion. However, in the 1990s it was still higher than that found in many other countries, for example, the USA (3.9 percent), Japan (10.7 percent), the UK (2.6 percent), West Germany (4.9 percent), South Korea (33.5 percent) and India (66.2 percent) (UNFAO, 1992). This was, to a large extent, the result of the long-standing government policy that exercised strict control over rural–urban migration. With little prospect for expanding cultivated land and a large and still growing population, the Chinese government began to recognize the urgency of shifting the rural labor force from farming to more productive non-agricultural sectors. However, the government also remained convinced that this occupational shift must be achieved without significantly enlarging the urban population through rural–urban migration. Accordingly, the period since the 1970s has witnessed the implementation of the policy entitled *"litu bu lixiang, jinchang bu jincheng"* (leave the soil but not the countryside, enter the factory but not the city).

The growth of the rural industrial sector has been extremely rapid and is largely responsible for the dramatic increases in income levels in rural China. Almost overnight, a large number of new industrial activities emerged and millions of private, shareholding or other enterprise (PSEs) and collectively-owned enterprises (COEs) were established in the countryside. Of particular importance in this respect is the rapid growth of enterprises that are collectively owned and operated by the townships and villages. The proliferation of township and village-based enterprises (TVEs) has had far-reaching consequences, because millions of rural workers have shifted from farming to industrial activities and in the process helped to transform the economic structure of rural China. For example, in 1978, rural non-agricultural workers accounted for only 7.12 percent of total rural workers. By 2000, however, the share of rural non-agricultural workers in the total rural labors had quadrupled to more than 30 percent.[3]

The growth in the number of the TVEs is extraordinary. In 1978, there were only 1.524 million TVEs in rural areas, whereas by 1995 the number of TVEs had increased dramatically – to 22.027 million. Output has grown by over 30 percent per annum since 1978. The share of value-added output in GDP rose from about 10 percent in the early 1980s to more than 30 percent in 1995 (SSB, 1996, pp. 387–90). The TVEs created a large number of jobs for the surplus rural workers and contributed significantly to the growth of the Chinese economy during the 1980s and 1990s. Total factor productivity in the TVEs is much higher than in the state sector and is growing by 5 percent a year, more than twice the rate in the SOEs (World Bank, 1996, p. 51). The factors that have contributed to the remarkable growth and superior efficiency record of the TVEs include the following:

(1) *Decentralization plus financial discipline.* The 1984 decentralization of fiscal power in China allowed sub-national governments to retain locally generated revenues, creating powerful incentives for the development of local industry. Under this system a non-performing

TVE becomes an unaffordable drain on a limited local budget. In the end persistent money-losers are closed and the workforce is transferred to more profitable lines.

(2) *Competition.* Studies also show intense competition for investment (including foreign investment) among communities with TVEs. Success in attracting investment is affected by reputation and local economic performance.

(3) *Market opportunities and rural saving.* A past bias against light industry and services has created vast market opportunities, buttressed by high rural savings and demand following the agricultural reforms of 1978 and by the limited scope for emigration from rural areas.

(4) *Links with the state enterprise sector.* The large state-owned industrial sector provides a natural source of demand, technology and raw materials for many TVEs.

Kinship and implicit property rights were characteristics of the TVEs (World Bank, 1996, p. 51). Strong kinship links among rural Chinese villagers, although encouraging responsibility in entrepreneurs, especially during the 1980s, have had potential risks thereafter since they do not exhibit the basic principles of market economic systems. The system of implicit, if fuzzy property rights was improved compared to the people's commune system (PCS) of the pre-reform period and this led to a productive combination of risk and reward sharing between entrepreneurs and local government. However, the incentives facing TVEs are less than those of private firms. In addition, the proliferation of industrial activities in rural China stemming from rural reform created numerous opportunities for China's rural population. The rural residents have seized these opportunities aggressively and shifted large amounts of resources from agricultural to more profitable non-agricultural activities. It appears that large amounts of "surplus labor" existing in China have facilitated the rapid rural industrial development. The problems that have emerged in the process of rural industrialization are, *inter alia*, the occupation of farmland by TVEs, the possible adverse effects of rural industrial production on agriculture, the waste of energy by TVEs, and environmental pollution.[4]

In the 1990s, increasing institutional checks and balances increased the security of foreign investors, and FDI replaced the TVEs as a major driver of manufacturing growth (Winters and Yusuf, 2007, p. 29). A detailed analysis of the FDI and its contributions to the development of the Chinese economy is given in Chapter 11.

9.2.3   Rural–urban labor migration

Since the late 1960s the Chinese economy has been characterized by a labor surplus problem – a result of the uncontrolled population growth during the 1950s and the 1960s. While China's urban unemployment rate is not as high as is found in the developed nations,[5] there have been greater unemployment problems in rural China. In 1952, more than 87 percent of the Chinese population lived in the countryside and earned their living from the land. By 1995, this figure had decreased gradually to 70.96 percent. Yet the total rural population increased from 503.19 million to 859.47 million over the same period (SSB, 1996, p. 69). It is inevitable that the situation of a rapidly increasing rural population combined with a limited amount of cultivable land will generate a large rural labor surplus, particularly with the increased productivity resulting from the introduction of advanced technologies.

Since the 1980s, the seasonal movement of tens of millions of rural laborers (*mingong*) between the rural and urban areas has created a special scenario for the Chinese economy. Following the Spring Festival – the Chinese New Year which begins in late January or early February and lasts for about a month – the rural laborers leave for the urban areas where they are employed as industrial workers or self-employed as retailers and servants. During the planting and harvesting seasons in the Summer and Autumn, some of them may return home to take part in agricultural work. As migration from the countryside to the cities is strictly controlled by the government through a system of registration of urban residents, most of the *mingong* are still treated as "agricultural residents." The *mingong* phenomenon has been having a dramatic effect on Chinese society. First of all, it has met the needs of the workers in urban construction and other labor-intensive sectors. Secondly, it has become an important source of increases in rural income level and been mainly responsible for the socioeconomic changes in rural China.

In any consideration of the factors that have contributed to China's dramatic urban growth, particular emphasis should be given to the role of the large numbers of rural workers. In Beijing, for example, each year there are more than one million temporary migrants from the countryside. As a permanent resident in Beijing, I have found that these rural workers have carried out most of Beijing's physical work. Without these workers, Beijing's urban construction projects (such as those of the Bird's Nest and other new facilities used during the 2008 Olympic Games) would have been impossible. By contrast, very few, if any, of Beijing's "officially registered" and economically active population are now to be found carrying out physical and menial jobs in the low-level service sectors of the economy.[6] This phenomenon stems mainly from the fact that China's "one-child" policy has been implemented more strictly in urban than in rural areas. It is expected that, over the course of the next few years, this part of the rural population will continue to contribute to China's urban development, especially in those areas experiencing physical expansion and therefore physical laborers play a crucial role.

9.3   A comparative analysis

In order to conduct an international comparison of China's industrial performance during the post-reform period, one may simply employ the results estimated by Hsueh (1994b, pp. 74–99) for China and the results estimated by Chenery and Syrquin (1975, pp. 20–1) for the international case. Both results are based on the same specification shown below:

$$X = \alpha + \beta_1 \ln Y + \beta_2 (\ln Y)^2 + \gamma_1 \ln N + \gamma_2 (\ln N)^2 + \sum (\delta_i T_i) \qquad (9.1)$$

where X denotes each of the variables shown in the first column of Table 9.3; Y is the per capita national income (RMB yuan) at 1980 constant prices in the case of China and per capita GNP (US dollar) in the case of other countries; N is population size (million persons); and T_i

Table 9.3   Industrialization at different economic stages, Chinese and international cases

Variable	International case[a]			Chinese case[b]		
	US$100 (1)	US$400 (2)	(2)–(1) (3)	¥250 (4)	¥1000 (5)	(5)–(4) (6)
Va	0.452	0.228	−0.224	0.513	0.196	−0.317
Vm	0.149	0.276	0.127	0.276	0.584	0.308
Vl				0.118	0.282	0.164
Vh				0.164	0.303	0.139
Lp	0.658	0.438	−0.220	0.892	0.462	−0.431
Lm	0.091	0.135	0.144	0.041	0.323	0.282
Ls	0.251	0.327	0.076	0.067	0.215	0.149

a: Chenery and Syrquin (1975, pp. 20–1);
b: Hsueh (1994b, p. 80).
Variables: Va = ratio of value-added agricultural output in NI (national income); Vm = ratio of value-added industrial output in NI; Vl = ratio of value-added light industrial output in NI; Vh = ratio of value-added heavy industrial output in NI; Lp = ratio of labor of primary sector in total social labor; Lm = ratio of labor of manufacturing sector in total social labor; and Ls = ratio of labor of service sector in total social labor.

denotes the time period. In Hsueh's analysis, two periods (i.e., 1980–84 and 1985–89) were selected. Arguably this is reasonable, because the year 1985 was generally regarded as a watershed for China's HRS-based agricultural reform and urban industrial reform, while it was the latter that significantly influenced industrialization. For most provinces, per capita national income ranged between ¥250 and ¥1,000 during the 1980s, which can be converted approximately to the per capita GNP of US$100 to $400 for the international case during the period 1950 to 1970 in Chenery and Syrquin (1975).

From Table 9.3, we find that the industrial structure of China was similar to that found in many other countries. For both versions, the ratios of value-added agricultural output were in decline, while those of industrial output were increasing. However, the only difference is that China had larger marginal changes in industrial structure with respect to economic growth than the international version. For example, when the per capita GNP ranged from US$100 to US$400, the changes of the ratio of value-added agricultural output and the ratio of value-added industrial output in GNP were –0.224 and 0.127, respectively, for the international case; while the changes of the ratio of value-added agricultural output and the ratio of value-added industrial output in national income for the Chinese case were –0.317 and 0.308, respectively, during the approximately same development stage. Furthermore, when the per capita national income increased from 250 yuan to 1,000 yuan, the ratio of value-added light industrial output and the ratio of value-added heavy industrial output in national income increased by 0.164 and 0.139, respectively, implying that light industry served as a stronger engine for the Chinese economy than heavy industry. In Table 9.3, when the per capita national income increased from 250 yuan to 1,000 yuan, the ratio of value-added agricultural output in national income decreased from 0.513 to 0.196, and the ratio of primary sector labor to total social labor decreased from 0.892 to 0.462 accordingly; in contrast, when the per capita national income increased from 250 yuan to 1,000 yuan, the ratio of value-added industrial output in national income increased from 0.276 to 0.584, while the ratio of labor of the industrial sector to total social labor increased from 0.041 to 0.323 accordingly.

Industrialization in China differs considerably from region to region, as is demonstrated by the figures given in Table 9.4. For instance, the Eastern belt, with only 12 provinces and 13.5 percent of the land area, has 244,183 industrial enterprises under an independent accounting system, 10.5 percent more than that of the Central and Western belts as a whole (18 provinces), which account for 86.5 percent of the nation's land area.

Table 9.4   Major industrial indicators[a] by the Eastern, Central and Western belts

Item	Eastern	Central	Western
Number of enterprises (N)	244,183	156,075	64,981
Employees (thousand persons) (L)	44,770	27,527	12,822
Fixed assets (billion yuan) (K)	1,921.51	933.25	489.39
Newly-added output (billion yuan) (O)	905.15	382.93	181.92
Pre-tax profits (billion yuan) (P)	296.93	126.88	69.72
Average (million yuan) (K/N)	7.87	5.98	7.53
Size (persons) (L/N)	183.3	176.4	197.3
Capital/labor (yuan/person) (K/L)	429,196	339,031	381,680
Output/capital ratio (O/K)	0.47	0.41	0.37
Labor productivity (yuan/person) (O/L)	202,178	139,111	141,881
Income/output share (%) (P/O)	32.80	33.13	38.32
Profit/capital share (%) (P/K)	15.45	13.60	14.25

a: for industrial enterprises under independent accounting system only.
Source: calculated by the author based on SSB (1996b, pp. 79–81).

These regional industrial differences can be explored in further detail. In 1994, the number of employees and fixed assets in the Eastern belt were 62.6 percent and 105.9 percent higher than that in the Central belt, and 249.2 percent and 292.6 percent higher than that in the Western belt, respectively; while the GVIO, newly-added output and pre-tax profit in the Eastern belt were 185.7 percent, 136.4 percent and 134.0 percent higher than that in the Central belt, and 536.5 percent, 397.6 percent and 325.9 percent higher than that in the Western belt, respectively. From Table 9.4, we find that the relative industrial indicators of the Eastern belt were the best among the three belts. A glance at the Central and Western belts reveals that, with the exception of the output/capital ratio (O/K), all other relative industrial indicators were better in the Western belt than in the Central belt.

In order to conduct an in-depth comparison of industrial performances between different regions, we may build a multiregional production function. The general form of a Cobb–Douglas function can be written as $Y = e^\lambda K^\alpha L^\beta e^\mu$, where, Y = output, K = capital, L = labor, α = elastic coefficient of capita, β = elastic coefficient of labor, λ = factor of technological progress, and μ = system error. If we use a regional variable, D_1 (where, $D_1 = -1$ denotes the Western belt, $D_1 = 0$ denotes the Central belt, and $D_1 = 1$ denotes the Eastern belt) and a sectoral variable, D_2 (where $D_2 = -1$ denotes the resource-exploiting enterprises, $D_2 = 0$

Table 9.5 The elasticities of *K* and *L* on the industrial production

Sector	Western belt ($D_1 = -1$)		Central belt ($D_1 = 0$)		Eastern belt ($D_1 = 1$)	
	K	L	K	L	K	L
Resource-exploiting ($D_2 = -1$)	0.68	−0.32	0.66	−0.30	0.64	−0.23
Resource-processing ($D_2 = -0$)	0.51	−0.13	0.50	−0.10	0.48	−0.07
High-tech ($D_2 = -1$)	0.35	−0.04	0.33	−0.01	0.31	0.02

Source: Derived from Equation 9.3.

denotes the resource-processing enterprises, and $D_2 = 1$ denotes the high-tech enterprises), the modified Cobb–Douglas production function may be written in the log form:

$$\ln Y = \lambda_0 + (\alpha_0 + \alpha_1 D_1 + \alpha_2 D_2) \ln K + (\beta_0 + \beta_1 D_1 + \beta_2 D_2) \ln L \quad (9.2)$$

where, λ_0, α_0, α_1, α_2, β_0, β_1, β_2 are constants to be estimated. Using the data of 500 top industrial enterprises compiled by CEEC (1990), we obtain a log-form regression:[7]

$$\ln Y = 6.87 + (0.50 - 0.02 D_1 - 0.17 D_2) \ln K + (-0.10 + 0.03 D_1 + 0.09 D_2) \ln L$$

$$(10.11) \ (-4.53)(-2.40) \qquad (-17.0)(4.94) \ (2.51) \qquad (9.3)$$

where ln represents a natural logarithm, R^2 is a multiple correlation coefficient, F is the F-statistic and the figures in the parentheses under the parameters are the *t* statistics. Using Equation 9.3, we may obtain the elasticities of capital (*K*) and labor (*L*) on production for each geographical belt and industrial sector (see Table 9.5).

From the perspective of geography, we may find that: (1) the capital elasticity of the Western belt is larger than that of the Central belt, which is in turn larger than that of the Eastern belt, which suggests that the Western belt has the highest efficiency for capital input in large enterprises; (2) the labor elasticity of the Eastern belt is larger than that of the Central belt, and the latter is larger than that of the Western belt, which suggests that the Eastern belt has the highest efficiency for labor input in large enterprises.

From the perspective of the industrial sector, we may observe that: (1) the capital elasticity of the resource-exploiting enterprises is larger than that of the resource-processing enterprises, and the latter is larger than that of the high-tech enterprises, which suggests that the resource-exploiting enterprises have the highest level of efficiency for capital input in the large enterprises; (2) the labor elasticity of the high-tech enterprises is larger than that of the resource-processing enterprises, and the latter is larger than that of the resource-exploiting enterprises, which suggests that the high-tech enterprises have the highest level of efficiency for labor input in the large enterprises.

In addition, it is rather surprising that the labor elasticity is negative for all enterprises, with the exception of high-tech enterprises in the Eastern belt of China, implying that China's larger enterprises must have experienced some problems in relation to labor productivity.

9.4   Technological progress

Technological innovation has been the most fundamental element in the promotion, either directly or indirectly, of economic development and social change. Although it is very difficult to measure its short-term impact precisely, nobody would reject the notion that technological progress is changing the world at an incredible rate. The most obvious contribution is transport and communication that have changed from the primitive means (such as horses, carriages and hand-written letters) to advanced methods such as superjets, telephones and faxes as well as the increasingly efficient computer networks, of which the Internet has increasingly been becoming the most important means for transmitting information.

Before the early twentieth century, technological innovations had been contributed mainly by individual inventors or small-scale entrepreneurs. But now the great bulk of it – such as the invention of the space shuttle and the Internet, to list but two – has been conducted by prominent firms with substantial budgets, as well as by governments. As a result, the process of technological innovation becomes more complicated than ever before. Specifically, the technological and related products are positively related to capital stock of and personnel engagement in technological innovation. In addition, technological innovation is also related to the educational level, as the content of education changes over time to accommodate the growing stock of knowledge. There has been a proliferation of specialized intellectual disciplines to facilitate the absorption of knowledge and to promote its development through research.

Chinese inventions, including papermaking, gunpowder, movable-type printing and the compass, have made enormous contributions to world civilization. For example, paper was introduced in China in the second century AD, came to Japan in the seventh century, and was then diffused westward to Central Asia in the eighth century, North Africa in the tenth, Spain in the twelfth and northern Europe in the thirteenth. Printing was invented in China in the eighth century AD and movable type in the eleventh century, but this technology only reached Europe in the fifteenth century. Another Chinese invention, gunpowder, made in the ninth century, disseminated to the Arabs after a few hundred years and reached Europe in the fourteenth century (Braudel, 1981, p. 14). In recent centuries, however, China has lagged far behind Western nations in terms of technological innovation.[8]

After the foundation of the PRC in 1949, China began to import advanced technology from the Soviet Union. Unfortunately, this process came to an abrupt halt following the worsening of Sino-Soviet relations in the late 1950s. Following its *rapprochement* with the United States and Japan, China began the gradual importation of advanced technology from the capitalist nations. But economic relations between China and the technologically advanced nations did not improve significantly until the late 1970s when the new CCP and the state leaders tried to abandon the "leftist" ideology (of self-reliance and independence). By the early 1980s, China's production technology in the iron and steel industry was still comparable to that used in the advanced nations in the 1950s; similarly, the scientific and technological level of the electronic industry was approximately 15 to 20 years behind advanced international standards (Liao, 1982, p. 138). According to the national industrial census conducted in 1985, 23 percent of the machines and equipment used by 8,285 large and medium-sized companies were produced during the period from 1949 to 1970 (SSB, 1987b, p. 100).

It must be mentioned that some important advances in science and technology had been achieved during the pre-reform period. Notable technological milestones include the development of the atomic bomb in 1964 and of artificial satellites in 1970, which granted China a political seat among the superpowers. However, as this kind of technology has been controlled by the Science and Technology Commission for National Defense (STCND) and guided by the State Council and the Military Commission of the CCPCC, the transfer of military technology to social and economic uses is to some extent limited. Other sectors of the economy, such as China's metallurgical, coal, machine-building, oil, chemical, power, electric and precision instrument industries, had acquired a

Table 9.6   Some industrial production indicators, China and the advanced nations

Item	Advanced nations (1)	China (2)	(2)/(1) (3)
A. *Labor productivity*			
Steel (ton/person)	600–900	30	0.03–0.05
Electricity (kW/person)	2132[a]	244	0.114
Synthetic rubber (ton/person)	200–300	20–50	0.067–0.25
Ethylene (ton/person)	150	30	0.2
B. *Energy consumption*[b]			
Steel (kg/ton)	629	1034	1.64
Oil refinery (kg/ton)	19	22	1.16
Ethylene (1000 kal)	420–550	840	1.53–2.0
Electricity (g/kWh)	150	30	1.28

Notes:
a: USA.
b: Standard coal equivalent.
Source: IIE (1996, p. 40 and tabs. A and B).

stock of relatively advanced equipment. This provided the foundation for industrial modernization. Taken as a whole, however, the level of productivity still remained very low, as did the level of labor productivity.

For a considerable period, China followed an extensive development pattern and paid more attention to the construction of new industrial projects than to the renovation of old ones. It is often reported that outdated machinery and equipment is being used by many Chinese factories. Technologically outdated machinery and equipment implies low levels of labor productivity and high levels of energy consumption. In Table 9.6 the labor productivity in the Chinese steel, electricity and petrochemical industries is shown to be only between 3 and 25 percent that of the advanced nations, while the energy consumption level of China is 16 to 100 percent higher than that found in advanced nations. The technologically outdated machinery and equipment also lead to the manufacture of poor-quality products. According to the sample survey conducted by the State Technological Supervision Bureau in 1995, only 86.8 percent, 75.1 percent and 24.2 percent of the commodities of the SOEs, the TVEs and the PSEs, respectively, had met national standards (Huang, 1996, p. 11).

The large number of small-scale plants, particularly those in the energy and heavy industries, contribute widely to this high level of energy consumption. In addition, the use of inefficient facilities and equipment has been encouraged by the country's low energy prices. In market economies the energy price provides an incentive under which the efficient production and use of energy resources are guided properly. However, for a long period, especially during the pre-reform era, China's energy price was fixed at an artificially low level. These lower energy prices encouraged people to operate those facilities in ways that used more energy than they would have done if managers had taken account of the true costs of energy. These results have been the wasteful production of excess energy, idle factories and other facilities when sufficient energy is not available, and emission of more CO_2, SO_2 and other pollutants than necessary.

The Chinese economy has been regarded as very efficient in terms of energy consumption. As of 2004, China's energy intensity – a term that refers to the total primary energy consumption per dollar of GDP at market exchange rates) – was 1.53 times that of India, 2.71 times that of South Korea, 4.26 times that of the USA and 8.69 times that of Japan (EIA, 2006). If all of the above assumptions and projections hold up, China's oil consumption will increase continually and will account for an increasing portion of the global oil demand in the coming decades. This will place energy security at the top of China's economic agenda, and thus never before has this country been more eager to compete and secure cheap and stable overseas energy supplies.

In fact, Chinese policy makers clearly recognized the increasing role of technology in the Chinese economy and have also paid considerable attention to the acceleration of research and development (R&D).[9] According to UNESCO (1986), during the 1980–85 period the R&D/GNP ratio of China was, although lower than that of USA, Japan, West Germany, the UK and Switzerland, whose R&D/GNP ratios exceeded 2.0, higher than that found in Pakistan, Indonesia, Thailand and the Philippines, whose R&D/GNP ratios ranged between 1.0 and 0.4, and very similar to that of Austria, Australia, Denmark, Italy and South Korea, whose R&D ratios ranged between 1.0 and 1.2. Since the mid-1980s, China has implemented a package of plans for the development of new technology, high-technology and traditional technology. These plans include, *inter alia*,

- *"863" Plan*, which aims to track the frontiers of the high and new technologies and research and development;
- *Torchlight Plan*, which aims to promote the commercialization, industrialization and internationalization of the high-tech products;
- *The Climbing Plan*, which aims to organize the research and application of new and high technologies;

- *Spark Plan,* which aims to spread applicable technologies to small and medium-sized enterprises, TVEs and other rural areas; and
- *Harvest Plan,* which aims to popularize various kinds of technology contributing to agriculture, animal husbandry and fishery.

However, many problems still exist in the Chinese science and technology sector, particularly during the 1990s. For example, China's R&D/GNP ratio declined rapidly alongside its GNP growth from the late 1980s to the mid-1990s. In 1995, China's expenditure on R&D was only 0.50 percent of GNP, compared with the R&D/GNP ratios of 0.93 percent in 1979 and 1.12 percent in 1986.[10] According to UNESCO (1995, tab. 5), the R&D/GNP ratio of China was much lower than that of many advanced countries, including the USA (2.9 percent, 1988), Japan (3.0 percent, 1991), France (2.4 percent, 1991) and the UK (2.1 percent, 1991).

Minami (1994, p. 116) have found that the R&D/GNP ratio rises sharply with respect to per capita GNP in developing countries when the per capita GNP is less than US$11,000 and in the newly industrialized economies (NIEs). However, this did not apply in the case of China in the years from the late 1980s to the mid-1990s. Nevertheless, since the late 1990s, there have been continuous increases of government expenditure on R&D activities, with the R&D/GDP ratio being grown at the rate of about 0.1 percentage point per year. In 2006, for example, China's R&D/GDP ratio was already 1.42 percent (NBS, 2007). Consequently, technological innovation has been accelerated significantly and been playing a positive role in China's economic growth.

Since the late 1970s, a large number of university graduates and PhD students have traveled to Western nations to pursue their advanced studies. A majority of them, living primarily in the USA, have remained abroad and these people constitute an important "brain-pool" for China's technological development. It is estimated that the total number of Chinese graduates now living in the USA may be in the range of 200,000–300,000. Of these, around 10,000 to 15,000 are world-class scientists and engineers (Sigurdson *et al.*, 2005, p. 65). Since the late 1990s, the Chinese government has sought to create a more favorable climate in order to encourage these overseas Chinese scholars to return home, in order to take over the running of laboratories, high-tech firms or scientific parks. In addition, universities are encouraged to establish science parks and research centers to speed up the commercialization of new technologies.

9.5 Summary

In this chapter, we have discussed China's progress in the areas of industrialization and technology. During the pre-reform period China's industrialization had been affected to a large extent by political movements. Generally, the poor industrial performances had been ascribed to the Chinese socialist construction of "self-reliance and independence" and the irrational industrial structure in which heavy industry was given priority.

Industrialization makes a direct contribution to economic development through an increase in income levels, job opportunities, exports, the availability of foreign capital and technology, and other related factors. In the newly industrialized economies (NIEs), industrialization has served as the key engine in the early period of economic take-off. Therefore, most developing nations (especially poor and agrarian nations) have placed great emphasis upon it. Despite its long history of civilization, over recent centuries China has lagged behind the advanced nations in industrial modernization. If the leapfrogging theory (explained in the case study in section 9.6 below) can be used to describe the dynamic pattern of the world economy, it appears likely that, in the decades to come, China's technological gap with advanced nations will be narrowed.

9.6 Case study: Technological and economic leapfrogging

Modern Western civilization has undoubtedly attained a far higher level of development than is to be encountered in the rest of the world. As mentioned in Weber (1904, pp. 1–2), only in the West has science attained such an advanced stage of development. However, a consideration of the evolution of the world's civilizations over the past many thousands of years clearly reveals that no civilizations (or countries) have been economic and technological leaders throughout the ages. If the current world growth pattern (see Figure 9.4) persists for two or more decades, we may be seeing the USA overtaken by China or India in the twenty-first century. The mechanism of international competition in securing technological leadership has been characterized by a leapfrogging process. Leapfrog is a game in which one player kneels or bends over while the next in line leaps over him or her. Economists have applied it to explain the international patterns of incremental technological change.[11] Theoretical

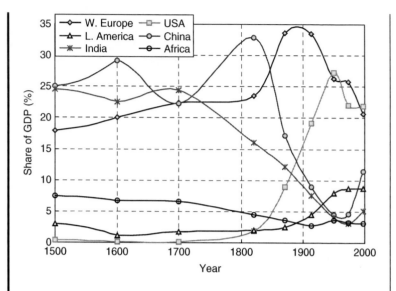

Figure 9.4   A dynamic view of the world economy
Source: Created by the author based on Maddison (2001).

and empirical analyses have concluded that, given their extensive experience with older technologies, leading nations may have no incentive to adopt new ideas; lagging nations, however, have less experience with the old technologies, and may grasp the opportunity to break into the market. If the new techniques eventually prove to be more productive than the old, there is a reversal of leadership.

When a new technology becomes available, however, it may not initially seem much better than the old one – and to a nation that has established a commanding lead in the old technology, it may well seem worse. Thus eighteenth-century Holland, with its established lead in shipping, banking and trading, was not attracted by the prospects of cotton spinning; it was the somewhat poorer English who moved into the new area and exploited its eventually far greater potential (Brezis *et al.*, 1993, p. 1212). Such a failure to take advantage of new technologies may seem in retrospect like short-sightedness. In fact, however, it may have been an entirely rational decision from the point of view of individual entrepreneurs. A country with an established lead will be a high-wage nation; new technologies or industries that are initially less productive than the old one are therefore not profitable. It is only in a lagging nation, where the old technology is less well developed and hence wages are lower, that the new, relatively untried techniques seem attractive.

Such economic and technological "leapfrogging" could be essentially random: lagging countries may simply get lucky, leading countries may be unlucky. And, indeed, the divergent patterns could be explained, at least partially, by what has been noted in Landes (1966, p. 563): "Prosperity and success are their own worst enemies". However, the above situation does not exist in all circumstances. Brezis *et al.* (1993, p. 1219) give a number of conditions under which there will be a leapfrogging process:

(i)   The difference in wage costs between the leading nation and potential challengers must be large.

(ii) The new technology must, when viewed by experienced producers, appear initially unproductive compared with the old one.

(iii) Experience in the old technology must not be too useful in the new technology.

(iv) The new technology must ultimately offer the possibility of substantial productivity improvement over the old.

10
The Quest for Sustainable Development

Xishi, known for her peerless beauty, was beset by some sort of heart trouble, and so she was often seen knitting her brows and walking with a hand on her chest. Now there was an ugly woman, named Dongshi, in the neighborhood who one day saw Xishi in the village street. In admiration she returned home determined to imitate Xishi's way of walking and mannerisms. But this only increased her ugliness. So much so that every time she walked abroad the rich would shut their doors tight and disdain to come out, while the poor with their wives and children would avoid her and quickly turn their steps away. Alas, that woman mistook frowning for something invariably beautiful, and was unaware that it only adds beauty to a real beauty.

– Zhuangzi (*c*.368–286 BC)

10.1 Background

It was not until the late 1960s and the early 1970s that the "environment" became a significant element on the political agenda in developed nations. This was largely a response not only to the spectacular growth of the Western economies, but also to the continued extensive industrialization of the rest of the world. The phrase "sustainable development" was firstly popularized by the World Commission for Environment and Development (WCED, 1987). Since that time, much attention for defining "sustainable development" has been given by the worldwide environmentalists and economists. For example, Pearce *et al*. (1988, p. 6) state "We can summarize the necessary conditions for sustainable development as constancy of the natural capital stock; more strictly, the requirement for non-negative changes in the stock of natural resources, such as soil and soil quality, ground and surface water and their quality, land biomass, water biomass, and the waste-assimilation capacity of the receiving environments". Another example cited by Solow (1991) from an UNESCO document is as "... every generation should leave water, air and soil resources as pure and unpolluted as when it came on earth". The above two passages involve a category mistake being to identify the determinants of well-being with the constituents of well-being (for example, welfare, freedom, and so on), as sustainable development is defined as an impossible goal by these authors.

To be sure, a number of authors writing on sustainable development have recognized that the starting point ought to be the realization of well-being over time. Based on this point, Dasgupta and Mäler (1995, p. 2394) give a more general interpretation of the idea of sustainable development that well-being (and, therefore, consumption) must never be allowed to decline over time. However, this definition also suggests that the sustainable development is very difficult or, sometimes, impossible to achieve. In what follows in this chapter, we will less strictly (but more practically) define sustainable development as "the maximization of the total well-being over a long period of time."

There are at least two characteristics for China: its population is huge and its economy has been growing very fast for at least a quarter of a century. China has become the world's major player in both output and input markets. The data on the total consumption of various primary products presented in Table 10.1 reinforce the importance of China in world consumption markets. In the areas of both metals and coal, China is always ranked first, with shares of between 15 percent and one-third of world consumption, and the United States is ranked either second or third; in other energies, the United States is first and China is either second or third. China is also an important consumer of agricultural commodities, leading the world in the consumption of wheat, rice, cotton, palm oil, and rubber. India is ranked first in terms of the consumption of sugar and tea. Increasing commodity demand from the giants obviously supports prices, other things being equal, but prices also depend upon supply. Most analysts hold that, in recent years, Chinese demand has increased the prices of most metals because the growth in supply has not kept pace with with the grow in demand (Winters and Yusuf, 2007, pp. 16–17).[1]

In recent decades, China's rapid economic development has resulted in a substantial improvement in the standard of living of ordinary people. However, it has also generated environmental problems at an impressively high rate. Carbon dioxide (CO_2), sulfur (SO_2), nitrogen

Table 10.1   Shares in consumption of primary commodities for China, India and the USA (%)

Commodity	China	India	USA
Metals 2005			
Aluminum	22.5 (1)	3.0 (8)	19.4 (2)
Copper	21.6 (1)	2.3 (11)	13.8 (2)
Lead	25.7 (1)	1.3 (15)	19.4 (2)
Nickel	15.2 (1)	0.9 (17)	9.5 (3)
Tin	33.3 (1)	2.2 (7)	12.1 (2)
Zinc	28.6 (1)	3.1 (8)	9.0 (2)
Iron ore	29.0 (1)	4.8 (5)	4.7 (6)
Steel production	31.5 (1)	3.5 (7)	8.5 (3)
Energy 2003			
Coal	32.9 (1)	7.1 (3)	20.6 (2)
Oil	7.4 (2)	3.4 (7)	25.3 (1)
Total primary energy	12.6 (2)	3.6 (5)	23.4 (1)
Electricity generation	11.4 (2)	3.8 (5)	24.3 (1)
Agriculture 2003			
Wheat	15.2 (1)	13.5 (2)	5.4 (4)
Rice	29.7 (1)	21.4 (2)	1.0 (12)
Maize	17.0 (2)	2.2 (6)	32.5 (1)
Soybeans	19.2 (2)	3.7 (5)	24.0 (1)
Soy oil	24.4 (2)	6.4 (4)	25.7 (1)
Palm oil	15.8 (1)	15.3 (2)	0.6 (37)
Sugar	6.6 (3)	15.2 (1)	12.5 (2)
Tea	14.4 (2)	17.5 (1)	3.8 (7)
Coffee	0.4 (45)	0.8 (27)	16.8 (1)
Cotton	31.2 (1)	12.8 (2)	6.9 (5)
Rubber	23.5 (1)	8.4 (4)	12.9 (2)

Note: Figures within parentheses are world rankings.
Source: Streifel (2006).

oxide (NO_x), methane (CH_4), chlorofluorocarbons (CFCs) and other hazardous waste and toxic materials have been increasingly produced in parallel with industrial growth in China. Air pollution stemming from the burning of coal – China's major primary energy – has reached the approximate level of the developed countries in the 1950s and 1960s. Today, air, water, noise pollution, and land erosion together with unprocessed garbage have had a considerable impact upon Chinese society. One striking example is that air pollution is estimated to have caused more than 400,000 excess deaths in 2003, and this figure will increase if no action is taken (Winters and Yusuf, 2007, p. 26).

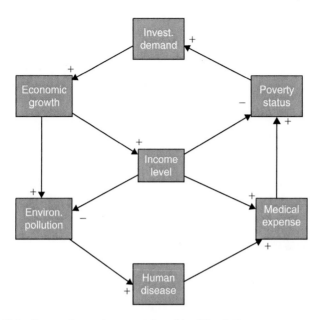

Figure 10.1 Economic, environmental, and health relations
Notes: "+" denote positive relations; "−" denote negative relation; "→" denotes causal direction.

Three elements have made substantial contributions to the environmental damage that has been wrought in China in recent decades: population growth, economic growth driven by highly polluting manufacturing industries and an energy industry that is dominated by coal. In 1949, the new government adopted the Soviet-style development model in which heavy industry was given priority while seeking the maximum level of self-sufficiency in the national economy. The Chinese leadership believed strongly that economic independence and national defense could only be guaranteed by the development of heavy industry. But the latter is also the main source of pollution within the country. Without good reason, the rapidly growing population, with its increasing demand for energy and food, will accelerate the deforestation and transference of forestland and wetland into cropland. But the fragile ecosystem can only accelerate the vicious circle of poverty (see Figure 10.1). If these problems are not addressed properly, all efforts to achieve the sustainable development of the Chinese economy would inevitably be jeopardized.

10.2   Natural resources

Natural resources (such as land, climate, biology, water, minerals, energy and so on) are the basic component among the factors that influence social and economic activities, especially for less-developed economies lacking capital and technology. Theoretically, in a nation whose manufacturing and other high-tech industries are not internationally competitive, one of the most feasible ways to eradicate poverty and backwardness is to develop the natural resource-based sectors. In recent decades, Chinese economic development has followed this path. Until recently, the natural resource-based sectors were still playing the most important role in the less-developed areas of China.

China's vast size, which is comparable to that of the USA or Canada, means that it possesses an abundance of natural resources. According to a report published by the World Resources Institute, China's cropland (96,615,000 ha) accounts for 6.8 percent of the world total, making it the fourth largest (after Russia, the USA and India); China has 9 percent of the world's total permanent pasture (exceeded only by Australia and Russia), 3.4 percent of the world's forestland and woodland (after Russia, Brazil, Canada and the USA), and 8.39 percent of the world's reserves of 15 major metals (copper, lead, tin, zinc, iron ore, manganese, nickel, chromium, cobalt, molybdenum, tungsten, vanadium, bauxite, titanium and lithium) (after Russia, South Africa and USA) (WRI, 1992, pp. 322–3 and 262–3).[2]

However, if population size is taken into account, China's natural resources are not richer than in the world as a whole. For instance, China's per capita cultivated land area is less than one-third the world's; its per capita forestland and woodland is approximately one-seventh the world's; and, with the exceptions of tin and tungsten, China's per capita metal reserves are fewer than the world's, as is shown in Table 10.2. In addition, China's natural resources are generally known to be low grade. For example, more than 95 percent of the iron ore reserves are ferriferously poor, and the iron-rich ore that can be directly processed by refineries accounts for only 2.4 percent of the proven reserves; about two-thirds of the proven copper ore reserves can be refined to only 1 percent copper products. The phosphoric ore with the composition of phosphorus pentoxide (P_2O_5) at or higher than 30 percent accounts for only 7.1 percent – while, in contrast, that at or lower than 12 percent accounts for 19 percent – of the proven reserves (Zhu, 1990, pp. 727–36).

The Chinese economy is characterized by heterogeneous and diversified natural conditions: the climate ranges from the tropical zone in

Table 10.2 Major metal reserves of China and the world

Item	Million tons of contents[a]			Per capita kg[b]		
	China (1)	World (2)	(1)/(2) (%)	China (3)	World (4)	(3)/(4) (%)
Bauxite	150	21,559	0.70	128.2	3934.1	3.26
Copper	3.00	321.00	0.93	2.56	58.58	4.37
Iron ore	3,500	64,648	5.41	2992	11797	25.36
Lead	6.00	70.44	8.52	5.13	12.85	39.92
Manganese	13.6	812.8	1.67	11.62	148.32	7.83
Molybdenum	0.55	6.10	9.02	0.47	1.11	42.34
Nickel	0.73	48.66	1.50	0.62	8.88	6.98
Tin	1.50	5.93	25.30	1.28	1.08	118.52
Titanium	30.0	288.6	10.40	25.64	52.66	48.68
Tungsten	1.05	2.35	44.68	0.90	0.43	209.30
Vanadium	0.61	4.27	14.29	0.52	0.78	66.67
Zinc	5.00	143.90	3.47	4.27	36.26	16.26

a: WRI (1992, pp. 322–3);
b: figures of population are 1.17 billion for China and 5.48 billion for the world in 1992.

the south to the frigid zone in the north and from the arid and semi-arid zones in the northwest to the humid and semi-humid zones in the southeast. As a result, the regional distribution of natural resources is extremely unequal in China. In general, the agricultural and biological resources diminish from the south to the north and from the east to the west. With the exception of hydropower resources, which are concentrated in the Southwest and Central South regions, energy resources are richer in the north than in the south; while metals are distributed principally in the transitional area (such as Sichuan, Gansu, Hunan and so on) between the plateau in the west and the mountain and hilly areas in the east. The regional distribution of China's major mineral resources (in order of reserves) is provided as follows:[3]

- Argentum (Ag): Jiangxi, Guangdong, Guangxi, Yunnan, Hunnan
- Bauxite: Shanxi, Henan, Shandong, Guangxi, Guizhou
- Bismuth (Bi): Hunan, Guangdong, Jiangxi, Yunnan, Inner Mongolia
- Chromium (Cr): Tibet, Inner Mongolia, Gansu
- Coal: Shanxi, Inner Mongolia, Shaanxi, Guizhou, Ningxia
- Cobalt (Co): Gansu, Yunnan, Shandong, Hebei, Shanxi
- Copper (Cu): Jiangxi, Tibet, Yunnan, Gansu, Anhui
- Gold (Au): Shandong, Jiangxi, Heilongjiang, Jilin, Hubei
- Hydragyrum (Hg): Guizhou, Shaanxi, Hunan, Sichuan, Yunnan

- Iron (Fe) ore: Liaoning, Sichuan, Hebei, Shanxi, Anhui
- Kaolin (Ka): Hunan, Jiangsu, Fujian, Guangdong, Liaoning
- Lead (Pb): Yunnan, Guangdong, Hunan, Inner Mongolia, Jiangxi
- Manganese (Mn): Guangxi, Hunan, Guizhou, Liaoning, Sichuan
- Molybdenum (Mo): Henan, Jilin, Shaanxi, Shandong, Jiangxi
- Natural gas: Sichuan, Liaoning, Henan, Xinjiang, Hebei, Tianjin
- Nickel (Ni): Gansu, Yunnan, Jilin, Sichuan, Hubei
- Petroleum: Heilongjiang, Shandong, Liaoning, Hebei, Xinjiang
- Platinum (Pt): Gansu, Yunnan, Sichuan
- Silica stone (SiO_2): Qinghai, Beijing, Liaoning, Gansu, Sichuan
- Stibium (Sb): Hunan, Guangxi, Guizhou, Yunnan
- Tantalum (Ta): Jiangxi, Inner Mongolia, Guangdong, Hunan, Sichuan
- Tin (Sn): Guangxi, Yunnan, Hunan, Guangdong, Jiangxi
- Titanium (Ti): Sichuan, Hebei, Shaanxi, Shanxi
- Tungsten (WO_3): Hunan, Jiangxi, Henan, Fujian, Guangxi
- Vanadium (V): Sichuan, Hunan, Gansu, Hubei, Anhui
- Zinc (Zn): Yunnan, Inner Mongolia, Guangdong, Hunan, Gansu

In order to have a general picture of the spatial distribution of mineral resources in China, let us use the monetary values of 45 major minerals estimated by Sun (1987, pp. 4–8).[4] Figure 10.2 shows that the five richest provinces are Sichuan, Shanxi, Inner Mongolia, Yunnan and Liaoning, while Guangdong, Jilin, Guangxi, Jiangsu, Hubei, Beijing, Tianjin, Fujian, Zhejiang, Tibet, Shanghai and Hainan as a whole account for only 5 percent of the total minerals.

In China, the distribution of water is extremely irregular. In general, the Northern part is poor in surface water, but modestly rich in groundwater in a few provinces, including Qinghai, Xinjiang, Inner Mongolia and Heilongjiang. The precipitation is more than 1,000 mm/yr in the Southern part and more than 1,600 mm/yr in the southern coastal area, while it ranges between 100 and 800 mm/yr in the Northern part. In particular, the Talimu, Tulufan and Chaidamu basins in the Northwest region have less than 25 mm of precipitation per annum. As a result of the suitable climate and adequate rainfall, the Southern part is the dominant rice producer; and wheat is the main foodstuff in the lower Yellow river (such as Henan, Shandong, Hebei, northern Jiangsu and Anhui provinces) and southern Great Wall areas. A selection of top five agriculturally based provinces is shown below:

- Rice: Hunan, Sichuan, Jiangsu, Hubei, Guangdong
- Wheat: Henan, Shandong, Jiangsu, Hebei, Sichuan

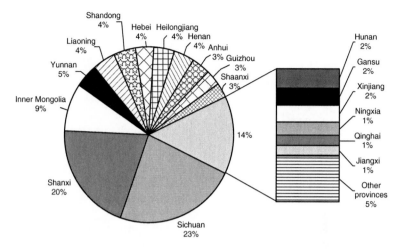

Figure 10.2   Spatial distribution of major mineral resources in China
Notes: "Other provinces" include Guangdong, Jilin, Guangxi, Jiangsu, Hubei, Beijing, Tianjin, Fujian, Zhejiang, Tibet and Shanghai. (2) Guangdong includes Hainan; and Sichuan includes Chongqing.
Source: Created by the author based on the monetary values of 45 major minerals estimated by Sun (1987, pp. 4–8).

- Maize: Shandong, Jilin, Hebei, Sichuan, Henan
- Soybean: Heilongjiang, Henan, Jilin, Shandong, Anhui
- Cotton: Shandong, Hebei, Henan, Hubei, Jiangsu
- Rapeseeds: Shandong, Sichuan, Anhui, Jiangsu, Henan
- Tobacco: Henan, Yunnan, Shandong, Guizhou, Hunan
- Tea: Zhejiang, Hunan, Sichuan, Anhui, Fujian
- Fruits: Shandong, Hebei, Guangdong, Sichuan, Liaoning

China faces almost all of the problems related to water resources that are faced by countries across the globe. China's rapid economic growth, industrialization, and urbanization have outpaced infrastructural investment and management capacity, and have created widespread problems of water scarcity. The degradation of underground water resources and the deterioration in the quality of underground water quality have become a considerable environmental problem in many of China's cities. In the areas of the North China Plain, where about half of China's wheat and corn is grown and there are extensive peach orchards, drought is an ever-looming threat. With 22 percent of the world's population, China has only 8 percent of the fresh water. In 2002, China's annual renewable water reserves were about 2.8 trillion cubic meters, which ranked it fifth in the world, behind Brazil, Russia, Canada and Indonesia, but ahead of the USA. However, in terms of per capita availability of water reserves, China is one of the lowest in the world – barely one-quarter of the world average (WRI, 2003). It is estimated that by 2030, in addition to its population reaching 1.6 billion, China will be under severe water stress as defined by the international standard of 1,700 cubic meters per capita (Qian and Zhang, 2001).

In addition to water scarcity for China as a whole, there is considerable unevenness in terms of the amount of water resources available in different regions of the country. The northern parts of the country are deficient in water, while the south is water-rich. The areas south of the Yangtze river, which account for only 37 percent of the country's total territory, have 81 percent of its total water resources. By contrast, the areas north of the Yangtze, which make up 63 percent of China's territory, possess only 19 percent of the country's total water resources (Chen and Cai, 2000). As a result of the uneven distribution in some areas in north China, the per capita water rate is as low as one-fifth of the national average (in the Liaohe river valley in the northeast) or one-sixth (in the Haihe river valley around Tianjin). Water shortage has become a major economic bottleneck to these areas (see Box 10.1).

Box 10.1   The South–North Water Diversion Project

China is plagued with unevenly distributed water and land resources: more water vis-à-vis less land in southern China and less water vis-à-vis more land in northern China. North China accounts for over one-third of the country's total population, nearly one half of cultivated land, but only one-eighth of the total water resources. Over 80 percent direct water runoff in China takes place in the south. Since the 1980s the Haihe and Yellow river valleys have been stricken by chronic drought. Yet, further south, large amount of water from the Yangtze empties into the sea each year.

Given the existence of surface water surplus in southern China and freshwater shortage in northern China, is it feasible to transfer water from the water-rich south to the north? Transfer project had been discussed for more than two decades before it was started on December 27 2002. The gigantic South–North Water Diversion project involves the construction of three canals running 1,300 kilometers across the eastern, middle and western parts of China, linking the country's four major rivers – the Yangtze, Yellow, Huaihe and Haihe rivers.

The South–North Water Diversion project is expected to cost US$59 billion and to take 50 years to complete. If all goes well, the South–North Water Diversion project will carry annually more than 40 billion tonnes of water from the Yangtze River basin to Beijing and the other north provinces. However, this project cannot completely solve the water shortage problems in northern China.

10.3   Energy production and consumption

Energy resources are also unevenly distributed in China (Table 10.3). For example, about 70 percent of the hydropower reserves are concentrated in the Southwest region, while the North, Northeast and East regions as a whole share less than 10 percent; more than 60 percent of coal reserves are distributed in the North region, with only a small portion, sparsely distributed, in the Northeast, East and Central South regions; the Northeast region accounts for nearly one half of the nation's petroleum and natural gas reserves, while the Central South and Southwest regions as a whole only share a mere 5 percent. Nevertheless, the Northwest is the only region which is modestly rich in coal, hydropower, petroleum and natural gas. In addition, the energy structure is disproportional among regions. For example, coal nearly monopolizes the North region, while the Southwest and Central South regions are mostly dominated by hydropower. Nevertheless, the East, Northwest and Northeast regions are principally served by coal rather than by petroleum, hydropower and natural gas.

Coal resources are concentrated in the North and Northwest regions, around 600–1,000 km away from the most industrialized provinces and municipalities in the Southeast. Coal is transported mainly by train and it accounts for more than 40 percent of the country's rail freight. On the other hand, the building of thermal power stations near the coal mines (*kengkou dianzhan*) seems to be an efficient way, but faces substantial obstacles because of the shortage of water needed for turbine cooling. With an annual production of near 2.5 billion tons in 2008, coal accounts for more than 70 percent of China's primary energy production (shown in Figure 10.3). This figure already makes China the world's leading coal producer. Furthermore, the Chinese coal industry is planning to increase its levels of annual coal production and it is unclear whether or not the Chinese government will be willing to introduce significant decreases in the current proportion of coal in total energy consumption in the foreseeable future. Environmental problems

Table 10.3 Composition of energy resources, by region and by type of energy (%)

Region	Coal	Hydropower[a]	Petroleum[b]	All energy[c]
North	64.0 (98.2)	1.8 (1.3)	14.4 (0.5)	43.9 (100.0)
Northeast	3.1 (54.6)	1.8 (14.2)	48.3 (31.2)	3.8 (100.0)
East	6.5 (72.9)	4.4 (22.5)	18.2 (4.6)	6.0 (100.0)
Central South	3.7 (44.5)	9.5 (51.8)	2.5 (3.7)	5.6 (100.0)
Southwest	10.7 (25.2)	70.0 (74.7)	2.5 (0.1)	28.6 (100.0)
Northwest	12.0 (66.7)	12.5 (31.3)	14.0 (2.0)	12.1 (100.0)
China	100.0 (85.9)	100.0 (13.1)	100.0 (1.0)	100.0 (100.0)

Notes: (1) The geographical scopes of the great regions are defined in Figure 2.1. (2) Figures in parentheses are energy structures. [a]The theoretical reserves multiplied by 100 years. [b]Includes natural gas and shale oil. [c]Standard coal equivalent conversion rates are as 0.714 t/t for coal, 1.43 t/t for petroleum, 1.33 t/1000 m^3 for natural gas, 0.143 t/t for oil shale, and 350 g/kWh for hydropower.
Source: MOE (1991, p. 101).

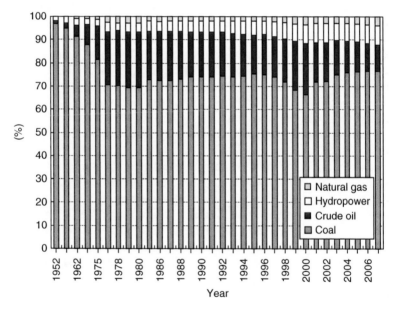

Figure 10.3   China's energy production structure

associated with the entire process of coal extraction, transportation, processing, and consumption will, therefore, continue to have a serious effect on the sustainable development in China if no measures are adopted.

China's dependence on coal continues amid the frequent occurrence of mining accidents, which cause thousands of casualties each year. Furthermore, China is much more inefficient in its coal exploitation than developed nations. At present, China uses about 3.3 tons of coal reserves in order to produce one ton of raw coal. In the USA, for example, the production of one ton of raw coal uses only 1.25 tons of reserves. According to a report released by the Chinese Academy of Social Sciences, the mining recovery ratio has been less than 44 percent in China's large state-owned coal mines and only 10 percent in the small and private coal mines; by contrast, those in developed nations including Australia, Canada, Germany and the United States reportedly achieve figures as high as 80 percent (Cui, 2007). The Chinese government has planned to raise the average recovery ratio of coal exploitation from the current figure of 30 percent to at least 50 percent by 2010 (Si, 2008). As part of its efforts to achieve these goals, China has decided to consolidate the coal industry by building several large mining conglomerates (each with a production capacity of 100 million tons of raw coal per year), as well as to shut down those small and inefficient coal pits. However, this seems to be a difficult task to achieve within a short period of time, since many stakeholders, especially local governments, would be unwilling to support this kind of reform.

Most of China's proven coal reserves are bituminous, with only a small proportion being lignite and anthracite. Therefore, coal is mainly responsible not only for the high CO_2 emissions, but also for the high emissions of SO_2, NO_x, and total suspended particulate (TSP). In addition, as the northern (especially urban) areas usually use coal for heating in the winter, it is unsurprising that the level of air pollution there is much more serious than that in the Southern part. All of these pollutants have posed serious threats to public health. There has been a rise in the share of chronic obstructive pulmonary disease and cancers. In addition, acid rain is becoming an increasingly critical issue. The high sulfur content of burning coal contributes widely to the high acidity levels of rainfall. Nationwide acid rain measurement, which has been carried out since 1982, shows that the situation is particularly serious in southern China, where the pH values are often lower than 5.6.[5] Another noticeable factor is that the wind coming from the Northwest region increases the neutralizing capability of atmosphere and transfers air pollutants to Southeast China and the neighboring countries. In addition, lead (Pb) emissions from vehicles will increase substantially, in line with the rapid increase of vehicles in urban China.

Petroleum is currently supplied mainly by the Northeast region, while the Northwest region is rich in oil reserves and is looking forward to becoming the world's major oil supplier in future. The locational disadvantages of the Northwest oil fields, however, will pose difficulties for oil exploitation and transportation in China. Theoretically, the structure of energy consumption may be largely readjusted through foreign trade. As a result of its rapidly growing consumption – and relatively stagnant production – of petroleum, in 1993 China became a net importer of oil. According to the Economist Intelligence Agency (EIA), China's consumption of petroleum increased by 3.44 times to 13.11 quadrillion BTU in 2004 from 3.81 quadrillion BTU in 1980, while its production of crude oil increased only 1.65 times to 7.50 quadrillion BTU in 2004 from 4.55 quadrillion BTU in 1980, creating an ever-growing oil shortage. In addition, China's oil deficit stood at 3.5 million barrels per day in 2006 and is expected to quadruple to 13.1 million barrels per day over the projection period to 2030, when the country's oil consumption is projected to reach 15.7 million barrels per day (EIA, 2006). That is to say, more than 80 percent of China's oil demand should be met by either imports or technological substitution.

The government hopes to reduce the share of thermalpower in its power generation mix through the construction of large hydroelectric dams. The main hydroelectric dams are Gezhouba Dam in Hubei province, followed by Liujiaxia Dam in Gansu province, Longyang Dam in Qinghai province, Manwan Dam in Yunnan province, Baishan Dam in Jilin province, and so on. China has now also completed the world's largest dam in the Three Gorges on the Yangtze river. This dam will increase the supply of affordable electricity throughout the Yangtze valley, as well as controlling floods, boosting the growing economy and reducing the levels of air pollution. The economic advantages coming from such a big dam, however, could also be reduced by the losses arising from the ecological and environmental costs and risks. The Chinese leadership realizes that the development of nuclear power is an appropriate solution to improve local energy shortages in those eastern and southern coastal areas that lack coal and petroleum resources. Currently, the nuclear power stations are at Qinshan in Zhejiang province, Daya Bay in Guangdong province, and Hongyanhe in Liaoning province. But the development of nuclear power stations also faces a series of uncertainties and risks, as well as domestic technological constraints.

With its large land mass and long coastline, China has relatively abundant wind resources. The windiest areas of the country are located mainly along the southeast coast and the nearby islands and in Inner

Mongolia, Xinjiang, western Gansu, and in some parts of Northeast China, Northwest China, North China, and the Qinghai-Tibetan Plateau. Apart from this, there are also certain areas in China's interior that are rich in wind resources. China also has large marine areas, and ocean-based wind resources are plentiful.

10.4   Environmental situation

China's environmental concerns stem from two kinds of human activities: (i) resource depletion, which covers the activities of the losses reflecting the deterioration of land and depleting reserves of coal, petroleum, timber, groundwater and so on; and (ii) resource degradation, which covers the consequences associated with air and water pollution, land erosion, solid wastes and so on. Resource depletion is a concern because it would mean the quantitative exhaustion of natural resources that are an important source of revenues, obtained through exploitation and the discovery of new reserves. In the case of resource degradation, the issue is not the quantitative exhaustion of natural resources, but rather the qualitative degradation of the ecosystem, for example, through, amongst other things, the contamination of air and water as a result of the generation and deposit of residuals, and as a result of the environmental impact of producing garbage and solid wastes.

In order to make an assessment of China's environmental situation, let us consider air, water, land and deforestation and desertification.

10.4.1   Air

Recent decades have seen a worsening of China's air quality, particularly in urban areas. According to European satellite data, pollutants in the sky over China have increased by about 50 percent between 1995 and 2005. The satellite data also revealed that the city of Beijing – China's capital – is one of the most serious environmental victims of China's spectacular economic growth, which has led to air pollution levels that have been blamed for more than 400,000 premature deaths a year. According to the European Space Agency, Beijing and its neighboring northeast provinces have the planet's worst levels of nitrogen dioxide, which can cause fatal damage to the lungs (Watts, 2005). An explosive increase in car ownership is blamed for a sharp rise in unhealthy emissions. By 2008 more than three million vehicles were clogging the capital's streets.

When discussing the situation of China's greenhouse gas (GHG) emissions, one comes across two different opinions: first, it is posited that

Table 10.4   Various indicators of GHG emissions, China and the USA

Item	China		USA	
	1990	2006	1990	2006
GDP (billion US$)[a]	372.4	2,626.3	5,672.6	13,194.7
GHGs (million ton)	2,524	6,200	5,163	5,800
GHGs/POP (ton/person)	2.18	4.72	21.0	19.4
GHGs/LA (ton/km^2)	262.9	645.8	551.6	619.7
GHGs/GDP (kg/US$)	6.78	2.36	0.91	0.44

Notes: [a]Measured in exchange rates (for China) and in current prices (for China and USA). GDP = gross national product, GHGs = greenhouse gases, POP = population, LA = land area.
Source: Calculated by the author based on WRI (1992, tables 13.4 and 24.1) and NEAA (2007).

the country's per capita emissions are very low in comparison with the industrially developed countries and that the *onus* of global warming must rest elsewhere; secondly, compared with other countries, China's GHG emissions per unit of GDP are already very high – approximately 5.36 times that of the USA in 2006, although this figure is lower than in 1990 (see Table 10.4). China's GHG emissions are composed of about 68 percent carbon dioxide (CO_2), 24 percent methane (CH_4), and 8 percent chlorofluorocarbons (CFCs) (WRI, 1992, tables 13.4 and 24.1; Perlack *et al.*, 1993, p. 78). With respect to CO_2, about 80 percent of emissions come from coal and other solid fuels, 14 percent from liquid petroleum fuels and the remainder from natural gas use and from chemical processes in the manufacturing of cement (CDIAC, 1990).

According to a preliminary estimate by the Netherlands Environmental Assessment Agency (NEAA), the largest national producer of GHG emissions since 2006 has been China, with an estimated annual production of about 6,200 million tons. China is followed by the USA with about 5,800 million tons (see Table 10.4). However, the per capita emission figures of China are still less than one-quarter of those for the US population. It has been projected that in the period from 2000 to 2010, China is expected to increase its CO_2 emissions by 600 million tons, largely because of the rapid construction of old-fashioned power plants in its poorer, internal provinces (source: http://en.wikipedia.org/wiki/Greenhouse_gas). Moreover, using the GREEN model built by the OECD, Burnaux *et al.* (1992, fig. 2) present a detailed scenario for the world's GHG emissions which suggests that China will constitute 29 percent, far ahead of the shares of the USA

(12 percent), the former USSR (13 percent), and the European Union as a whole (7 percent) by the year 2050.

In China, atmospheric pollution comes mainly from the burning of coal and its associated products which, under the most optimistic scenario, will be unlikely to contribute less than the current three-quarters of total primary energy consumption by the year 2025 (Huang, 1990) or even by the year 2050 (Wang and Li, 1996; Wang, 1995). China's CFC and halon compound use is relatively minor given the size of the country. However, the potential for much greater use of CFCs is enormous. Moreover, it is projected that CFC emissions are projected to increase as a result of both China's economic growth and its increases in population. The specific sources of these emissions are, in order of quantity produced, livestock, wet rice, natural gas pipeline leakage, solid waste disposal, and coal mining. In addition, China's large and still expanding population also suggests a concomitant increase of CH_4.

10.4.2 Water

Water scarcity, a matter of worldwide concern, is also presenting serious problems for China. Today, water scarcity is often viewed as a major threat to China's long-term security. Large-scale underground water extraction began in the 1950s and has increased significantly over the course of the past 20 years. Accordingly, underground water use as a percentage of the total water supply also increased – from 14 percent in 1980 to 20 percent in 2001 (Chen and Cai, 2000). The over-exploitation of groundwater has led to a marked and continuous drawdown of underground water levels in China. From time to time deeper wells have to be installed. A recent survey indicates that the cones of depression in the deep aquifers have joined together to form a huge interprovincial cone of depression in the North China Plain. There is growing competition for water between communities, sectors of the economy, and individual provinces (Jiao and Wen, 2004).

There are already more than ten seawater desalination plants in China, with a total capacity of 5,000 cubic meters per day. China has also invested in a seawater desalination project to carry desalinated seawater to the Beijing municipality. In some countries the production cost per ton of seawater ranges between US$1.1 and US$2.5. In China, it can be reduced to ¥5.0, or even lower (¥3.7) for larger seawater desalination plants.[6] However, the problem with respect to the wide utilization of the desalinated seawater in the vast rural area is the cost. Many farmers in China are still neither able nor willing to offer such a high price, since, in traditional cultures, the waters in rivers and lakes have been free of any such charge.

The constant and excessive extraction of groundwater has led to the continuous fall in the level of the watertable and the subsidence of land. The area of subsidence around large municipalities such as Beijing, Tianjin and Shanghai has been reported to be the most serious. In the coastal areas of Hebei and Shandong provinces, the excessive drop in the groundwater level has led to the leeching of saline water into the freshwater aquifers. In the loess plateau area of Northwest China, the drawing of underground water for irrigation is becoming extremely difficult, with increasing energy costs.

The excessive use of water without adequate drainage leads to waterlogging, salinization and soil erosion. Salinization and alkalization are increasingly affecting irrigated farmland. In the Northeast region, cropping activities have increased the soil alkalinity to such a high level that it is very difficult to put them back into pasture. In the sandy soils of the Northwest region, where the irrigation water seeps away quickly, strong winds and high evaporation contribute to alkalization of the soil. The rapid development of individually- and collectively-owned industrial enterprises are generally known to be responsible for the increasing levels of water pollution in rural areas. More than two-thirds of China's industrial wastewater has flown directly into rivers, lakes, seas and reservoirs. The chemical industry is the largest wastewater producer. Other main sectors discharging wastewater include ferrous metals, papermaking and paper products, the production and supply of power, steam and hot water, and so on.

Another key issue is the pollution of drinking water in both urban and rural areas. Many groundwater sources have been affected as a result of infiltration of polluted surface water in urban areas. Rural water resources are even more contaminated due to fertilizers and pesticide runoff, human and animal waste, and pollutants from the township and village-owned enterprises. As a result, only one in seven people residing in the rural areas have access to safe drinking water (UNDP, 1994, p. 3). 76 percent of the population drink water with fecal coliform counts that are above the Chinese national drinking water quality standards, and 59 percent drink water exceeding the less stringent WHO standard. About 60 percent of the country's inhabitants have no access to potable water (WRI, 1992, p. 410).

River water pollution in those sections of rivers that run through or near cities is the most serious in terms of ammonia nitrogen, fecal bacteria, volatile phenols, and biological oxygen demands (BOD).[7]

The Yangtze river, which links China's large industrial bases such as Chongqing, Wuhan, Nanjing and Shanghai, is estimated by many observers to be seriously polluted, if no countermeasure is carried out. The Huaihe river, which many people now refer to as the *black river*, is believed the most polluted river in China. In all of the 96 monitoring stations established by the National Environmental Protection Agency (NEPA), only 35 monitoring stations obtained dissolved oxygen of more than 5 mg/l – a level that supports fishes; for BOD, only 24 of the 91 monitoring stations met the standard (i.e., 5 mg/l), while 21 stations violated it (NEPA, 1994, p. 4). In addition, pollution from heavy metals, such as mercury (Hg) and lead (Pb) and other toxic chemicals, are also having a serious impact on river water.

Nitrogen and phosphorus pollution is common in China's lakes. Water pollution has not only endangered the local fishery and the collection of limnological plants, but has also affected the daily lives and health of the nearby residents. In addition, petropollutants, inorganic nitrogen and inorganic phosphorus are common in the coastal water sources. Marine environments near large coastal cities are degraded as a result of the discharge of raw sewage and coastal construction. As a result, incidences of red tides have become frequent in many coastal areas, contaminated fish and molluscs have been commonplace and, consequently, many fragile marine environments have been destroyed. Marine pollution in northeastern and southern China is of particular concern since the industrial development is outpacing the environmental protection efforts in these areas.

10.4.3 Land

China has provided sustenance and other basic necessities for 22 percent of the world's population, although it has only 7 percent of the world's cultivated land. But this kind of development pattern has also created many serious environmental problems that are the result of inappropriate policies and approaches in agricultural production. During the 1960s and 1970s, the Chinese government saw "taking grain production as the key link" (*yi liang weigang*) in order to maximize self-sufficiency in the supply of foodstuffs. This policy has been generally seen as ignoring the comparative advantages between the regions in natural conditions, and accelerated the conversion of forestland, wetland, and marginal land into cropland.

Since the introduction of economic reforms in the late 1970s, the transference of farmland to residential and industrial uses has been promoted.

Consequently, the area of land under cultivation has decreased substantially. This meant that in order to increase the level of agricultural production, the only way was to increase the levels of land productivity, which resulted in the intensive use of chemical fertilizers, continuous cropping, greatly expanded irrigation, and the use of improved plant varieties. As reported by the SSB (1996, p. 361), the total consumption of chemical fertilizers almost quadrupled between 1983 and 1995. In practice, it is almost impossible for farmers to make an accurate count of the proportion of nutrients that is required by the soil. In most cases, the marginal cost and benefit do not determine the use of fertilizers. The government's subsidies on fertilizer consumption could distort the pricing mechanism and induce farmers to the even more excessive and inefficient use of chemical fertilizers, which has, through the leaching of nitrates, caused the contamination of groundwater and the deterioration of soil structure.

Organic manure and the leavened crop residues, stalks, and straws have many advantages when used as fertilizers, even if their value of nutrient per unit volume is lower than that of chemical fertilizers. Many farmers, however, have ignored the advantages of these *clean* fertilizers. In addition, in rural China the shortage of fuelwood for both cooking and heating results in the burning of straws, stalks, and crop residues. Continuous cropping, instead of crop rotation, may cause the soil to be deficient in some nutrients. For example, the cropping of soybeans causes a deficiency of phosphorus and potassium in the soil. The use of high-yielding and improved plant varieties has made crops more vulnerable to pest damage, which in turn results in the use of pesticides. Since the 1970s the use of pesticides has increased in both tonnage and concentration of active ingredients and, as a result, has had a serious effect on water, soil and food.

The more widespread use of plastic sheeting is a further threat. Farmers have been increasingly interested in the application of plastic sheets to conserve soil moisture and speed up the maturation of crops, particularly in northern China. But many farmers have ignored the fact that plastic sheets, if not treated properly after cropping, may be mixed with the soil and hence hinder the flow of water and root growth. Farmland is also suffering from the damage of industrial wastes and urban rubbish, occupied by piles of solid waste and seriously damaged as a result of the improper use of garbage and sludge. The sum of these circumstances has led to soil loss, especially in those areas where ground cover was removed. The ecosystems of forests, wetlands, sloping and marginal lands are particularly fragile. Another form of soil contamination is the use of wastewater for irrigation, which ignores the fact that acids and toxic heavy metals in much of this water impair the soil chemistry and render it useless for agriculture.

Apart from the soil loss deriving from the erosion process, another consequence of soil over-exploitation and removal of ground cover is the increase of silt materials flowing into rivers. This leads to the rising of riverbeds undermining flood control, navigation and power generating capacity. The loess plateau area between Gansu, Shaanxi, and Shanxi provinces has been cultivated since the Neolithic period and is now perhaps one of the most erodible areas in the world. Through this area, the Yellow river carries 1.6 billion tons of sediment into the Bohai sea by degrading a land from 260 to 330 square kilometers annually (Vaclav, 1992, p. 433). The average riverbed has been rising by approximately one meter per decade, with a consequent growing risk of catastrophic flooding. The Yangtze river's load raises lake levels, particularly in Hubei and Hunan provinces. As a result, over the course of recent decades most lakes in East Hubei have disappeared, owing to the combination of silting and conversion to farmland.

With the formation of cones of depression, many cities, especially those coastal cities which have thick unconsolidated soft soil layers, are suffering from land subsidence caused by the withdrawal of underground water from deep aquifers. The cities of Shanghai and Tianjin, with a maximum subsidence of about three meters, are the most severe cases. Ground subsidence has caused a series of problems, such as the sinking and splitting of railway bases, buildings, and underground pipelines, and an emerging flooding crisis in areas near major rivers or the sea. For example, embankments have had to be constructed to prevent flooding of seawater into some areas of Tianjin after significant ground subsidence.

10.4.4   Deforestation and desertification

In spite of different estimates about the actual extent of forestland area,[8] the rapid decrease in forestland has meant that China faces up to the shortage of timber. The causes of deforestation come mainly from the rapidly growing population in rural areas and the economic interests of the state. As the size of population expands, the needs of food, housing, and energy will increase accordingly. The conversion of forestland, grassland and wetland to cropland, as well as the illegal felling of trees for lumber and fuel, increases. In the rural areas, the lack of fuels led to use of wood for both heating and cooking. But the traditional rural stoves have low combustion efficiency. In addition, much of the fuelwood consumed is low-quality brush and weeds collected from already deforested hills.

From the 1950s to the 1970s, a period during which a series of political and social movements (such as the Great Leap Forward and the Cultural Revolution) were under way, many of China's natural and tropical forests were suffering serious damage. For example, the natural tropical forest in Hainan island decreased by 72 percent – from 8,630 square kilometers in the 1950s to 2,450 square kilometers in 1980 (Vermeer, 1984, p. 10). In Sichuan province, the level of forestland cover decreased from 19 percent of the province's land area in the early 1950s to 12.6 percent in 1988. During the 1980s the total area of forestland decreased by 128,000 square kilometers (nearly 10 percent of the total area) in Tibet Autonomous Region. From 1950 to 1985 some $54 billion worth of Tibetan timber was felled and processed, and 90 percent of the timber, meat and minerals culled from the plateau are exported to other parts of China (Denniston, 1993, p. 9). In Tibet and many other provinces and autonomous regions, the process of forest degradation began with the large-scale cutting of forests by the state or its contractors for commercial logging. This large-scale cutting combined with fuel necessities has denuded hillsides, resulting in soil erosion and water loss. Vaclav (1992, p. 435) estimates that between 1979 and 1986 there was a 25 percent increase in timber logging in China. The remaining natural forests in the Northeast and Southwest regions and Hainan island are still being excessively logged in order to meet the increasing industrial and commercial demands.

Covering about one-third of its total land area, China's grassland is concentrated in the Inner Mongolia, Xinjiang, and Tibet autonomous regions and a few other provinces and autonomous regions, located mostly in the North and Northwest regions. As grassland is usually regarded as "wasteland," the conversion of it into productive uses has been promoted in recent decades as a result of the growth in population. The conversion of grassland into crop cultivation has led to a continuing decrease in the amount of grassland. The Eighth Five-Year Plan (1991–95) proposed a plan to transfer, while among other provinces and autonomous regions, 1,250 square kilometers of grassland in Inner Mongolia, 200 square kilometers in Xinjiang. At the same time, overgrazing is widely visible. Since the early 1980s, peasants have been allowed to raise their own animals. When the number of heads grows, the grassland decreases accordingly.[9]

During the recent decades, desertification has become an increasingly serious problem, with some 176,000 square kilometers of land being desertified in northwestern China. Still expanding at a rate of 1,560 square kilometers per annum, the area of deserts and desertified lands is now estimated to be some 1,490 thousand square kilometers (that is, 15.5 percent of China's total land area), with, specifically, 41.8 percent of rock and gravel (*gobi*) and 58.2 percent of sandy (*shamo*) (Fullen and Mitchell, 1994, p. 131).

Heavy and frequent sand storms in northern China have resulted in damage to the sustainability of the Chinese economy. Dust storms are caused by turbulent wind systems which contain particles of dust that reduce visibility to less than 1,000 m. A dust storm may cause soil erosion, loess formation, climate change, air pollution, and a reduction in the level of solar irradiance. Although the number of annual dust days has decreased over past decades, the frequency of severe dust storms (where visibility <200 m) has increased during the same period in northern China, with four in the 1950s, seven in the 1960s, 13 in the 1970s, 14 in the 1980s, and 23 in the 1990s (Qian and Zhu, 2001; and Chen *et al.*, 2003). An extremely dry environment can induce more severe dust storms such as the "Black Storm" (in which visibility <10 m).

The variability of dust storms over time is associated with climate fluctuations in terms of both temperature and precipitation. The arid and semi-arid areas of northern China make up 30 percent of the country's total land area; and for much of the year the dry mid-latitude climate is dominated by continental polar air masses. Most dust events occur during the spring season from March to May when cyclonic cold fronts meets warm air mass influxes, leading to strong seasonal atmospheric instability, a favorable synoptic condition for dust storms. However, human activities have also had a substantial impact on dust storms at both regional and local levels. In northern China, there was a rapid escalataion of the level of decertified land, as a direct result of human activity. In recent decades the Chinese government has invested substantial social and economic resources to suppress dust storms. Despite some successful cases, the present-day desertification situation is not optimistic. It can be summed up in the phrase "locally improved, but wholly deteriorated" (Chen *et al.*, 2003).

10.5   Chinese environmental policy

Using a way to fish by drying up lakes – how cannot you catch the fisheries? Then there would be no fisheries next year. Using a way to hunt by firing woods – how cannot you catch the animals? Then there would be no animals next year.

– *Lvshi Chunqiu* (Yishang, 2)

Since the late 1970s, several changes have taken place in the legislation of environmental protection in China, along with the economic reform and opening up to the outside world. in the year 1978 saw the first insertion of a clause for environmental protection in the Constitution of the People's Republic of China. China's first Law on Environmental Protection (*huanjing baohu fa*) was formally promulgated in 1989 and was further revised in 1995. Since the early 1980s, a series of laws, regulations, and national standards (*guobiao*, or GB) concerning environmental protection (including four environmental laws, eight natural resource protection laws, more than 20 administrative decrees, more than 30 ministerial regulations for pollution prevention, and 300-plus environmental standards) have been promulgated in China.[10] A relatively comprehensive legal system concerning environmental protection has initially taken shape, ending the past situation of no laws in this regard. Since 1980, China has joined or approved many international protocols on environmental protection, including the United Nations Convention on the Law of the Sea, the Antarctic Treaty, the Convention on International Trade in Endangered Species, the Vienna Conference for the Protection of the Ozone Layer, the Basel Convention on Transboundary Hazardous Waste Disposal, and the Montreal Protocol for Limiting use of CFCs, the Kyoto Protocol, and so on.

However, a number of problems still remain. For example, in the field of the environment and resources, for a long period up to the late 1990s there was no appropriate legislation in relation to solid wastes and toxic chemicals, radioactive pollution prevention, and the sustainable management of natural resources. Chinese legislation also faces problems of attempting to achieve coordination and consistency with international treaties and conventions. Moreover, as the Chinese legislation relating to sustainable development was to a large extent promulgated on the basis of a centralized planning system, many problems arose from China's economic transition. For example, there have been no environmentally related laws and regulations that are directly applicable to diversified economic sectors, that is, for the environmental administration of township and village-based enterprises, foreign-funded enterprises and the tertiary sector.

In China, environmental concerns have stemmed from two kinds of human activities: resource depletion, which covers the activities of the losses reflecting the deterioration of land and depleting reserves of coal, petroleum, timber, groundwater, and so on; resource degradation, which covers the activities associated with air and water pollution, land erosion, solid waste, and so on. Resource depletion is a concern because it would lead to the quantitative exhaustion of natural resources that are an important source of revenues, obtained through exploitation and the discovery of new reserves. In the case of resource degradation, the issue is not the quantitative exhaustion of natural resources, but rather the qualitative degradation of the ecosystem – for example, through the contamination of air and water as a result of the generation and deposit of residuals, and as a result of the environmental impact of producing garbage and solid waste (see Box 10.2).

To preserve the richness of forestry and stabilize the soil structure, the Chinese government has begun a massive reforestation program. The first afforestation project was initiated in 1978 to plant 667,000 square kilometers of trees covering 551 counties, cities and townships of 13 provinces and autonomous regions in the northern, western, central and eastern China areas. The other afforestation projects include: (1) "Forest System of the Upper and Middle Reaches of the Changjiang River", with a planned afforestation space of around 66,000 square kilometers; (2) "Coastal Shelter-Forest System" with 25,000 square kilometers; and (3) "Afforestation Project of the Taihang Mountains between Shanxi, Hebei and Henan provinces and Beijing and Tianjin Municipalities", with 33,000 square kilometers (NEPA, 1992). Unfortunately, some plantings claimed by the government in the mass reforestation programs have managed to survive.

There are further constraints on Chinese sustainable development. For example, China has expressed a willingness to participate in an international global warming treaty. However, it is unlikely that the Chinese are going to push GHG reductions up to the "no-regrets" level, because they have more pressing problems. In addition, China has also promised to protect the endangered species in order to maintain a diversified ecosystem. Nevertheless, the relevant treaties and laws in this regard will have relatively little impact on those people who are in the habit of "having wild animals in the tables". The gains of today might eventually become the costs of tomorrow. The environmental costs resulting from industrialization often build up slowly and do not become critical in the first few years. By contrast, the benefits of industrialization are usually immediate. However, if the government, industrialists, and consumers are prepared to continue with various practices and leave future generations to worry about their environmental consequences, the problem is therefore a re-election of the importance that people attach to the present relative to the future.

Box 10.2   What is the environmental Kuznets curve?

There is a long line of thought suggesting that environmental quality changes with respect to income level. Theoretical papers by Gruver (1976), John and Pecchenino (1992), and Seldon and Song (1995) have derived transition paths for pollution, abatement effort and development under alternative assumptions about social welfare functions, pollution damage, the cost of abatement, and the productivity of capital. Empirical studies (Hettige *et al.*, 1997; Shafik, 1994; Selden and Song, 1994; and Grossman and Krueger, 1995) have searched for systematic relationships by regressing cross-country measures of ambient air and water quality on various polynomial specifications of income per capita.

In the empirical studies based on the cross-national data of the 1980s, Grossman and Krueger (1991) and Shafik and Bandyopadhyay (1992) demonstrate three types of relationships: (i) environmental quality (as indicated by "municipal wastes per capita" and "carbon dioxide emissions per capita") declines steadily as incomes increase; (ii) environmental quality (as indicated by "population without safe water" and "urban population without adequate sanitation") increases steadily as incomes increase; and (iii) environmental quality (as indicated by "urban concentration of particulate matter" and "urban concentrations of sulfur dioxide") first declines but then increases with incomes increase.

In a more synthesized term, the relationship between environmental pressures and income levels has been summarized to follow an inverted-U curve (See, for example, Lucas *et al.*, 1992, World Bank, 1992 and 1995, Panayton, 1993, Selden and Song, 1994, Shafik, 1994, Grossman and Krueger, 1995, Holtz-Eakin and Selden, 1995, and Rock, 1996). This phenomenon is known as the environmental Kuznets curve (EKC), due to the similarity with the relationship between the level of inequality and income per capita considered by Kuznets (1955). According to the EKC hypothesis, environmental pressures increase as income level increases at the initial stage of economic development, but later these pressures diminish along with the income levels. The simplest form of mathematical expression can be written as $y = a + bx + cx^2 + \varepsilon$, where y is the level of environmental damage, x is the current level of per capita output, ε is the unobservable residual, a is constant, and $b > 0$ and $c < 0$.

It should also be noted that some articles of the laws relating to the environment have only been defined in principle, but were not able to be put into practice. For example, Article 44 of the Law on Mineral Resources (*kuangcan ziyuan fa*), issued in 1986, states: "... those who use destructive methods to extract mineral resources should refund the loss of damages and be additionally charged if the resources have been seriously damaged, till the withdrawal of their certificates for mining permission at the most serious situation," these should be further clarified at least in the following aspects: (i) which kinds of extraction methods should be defined as "destructive" to mineral resources; (ii) how to set up the standard of the "serious damages" to resources; (iii) how to calculate the "loss of damages"; (iv) how to determine the amount of "additional charges"; and (v) what should be defined as the "most serious situation", and so on.

Before the early 1980s, China had no formal administrative organs in charge of environmental protection. In 1984, the National Environmental Protection Agency (NEPA) was established. Thereafter, environmental protection bureaus, divisions, or offices have been established at all governmental levels, including the "environmental protection offices" of the Commissions, ministries, and other government branches and the state-owned corporations at ministry or semi-ministry level, the "environmental protection bureaus" of the provinces and autonomous regions, and so on. In 2008, the NEPA was upgraded, becoming the Ministry of Environmental Protection (MEP).

China's environmental protection network has thus become reasonably comprehensive. Directly under the State Council, the MEP – which has eight specific departments of planning, policy regulation, development supervision, pollution control, science and technology, nature conservation, personnel, and foreign affairs – supervises China's environmentally related activities through two parallel channels:

(1) Provinces and autonomous regions → prefecture or municipalities → counties and urban districts → non-state and private enterprises; and
(2) State commissions → ministries and other government branches and state corporations at ministry and semi-ministry levels → state-owned enterprises.

However, China's current administrative organs in charge of environmental protection and its environmentally related law enforcement are still weak, particularly at the grassroots level, compared to its increasing economic growth and social demands for environmental quality. The MEP can only exert its policy and professional directions to the provincial environmental protection bureaus, while the latter are appointed by and, naturally, mainly responsible to *their* respective provincial governments. Furthermore, the importance of coordinating the economic development and environmental protection has not been brought home to some local governments and enterprises, because of their lack of awareness of their responsibility for the implementation of the environmental protection laws. Motivated by partial economic interest, the government officials and enterprise managers often ignore environmental costs and benefits, as the yardstick of their achievements has been largely confined to the economic growth index. They are reluctant to make a careful study of whether such growth could be sustained, and have even seen the developing economy as an excuse to evade the restraints of laws and regulations. The irrational aspects of the administrative system and unclear defined responsibility in various departments have impaired the efficiency of environmental management.

10.6 Summary

The uneven distribution of natural resources in China has had a considerable influence on the disequilibrated regional structures of exploitation and the supply of those resources used as inputs of production to produce desired final goods and services for the society. China's mineral and energy resources are distributed principally in the northern and western inland areas, while the largest industrial consumers are located in the eastern and southern coastal areas. Therefore, the long-distance transfers of raw materials and semi-finished products from the northern and western inland areas to the eastern and southern coastal areas should be the only feasible approach by which to efficiently create an equilibrium between supply and demand in the Chinese economy. The Chinese government should recognize this fact and try to deal carefully with national economic cooperation.

In contrast to the development pattern of most industrialized economies, the Chinese economy has been fueled principally by coal rather than by petroleum and natural gas. Given its abundance in reserves compared with other energy resources such as hydropower, petroleum and natural gas, coal, which accounts for more than 80 percent of China's total energy resources, has until recently supplied almost 70 percent of the nation's total energy supply. Without stressing the low heating conversion rate of coal consumption, the serious environmental damage resulting from the exploitation, transportation and consumption of coal resources has already posed challenges to the sustainable development of the Chinese economy.

China's economic development has essentially followed a traditional development model that is characterized by high resource and energy (mainly coal) consumption and extensive management. This has led not only to a series of events that have damaged the present-day environment, but has also affected its economic sustainability. Therefore, shifting the development strategy and embarking on the path to sustainable development is the only correct choice for the Chinese economy. In this chapter we have posed questions about China's natural resources and environmental issues rather than drawing up any conclusions. It should be noted that China, like many other developing countries, is facing many pressing problems related to the economic development which might, at least in the short run, be contradicted by a system of environmental protection. However, environmental policies and measures should never be treated independently of economic policies. Moreover, they can serve as a dynamic mechanism for the maximization of the real well-being of the whole people.

10.7   Case study: Should Chinese legislation be revised?

The period since the 1980s has seen the introduction of a number of pieces of legislation relating to the exploitation and protection of natural and environmental resources. But the legislative foundation of the Chinese economy is still weak. For example, China has not introduced any comprehensive weather modification laws. It has only enacted the "Regulations of the People's Republic of China on Meteorological Services" promulgated by the State Council on August 18 1994, and the "Regulations on Administration of Weather Modification" adopted at the 56th Executive Meeting of the State Council on March 13 2002. The Meteorological Law was adopted at the 12th Meeting of the Standing Committee of the Ninth National People's Congress of the People's Republic of China on October 31 1999 and came into effect as of January 1 2000 (NPC, 2000). However, there are many contradictory articles in the law. For example, in Article 5, the Law states:

> The competent meteorological department under the State Council is responsible for meteorological work nationwide. Local competent meteorological departments at different levels are responsible for meteorological work in their own administrative

regions under the leadership of the competent meteorological departments at a higher level and the people's governments at the corresponding level.

This article defines a dual-track system of leadership for the provincial and local meteorological departments. The problem with this system is its administrative inefficiency, given that provincial and local meteorological departments are simultaneously subordinate to two different administrative organs. Regarding the prevention of meteorological disasters, Article 28 of the Law states:

> Competent meteorological departments at all levels shall make arrangements for joint monitoring and forecast of significant weather events among regions or departments, propose timely measures for preventing meteorological disasters and make assessment of severe weather disasters, which shall serve as the decision making basis for the people's governments at the corresponding levels to arrange prevention of meteorological disasters.

Obviously, this article does not define the geographic scopes of and manners for interregional coordination in case that a meteorological disaster occurs. Our most serious concern now arises from the fact that there is no article relating to cross-border activities of weather modification in the Chinese laws. In 2002, it appears in the "Regulations on Administration of Weather Modification" (*rengong yingxiang tianqi guanli tiaoli*) adopted at the 56th Executive Meeting of the State Council on March 13 (State Council, 2002). As defined in Article 14 of this Regulations,

> Where weather modification operations are to be implemented crossing the boundaries of different provinces, autonomous regions or municipalities directly under the Central Government, the relevant people's governments of the provinces, autonomous regions or municipalities directly under the Central Government shall make a decision thereon through consultation; if no agreement is reached through consultation, the decision shall be made by the competent meteorological department of the State Council in consultation with the relevant people's governments of the provinces, autonomous regions or municipalities directly under the Central Government.

Clearly, this is an invalid article. And, therefore, its enforcement is weak. In most circumstances, the weather modification activities of a province may not be carried out across land borders, but they could have serious impacts on the neighboring provinces. Because of the geographical proximity in cross-border areas, weather modification activities carried out on either side of a border may affect the territory of the other side (see Section 8.6 of Chapter 8 for more detail).

In contrast to the Chinese regulations on weather modification, the "Agreement between the United States of America and Canada Relating to the Exchange of Information on Weather Modification Activities," signed by the Government of the United States of America and the Government of Canada, is much more clearly defined.[11] For example, in Article I(b) of the Agreement, the term "weather modification activities of mutual interest" is defined as

...carried out in or over the territory of a Party within 200 miles of the international boundary; or such activities wherever conducted, which, in the judgment of a Party, may significantly affect the composition, behavior, or dynamics of the atmosphere over the territory of the other Party.

In Article IV, "each Party agrees to notify and to fully inform the other concerning any weather modification activities of mutual interest conducted by it prior to the commencement of such activities. Every effort shall be made to provide such notice as far in advance of such activities as may be possible...". Furthermore, the agreement states:

The Parties agree to consult, at the request of either Party, regarding particular weather modification activities of mutual interest. Such consultations shall be initiated promptly on the request of a Party, and in cases of urgency may be undertaken through telephonic or other rapid means of communication.

11
International Economic Influences

A frog that lived in a shallow well said to a turtle coming from the East Sea: "I am so happy! When I go out, I jump about on the railing beside the mouth of the well, and I rest in the holes on the broken wall of the well when I come home. If I jump into the water, it comes up to my armpits and holds up my cheeks. If I walk in the mud, it covers up my feet. I look around at the wriggly worms, crabs and tadpoles and none of them can compare with me. Moreover, I am lord of this trough of water and I stand up tall in this shallow well. My happiness is full. Why wouldn't you come here often and look around my place?"[1]

– Zhuangzi (c.369–286 BC)

11.1 Historical review

China had been a typical autarkic society for a long time before it was forced to open up to the outside world at the end of the First Opium War (1840–42). According to the *Guangxu Da Qing Huidian Shili* (vol. 775, p. 4 and vol. 776, p. 13), *haijin* (ban on maritime voyages) included: (1) the export of cereals and five metals (gold, silver, copper, iron and tin) were strictly prohibited; (2) private trade and contacts between Chinese and foreign businessmen were illegal; (3) foreigners' activities in China were only allowed on the conditions that "At most ten foreigners may take a walk together near their hotel on the 8th, 18th and 28th days a month", "Overseas businessmen should not stay in Guangdong in winter", and "Women from foreign countries are prohibited to enter this country" and so on; (4) Chinese businessmen going abroad were subject to the conditions that "At most one liter of rice may be carried by a seaman a day" and "At most two guns may be installed in a ship"; and (5) the manufacture of seagoing vessels of more than 500 *dan* (hectoliters) in weight and eight meters in height was prohibited.

Western influence in China came about at the beginning of the fifteenth and sixteenth centuries due to the increased trade in Chinese products, such as silk and tea through the Silk Road that stretched from northwestern China to eastern Europe. The Europeans were interested in Hong Kong's safe harbor located on the trade routes of the Far East, thus establishing a trade enterprise between Western businessmen and China. The Portuguese were the first to reach China in 1555, but the British dominated foreign trade in the southern region of Guangdong during the early stages of Western connections with China. Ships from the British East India Company were stationed on the Indian Coast after Emperor Kangxi (reign 1654–1722) of the Qing dynasty (1644–1911) opened trade on a limited basis in Guangzhou. Fifteen years later, the company was allowed to build a storage warehouse outside Guangzhou. The Westerners were given limited preferences and had to adhere to many Chinese rules and policies. In addition, Chinese rulers also banned foreigners from learning the Chinese language in fear of their potential bad influences.

Chinese commodities, principally porcelains, were popular among European aristocrats. However, the level of European imports from China were far greater than its exports. As a result, the British East India Company tried to equalize its huge purchases from China by doubling its sales of opium to China. The sale of opium saw a great increase by the turn of the nineteenth century. Fearful of the outflow of silver, the Chinese emperor banned the drug trade in 1799 but to no avail. Following the end of the first Opium War, the Treaty of Nanjing in 1842 ceded Hong Kong to Britain in perpetuity. With the involvement of the British, many companies transferred from Guangzhou to Hong Kong, enabling the British colony to begin a prime Asian entrepôt. Hostilities between the British and the Chinese on the mainland continued to heighten, leading to the Second Opium War. In 1860, under the "Convention of Peking", Britain gained Kowloon, Stonecutters Island and some other small islands.

Since the middle of the nineteenth century, the Chinese economy has been transformed as a result of the gradual destruction of the feudal system. There was a flow of foreign capital into the mainland, which was followed by the penetration of Western culture, which represented the first stirrings of Chinese industrialization. Unfortunately, because of long civil wars as well as the invasion by the Japanese, China's economic development had not been given a high priority during the first half of the twentieth century. During the period of the first Five-Year Plan (1953–57), some economic progress was achieved. Thereafter, however, difficulties took place due to China's frequent domestic political struggles and the "closed-door" policies towards both the US-dominated capitalist bloc and the USSR-dominated socialist bloc.

As soon as the PRC was founded on October 1 1949, the Chinese government severed almost all economic ties with the capitalist world. Affected by the Korean War (1950–53) and the Taiwan Strait crisis, the Eastern belt stagnated, in comparison with most parts of the Western belt – which benefited geographically to a large extent from China's close relations with the former USSR. However, it should be noted that China's foreign trade with the centrally planned economies (CPEs) usually remained at a minimum level, aiming at just supplementing any gap between domestic supply and demand. Such trade reflected natural resource endowments more than anything else. Therefore, China's close ties with the socialist economies did not result in significant economic effects on the Western belt. During the period from the early 1960s to the late 1970s, China practised autarkic socialism as a result of the Sino-USSR disputes as well as the implementation of the "self-reliance and independence" strategy thereafter.

For thousands of years, Chinese culture has aimed at achieving a harmonious balance between Confucianism, Buddhism and Taoism, which worked quite well for a very long time. Probably as a result, the Chinese were too intoxicated with their past prosperity and still had proudly treated themselves as the "center of the world" even when it was clear that in economic terms they lagged well behind Western nations. This kind of ethnocentrism and self-satisfaction meant that China remained a typical autarkic society. With regards to the cultural differences between the Chinese and Japanese economies, Maddison (1996, p. 53) states:

> In China, the foreigners appeared on the fringes of a huge country. The ruling elite regarded it as the locus of civilization, and considered the 'barbarian' intruders as an irritating nuisance. In Japan, they struck in the biggest city, humiliated the Shogun and destroyed his legitimacy as a ruler. The Japanese had already borrowed important elements of Chinese civilization and saw no shame in copying in a Western model which had demonstrated its superior technology so dramatically.

China's economic internationalization strategy began to experience dramatic changes in the late 1970s when the top Chinese policy makers suddenly found that the Chinese economy, having been constructed along socialist lines for almost 30 years, lagged far behind not only the

Western nations but also those formerly backward economies along the western coast of the Pacific Ocean. In order to attract foreign investment, China enacted the "Law of the People's Republic of China Concerning the Joint Ventures with Chinese and Foreign Investment" in 1979. In the same year, the CCPCC and State Council decided to grant Guangdong and Fujian provinces "special policies and flexible measures" in foreign economic affairs. On December 26 1979, the People's Congress of Guangdong province approved the proposal of the provincial government that a part of Shenzhen next to Hong Kong, Zhuhai next to Macau, and Santou should all be permitted to experiment with a market-oriented economy with Chinese characteristics, namely, special economic zones (SEZ). This proposal was finally accepted by the NPC on August 26 1980. At the same time, Xiamen in Southeast Fujian province, with its close proximity to Taiwan, also became a SEZ with the approval of NPC.

Thereafter, a series of open-door measures were implemented in the coastal area: in October 1983, Hainan island, Guangdong province, was allowed to adopt some of the special foreign economic policies implemented by the SEZs; in April 1984, 14 coastal cities (Tianjin, Shanghai, Dalian, Qinhuangdao, Yantai, Qingdao, Lianyungang, Nantong, Ningbo, Wenzhou, Fuzhou, Guangzhou, Ganjiang and Beihai) were designated by the CCPCC and the State Council as "open cities"; in February 1985, the three deltas of the Yangtze river, the Pearl river and South Fujian were approved as coastal economic development zones (EDZs); in March 1988, the expansion of the EDZs of all three deltas was again approved while at the same time some cities and counties in Liaodong and Shandong peninsulas and Bohai Basin area were allowed to open up economically to the outside world; in April 1988, the NPC approved the establishment of Hainan province which was organized as an SEZ operating under even more flexible policies than other SEZs; in April 1990, Shanghai's suggestion to speed up the development of Pudong area using some of the SEZ's mechanisms was approved by the CCPCC and the State Council.

In addition to its 14,500 km coastline, China has more than 22,000 km of international land boundaries. Specifically, nine provinces are directly exposed to the outside world. These frontier provinces, the neighboring nations and the lengths of their respective borderlines are as detailed below:

- Gansu (with Mongolia, 65 km)
- Guangxi (with Vietnam, 1,020 km)
- Heilongjiang (with Russia, 3,045 km)
- Inner Mongolia (with Mongolia, 3,640 km; and Russia, 560 km)

- Jilin (with North Korea, 870 km; and Russia, 560 km)
- Liaoning (with North Korea, 546 km)
- Tibet (with India, 1,906 km; Nepal, 1,236 km; Bhutan, 470 km; and Myanmar, 188 km)
- Xinjiang (with Russia, 40 km; Mongolia, 968 km; Pakistan, 523 km; Kazakhstan, 1,533 km; Kyrgyzstan, 858 km; Tajikistan, 540 km; Afghanistan, 76 km; and India, 1,474 km)
- Yunnan (with Myanmar, 1,997 km; Laos, 710 km; and Vietnam, 1,353 km)

Generally, cross-border economic cooperation and trade are facilitated by both geographical factors and also the fact that people on both sides of the border often belong to the same minority group and share a number of cultural characteristics. China's border development has mainly benefited from its "open-door" policy and *rapprochement* with the neighboring countries since the mid-1980s. In 1984 the Chinese government promulgated the "Provisional Regulations for the Management of 'Small-volume' Border Trade" and opened up hundreds of frontier cities and towns. In contrast to the eastern coastal development, which was fueled principally by FDI, China's inland frontier development has been characterized by border trade with its foreign neighbors. Inspired by Deng Xiaoping's Southern Speech in early 1992, China has embarked on a deeper outward-looking policy in an attempt to promote development in the frontier regions of the four provinces of Heilongjiang, Yunnan, Jilin and Liaoning and the four autonomous regions of Inner Mongolia, Xinjiang, Tibet and Guangxi. Since the early 1990s, a series of favorable and flexible measures to manage cross-border trade and economic cooperation have been granted to those frontier provinces. They include:

- "Measures Concerning the Supervision and Favourable Taxation for the People-to-People Trade in Sino-Myanmar Border" (January 25, 1992, Office of Custom, PRC);
- "Notification Concerning the Further Opening up of the Four Frontier Cities of Heihe, Shuifenhe, Hunchun and Manzhouli" (1992, State Council);
- "Notification Concerning the Further Opening up of the Five Frontier Cities and Towns of Nanning, Kunming, Pingxiang, Ruili and Hekou" (June 1992, State Council);
- "Some Favourable Policies and Economic Autonomy Authorized to the Frontier Cities of Heihe and Shuifenhe" (June 1992, Heilongjiang);

- "Resolution of Some Issues Concerning the Extension of Open-door and Promotion of Economic Development" (April 20, 1991, Inner Mongolia);
- "Notification of Promoting Trade and Economic Cooperation with Neighbouring and Eastern European Countries" (February 9, 1992, Xinjiang);
- "Resolutions Concerning the Further Reform and Opening up to the Outside World" (July 14 1992, Tibet);
- "Provisional Regulations Concerning the Border Trade" (1991, Yunnan province).[2]

Box 11.1   A guide to applying for visas

Since the late 1970s when the open-door policy was introduced, Chinese citizens have had fewer restrictions on travelling abroad. However, problems still remain due to both the border control policy of China and the unavailability of visa-free access to most foreign nations. Chinese citizens going abroad for public affairs are able to apply for "public affairs passports" (*gongwu huzhao*), while those who intend to go abroad for personal matters have to apply passports and visas through a more complicated procedure. The diagram below shows a visa application process in the mid-1990s when I was invited by a European institution to write the first edition of this book:

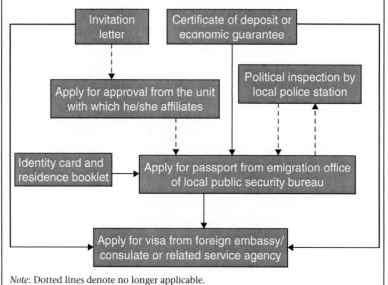

Note: Dotted lines denote no longer applicable.

Since the introduction of reform and open-door policies in 1978, China has basically formed a pattern featuring gradual advances from east to west, viz., from the SEZs, then to other coastal areas and finally to the inland area. Since 1992, further progress has been made in opening up border, riparian and inland areas to the outside world. This has also spread from processing industries to basic industries, infrastructure facilities and service trades, and is intended to develop toward a multi-level and universal opening pattern. One glance at the history of the PRC reveals that China's economic stagnation and prosperity have been closely related to its policy of economic internationalization. More specifically, when the autarkic policy was implemented, economic stagnation occurred; when the outward-looking policy was introduced, economic prosperity would be achieved accordingly. China's regional economic performances have also been decided in this way.

Along with the increasing global participation of economic activity, the concept "economic integration" has become a burning issue in the political agenda of both developed and developing nations since the end of World War II, particularly in the late 1980s when the Cold War came to an end. During the past few decades, international economic integration has achieved substantial progress, including the establishment of the European Community (EC) and its transformation into the European Union (EU), the North America Free Trade Agreement (NAFTA), Asia-Pacific Economic Cooperation (APEC), the Association of Southeast Asian Nations (ASEAN), and so on.

In pre-reform China, tariffs were high and represented the only form of protection. When China initiated significant trade reforms in 1992, the rates of tariff were still high, averaging 44.05 percent. Since 1992, China has cut its tariff rates substantially every year. For example, the average tariff rate fell to 17.1 percent in 1998. On the other hand, non-tariff barriers were introduced in the early 1980s. Subsequently, an increasing number of goods were placed under licensed trading and quota. In 1992, some 25 percent of imports and 15 percent of exports were managed under licenses. However, the scope of license and quota management has been narrowed since 1992. By 1997, only 384 categories of imports, only 5 percent of the total, were managed under quota and licenses. China's import-regulating tax system was finally abolished in 1992. Since this time, the Chinese government has reduced the tariffs on three occasions. However, before April 1996 the average tariff rate was still higher than that of other developing countries. At that time China began to reduce the tariff rates on more than 4,000 items of imported commodities with an average reduction of over 30 percent. Meanwhile, tax exemption and reduction for the foreign-funded enterprises have also been abolished. After the reduction, China's average tariff rate was cut to 23 percent from the previous level.[3]

On December 11 2001, China became the 143rd member of the WTO at the Fourth Ministerial Conference of the World Trade Organization (WTO) held in Doha, Qatar. In order to accede to the WTO, China agreed to take concrete steps to remove trade barriers and open up its markets to foreign companies and their exports in virtually every product sector and for a wide range of services as represented in the Protocol of Accession of the People's Republic of China (Document No. WT/L/432, 2001). With China's consent, the WTO created a special multilateral mechanism for the purpose of reviewing China's compliance on an annual basis. Known as the Transitional Review Mechanism, this mechanism will operate annually for eight years after China's accession, with a final review in the tenth year. The WTO membership will give China an improved external environment under which the import of new technologies and capital inflows have given a boost to China's industry. Exports have also been growing faster as China has been less strictly bound by trade quotas. For the first time in the last few decades China no longer needs to be concerned about the annual renewal of its most-favored nation (MFN) status by the US Congress. Furthermore, in accordance with WTO requirements, banks, insurance companies, telecommunications and other service industries of the rest of the world will be allowed to operate in China according to the negotiated timetable. The impact may eventually break up the status of monopoly and state control that have existed in China for around half a century. In the long run the impact on social and political reforms can be highly significant.

On January 1 2002, China cut the import tariffs on more than 5,000 goods. The average tariff rate was reduced to 12 percent from a level of 15.3 percent in 2001. The rate for manufacturing goods was reduced from 14.7 percent to 11.3 percent, while that for agricultural goods, excluding fisheries, fell from 18.8 percent to 15.8 percent (Wan *et al.*, 2004). At the same time, China abolished the quota and license arrangement for grains, wool, cotton, chemical fertilizers and so on. In addition, China modified or abolished those laws and regulations that are inconsistent with WTO rules. Since January 1 2002 new laws on anti-dumping and anti-subsidy have been implemented. The average tariff rate was cut further from 12 percent in 2002 to 9.3 percent in 2005. Non-tariff barriers were also removed for most manufacturing goods by the end of 2004. Small and medium-sized enterprises and foreign invested companies have also been entitled to participate directly in international trade.

11.2 Foreign direct investment

The trends in foreign direct investment (FDI)[4] can be distinguished according to changes in the direction of overall policy. During the late 1970s and the early 1980s, the Chinese government established four special economic zones (SEZs) in Guangdong and Fujian provinces, and offered special incentive policies for these SEZs to attract FDI. China has made continuous efforts to attract foreign capital in the forms of both foreign loans and FDI. Foreign loans include foreign government loans, loans from international financial institutions, and buyers' credits and other private loans. In order to attract foreign investment, the NPC enacted the "Law of the People's Republic of China Concerning the Joint Ventures with Chinese and Foreign Investment" in 1979. In the SEZs and other economic and technological development zones, foreign investors were afforded preferential treatment. Moreover, the government assumes responsibility for improving the landscape and constructing infrastructure such as water-supply and drainage systems, electricity, roads, post and telecommunications, warehouses, and so on. While FDI inflows into China were highly concentrated in these SEZs, the amount was rather limited during this period.

Since the early 1980s, when Hainan island and 14 coastal cities across ten provinces were opened up, the previously recorded modest FDI levels started to take off. Total FDI inflows amounted to US$10.3 billion in the 1984–88 period, with an annual average growth of US$2.1 billion. This remarkable upward trend, however, dropped steeply in 1989, mainly due to the impact of the Tian'anmen incidents. The growth of FDI inflows into China slowed down at a meager 6.2 percent level in 1989 and only 2.8 percent in 1990. Even though FDI resumed its growth path in 1991, by recording an increase of 25.2 percent over the previous year, the annual growth rate for this overall period fell to 11.0 percent, which paled in comparison with the 38.1 percent recorded during the period 1984 to 1988 (OECD, 2000).

The third phase began in the Spring of 1992, when Deng Xiaoping went on a tour of China's southern coastal areas and SEZs. His visit, whose principal intention was to push forward China's overall economic reform process and to emphasize China's commitment to the open-door policy and market-oriented economic reform, also proved to be a success in terms of increasing the confidence of foreign investors in China. China adopted a new approach, turning away from special regimes toward a more nationwide implementation of open policies for FDI. The government issued a series of new policies and regulations to encourage

FDI inflows. The results were remarkable: Since 1992 the inflows of FDI into China have accelerated and reached the peak level in the early 2000s.

Since it made its first calls for foreign capital participation in its economy in 1979, China has received a large proportion of international direct investment flows. China has become the second largest FDI recipient in the world, behind the United States, and the largest host country among the developing countries. China's position as a host to FDI is in fact too far removed from any other developing country – and most developed countries – to be subject to any serious challenge. China has been the largest recipient of FDI among developing countries since 1993. China's joining of the WTO in 2001 provided a strong push for a new wave of foreign investment into China. In 2003, China overtook the United States as the world's biggest recipient of FDI, attracting a figure of US$53 billion. By the end of 2004, the number of established foreign-invested enterprises had reached more than half a million with contracted foreign investment of more than US$1,000 billion and actual use of foreign investment of more than US$500 billion (NBS, 2005), which is equivalent to 10 percent of direct investment worldwide and about 30 percent of the combined investment amount for all developing countries.

The three major forms of foreign investment in China are: joint venture, cooperative and foreign enterprises. The scope of foreign investment has now extended from investments in tourism, textile and building industries to cooperative ventures in oil exploration, transportation, telecommunications, machine building, electronics, and other industries. Regarding the origins of FDI, Hong Kong and Macau were the largest investors, contributing 43.30 percent of the total foreign investment. They were followed by Japan (10.62 percent), Taiwan (6.58 percent), USA (6.51 percent), Singapore (3.87 percent), South Korea (2.47 percent) and UK (2.10 percent) in 1995. In 2005, the top ten countries and regions with investments in China were as follows (in order of shares): Hong Kong, Virgin Islands, South Korea, Japan, the United States, Taiwan, Singapore, Cayman Islands, West Samoa and Germany, the total of which accounted for more than 80 percent the total actual use of foreign investments in the country.[5]

During the 1980s, FDI was concentrated in traditional labor-intensive manufacturing industries (light industry), especially textiles, garments and real estate companies. Since 1992, it has gradually shifted to capital- and technology-intensive sectors, such as chemicals, machinery, transport equipment, electronics and telecommunications. In the second half of the 1990s, while there was stagnation in foreign investment in traditional labor-intensive manufacturing industries, the IT industry became a new focus of investment. Investments in technology-intensive industries have become a new focus of investment. The goal to attract FDI inflows has been to introduce advanced technology, improve management and expand markets. The modes of foreign investment have undergone some systematic changes. The basic option in the early period of reform was to set up a contractual joint venture. Since 1986, equity joint ventures and wholly foreign-owned enterprise investments have become the main forms of foreign investment. Since the 1990s, the share of wholly foreign-invested enterprises has increased gradually, as has the level of foreign control of joint ventures. By 2000, the actual investment share of wholly foreign-owned enterprises exceeded that of joint ventures; the former became the main force in impelling growth in foreign trade. A related fact is that, with the exception of a few sectors, the Chinese government repealed restrictions on foreign control in joint ventures.

Foreign investment has been unevenly distributed in China. FDI inflows have been heavily concentrated in China's coastal provinces, while the Central and Western Regions have attracted only marginal shares. By 2000, foreign investments were felt in all parts of China, except in Tibet. Throughout the period the southeast coastal area has dominated as a recipient of inward foreign investment. Not surprisingly, the most important determinant for the irregular absorption of foreign capital is geographical location. For example, the Eastern belt received most of the foreign capital, while less than 10 percent of the total foreign capital flowed into the Central and Western belts, which cover more than 85 percent of China's territory. Nevertheless, this uneven pattern has improved gradually as a result of the government efforts to internationalize the inland economy.

This inequality stems from the FDI policies taken by the Chinese authority. The open door began with the creation of SEZs and preferential regimes for 14 coastal cities. This has resulted in an overwhelming concentration of FDI in the east. With the adoption of more broadbased economic reforms and open-door policies for FDI in the 1990s, FDI inflows into China have started to spread to other provinces. Among the eastern region provinces, Guangdong's performance in attracting FDI has been particularly impressive. Its share of accumulated FDI stock from 1983 to 1998 was 29.4 percent of the national total, far exceeding all other provinces including Jiangsu and Fujian, each of which possessed around 10 percent of the national total, ranking them second and third among China's thirty provinces. However, if we analyze this province group one step further, we find that the shares of each province have changed gradually. The share of Guangdong has declined from 46.13 percent in the 1980s to 27.98 percent in the 1990s. In contrast, the shares of other coastal provinces (such as Jiangsu, Fujian, Zhejiang, Shandong, Tianjin and Hubei) have increased steadily.

In recent years the share of the central provinces in the national total of accumulated FDI stocks has increased gradually – from 5.3 percent during the 1980s to 9.2 percent during the 1990s. The main contributors are Henan, Hubei, and Hunan provinces, with their shares of accumulated FDI in the national total doubling between the 1980s and the 1990s. These figures suggest that the provincial distribution of FDI inflows has spread somewhat from the opened coastal provinces into the inland provinces. The western, less developed provinces received only a very small amount of FDI inflows, with their share in the national accumulated FDI stocks declining from 4.7 percent in the 1980s to 3.2 percent in the 1990s. However, Sichuan and Shaanxi attracted relatively higher levels of FDI inflows than the other provinces in this group. In the final analysis, FDI inflows in the 1990s have diffused from the initially concentrated southern coastal areas toward the southeastern and eastern coastal areas as well as toward inland areas. The three provincial groups of the Eastern, Central and Western belts experienced different patterns of FDI inflows. For the provinces of the eastern region FDI inflows have been increasing steadily, with a remarkably high growth rate particularly in the period from 1992 to 1998. For the other two provincial groups, the inflows of FDI have been much lower, especially for the western region provinces. As a result, in terms of the absolute magnitude of annual FDI inflows the gap between the Eastern belt and the Central and Western belts has actually broadened since 1992.

Foreign investment has played an increasing role in the Chinese economy. In 1990 the shares of foreign trade, gross value of industrial output (GVIO) and employees of the foreign-funded enterprises to China were only 17.4 percent, 2.1 percent and 1.4 percent, respectively. By 1995, they had increased dramatically – to 39.1 percent, 16.6 percent and 10.8 percent, respectively (IIE, 1996, pp. 274–5). What is more, the foreign enterprises have promoted the importation of advanced technology, equipment, and management and, above all, competition mechanisms from the advanced economies. Moreover, they have generated nearly one-fifth of the total tax revenues and millions of job opportunities, employing around 10 percent of all urban workers.

Table 11.1 The effects of foreign direct investment (FDI) on the Chinese economy

A. External effects	B. Domestic effects
1. China's comparative advantages	1. An increasingly important source of capital
2. Increased participation in the international segmentation of production	2. Create jobs
3. Impact on China's trade growth	3. Upgrade skills
4. Role of FIEs in processing trade	4. Paid higher wages to employees
5. Comparative trading performance of FIE firms	5. Raise factor productivity and increased technology transfer
6. Building dynamic specialization	6. Modify China's industrial structure
7. Domestic penetration of FIEs	7. Foreign and domestic firms are different
8. Rising local content	8. FDI has increased domestic competition
9. FIE export competitiveness and exchange rate policy	9. FDI has increased industrial performance
10. Domestic firms have lagged behind	
11. Regional disparities have increased	
12. Impact on China's balance of payments	

Note: FIEs = foreign (including Taiwan, Hong Kong and Macau) invested enterprises.

Most of the foreign investments came from small and medium-sized enterprises based in Hong Kong. The dominant position of Hong Kong is apparent from several factors. First, Hong Kong is geographically adjacent to Guangdong province, where Shenzhen – the most important China SEZ – is located. Secondly, it was in the 1980s that Hong Kong made the transfer of its export-oriented labor-intensive manufacturing industry to mainland China. This is the typical "Flying Geese Paradigm" of the international division of labor. Thirdly, especially since 1992, investments from Hong Kong took advantage of the preferential treatment given to foreign investors.

Table 11.1 summarizes the main findings of the research conducted under the cooperation program by the Ministry of Foreign Trade of China and the OECD (2000).

There is a substantial literature on the subject of FDI and exports as the driving force behind China's success (see, for example, Berthelemy and Demurger 2000; Lemione 2000; and Demurger 2000). In this connection the roles of overseas Chinese and of Hong Kong and Taiwan are often emphasized. In contrast to the above view, Qian (2002) presents a quite different conclusion after simply considering a parallel experience in Germany. If Hong Kong or Taiwan could play such a powerful role on mainland China, West Germany should have had an even greater impact on East Germany, given that West Germany is much larger and stronger than Taiwan and Hong Kong combined and East Germany is much smaller than mainland China.[6] We argue that Qian's (2002) judgment would have been correct if it were only taking into account the direct influences of the FDI and foreign trade. However, the indirect effects of the FDI, although following a decreasing geographical order from coastal to middle and to western China, are also enomous. In addition, social and cultural influences of the open-door policy should never be neglected, since they also significantly determined the rates of economic development. Anyone who has ever traveled to western and inland cities cannot fail to notice that their vibrant local economies were due largely to their interactions with the outside world. More important is the great potential of comparative advantages as well as the close cultural linkages between Hong Kong, Macau, Taiwan and mainland China.

11.3 Foreign trade

A country may benefit from the export of those commodities it can produce more cheaply and importing those which can be produced more efficiently abroad. This is particularly useful for China – a country with abundant natural and agricultural resources but a comparative lack of capital and technology – to import advanced scientific innovations, production techniques and management experience from advanced nations. To bring about socialist modernization in its own way, China did not adopt the strategy of "founding a nation on trade" used by many industrially developed nations; rather, it was based on the principle of "independence and self-reliance" during the first decades of the PRC. As a result, China lagged far behind the advanced nations. In order to achieve rapid economic modernization, the Chinese government has clearly recognized the importance of seeking new technologies through foreign trade and international cooperation.

During the early stages of the PRC China's foreign trade and economic relations reflected, to a large extent, the basic characteristics of a socialist economy. In the 1950s, because of a trade embargo imposed by the USA and other Western nations, most foreign trade was restricted to the countries of the Soviet bloc. Following the Sino-Soviet split in the early

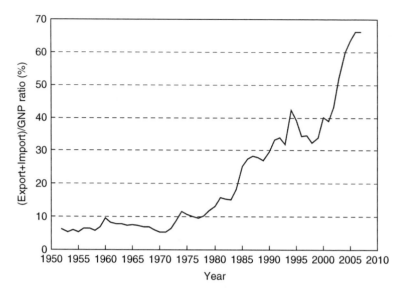

Figure 11.1　China's economic openness

1960s, there was a dramatic fall in the level of foreign trade. Guided by the principle of "self-reliance and independence," China's foreign trade and economic relations were not improved significantly before the early 1970s. Since then, its trade with the capitalist nations has increased gradually, as a result of the *rapprochement* with Japan, the USA, and some EU countries. However, because the autarkic economic policy was still in operation before the late 1970s, both the volume of Chinese foreign trade and its ratio to GNP were still very small at that time (see Figure 11.1).

Since the early 1980s, there has been a remarkable growth in terms of both exports and imports. In 1978, China ranked 32nd in the world in terms of international trade. Its ranking improved to 15th in 1989, 10th in 1997, 6th in 2001 and 2nd in 2007. The ratio of international trade to GDP also rose from less than 10 percent in 1978 to as high as more than 50 percent in 2004. The growth trend was maintained even during the Asian financial crisis in the late 1990s and in the US financial crisis of 2008.

Since the late 1970s, China has made many efforts to import advanced production equipment from abroad in order to use it to kick-start its economic take-off. Except for a few years, for example, 1982–83 and 1989–90, China's foreign trade during the reform period has grown

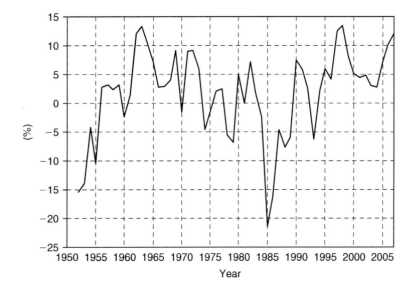

Figure 11.2 Foreign trade surplus (deficit) as percentage of total trade

with exceptional rapidity. When exports exceed imports, a trade surplus occurs. During the early period of the PRC, the Chinese economy sustained a large trade deficit. This seems to be reasonable because, after many years of wars, China's demand for both more consumer goods and more production materials was greater than it could possibly supply. From 1955 to 1977, China obtained a high level of trade surplus, with the exceptions of 1960, 1970, and 1974–75. Obviously, this beneficial foreign trade pattern had to a large extent been shaped by China's "self-reliance" policy for much of that period. China's attempt at speeding up economic development based on the "imported" method was mainly responsible to the trade deficit in the late 1970s. A long-lasting trade deficit occurred between 1984 and 1989. Trade surplus has accompanied the strong and growing exports since 1990, with the exception of 1993 (see Figure 11.2). This has also increased China's foreign deposits. However, this trade surplus has also led to large trade deficits for its trade partners, sometimes resulting in retaliations.[7]

Generally, foreign trade can be classified into four types according to its composition in terms of imported and exported commodities: (1) both imports and exports are dominated by primary goods; (2) imports are dominated by primary goods while exports are dominated by

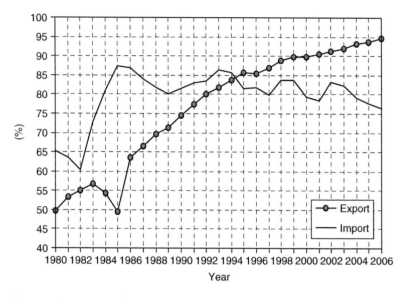

Figure 11.3   Shares of manufactured commodity imports and exports (%)

manufactured goods; (3) exports are dominated by primary goods while imports are dominated by manufactured goods; and (4) both imports and exports are dominated by manufactured goods. Over recent decades China's foreign trade has effectively transformed from pattern (1) to pattern (4). In the early 1950s, the shares of primary and manufactured goods were about 80 percent and 20 percent of total exports, respectively. Since then, the share of manufactured products to total exports has grown steadily and it eventually overtook that of primary products in the early 1980s. Since 1995, the share of manufactured goods to total exports has increased to more than 80 percent (see Figure 11.3).

In summary, China's export of manufactured goods has accounted for an increasing share since the mid-1980s, while the corresponding level of imports has declined, although at a slower rate. Clearly, China has been industrializing and is becoming a major exporter of manufactured goods. This structural change of exports has been largely ascribed to China's strong push toward industrialization since 1949 (as discussed in Chapter 9). The composition of imported commodities includes a very small share of primary products compared with that of manufactured products, as a result of China's abundance in natural resources as well as its large agricultural sector.

11.4 A quantitative analysis

It has been generally assumed that a country's economic dependence on the outside world is negatively related to its land area. For example, in an estimation of international trade, Frankel and Romer (1996, table 1) find that, for every 1 percent increase in land area, trade falls by about 0.2 percent. This may be illustrated unambiguously by the relationship between the supply and demand of some basic resources for countries differing in size (land area). Generally speaking, in comparison to large economies, small economies have a relatively limited range of natural resources. Therefore, they have to import those resources that they lack and that are essential to meeting diversified production and consumption needs. Eventually, the increased imports will stimulate exports in order to attain a balance.

In addition to geographic area, a country's economic size (output) and population also have an influence on its external economic activities. Generally, the larger the GDPs (or GNPs)[8] of trading partners, *ceteris paribus*, the larger the volume of trade between them; by contrast, population is a negative factor in the determination of international trade. This captures the well-known phenomenon that larger countries tend to be relatively less open to trade as a percentage of GDP (or GNP). Therefore, it is easy to understand that Hong Kong, Singapore, and Luxembourg are more highly dependent on international trade than the United States, China, or India. The former lack not only natural endowments but also the room to exploit economies of scale in the domestic market, while the latter, engaging in far more trade in absolute terms (*versus* less trade as a percentage of GDP or GNP), can find an increasing number of business opportunities within their own borders.

Without considering geographic factors, it could be very difficult to understand the current patterns of both global and regional trade. For instance, bilateral trade flows across the US–Canadian border, between France, Italy, the UK, Germany and the Netherlands, and along the western coast of the Pacific Ocean (including, *inter alia*, South Korea, Taiwan, Hong Kong and the mainland of China) have risen a great deal more quickly than between more remote and isolated economies. In addition to distance, another proxy of geographic factor that influences international trade is adjacency. For example, bilateral trade between France and the United Kingdom will be the result of their proximity, but trade between France and Germany will be further boosted by their common border.[9] Figure 11.4 shows a spatial pattern of foreign trade in which

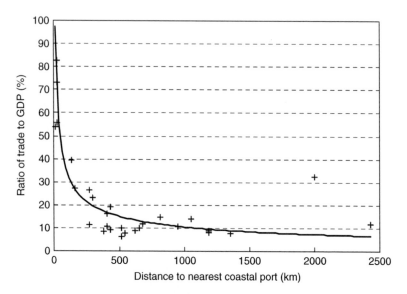

Figure 11.4   The spatial pattern of foreign trade in China

Notes: (1) Data on "ratio of trade to GDP" are based on NBS (2002). (2) Data on "distance to nearest coastal port" are estimated by the author based on the locations of China's 31 provincial capitals.

provinces' ratios of trade to GDP are negatively related to their distances to the nearest coastal port.

Past theories of the determinants of international trade seem controversial, or at best incomplete. The Heckscher-Ohlin (H-O), or factor-endowment, theory can be expressed in terms of two theorems. According to the H-O theorem, a nation will export the commodity produced by its relatively abundant and cheap factor and will import the commodity produced by its relatively scarce and expensive factor (see Heckscher, 1919; and Ohlin, 1933). The factor-price equalization theorem was proved rigorously by P.A. Samuelson and is therefore also called the Heckscher-Ohlin-Samuelson (H-O-S) theorem (Samuelson, 1948, 1949). According to the H-O-S theorem, international trade will bring about equalization in the relative and absolute returns to homogeneous factors across nations. The first empirical test of the H-O model was conducted by Leontief (1954) using 1947 US data, which demonstrates that US import substitutes were about 30 percent more capital-intensive than US exports. Since the United States is the most capital-intensive nation, this result was the opposite of what the H-O model had predicted and thus it became known as the Leontief paradox. This paradox could be explained in a number of ways: (1) 1947 being a nonrepresentative year; (2) the use of a two-factor (labor and capital) model; (3) the fact that US tariffs gave more protection to labor-intensive industries; and (4) the exclusion of human capital from the calculations. Some empirical studies, however, give conflicting results.[10]

However, past studies have raised more questions than they have answered. For example, the effects of geographic proximity on trade have not been shown to fall over time. Rather, for the period 1950–88 (Boisso and Ferrantino, 1997) and 1965–92 (Frankel *et al.*, 1997b) these effects have been shown to increase over time. In their analyses of the negative correlation between distance-related costs and the interdependence for sovereign countries, Frankel *et al.* (1997a) use the data from the 1980s and obtain slightly larger coefficients (around 0.5 to 0.6) on distance compared with Eichengreen and Irwin's (1995) interwar estimates (around 0.3 to 0.6) based on data from the 1930s. Similarly, using panel data from 1970, 1980 and 1990, Rauch (1999) finds little evidence that the effects of distance-related barriers declined between 1970 and 1990. Clearly, this provides no evidence that, as a result of technological innovation, declining distance-related transactions costs should have led to increased trade flows. One possibility is that these analyses exclude important explanatory variables, thereby biasing the estimates. To clarify related issues, it is necessary to isolate the influences of all distance-related variables on trade. In particular, the inclusion of some relevant cultural variables might allow us to gain a better understanding of the 'black box' containing the distance-related transactions costs that affect foreign trade.

Since the 1990s, numerous quantitative studies have examined the role that cultural factors play in international trade (for example, Havrylyshyn and Pritchett, 1991; Foroutan and Pritchett, 1993; Frankel and Wei, 1995, Table 5; Frankel *et al.*, 1997b; Rauch, 1999). These studies used linguistic links as one or more explanatory variables. The estimated results suggest that countries which have linguistic similarities have been more likely to trade with each other in the postwar period. In other words, there is some evidence of linguistic barriers to trade. However, linguistic variables have been highly simplified in these studies. For example, the links between countries were only measured with dummy variables in the above studies. As most countries do not share the same language, the international (or interregional) links should not be simply expressed by a dummy variable.[11] Last but not least, the existing literature omits another cultural variable – religion – that could play, at least

Table 11.2   Determinants of foreign trade, China and East Asia

Coefficient	East Asia		China	
	1985	1995	1985	1995
Constant	−17.282	−29.303	−2.122	−15.220
	(1.666[a])	(1.225[a])	(7.664)	(2.823[a])
ln(GDP$_i$GDP$_j$)	1.162	1.236	1.418	1.081
	(0.032[a])	(0.027[a])	(0.166[a])	(0.065[a])
ln(GDPPC$_i$GDPPC$_j$)	0.722	0.868	−0.689	0.145
	(0.059[a])	(0.047[a])	(0.330[b])	(0.117)
ln(DISTANCE$_{ij}$)	−1.440	−0.648	−1.364	−0.423
	(0.147[a])	(0.103[a])	(0.631[b])	(0.218[b])
LANGUAGE$_{ij}$	−9.048	2.860	14.375	2.600
	(2.096[a])	(0.862[a])	(4.432[a])	(1.017[a])
RELIGION$_{ij}$	0.192	1.242	−26.770	5.919
	(0.410)	(0.330[a])	(11.358[b])	(4.069)
R square	0.570	0.633	0.489	0.770
F-statistic	425.917	841.41	22.737	98.54
Number of observations	1612	2446	124	152

Notes: All regressions are based on ordinary least squares (OLS). Dependent variable is the natural log of bilateral trade (sum of exports and imports) in 1984 (since many East Asian economies suffered from bad recessions in 1985). Figures within parentheses are standard errors. "[a]" and "[b]" denote statistically significant at the 1% and 5% levels, respectively.
Source: Guo (2007) for "East Asia" and estimated by the author for "China".

in some cases, a more important role in economic activities than the linguistic variable (Guo, 2006, pp. 96–102).

The following result is based on the data from a panel of East Asian economies and on the model built in section 11.6. A comparison of the estimated coefficients on the log of DISTANCE in 1985 and 1995 (see Table 11.2) provides evidence that supports the view that geographic influence on trade also tends to be reduced in China and East Asia during the last decades of the twentieth century. One of the major driving forces contributing to this tendency might be technological advances in transportation and communications. Intuitively, the widespead application of e-commerce and the decline in distance-related transactions cost have increasingly contributed to the growth of international trade in East Asia.

The estimated results reveal that, between 1985 and 1995, five individual languages (Bahasa, Chinese, English, Khmer and Thai) have played different roles in foreign trade in East Asia (see Table 11.3). In the case of interregional trade, Chinese and English, the only two languages with

Table 11.3 The growing role of "Chinese" in foreign trade

Explanatory variable	Intra-regional trade		Inter-regional trade	
	1985	1995	1985	1995
Constant	−46.816	−39.547	−12.519	−33.077
	(4.716[a])	(3.079[a])	(2.232[a])	(1.833[a])
ln(GDP$_i$GDP$_j$)	1.147	1.107	1.148	1.260
	(0.126[a])	(0.079[a])	(0.034[a])	(0.029[a])
ln(GDPPC$_i$GDPPC$_j$)	1.313	1.093	0.642	0.742
	(0.219[a])	(0.169[a])	(0.063[a])	(0.053[a])
ln(DISTANCE$_{ij}$)	1.069	0.601	−1.795	−0.112
	(0.288[a])	(0.210[a])	(0.217[a])	(0.178)
RELIGION$_{ij}$	2.697	2.332	−0.206	0.454
	(1.659)	(0.901[b])	(0.419)	(0.360)
BAHASA	1.893	1.478	Excl.	Excl.
	(1.036[c])	(0.753[b])		
CHINESE	0.056	1.755	0.529	1.012
	(0.694)	(0.483[a])	(0.641)	(0.383[a])
ENGLISH	1.734	−0.419	0.258	0.679
	(0.710[b])	(0.527)	(0.218)	(0.159[a])
KHMER	6.806	5.922	Excl.	Excl.
	(2.277[a])	(1.191[a])		
THAI	−3.406	−1.211	Excl.	Excl.
	(4.114)	(1.137)		
R square	0.565	0.641	0.569	0.625
F-statistic	19.341	48.71	322.188	605.96
Number of observations	143	255	1468	2190

Notes: All regressions are based on ordinary least squares (OLS). Dependent variable is the natural log of bilateral trade (sum of exports and imports) in 1984 (for 1985's regressions) and 1995 (for 1995's regressions). Hong Kong is excluded from regressions in 1985. Figures within parentheses are standard errors. "Excl." denotes the left-hand variable is deleted from the analysis since it has missing correlation. "[a]", "[b]" and "[c]" denote statistically significant at the 1%, 5% and 10% levels, respectively.
Source: Guo (2007).

no missing correlation in the regressions, are statistically insignificant in 1985; but they become statistically significant in 1995. In the case of intra-regional trade, Bahasa has a decreasing role between 1985 and 1995; English and Khmer are statistically insignificant in 1995 and statistically significant in 1985. For both years, Thai is not statistically significant. By way of contrast, the Chinese language plays a dramatically increasing role from 1985 (with a statistically insignificant coefficient of only 0.056) to 1995 (with a statistically significant coefficient of 1.755).

Why does Chinese play a more important role in international trade than the other languages? I suspect that the stronger effect of linguistic influence on foreign trade might be attributable to the Chinese Diaspora. Rauch and Trindade (2002), for example, find that ethnic Chinese networks have a quantitatively important impact on bilateral trade through the mechanisms of market information and matching and referral services, in addition to their effect through community enforcement of sanctions that deter opportunistic behavior. Their estimated results show that for trade between countries with ethnic Chinese population shares at the levels prevailing in Southeast Asia, the smallest estimated average increase in bilateral trade in differentiated products attributable to ethnic Chinese networks is nearly 60 percent.

11.5   Summary

In *The Wealth of Nations* (1776), Adam Smith explained not only the critical role that market played in the relocation of a nation's resources but also the nature of the social order that it achieved and helped to maintain. Applying his ideas about economic activity within a country to specialization and exchange between countries, Smith concluded that countries should specialize in and export those commodities in which they had an absolute advantage and should import those commodities in which the trading partner had an absolute advantage. Each country should export those commodities it produced more efficiently because the absolute labor required per unit was less than that of the prospective trading partner. According to Smith, there is a basis for trade because nations are clearly better off specializing in their lower-cost commodities and importing those commodities that can be produced more cheaply abroad.

China's foreign economic affairs have not been guided by a *laissez-faire* approach even since the implementation of the outward-oriented development strategy in the 1980s. Intervention in the form of trade restrictions such as tariffs and licensing, subsidies, tax incentives and active contact with the world economy exists on the sides of both imports and exports. China used to manage its foreign trade through a policy of high tariff rates. This policy had effectively promoted the developments of China's immature, domestic industries. However, it also had a negative effect upon the Chinese economy. For example, under the system of high tariff rates, products made abroad do not have an equal opportunity to enter the Chinese market as that made in China, which will inevitably prevent the importation of high-quality and cheap commodities from advanced nations, harming the interests of Chinese consumers, and finally providing fewer incentives for Chinese producers to improve their competitiveness.

Throughout the 1980s and most of the 1990s, China's economic liberalization had been hindered by both "super-national remuneration" and "sub-national remuneration." On the one hand, the foreign-funded enterprises were greeted by a series of favorable policies such as tax exemption and low tax rates; on the other hand, they also faced some unequal treatments and economic discrimination in fields such as communication, transportation, housing, and advertising. Around the time of China's entry into the WTO, China issued new laws and regulations concerning service trade, covering legal services, telecommunications, financial institutions, insurance, audio and video products, tourism, and other related areas. Laws regarding the entry of foreign sales companies and joint ventures of stock exchange are being drawn up. However, further measures are still needed to ensure compliance with rules of the WTO on intellectual property, foreign investment, and information transmission.

Before ending this chapter, let us complete our recounting of the story told by Zhuangzi at the beginning of this chapter:

> Before the turtle from the East Sea could get its left foot in the well, its right knee got struck. It hesitated and retreated. The turtle told the frog about the East Sea: "Even a distance of a thousand *li* [500 km] cannot give you an idea of the sea's width; even a height of a thousand *ren* [approximately 666.67 m] cannot give you an idea of its depth. In the time of King Yu of the Xia dynasty, there were floods nine years out of ten, but the waters in the sea did not increase. In the time of King Tang of the Shang dynasty there were droughts seven years out of eight, but the waters in the sea did not decrease. The sea does not change along with the passage of time and its level does not rise or fall according to the amount of rain that falls. The greatest happiness is to live in the East Sea."

11.6 Case study: Cultural influences on foreign trade[12]

There is a widely held view that easily observable impediments, such as transportation costs, do not adequately capture the transactions costs of international trade. One response has been to offer direct investigations of the possible role of transborder business networks or ethnic diasporas in reducing transaction costs (Rauch, 2001; Rauch and Trindade, 2002; and Combes *et al.*, 2005). In addition, Guiso *et al.* (2004) and Guo (2006) suggest that more diffuse cultural affinity or similarity may be another channel. They argue that cultural distance – as proxied by, among other things, the genetic differences across national populations – is a robust determinant of the volume of international trade in the context of a conventional gravity model.

The gravity model is most commonly used by economists to make a quantitative estimate of the determinants of foreign trade. The classic early application of the model was by Linnemann (1966), who continued work first reported in Tinbergen (1962) and then in Pöyhönen (1963).[13] Some of the most recent work on the application of the model was undertaken by Frankel *et al.* (1997a, 1997b), Rauch (1999), and Rose (2004), among others. Generally, a gravity model assumes that the volume of trade between any two economies will be directly proportional to the product of their economic masses (measured by GDP or GNP) and inversely proportional to the distance between them. Per capita incomes (measured by product of per capita GDPs or GNPs) have become a standard covariate in the gravity models of, for example, Eaton and Tamura (1994), Frankel *et al.* (1997a, 1997b), and Rauch (1999).

In order to apply the gravity model in order to test the effects of the cultural influences on trade, we analyze the influences of linguistic and religious variables. The assumption here is that language is an effective tool of communication and that religion can provide the insights into the characteristics of culture. The basic form of the gravity model to be used in my empirical analysis is as the following:

$$\ln(\text{TRADE}_{ij} + 1) = \alpha_0 + \alpha_1 \ln(\text{GDP}_i \text{GDP}_j) + \alpha_2 \ln(\text{GDPPC}_i \text{GDPPC}_j)$$

$$+ \alpha_3 \ln \text{DISTANCE}_{ij} + \alpha_4 \text{LANGUAGE}_{ij}$$

$$+ \alpha_5 \text{RELIGION}_{ij} \tag{11.1}$$

In Equation (11.1), "ln" represents natural logarithm; TRADE_{ij}, measured in thousands of US dollars, is the sum of exports and imports between economies i and j. In order to make the natural logarithm of TRADE become mathematically meaningful when

TRADE $= 0$, ln(TRADE $+ 1$) is used to approximate ln(TRADE).[14] This seems to be reasonable since the size of TRADE is, if not zero, always far larger than US\$1,000. GDP_iGDP_j is the product of purchasing power parity (PPP)-adjusted GDP of the ith and jth economies. $\text{GDPPC}_i\text{GDPPC}_j$ is the product of PPP-adjusted GDP per capita of the ith and jth economies. DISTANCE_{ij} represents the distance between the geographic centers of gravity of the ith and jth economies (in kilometers). LANGUAGE_{ij} and RELIGION_{ij}, the measurement of which will be discussed later, denote the extents to which the ith and jth economies are linguistically and religiously linked each other, respectively.

Linguistic differences have clearly, to some extent, influenced international trade and marketing. Although it is not the only tool for building trusting relationships, doors usually open more quickly when knocked on by someone who speaks a familiar language. Sharing a common language, however, does not necessarily mean effective communication in technical terms. Compared to language, religion can provide more insights into the characteristics of interpersonal behavior. More importantly, religion can have a deep impact not only on attitudes toward economic matters but also on values that influence them. Specifically, religious attitudes and values help to determine what one thinks is right or appropriate, what is important, what is desirable, and so on.

As discussed later, the data on some, if not all, linguistic groups are probably subject to a wider range of error than the other variables in Equation (11.1). Therefore, the ability to use five international languages of, in the case of East Asia, Bahasa (Indonesian or Malay), Chinese, English, Khmer and Thai, is measured with dummy variables. Consequently, the gravity model on trade is written as:

$$
\begin{aligned}
\ln(\text{TRADE}_{ij} + 1) = {} & \beta_0 + \beta_1 \ln(\text{GDP}_i\text{GDP}_j) + \beta_2 \ln(\text{GDPPC}_i\text{GDPPC}_j) \\
& + \beta_3 \ln\text{DISTANCE}_{ij} + \beta_4 \text{RELIGION}_{ij} + \beta_5 \text{BAHASA} \\
& + \beta_6 \text{CHINESE} + \beta_7 \text{ENGLISH} + \beta_8 \text{KHMER} \\
& + \beta_9 \text{THAI} \quad\quad\quad\quad\quad\quad\quad\quad\quad\quad (11.2)
\end{aligned}
$$

In Equation (11.2), BAHASA $= 1$, CHINESE $= 1$, KHMER $= 1$ and THAI $= 1$ means that economies i and j both speak the language in question; otherwise these dummies take the value 0. It has been recognized that most international trade contracts and documents are processed in English, especially in East Asia where different phylums exist.[15] As a result, English reading/writing ability has been an important linguistic trait that reduces trade-related transaction costs. To reflect this fact, the English dummy is defined to include not only English as a mother tongue but also lingua franca and bilingual Englishes.

Equations (11.1) and (11.2) can be estimated by using standard statistical techniques. In order to further account for the potential impacts of multicollinearity between geographic and linguistic and religious variables, additional regressions are estimated by excluding the linguistic and religious variables. Specifically, if correlation coefficients of each pair of explanatory variables are fairly large, they could suggest potential multicollinearity that can cause imprecise regression results (Greene, 2002, pp. 255–8). Because this section employs cross-sectional data, it is also necessary to conduct tests for heteroscedasticity. More specifically, while ordinary least squares (OLS)-estimated coefficients are unbiased, weighted least squares (WLS) estimation can provide more efficient results in terms of smaller coefficient standard errors (Greene, 2002, p. 499). After each OLS run, heteroskedasticity tests are performed for each individual regression model. If heteroskedasticity is significant, WLS estimation should be performed to correct this problem.

Linguistic and religious similarity indexes can be constructed in different manners. The simplest method is to use a dummy index; i.e., using "1" for economies to be linguistically or religiously linked with each other, and using "0" otherwise. Although it has been applied in a number of studies (see, for example, Havrylyshyn and Pritchett, 1991; Foroutan and Pritchett, 1993; Frankel and Wei, 1995; Frankel *et al.*, 1997b), this method cannot precisely measure the extent to which economies are linguistically or religiously linked to each other, particularly when the economies are linguistically or religiously diversified.

A comprehensive method can be used to construct linguistic and religious similarity indexes. Suppose that the population shares of N linguistic (religious) groups are expressed by $(x_1, x_2, ..., x_N)$ and $(y_1, y_2, ..., y_N)$ for economies X and Y, respectively. x_i and y_i (where, $x_i \geq 0$ and $y_i \geq 0$) belong to the same linguistic (religious) group. Mathematically, the linguistic and religious similarity indexes (denoted by LANGUAGE and RELIGION, respectively) between the economies

X and *Y* can be measured according to the following formula:[16]

$$\sum_{i=1}^{N} \min(x_i, y_i) \qquad (11.3)$$

In Equation (11.3), min (•) denotes the minimization of the variables within parentheses.[17] The values of LANGUAGE and RELIGION range between 0 and 1. In the extreme cases, when LANGUAGE (RELIGION) = 1, the two economies have a common linguistic (religious) structure (i.e., for all i, $x_i = y_i$); when LANGUAGE (RELIGION) = 0, the two economies do not have any linguistic (religious) links with each other (i.e., for all i, x_i (or y_i) = 0 and $x_i \neq y_i$). In the other words, greater values of LANGUAGE or RELIGION indicate greater linguistic or religious similarity between two economies.

12
The Greater China Area: Retrospect and Prospect

> The king of the state of Wei intended to attack Handan. Ji Liang heard of this and went to see the king, and said: "Your majesty, on my way here I saw a man driving his carriage which was facing north. He told me that he wanted to go to the state of Chu. 'Why are you going north?' I asked. 'I have fine horses,' he said. 'Even though you have good horses, this is not the road to Chu,' I pointed out. 'I have plenty of money for my journey,' he said. 'But this is not the right direction,' I said. 'I have an excellent driver for my carriage,' he said. The better are the resources, the further he was going from Chu. Now you seek to raise above all the kings and win the support of the common people everywhere. However, you plan to extend your territories and raise your prestige by attacking Handan, relying on the powerful strength of your state and the well-trained soldiers. This is as effective as going north hoping to reach the state of Chu."
>
> – Zhanguoce (475–221 BC)

12.1 Historical evolution

The Greater China area is defined in this chapter as one which includes Taiwan, Hong Kong, Macau and mainland China.[1] In spite of their common history, cultural and linguistic homogeneity, in recent decades the four economic areas have followed divergent political systems, which have resulted in different social and economic performances. As soon as the PRC was founded in 1949, mainland China had effectively adopted and practised a Marxist-Leninist command economy as imposed by the Soviet Union, before it decided to introduce structural reform in the late 1970s. Two former colonial economies under the British and Portuguese administrations, respectively, Hong Kong and Macau have been fundamentally incorporated into the Western-style society, albeit that Chinese culture and language are still accepted by most of the citizens that live there. Taiwan had been under the colonial rule of the Japanese for 50 years before it was liberated and returned to China in 1945. With the Civil War (1946–49) coming to an end, however, the newly reunified nation was separated by two ideologically rival regimes – the Nationalists (Kuomintang, or KMT) in Taiwan and the Communists (CCP) on the mainland. Backed by the United States, the Taiwanese economy followed the capitalist road of economic development. While both sides of the Taiwan Strait have declared that there is only one *China* in the world and that their motherland should be reunified sooner or later, many of the political issues arising from the bloody war which was eventually detrimental to national cooperation still remain unresolved.

The end of the Cold War and the implementation of economic reform and the open-door policy in mainland China in December 1978 heralded a new era. In January 1979 the USA established diplomatic relations with mainland China and broke off its long-standing diplomatic relations with Taiwan. Ties between Hong Kong and the mainland developed very rapidly. The development of mainland–Taiwan ties mainly took place after November 1987 when Taiwan lifted its ban on visits to the mainland. Hong Kong and Macau reverted to Chinese sovereignty in 1997 and 1999, respectively, while preserving their capitalist system for 50 years under the formula of "one country, two systems." From an economic viewpoint, Hong Kong and Macau, each as an autonomous entity, are separate customs territories and founding members of the WTO. Each has an independent fiscal and monetary system, issuing their own currencies that are linked to the US dollar. It issues its own passport and retains its legal system, maintaining its own court of appeal. It runs its internal affairs without interference from the central government, except in matters of defense and foreign affairs.

In order to have an in-depth understanding of the economic mechanisms of the greater China area, let us briefly review the historical evolution of Hong Kong, Macau and Taiwan and the current situations of their economic relations with mainland China.

12.1.1 Hong Kong

In ancient China, Hong Kong was initially included in Bao'an county, while the latter today also included Donguan county and Shenzhen municipality, Guangdong province. In 1573, Xin'an county was established and was entitled to administer Hong Kong for more than two hundred years since that time. Following the end of the first Opium War, the Treaty of Nanjing in 1842 ceded the island of Hong Kong to Britain in perpetuity. Kowloon, Stonecutters' Island and and some small islands were annexed in 1860. In 1898, Britain acquired, under the "Treaty of Peking," what is known as the New Territories and 236 associated islands, which were mainly agricultural lands, were leased from the Qing dynasty (1644–1910), on a 99-year lease. At present, Hong Kong consists of the island of Hong Kong (83 sq. km), Stonecutters' Island, Kowloon Peninsula and the New Territories on the adjoining mainland, with 1,068 sq. km of land and a population of just over six million.

Over the past few decades, there has been a special geopolitical scenario between the two sides of the Shenzhen river. Even though the Chinese character, Shenzhen, means a deep gutter, no one would have expected that the "gutter" would serve as a forbidden frontier between the socialist mainland China and the capitalist Hong Kong in the mid-twentieth century, and that it would also create economic prosperity for Hong Kong and continue to fuel the industrialization of the South China area.

China has always maintained that the three treaties on Hong Kong were signed under coercion, and were therefore unjust. On December 19 1984, the Chinese and British governments issued a joint declaration in relation to the question of Hong Kong. As a result, the sovereignty of Hong Kong was transferred from the UK to PRC on July 1 1997.[2] Upholding national unity and territorial integrity, maintaining the prosperity and stability of Hong Kong, and taking account of its history and realities, China has made Hong Kong a Special Administrative Region (SAR) of the People's Republic of China (PRC) in accordance with the provisions of Article 31 of the Constitution of the PRC. The Joint Declaration also provides that for 50 years after 1997, Hong Kong's lifestyle will remain unchanged. The territory will enjoy a high degree of autonomy, except in relation to foreign and defense affairs, and China's socialist system and policies will not be put into practice in the SAR. Under the principle of "one country, two systems," "the socialist system and policies shall not be practised in the Hong Kong special administrative region, and the previous capitalist system and way of life shall remain unchanged for 50 years."[3]

12.1.2 Macau

Located on the west side of the Pearl river (Zhujiang), in ancient times Macau was included in Xiangshan county, Guangdong province. In 1533 Macau was colonized by the Portuguese, who extended their possessions after the Opium War (1840–42). Macau became a formal Portuguese colony in 1887. Bordering on Zhuhai municipality, Guangdong province, Macau now has an area of 16.92 square kilometers, including Macau peninsula and Taipa and Toloane islands. Macau has a population of more than 400,000. In accordance with the Sino-Portugal Joint Declaration signed on January 15 1988, Macau was handed over from the Portuguese administration to mainland China on December 20 1999. Since this time, Macau has become the second SAR of the PRC, operating like Hong Kong under the principle of "one country, two systems."

12.1.3 Taiwan

With 36,000 square kilometers of land and a population of more than 20 million, Taiwan is composed of Taiwan, Penghu, Mazu and other small islands adjacent to mainland China. The Sino-Japanese War was ended with the signing of the Shimonoseki Treaty on April 17 1895. Under the Treaty, Japan seized Taiwan and the Penghu islands from the Qing dynasty (1644–1911), subjecting Taiwan to colonial rule for half a century. At the end of World War II, in cooperation with the Allied forces, China defeated Japan. On October 25 1945, Taiwan and Penghu islands returned unconditionally to the Chinese government, marking the end of Japan's colonization. However, with the civil war coming to an end, Taiwan and mainland China were again politically separated in 1949 when the Nationalist-led government fled to Taiwan and the Communists took power in the mainland.

Since the late 1940s, in practice China has been ruled by two ideologically antagonistic regimes, each of which has laid claim to the sole sovereignty of the whole nation and treated the other side as its "rebel" local government.[4] The division of the Chinese nation extends through many phases of Chinese life – political, economic, and social. The 50-year-long cross-Taiwan Strait separation destroyed national unity, led to a series of tragic conflicts and produced mutual distrust and many other human and national agonies. Since the 1980s, it has become the inviolable mission and long-term goal for the two regimes to achieve peaceful reunification and to promote the all-round revitalization of the nation.

It can be seen that since the 1980s the greater China area has been undergoing a major transformation. Since 1997 and 1999, respectively, Sino-Hong Kong and Sino-Macau relations are no longer treated as international in nature. Regardless of the political separation, non-governmental relations between the two sides of the Taiwan Strait have been developed gradually since 1980 when the Standing Committee of the NPC firstly publicized "Message to the Taiwan Compatriots", especially since 1988 when private visits from Taiwan to the mainland were permitted by the Taiwanese government. In the remainder of this chapter, we will try to analyze economic performances and relations between Hong Kong, Macau, Taiwan and mainland China.

12.2   Social and economic differences

Despite the historical, cultural and linguistic homogeneity, the greater China economic area has adopted different patterns of economic development. Hong Kong and Macau have been under the colonial administrations of the UK and of Portugal, respectively. Taiwan was a Japanese colony between 1895 and 1945 and, following a short period of reunification with mainland China, has been operating independently from the rest of the world. As a result, significant social and economic differences have been present in the four parts of the area, especially since 1949. In what follows we will analyze them in detail.

Table 12.1 shows the basic social and economic indicators of greater China in the early years of the twenty-first century. In 2003, Taiwan's GDP was 1.8 times that of Hong Kong. The GDP of the mainland was 4.9 times that of Taiwan and 8.9 times that of Hong Kong. The mainland's

Table 12.1   Basic indicators of the greater China area

Indicator	Taiwan	Hong Kong	Macau	Mainland
Area (sq. km)	36188	1098	19	9600000
Population (million persons)	22.5	6.8	0.4	1284.5
GDP (2003, billion US$)	286.8	158.6	7.9	1416
GDP per capita (2003, US$)	12751	23311	17782	1090
Average growth rate of GDP per capita (1978–2002, %)	5.50	3.98	2.03[a]	8.04
Exports (2003, billion US$)	144.2	224.6(15.7[b])	2.6	438.4
Life expectancy (1990s, Female/ male, years)	77/71.8	81.2/75.8		71/68
Adult literacy rate (1990s, Female/ male, %)[c]	86/96	88/96	95.7[d]	73/90

Notes:
(a): Growth rate for 1982–2002.
(b): Exports of Hong Kong goods (re-exports are excluded).
(c): ADB (1996, pp. 11 and 28), SSB (1996, pp. 769, 781 and 803);
(d): Xie (1992, p. 115) for labor population.
Source: Websites of the respective governments, except those that are noted otherwise.

2003 exports of US$438 billion surpassed Taiwan's exports of US$144 billion and also substantially surpassed the level of Hong Kong's domestic exports (that is, exports made domestically in Hong Kong) of US$16 billion. The figure for Hong Kong's total exports (that is, including re-exports) of US$225 billion is large because Hong Kong is re-exporting Chinese products to third countries and third-country products to China. In other words, Hong Kong is China's gateway to the world in commodity trade.

From Table 12.1, one can also see that all parts of the greater China area have enjoyed higher annual GNP growth rates than most of the remaining economies in the world. Particularly noteworthy is the fact that mainland China's GNP growth rate is among the highest of all of the world's dynamic economies. If all goes according to plan, mainland China's economic size and per capita GNP will continue to increase at a higher rate than those of the other parts.

Hong Kong's economy was seriously affected by the Japanese invasion during World War II. The population decreased sharply from 1.6 million in 1940 to 0.60 million in August 1945 and 60 percent of the buildings were destroyed (Wu and Liang, 1990, p. 235). By the 1950s and 1960s the constant influx from China of capital and manpower led to the establishment of light manufacturing in Hong Kong. At the same time, Hong Kong's tax policies began to attract growing levels of foreign investment, adding further impetus to the rapid growth of the territory. In the 1950s Hong Kong began in earnest a new career as a manufacturing and industrial center. Textiles, electronics, watches, and many other low-priced goods stamped "Made in Hong Kong" flowed from the territory in ever-increasing amounts. Restricted by the shortage of land and other natural resources of its own and the closed-door policy in mainland China, Hong Kong's economy grew very slowly in the period before the 1970s.

Since the late 1970s, Hong Kong's economy has grown rapidly, as a result of its favorable geographical location in terms of international trade and its proximity to mainland China. During the 1980s Hong Kong started to work with China on a series of joint projects that brought the two closer together. Today the financial service industries have taken over from manufacturing as Hong Kong's main enterprise. This small territory was the first developing economy to enter the world's top ten economies and the most successful of the "four Asian dragons" in terms of per capita GNP. And while much of the manufacturing is now likely to be done either in the region across the border or further afield, Hong Kong is still one of the world's largest exporters. Social programs continue to raise the standard of living, which is comparable to that found in many Western countries.

In mid-1997 the Asian financial crisis struck Hong Kong shortly after Hong Kong's reversion to China. Hong Kong's GDP contracted by more than 5 percent in 1998, the first recorded instance of negative annual growth since official GDP figures became available in 1961. Though the Hong Kong economy recovered in 1999–2000, the slowdown of the US economy and the September 11 terrorist attack led to another recession, and GDP growth fell to 0.5 percent in 2001. Recovery in the second half of 2002 was interrupted by the outbreak of SARS in March 2003. Since the Asian financial crisis, Hong Kong has tried to exploit its connections with mainland China in order to boost its economy. The measures introduced included the relaxation of controls against tourists and skilled workers from the mainland, and the promotion of economic integration with the Pearl River Delta. Hong Kong also proposed the formation of an FTA (free trade area) with the mainland. The closer economic partnership arrangement (CEPA) was signed by the mainland and Hong Kong on June 29 2003. This was the first free-trade agreement for either the mainland or Hong Kong.

For the past 400 years, the mixture of the Western and Chinese societies has resulted in Macau developing a unique cultural landscape. However, Macau's industrialization only began during the 1960s and it has been restricted by the trade protectionism that was imposed upon Hong Kong by the USA and the EU before the 1980s. Since the early 1980s, the economic development of Macau has benefited greatly from its proximity to both Hong Kong (one the freest markets in the world) and mainland China (one of the world's cheapest sources of labor and raw materials). Today, Macau's three major industries are trade, tourism and casinos and property and construction.

In recent decades, Taiwan has been successfully transformed from a colonized and agriculturally based economy to a newly industrialized economy and has become known as one of the "four Asian economic dragons." In 1953, its per capita GNP was less than US$200, a figure that grew dramatically to more than US$15,000 in the 2000s. Economic development in Taiwan faced many obstacles, including a lack of energy and industrial resources, high population density, and the need to fund a high level of spending on defense in order to sustain a balance with mainland China (as shown in Table 12.3), a series of failures in foreign affairs as well as the increasing political pressure coming from the mainland, the effects of regional protectionism, and so on. The Taiwan miracle, however, has been ascribed mainly to the indomitable spirit of the Taiwanese people themselves, embodied in the phrase by Kao and Shong (1992, p. 10): "the more difficulties they faced, the harder they would work."

With the heterogeneous natural and social conditions, there exist substantial differences of real living standards in the greater China area. However, owing to the differing personal consumption structures as well as their purchasing powers, it is very difficult for us to conduct a complete and reasonable comparison of the four parts. In brief, Hong Kong and Macau, as two municipal economies, have the highest living standards in the greater China area. Nevertheless, the socioeconomic gap between Taiwan and mainland China wouls be narrowed substantially if the purchasing power differences are taken into account.

Other indicators, such as life expectancy, literacy and other physical quality-of-life indexes, not to mention the political freedom of the individual (which is the most valuable criterion in Western nations), seem to indicate that there exist significant differences within the greater China area.

12.3 Complementary conditions

Obviously, the mutually complementary conditions exist in the greater China area in terms of natural resources, labor force, technology, and industrial structure, as demonstrated in Table 12.2. For example, mainland China has adequate and various agricultural products and oil, coal, building materials, some high-tech products, excess and cheap labor and a huge domestic market. However, mainland China lacks capital, advanced equipment, technology, and management experience, especially in its western, inland areas. Taiwan, with its high levels of capital saving, its portable advanced equipment, and vanguard agricultural and industrial products and management experience, suffers from a shortage of energy and industrial resources, and facing increasing insufficiency and high costs of labor supply. Furthermore, its economic development seems to have been restricted by the limited domestic market. As the freest economies in the world, Hong Kong and Macau have capital surplus, favorable conditions for international trade and advanced management experience in commercial and financial markets; at the same time they are severely lacking agricultural and industrial resources, especially fresh water, foodstuffs, energy and land. In addition, like Taiwan, Hong Kong and Macau are also facing a serious deficiency and high cost of labor.[5]

Both Hong Kong and Taiwan have been strong in traditional labor-intensive, export-oriented industries: Hong Kong's niches are in

Table 12.2   Mutually complementary conditions in the greater China area

Economy	Advantages	Disadvantages
Mainland China	Adequate and various agricultural products, energy, industrial materials, excess labor, some high-tech products, and huge domestic market.	Relatively shortage of advanced equipments; shortage of international management experience and economic infrastructures, especially in the western, inland provinces.
Taiwan	High capital saving, advanced equipment ready to move out, vanguard agricultural and industrial products, and management experience.	Shortage of energy and industrial resources, limited domestic market, and insufficiency of and high costs of labor supply.
Hong Kong and Macau	Capital surplus, favorable convenient conditions for international trade, the freest economic environment, and management experience in commercial and financial markets.	Severe shortage of agricultural and industrial resources, especially fresh water, foodstuff, energy, and land and deficiency of labor; limited domestic market.

clothing, toys, watches, and electronics, while Taiwan's are in footwear, umbrellas, textiles, and electronics. Such traditional industries have now all but relocated to the mainland. The opening up of the mainland came at the right time for Hong Kong and Taiwan as they had accumulated valuable human capital in the management and manufacturing of labor-intensive products for exports from the 1950s to the 1970s. However, successful export-oriented industrialization had raised the levels of their wages, and their labor-intensive industries were threatened in the 1980s. The majority of manufacturing firms in Hong Kong and Taiwan were small, and lacked the ability to operate internationally; for example, to relocate to Southeast Asia. Without the opening of the mainland, the vast majority of these small firms would have gone bankrupt. However, the opening of the mainland allowed small firms to relocate to a cultur-ally familiar environment and thereby utilize their valuable know-how to build a "global factory" (that is, a production base dominating the world market) (Sung, 2004, p. 3).

Under the mutually complementary conditions, the multilateral eco-nomic cooperation may generate a series of positive effects on the economic development of the greater China area. Through trade and the spatial relocation of such production factors as labor, raw materials, technology and capital, economic optimization will be undoubtedly increased in the greater China area.

12.4　Cross-Strait economic relations

> The state of Zhao was going to assault the state of Yan. Su Dai came to see King Hui of the Zhao, and said, "On my way here I saw a clam just coming out to bask in the sun on the shore of the Yishui river. A snipe came over to peck at the flesh of the clam, which closed its shell and gripped the snipe's beak. The snipe said: 'If it does not rain today and tomorrow, you will become a dead clam.' 'If you cannot free yourself today and tomorrow, you will become a dead snipe,' replied the clam. Neither one would give way and eventually a fisherman caught them both." Su continued, "Now if Zhao is ready to attack Yan but if both states were locked in a long stalemate with neither side ready to yield, I am afraid then the powerful Qin will turn up as the fisherman. Therefore, I do hope that you will give this matter careful consideration before you act." "Well said," nodded the King. And he gave up his military plan.
>
> – Zhanguoce (475–221 BC)

12.4.1　Historical evolution

The Taiwan Strait became a "forbidden" boundary in 1949 when the Nationalist-led government fled to Taiwan and, at the same time, the Communist-led government was founded on the mainland. Since then, Taiwan and mainland China have been two divergent regimes. Against the common cultural and linguistic homogeneity, mainland China chose essentially to pursue a socialist line, while Taiwan followed the route of market-oriented capitalism. Furthermore, the two sides have also treated each other antagonistically, particularly during the high tide of military confrontation, when the mainland claimed that it would liberate the Taiwan compatriots from the *black* society sooner or latter, while in turn Taiwan maintained that they would use the "three democratisms" to reoccupy the mainland eventually.

Throughout the 1950s and the 1960s the Taiwan-based Nationalists had been the internationally recognized government representing China as a whole. On October 15 1971, the United Nations seat was changed from Taiwan to mainland China in accordance with UN Resolution No. 2758. Since this time, the international positions of Taiwan and mainland China have been reversed. Following the United States' transference of its diplomatic relations with China from the KMT-led Taiwan to the CCP-led mainland in December 1978, an increasing number of Western nations began to establish their own formal ties with the mainland. As a result, Taiwan lost most of its friends.

Even though "[the cross-Taiwan straits] reunification does not mean that the mainland will swallow up Taiwan, nor does it mean that Taiwan will swallow up the mainland" (Jiang, 1995, p. 2), many critical issues concerning the cross-Taiwan Strait relations still remain unresolved. For instance, even though both mainland China and Taiwan have declared to the outside world that they are pursuing the "one China" policy, the contents of which are absolutely different from each other. Mainland China proudly stresses that the "People's Republic of China" (PRC) has been one of the five permanent members of the UN's Security Council and of course should be – and has already been – the only legal government representing China of which, to be sure, Taiwan is only a province.[6] The Taiwanese government, however, strongly argues that the "Republic of China" (ROC) founded by Dr Sun Yatsen has existed since 1911 and is still in *rapport* with a certain number of independent nations. More importantly, in addition to Taiwan's remarkable economic growth and social progress, the Taiwanese government, after a long period of silence, has increasingly felt that it is time to expand its international presence and to let the outside world know the fact that there exists the "Republic of China on Taiwan" at least in parallel with the "People's Republic of China" in the mainland.

A comparison of military expenditures between Taiwan and mainland China is shown in Table 12.3.

Table 12.3   Military expenses, Taiwan and mainland China

Item	Taiwan	Mainland China
Defense expense (US$100 million)	104	562
Forces (1,000 persons)	442	3,031
Defense expense as % of GNP	4.7	2.7
Defense expense as % of budget	20.0	16.2
Per capita defense (US$)	494	48
Forces per 1,000 population	21.0	2.6

Sources: The US Academy of Defense Agency (1993) and SSB (1996, pp. 230 and 580).

Nevertheless, progress toward peaceful reunification has been registered in negotiations over a number of specific issues. In order to find a practical way to maintain contacts, each of the two sides established a "non-governmental" institution, viz., the Foundation of the Taiwan Straits Exchanges (FTSE) in Taiwan and the Association for the Taiwan Straits Relations (ATSR) in the mainland. During the early 1990s, the ATSR–FTSE talks represented forward steps in the relations between the two sides of the Taiwan Strait. However, after 1996, the cross-Taiwan Strait relations became strained by two significant developments: (i) the Taiwanese president, Lee Tenghui, insistence on seeking to expand Taiwan's "international living space" which is aimed at, as claimed by mainland China, creating "two Chinas" or "one China, one Taiwan"; and (ii) mainland China's missile tests within the Taiwan Strait area.

Taiwan's economy suffered from the Asian financial crisis during the late 1990s, from the September 11 terrorist attack in 2001 and from the Severe Acute Respiratory Syndrome (SARS) in 2003. While economic difficulties have spurred Taiwan toward the establishment of closer links with the mainland, Taiwan was less active than Hong Kong in terms of capturing the mainland market, owing to high levels of political antagonism. Taiwan's GDP contracted by 1.9 percent in 2001, the first record of negative annual growth since data were first made available in 1951. Taiwan's unemployment rate rose about 5 percent in 2002, the highest since 1964, when statistics on unemployment were regularly available (Sung, 2004, p. 7). While Taiwan's business community has been eager to improve relations with the mainland, the election and re-election of Chen Shui-bian (representing the pro-independence Democratic Progressive Party, or DPP) to Taiwan's presidency in 2000 and 2004, respectively, exacerbated political tensions across the Taiwan Straits.

However, where there is patience and willingness to compromise, there is still hope. The hope emerges when the two sides find that their differences are not really so fundamental. The long-awaited breakthrough on direct links has been achieved since the election of Ma Ying-jeou (representing the Kuomintang, or KMT) to Taiwan's presidency in 2008. Both sides have come to understand this "sameness" and their essential heterogeneity if they can make further progress in the cross-Taiwan Straits cooperation by establishing exchanges of, *inter alia*, sport, culture, education, science and technology and high-level political groups.

12.4.2   Bilateral trade and economic exchanges

Bilateral trade and economic exchanges between Taiwan and mainland China had been frozen before 1979, except for small amounts of indirect trade of, among others, Chinese medicine and other native products from mainland China to Taiwan (mainly conducted via Hong Kong). In 1979, mainland China's "Taiwan policy" was transformed from "liberating Taiwan" to "peaceful reunification". Since this time, indirect trade between the two sides of the Taiwan Strait and the Taiwanese investment in mainland China via Hong Kong and other regions have grown rapidly as a result of the cross-Taiwan Strait *détente*. In addition, tourism, technological and labor cooperation between the two sides have also achieved considerable progress.

Since 1985, when the Taiwanese government instituted the "non-interference" policy to Taiwan's exportation to mainland China, the restrictions on cross-Taiwan Strait trade have been gradually worn away under the principle of "indirect trading" – that is, the direct trade partners should be located outside mainland China and trade movements should be via third countries (regions). Until the 1990s, the cross-Taiwan Strait trade had still been managed through a "concentrated" approach in mainland China, not allowing the mainland's foreign trade companies to deal directly with Taiwanese companies outside Hong Kong and Macau. This policy, nevertheless, has promoted the two sides' foreign trade companies to open up either sub-companies or branches of their own in Hong Kong and Macau.

During the early period, Taiwanese investment in mainland China was usually conducted under the names of investors from Hong Kong, Macau, overseas Chinese and others who would nominally be accepted by the two sides.[7] In order to overcome the lack of foreign capital, mainland China introduced a flexible policy entitled "attraction of the Taiwanese capital via Hong Kong and overseas Chinese" (*yi gang yin tai, yi qiao yin tai*) which was intended to encourage Taiwanese businessmen to invest in mainland China. Since October 1990, when the Taiwanese government formally allowed Taiwanese businessmen to invest in mainland China, it has always required that the Taiwanese investors should be under the names of their sub-companies housed in the third areas. In order to encourage Taiwanese businessmen to invest in the mainland, mainland China promulgated the "Regulations Concerning the Promotion of the Taiwanese Compatriots' Investment" in July 1988 and the "Law of Protecting the Taiwanese compatriots investment" in March 1994.

Financial movements between Taiwan and mainland China had been strictly prohibited by the Taiwanese government before May 1990 when the South China Bank (in Taiwan) was allowed to indirectly (via a British bank in Hong Kong) offer individual financial businesses from Taiwan to mainland China. Since this time the level of Taiwanese investment in mainland China has increased dramatically. In July 1993, financial movements were able to extend from individual to business activities, and furthermore banks in the Taiwan area were able to receive funds sent indirectly from mainland China. As Taiwanese businessmen were only allowed to invest in mainland China via third regions or countries, this kind of "indirect investment" is, in theory, one between a third region (country) and mainland China, which might lead to many as yet unresolved issues.

In Taiwan, the population is identified mainly by two groups – native Taiwanese and Han- and other ethnic Chinese who fled to Taiwan when the Nationalists (KMT) lost the mainland in 1949. In addition to the cross-Taiwan Strait trade and Taiwanese investment on the mainland, other exchanges between the two sides of the Taiwan Strait have also grown rapidly since many Taiwanese have relatives in mainland China. Since November 1987, when Taiwanese citizens were first allowed to pay private visits to mainland China, there has been a considerable increase in the numbers of visitors from Taiwan to the mainland, resulting in a large amount of expenditure including traveling expenses, donations and others. In addition, there have been rapid developments in terms of the exchanges in labor, science and technology between the two sides.

12.4.3   Direct links for air and shipping services

Dividing the Chinese nation into two economically complementary but politically antagonistic counterparts, the Taiwan Strait has been perhaps one of the most special borders in the world. The nearest distance between Taiwan and mainland China is less than 1.8 km. Since the 1980s, efforts have been made to promote negotiations on the basis of reciprocity and mutual benefit. These have included the signing of non-governmental agreements relating to the protection of industrialists and businessmen. For years, Taiwan businesses had been asking for direct links across the 160-km wide Strait. But the pro-independence Democratic Progressive Party (DPP) had refused to re-establish direct links with the mainland. In the past, planes from the two sides had to fly through Hong Kong or Macao airspace, and cargo ships usually sailed via Japan's waters. Direct links for postal, air, and shipping services and trade between the two sides are the objective requirements for their economic development and contacts in various fields, and since they are in the interests of the people on both sides, it is absolutely necessary to adopt practical measures to speed up the establishment of such direct links.[8]

The "three direct links" across the Taiwan Strait were finally established in 2008. According to agreements signed between Taiwan and mainland China on November 4 2008, daily passenger flights have been launched.

The two sides have agreed to increase the number of direct charter flights to 108 a week and the frequency from four to seven days a week between 21 mainland cities (Beijing, Shanghai, Guangzhou, Xiamen, Nanjing, Chengdu, Chongqing, Hangzhou, Dalian, Guilin, Shenzhen, Wuhan, Fuzhou, Qingdao, Changsha, Haikou, Kunming, Xi'an, Shenyang, Tianjin, and Zhengzhou) and eight Taiwan cities (Taipei, Taoyuan, Kaohsiung, Taichung, Penghu, Hualien, Kuemen, and Taidong). In addition, 48 ports in mainland China have been approved for the establishment of direct links with Taiwan: Dandong, Dalian, Yingkou, Tangshan, Jinzhou, Qinhuangdao, Tianjin, Huanghua, Weihai, Yantai, Longkou, Fengshan, Rizhao, Qingdao, Lianyungang, Dafeng, Shanghai, Qingbo, Zhoushan, Taizhou, Jiaxing, Wenzhou, Fuzhou, Shongxia, Ningde, Quanzhou, Xiaocuo, Xiuyu, Zhangzhou, Xiamen, Shantou, Chaozhou, Huizhou, Shekou, Yantian, Chiwan, Mawan, Humen, Guangzhou, Zhuhai, Maoming, Ganjiang, Beihai, Fangcheng, Qinzhou, Haikou, Shanya and Yangpu and 15 river ports of Taichang, Nantong, Zhangjiagang, Jiangyin, Changshu, Changzhou, Taizhou, Zhenjiang, Nanjing, Wuhu, Ma'anshan, Jiujiang, Wuhan, and Chenglingji. Taiwan's ports granted to set up direct links with the mainland China include six ports (Keelung (including Taipei), Kaohsiung (including Anping), Taichung, Hualien, Mailiao and Budai) on Taiwan island as well as five other ports on Kuemen, Shuitou, Mazu, Baisa and Penghu islands.

On December 15 2008, a Trans-Asia Airways jetliner took off from Taipei's Sungshan airport, carrying 148 Taiwanese tourists and businesspeople on the 80-minute flight to Shanghai. Taiwan's ERA Cable Station also aired footage of a China Eastern Airline jetliner at Shanghai airport that was preparing to depart for Taipei. The flight time is now cut by an hour because the planes are no longer required to fly south through Hong Kong's airspace, a detour that Taiwanese authorities had insisted on previously for security reasons. Cargo ships had been required to stop at the Japanese island of Okinawa north east of Taiwan (see Figure 12.1). The distance and time for direct air travel across the Strait have been shortened significantly. A plane taking off from Beijing to Taipei, for instance, will fly 1,100 km less with its flying time becoming shortened by 80 minutes. Meanwhile, direct shipping lanes will cut costs and reduce time for businesspeople. Taiwan authorities are anticipating that shipping companies will save T$1.2 billion (US$36 million) and airlines at least T$3 billion a year.[9] The direct postal link will cut the time it takes to send express mail from around a week to only two or three days. The convenience will greatly facilitate cross-straits trade, economic cooperation, and personnel exchanges.

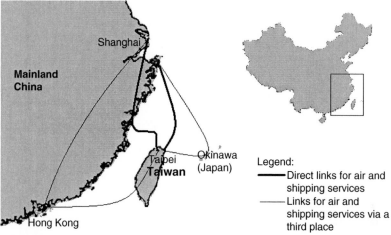

Figure 12.1   Links for air and shipping services between Taiwan and mainland China

---

Box 12.1   How to solve the cross-Strait equation?

The two sides of the Taiwan Strait have been separated politically for more than fifty years due to the mutual distrust and hostile strategies arising from the bloody conflict between the Nationalists and the Communists at the end of World War II. With the Cold War coming to an end and the surging tide of global participation in economic development, the levels of cross-Strait trade and economic cooperation have developed rapidly. However, it is still unclear when the national reunification may eventually become a possibility.

At present, there are five choices for Taiwan and mainland China: (i) PU (peaceful reunification); (ii) FU (forced reunification); (iii) peaceful independence (PI); (iv) SQ (to maintain the status quo); and (v) FI (forced independence). They are assumed to follow:

(1) PU>SQ>FU>FI>PI (preferred by mainland China)
(2) PI>FI>SQ>FU>PU (preferred by pro-independence clique in Taiwan)
(3) SQ>PI>PU>FI>FU (preferred by pro-reunification clique in Taiwan)
(4) PI>SQ>FI>PU>FU (preferred by "hawks" in the USA)

(5) SQ>PI>PU>FI>FU (preferred by "doves" in the USA)

Given the above preference ranking, what are the most likely solutions to the cross-Strait equation?

12.5   Future perspective

Despite their common history and cultural and linguistic homogeneity, over the course of recent decades the greater China area (including Taiwan, Hong Kong, Macau, and mainland China) has followed divergent political and economic systems, which has resulted in different social and economic performances. Along with mainland China's economic renaissance and the returns of Hong Kong and Macau, from the British and Portuguese governments, to China in 1997 and 1999, respectively, the economic ties between the three parts as a single sovereign nation have been accelerated under the principle of "one country, two systems". The two sides of the Taiwan Strait, however, have been politically separated for more than fifty years due to the mutual distrust and hostile strategies arising from the bloody conflict between the Nationalists and the Communists at the end of World War II.

In view of the development of the world economy in the twenty-first century, the cross-Strait economic exchange and cooperation should be accelerated further. Only this can achieve prosperity for both sides and benefit the entire nation. The two sides have promised that political differences should not affect or interfere with economic cooperation between the sides. Under the principles of peace, equality and bilateralism, the Taiwanese government is willing to promote cross-Taiwan Strait economic exchanges and to treat the mainland as its hinterland. In order to seek the most efficient way of raising the level of the national economy, the PRC's government seems intent to continue to implement, over a considerable period of time, the policy of encouraging industrialists and businesspeople from Taiwan to invest in the mainland. Along with the enforcement of the "Law of the People's Republic of China for Protecting the Investment of the Compatriots of Taiwan" and safeguarding the legitimate rights and interests of industrialists and businesspeople from Taiwan, the contacts and exchanges between the two sides will definitely increase and, surely, so too will the level of mutual understanding and trust.

It is close to a rule among practitioners and theorists that multilateral conflicts frequently arise from narrow individual interests and the expectations of different communities on the one hand, and a chaotic interdependent system on the other. Notwithstanding the political, economic, and social differences within the greater China economic area, it appears to be increasingly possible for all Chinese, under increasing comparative advantages, mutual complementary conditions as well as the tendency toward the development of unanimity in relation to political, social, and especially economic points of view across different parts of the area, to find an appropriate approach that can maximize the benefits for all of the parties concerned, while also taking into account their respective articulated objectives.

Following the restoration of Hong Kong and Macau from the British and Portuguese governments to mainland China in 1997 and 1999, respectively, the economic development of the PRC seems to be assured. However, nobody can predict when the reunification of greater China will become a realistic possibility.[10] With the Cold War coming to an end and private and semi-official cross-Taiwan Strait contacts being guaranteed by the both sides, all Chinese see no reason why their country should be left out of the surging tide of *détente* and further divided by man-made barriers.

While the Chinese economic areas are developing at a remarkable rate, no Chinese people have ever forgotten that their motherland is still being divided artificially. Nevertheless, the creation of political harmony and reunification between Taiwan and mainland China may still require time and patience on the part of both parties. It is a hopeful sign that the political regimes have promised to reunify peacefully as a single nation. Chinese people on both sides of the straits, and also the outside world, will watch carefully.

12.6 Case study: Overseas Chinese economics

There have been more than 50 million overseas Chinese living in over one hundred countries (regions). Since World War II, and especially since the 1970s, the wealth of the overseas Chinese has been growing rapidly and it has played an increasing role in the world economy. According to an incomplete estimate from *The Economic Research Materials* (1996, p. 62), the overseas Chinese already had US$223.1 billion of foreign currency deposits by the end of 1993, which is distributed mainly in Taiwan (US$90.6 billion), followed by Hong Kong (US$32.7 billion), Singapore (US$43.7 billion), Thailand (US$23.4 billion), Malaysia (US$15.4 billion), Indonesia (US$11.0 billion), the Philippines (US$4.3 billion) and other nations (US$2.0 billion). Furthermore, *The Economist* (1992, p. 17) offered an even more optimistic estimation that, excluding Taiwan and Hong Kong, the total capital owned by overseas Chinese could exceed US$150 to $200 billion.

Briefly, several factors can explain this remarkable growth of the overseas Chinese economy. These include:

(1) the thriftiness and hard-working nature of the overseas Chinese;
(2) an elite group of intellectuals;
(3) a positive role of overseas Chinese organizations; and
(4) closer socioeconomic ties with mainland China.

Since the early 1980s, when the open-door policy was implemented in mainland China, the overseas Chinese have made great contributions to the economic development of mainland China, and in particular the coastal area with which they had the closest relations. Studies show that overseas Chinese investment has provided more than two-thirds of the total foreign direct investment (FDI) in mainland China in recent decades. In addition, China's growing exports have also been widely promoted by the overseas Chinese networks (Rauch and Trindade, 2002).

Following the return of Hong Kong and Macau from the British and Portuguese governments to mainland China in 1997 and 1999, respectively, the economic development of the PRC has been accelerated by approximately two to three years, given an average per capita GNP growth rate of 6 to 9 percent for mainland China. Moreover, the eventual reunification of Taiwan with mainland China will accelerate the development of unified China by four to five years. These estimates are based on the following equation:

$$\frac{GNP_{MC} + GNP_x}{POP_{MC} + POP_x} = \frac{GNP_{MC}}{POP_{MC}}(1 + R_{MC})^{T_x}, \text{ with } \frac{GNP_x}{POP_x} \gg \frac{GNP_{MC}}{POP_{MC}}$$
$$\text{and } R_{MC} > 0.$$

Where GNP = gross   national   product, POP = population, MC = mainland China, x = Hong Kong, Macau, or Taiwan, R_{MC} = the average annual growth rate of per capita GNP for mainland China within a certain period in the future, and T_x = time period (in years) by which the per capita GNP of mainland China will reach that of mainland China and x as a whole. Solving the above equation with the data in Table 12.1, we can obtain T_x (for a constant rate of R_{MC} = 7%): $T_{HongKong}$ = 2.51 years, T_{Macau} = 0.03 year and T_{Taiwan} = 4.58 years.

Appendixes

A1 Basic Conditions of the Ethnic Minorities

Ethnicity	Geographic distribution	Language(s)	Religion(s)
Achang	Yunnan	Achang	Buddhism
Bai	Yunnan, Guizhou	Bai, most also speak Chinese	animism
Baonan	Gansu	Baonan, Chinese (spoken and written)	Islam
Blang	Yunnan	Blang, Dai	Buddhism
Bouyei	Guizhou, Yunnan, Guangxi		Buddhism
Dai	Yunnan	Dai, most also speak Chinese	Buddhism
Daur	Inner Mongolia, Heilongjiang, Xinjiang	Daur (spoken), Chinese (written)	Lamaism
Deang	Yunnan	Deang	Buddhism
Dong	Guizhou, Hunan, Guangxi	Dong, Chinese	animism
Dongxiang	Gansu, Xinjiang	Dongxiang, most also speak Chinese	Islam
Drung	Yunnan	Drung	
Ewenki	Inner Mongolia, Heilongjiang	Ewenki (spoken), Mongolian (written), Chinese (written)	shamanism
Gaoshan	Taiwan, Fujian	Gaoshan (spoken), Chinese	
Gelao	Guizhou, Guangxi	Gelao, Chinese	Islam
Hani	Yunnan	Hani	animism
Hezhe	Heilongjiang	Hezhe (spoken), Chinese	
Hui	Ningxia, Gansu, Henan, Hebei, Qinghai, Shandong	Chinese	Islam
Jing	Guangxi	Jing, Chinese (spoken and written)	
Jingpo	Yunnan	Jingpo	animism
Jino	Yunnan	Jino	
Kazak	Xinjiang, Gansu, Qinghai	Kazaki	Islam
Kirgiz	Xinjiang, Heilongjiang	Kirgiz, Uygur (written), Kazaki (written)	Islam, Lamaism
Korean	Jilin, Liaoning, Heilongjiang	Korean, Chinese	individual choice
Lahu	Yunnan	Lahu	animism
Lhoba	Tibet	Lhoba (spoken)	Lamaism
Li	Hainan	Li, males and a small number of females also speak Chinese	animism
Lisu	Yunnan, Sichuan	Lisu	

A1 Continued

Ethnicity	Geographic distribution	Language(s)	Religion(s)
Manchu	Liaoning, Jilin, Heilongjiang, Beijing, Inner Mongolia	most speak Chinese; only a small portion speak Manchu in Jilin and Heilongjiang	individual choice
Maonan	Guangxi	Maonan, Zhuang, Chinese (written)	Islam
Miao	Guizhou, Sichuan, Hunan, Hubei, Guangdong	Miao; the majority also assimilated into mainstream Chinese language	animism
Monba	Tibet	Monba, Tibetan	Lamaism
Mongol	Inner Mongolia, Xinjiang, Liaoning, Jilin, Heilongjiang, Gansu, Hebei, Henan, Qinghai	Mongolian, Mandarin	Lamaism
Mulam	Guangxi	Mulam and Zhuang (spoken), Chinese (written)	Lamaism
Naxi	Yunnan, Sichuan	Naxi, most also speak Chinese	Dongba
Nu	Yunnan	Nu	
Oroqen	Inner Mongolia, Heilongjiang	Oroqen (spoken), Chinese (written)	shamanism
Pumi	Yunnan	Pumi	
Qiang	Sichuan	Qiang (spoken)	Lamaism
Russian	Xinjiang, Heilongjiang	Russian	Eastern Orthodox
Salar	Qinghai, Gansu	Salar (spoken), Chinese (spoken and written)	Islam
She	Fujian, Zhejiang, Jiangxi, Guangdong	Chinese	animism
Shui	Guizhou, Guangxi	Shui, most also speak Chinese	animism
Tajik	Xinjiang	Tajik (spoken), Uygur	Islam
Tatar	Xinjiang	Tatar, Uygur, Kazaki	Islam
Tibetan	Tibet, Qinghai, Sichuan, Gansu, Yunnan, Xinjiang	Tibetan	Lamaism
Tu	Qinghai, Gansu	Tu, Chinese	Lamaism
Tujia	Hunan, Hubei	Tujia, most also speak Chinese	animism
Uygur	Xinjiang	Uygur	Islam
Uzbek	Xinjiang	Uzbek, Uygur, Kazaki	Islam
Va	Yunnan	Va	animism
Xibe	Xinjiang, Liaoning, Jilin	Xibe	Islam
Yao	Guangxi, Hunan, Yunnan, Guangdong	Yao, most also speak Chinese	animism
Yi	Sichuan, Hunan, Guizhou, Guangxi	Yi (spoken), males also speak and write Chinese	animism
Yugur	Gansu	Yugur, Chinese (spoken and written)	Lamaism
Zhuang	Guangxi, Guangdong, Yunnan and Guizhou	Zhuang (spoken), most males also speak Chinese; Chinese (written)	animism

A2 A List of Major Reforms from 1978 to 2008

Year/M/D	Organizer(s)	Program
1978/12/18	Third Plenum of the 11th CCPCC	"Decision of the CCPCC Concerning the Reform of Economic System"
1979	NPC	"Law of the People's Republic of China Concerning the Joint Ventures with Chinese and Foreign Investment"
1979	CCPCC and State Council	Guangdong and Fujian provinces were granted with "special policies and flexible measures" in foreign economic affairs.
1979/12/26	People's Congress of Guangdong province	Shenzhen next to Hong Kong, Zhuhai next to Macau, and Santou were designed as the SEZs, to experiment a market-oriented economy.
1980	State Council	Starting of the fiscal contract system
1980/8/26	NPC	Xiamen in Southeast Fujian province vis-à-vis Taiwan became a SEZ
1980/9	CCPCC and State Council	Household Responsibility System (HRS)
1984	State Council	"Provisional Regulations for the Management of 'Small-volume' Border Trade"
1984/4	CCPCC and the State Council	Design of 14 coastal open cities
1984/5/10	State Council	"Provisional Regulations on the Enlargement of Autonomy of State-owned Industrial Enterprises"
1984/10/21	CCPCC	"Decision of the CCPCC Concerning the Reform of Economic Structure"
1985/2	State Council	The Yangtze River, Pearl River and South Fujian were approved as coastal economic development zones
1986	State Council	Regulations of Issues Concerning the Extensive Regional Economic Cooperation
1986/12	NPC	"Bankruptcy Law Concerning the SOEs"
1986/12	State Council	Encouraging the SOEs to adopt the contract system.
1988/3	State Council	Liaodong and Shandong peninsulas and Bohai Basin area were allowed to open up to the outside world
1988/4	NPC	Hainan province was approved as a SEZ with even more flexible policies than other SEZs
1990/4	CCPCC and the State Council	Shanghai's Pudong area was granted to enjoy some of the SEZ's mechanisms
1991	Yunnan province	"Provisional Regulations Concerning the Border Trade"
1992/7/14	Tibet autonomous region	"Resolutions Concerning the Further Reform and Opening up to the Outside World"
1991/4/20	Inner Mongolia autonomous region	"Resolution of Some Issues Concerning the Extension of Open-door and Promotion of Economic Development"
1992	State Council	"Notification Concerning the Further Opening up of the Four Frontier Cities of Heihe, Shuifenhe, Hunchun and Manzhouli"
1992/1/25	Office of Custom, PRC	"Measures Concerning the Supervision and Favourable Taxation for the People-to-People Trade in Sino-Myanmar Border"

A2 Continued

Year/M/D	Organizer(s)	Program
1992/2/9	Xinjiang autonomous region	"Notification of Promoting the Trade and Economic Cooperation with the Neighbouring and Eastern European Countries"
1992/6	State Commission for Restructuring the Economic Systems	"Provisional Regulations on Joint-Stock Companies"
1992/6	State Council	"Notification Concerning the Further Opening up of the Five Frontier Cities and Towns of Nanning, Kunming, Pingxiang, Ruili, and Hekou"
1992/6	Heilongjiang province	"Some Favourable Policies and Economic Autonomy Authorized to the Frontier Cities of Heihe and Shuifenhe"
1992/7/22	State Council	"Regulations on the Transformation of the Operating Mechanisms of State-owned Industrial Enterprises"
1993/11	Third Plenum of the 14th CCPCC	Establishment of the Modern Enterprise System
1993/11/14	Third Plenum of the 14th CCPCC	"Decision of the CCPCC on Several Issues Concerning the Establishment of a Socialist Market Economic Structure"
1994	People's Bank of China	Separation of banking from policy lending; reducing of the number of the central bank's regional braches from 30 or more to only six
1994	State Council	Introduction of "tax-sharing system" into all provinces
1994/1/1	People's Bank of China	Establishment of a new unitary and floating exchange-rate system
1995/9	Fifth Plenum of the Fourteenth CCPCC	Policy of grasping the large and releasing the small SOEs
1998/3	The Ninth NPC	Amendment was to Article 6 of the Chinese Constitution: "public, instead of state, ownership as the main part of ownership of the means of production"
1999	State Council	Debt-equity swap scheme (zhai zhuan gu) in four large state-owned banks
2000/4/1	People's Bank of China	Adoption of "real name" banking system
2001/11	WTO	China's access to TWO
2004/4	State Council	The abolishment of agricultural tax within 3 years
2003/12	State Council	Transformation of Bank of China and China Construction Bank into joint stock ownership
2008/7	State Council	Privatization of forestland for 70 years of tenure in selected areas
2008/8	People's Bank of China	More flexible foreign exchange policies
2008/10	Third Plenum of the 17th CCPCC	De facto land privatization in rural areas

Sources: (1) Bulletins of the State Council, People's Republic of China, various issues; (2) Bulletins of the National People's Congress, various issues; and (3) the author's collection.

Notes

1 A Brief History of China

1. According to the Zhongfa system, the eldest son of the highest-ranking wife of a member of the royal household or nobility was called the "major branch" and inherited the right of succession to his father's throne or noble title. Other son(s) was (were) known as "minor branch(es)."
2. Historically, the Han dynasty is divided into two periods: the Western Han had its capital in Chang'an in the west; the Eastern Han had its capital in Luoyang in the east.
3. The major events that occurred in Chinese society during the twentieth century are listed below in chronological order: 1912, China's final dynasty, the Qing, was replaced by the Republic of China (ROC); 1937, Japan invaded China and the War of Resistance against Japan began; 1945, Japan surrendered unconditionally and, thereafter, the Civil War between the Nationalists and the Communists broke out; 1949, the People's Republic of China (PRC) was founded, followed by the large-scale land reform and socialist transformation of capitalist industry and commerce in mainland China.
4. Cited from Mencius (c.300 BC, Teng Wen Gong II). Note that the term "dragon," which was also known as the "God of water or rain" in traditional Chinese culture, was probably a reference to a crocodile or some other amphibious lizard.

2 Spatial and Administrative Divisions

1. The book *Yugong* probably was written or revised in the middle period of the Warring States (475—221 BC) since one tribute mentioned in this book, iron, had not been found until that period.
2. Notice that the Chinese character *dao* is still being used as "province" in both North and South Korea.
3. More detailed discussions can be found in section 2.5.
4. See section 2.7 for a case study of interprovincial territorial disputes.
5. For example, as reported in Liu (1996, pp. 153–6), the optimum numbers of China's provinces have been suggested as 58 by Hong (1945a and b), 40–3 by Hu (1991) and 43 by Guo (1993).
6. Examples of literature on the application of the six great regions would include Hu *et al.* (1988, pp. 171–381), Yang (1989, p. 92), and Wei (1992, pp. 62–3). Besides, regional scientists and economic geographers have also defined Chinese great regions, with differing numbers and geographical scope, for their own purposes. These include, for example, Wright (1984, p. 78), Yang (1993, p. 270), Hu (1993, pp. 193–203) and Liu (1994, pp. 36–7) for six great regions; Li *et al.* (1994, pp. 139–65), Keidel (1995) for seven great

regions; and Yang (1989, pp. 238–40), Yang (1990, pp. 38–40) and Liu (1994, p. 36) for ten great regions.

7. See *Guangming Daily*, April 6 1986, p. 1.

8. For example, Wu and Hou (1990, p. 116), Hu *et al.* (1988, pp. 182–4), Yang (1990, pp. 38–43), Liu (1994, pp. 1–13) and Hsueh (1994a, pp. 22–56) give the same definition.

9. Information about all these county-level autonomous administrations can be found on China's official websites.

10. Based on two field surveys conducted during 2001–02. I thank Professor Hu Xuwei for joining me on my first field trip to Lake Weishan and Dr David Lawerence and Mr Guo Liqing for their helpful assistance. A longer version of this section can be found in Chapter 10 of my monograph (*Cross-Border Resource Management*, Amsterdam and Boston: Elsevier, 2006, pp. 197–226).

11. *Weishan Statistical Yearbook 2001*, Statistical Bureau of Weishan country, May 2002, p. 1.

12. This proposal was submitted to the Ministry of Civil Affairs (MCA) by the Administrative Commission of East China Region on July 17 1953 (dongbanzi [53] official letter, No. 0643) and supported by the People's Government of Shandong province on May 4 1953 (luminzi [53] official letter, No. 1533).

13. Source: The State Administrative Council of the PRC (under the form of Letter zhengzhengbuzi, No. 136), August 22 1953. According to the *Weishan Statistical Yearbook 2001* (p. 1), the total number of villages was 302.

14. Source: *Weishan Statistical Yearbook 2001*, p. 2.

15. See "Statistics on Status of the Lakeside Land and Lake-related Resources in Lake Weishan, Peixian County" (peixian guanyu zai weishanhu nei hutian, huchan qingkuang tongji), Office of Lakeside land, Peixian county, June 8 1996.

16. Ibid.

17. See "Report on the Work of the Delimitation between Peixian and Weishan Counties" (guanyu peiwei bianjie kanjie gongzuo de huibao), the Working Office of Lake Area, Peixian County, February 17 1998.

18. Based on the author's two talks with officials in Weishan and Peixian counties on June 1 and 2 2000, respectively.

19. Source: "Report on the Work of the Delimitation between Peixian and Weishan Counties."

20. See "The Village Surrounded by Polluted Water" (bei wushui baowei de cunzhuang), *Qilu Evening News*, December 14 1997.

21. Based on the author's talks with county officials in Peixian township, Jiangsu province on June 2 2000.

22. Cited from "Comrade Wan Li's Speech at the Meeting of Report Delivered by Comrade Cui Naifu of Minister of Civil Affairs on the Issues Concerning the Resolution of the Disputes over Lake Weishan."

23. See "Report on the Work of the Delimitation between Peixian and Weishan Counties."

24. For instance, Article 12 of "Temporary Regulations Concerning the Resource Taxation of the People's Republic of China" (Beijing, State Council, No. 139 document, December 25 1993) states that: "Tax payers shall pay taxes to the taxation bureau in charge of places from which the taxed products originate."

25. Source: "Report on the Work of the Delimitation between Peixian and Weishan Counties."

3 Human and Cultural Contexts

1. Wakabayashi (1989, p. 14) estimates that 14 million people died from starvation between 1959 and 1961. In addition, Minami (1994, p. 197, fn. 8) puts a higher figure on the number of deaths.
2. The literature on this argument would include Wang and Dai (1958, pp. 10–14), He *et al.* (1960, pp. 20–5), and Zhang (1982, pp. 12–14).
3. According to the PRC's Constitution, women and men shall have the same right to be employed and be paid the same wage if they do the same job.
4. According to Chenery and Syrquin (1975, p. 20), when the per capita GNP grows from US$100 to US$400 in developing countries, the ratio of educational expenditure to GNP increases from 3.3 percent to 3.5 percent accordingly.
5. They are, for example, the Huns (Xiongnu) and Xianbei between the third and fifth century AD, the Eastern Hu and the Jurchens (ancestors of the Manchus) from the tenth through the early thirteenth century, and the Manchus through their conquest of China in the seventeenth century.
6. For example, the Chinese character for the tree that produces tung oil is composed of an ideogram on the left representing a tree, and a phonogram on the right indicating that the word should be pronounced tong (as would this phonetic element if it were an independent character).
7. See North and Thomas (1973), North (1981, 1990), and Abramovitz (1986) for the varieties of European experience on the importance of institutions or differential social capability.
8. Based on two surveys conducted in January 2001. Zhao Gongzheng and Guo Liqin joined these surveys and helped me to compile the data. Chen Tianchi and Tian Guogang, Director and Deputy Director of the General Managers' Office of the Kailuan Group, accompanied me during my stay at these two firms. As requested, the two firms are named as two abbreviated letters, J and L, respectively.
9. In China, females are not allowed to work as underground miners.
10. It should be noted that this does not mean that wages decrease with an increase in educational levels. As a matter of fact, the staff in each educational group are also characterized by other variables such as age, gender, and occupation – each of the latter also decides the level of wages. We will discuss this issue in more detail later in the volume.

4 Political Economic Systems in Transition

1. To be continued at the end of this chapter.
2. For example, the gross value of industrial output (GVIO) grew at 18 percent annually, higher than the planned rate (14.7 percent); the annual gross value of agricultural output (GVAO) growth rate (4.5 percent) exceeded the planned rate (4.3 percent) during this period (SSB, 1990b).
3. See, for example, Liu (1982, pp. 28–51) for more detail.

4. This repetitive bargaining between the state planners and the managers usually reached a high tide during the annual national planning meetings arranged by the State Planning Commission (SPC).

5. This is mainly due to the fact that, as will be discussed in detail later in subsection 4.3.1, China's agricultural reform was usually accompanied by price rises, since the prices of agricultural products were always kept at a very low level, especially during the early period of reform.

6. See Liew (2000), which also gives other references.

7. As noted by Lin (1995), China's SOEs enjoyed far less autonomy than their Soviet antecedents, since the Soviet enterprises operated under the Economic Accounting System (*khozraschet*) which endowed state enterprises with a limited degree of financial autonomy with them being allowed to retain a proportion of profits, depreciation reserves, and major repair funds. However, national shortages of productive resources and severe weaknesses in enterprise management in China during the 1950s compelled a much more centralized system which left SOEs without any substantive decision-making or financial autonomy.

8. Notice that as soon as the Tian'anmen Square incident (May–June 1989) was calmed down, the Chinese leadership began to re-emphasize the role of the working class in the Chinese economy.

9. A case study of the ownership of the SOEs can be found in section 6.6 of Chapter 6.

10. Note that the state ownership only includes the SOEs, while the public ownership include the SOEs and COEs (see Figure 4.4).

11. The literature of the evolution in central–local fiscal arrangement over the pre-reform era would include Lardy (1975, pp. 25–60), Donnithorne (1976, pp. 328–54), and Oksenberg and Tong (1991, pp. 1–32).

12. That is, the marginal and average propensity to tax each province from its collected revenue ranged between 12 percent and 90 percent (Oksenberg and Tong, 1991, p. 24).

13. They are Shanghai, Tianjin, Shenyang, Nanjing, Ji'nan, Wuhan, Guangzhou, Chengdu, and Xi'an, with additional two administrative departments housed in Beijing and Chongqing municipalities.

14. Before the crisis, there had been a crying call for the SOEs to be reconstructed according to the Korean model. But obviously this idea has been abandoned as soon as South Korea's chaebols met difficulties.

15. Sachs and Warner (1995) define a closed economy as one that has at least one of the following characteristics: non-tariff barriers cover 40 percent or more of trade; average tariff rates of 40 percent or more; a black-market exchange rate that is depreciated by 20 percent or more relative to the official rate, among others.

16. For example, they have the authority to approve foreign investment projects up to US$30 million, while other regions' authority remained much lower (Montinola *et al.*, 1995).

5 Understanding Chinese Economic Reform

1. Even though the term "commodity" in the Chinese understanding is closely related to the concept of market economy, we may assume that it was used

here to distinguish the Chinese economy literally from the Western-style market system.

2. The term was firstly publicized in bold headlines in the CCP's official newspapers (such as *People's Daily* and *Workers' Daily*) in early 1988.

3. For details of the Speech, see Deng (1992, pp. 370–83).

4. See Appendix 2 at the end of the volume for a list of major reforms from 1978 to 2008.

5. In fact, it is difficult to consistently identify the radicals and conservatives throughout the whole period of reform. Those who had been treated as radicals during one period might become conservatives at a later stage; furthermore, a CCP senior who can be a radical reformer in respect of one agenda (such as agricultural or other domestic sector reform) might be considered as a conservative in another (such as external economic sectors or political reform in general).

6. Note that this result does not depend on the process through which the redistribution of incomes from the radicals and conservatives has been determined.

7. Cited from http://edition.cnn.com/SPECIALS/1999/china.50/inside.china/profiles/li.peng/.

8. Since the institutional decentralization and concentralization might occur simultaneously in different sectors, authors with different analytical purposes may identify the *fang-shou* circle differently. For example, Baum (1994, pp. 5–9 and pp. 369–76) offers a plausible explanation of the *fang–shou* cycle during 1978–93: the decentralization (*fang*) policy was concentrated on 1978, 1980, 1982, 1984, 1986, 1988, and 1992; while the over-centralization (*shou*) policy was concentrated on 1979, 1981, 1983, 1985, 1987, 1989, and 1993. Shirk (1993), Dittmer and Wu (1993, pp. 10–12) reach a similar conclusion, sketching out four relatively complete, synchronous cycles of *fang* and *shou* during 1980 to 1989: *fang* predominated in 1979–80, 1984 and 1988, while *shou* predominated in 1981, 1985–86, 1987, and 1988–89.

9. Note that this result does not depend on the process through which the redistribution of incomes from the radicals and conservatives has been determined.

10. In a survey conducted in 1992, 30 percent of surveyed officials were thinking about *xiahai* (Chen, 1993). In another survey of local government officials in 1995, close to 20 percent were planning on *xiahai* (SCSR, 1996). Of those, 35 percent were looking for joint-venture enterprises, 21 percent for private enterprises, and 1.5 percent for SOEs. Tang and Parish (1998) find in their large survey that 99 percent of those officials who planned to quit the bureaucracy wanted to join businesses. Cited from Li (1998).

11. This can be witnessed by, for example, Yu's (2004) article in which some influential Chinese economists are criticized for their favoritism to the rich vis-à-vis the poor.

12. Note that as a result of three decades of effective CCP control on the one hand and of the closed-door policy on the other, most, if not all peasants in rural China had been accustomed to obeying political and economic orders coming from Beijing.

13. For example, according to a World Bank report, before reform, China's "bare-foot doctor" approach in its rural areas had been an important model for primary health care worldwide (Hammer, 1995).

14. I still remember that, upon hearing the news about price reforms in August 1988, I rushed to an electrical appliances shop to buy a radio-recorder, which was worthy of my ten-month salary but seldom used in the following years.

15. The resulting near-zero incentives in post-reform Russia look similar to the pre-reform China but stand in sharp contrast to the post-reform China (Qian, 2002).

16. More detailed analysis can be found in Shen and Dai (1990), Li (1993) and Wedeman (1993).

17. Discussions in this regard would include, for example, Garnaut and Huang (1995), Corbet (1996), Keidel (1995), Wu (1996), Mastel (1996, 1998) and Morici (1997).

18. Examples that support "Big bang" reforms would include Lipton and Sachs (1990), Åslund (1991), Berg and Sachs (1992), Boycko (1992), Murphy *et al.* (1992), Sachs (1993), Frydman and Rapaczynski (1994), and Woo (1994).

19. Examples that support gradual reforms would include Svejnar (1989), Portes (1990), McKinnon (1991b), Roland (1991), Dewatripont and Roland (1992a, 1992b, and 1995), McMillan and Naughton (1992), Murrell (1992), Aghion and Blanchard (1994), Litwack and Qian (1998), and Wei (1993).

20. Cited from www.wsws.org/articles/2002/nov2002/chin-n13.shtml.

21. From November 2002 to 2003, SARS infected over 8,000 people in 30 countries and killed more than 500. In addition to the human toll, it inflicted significant economic damage across Asia. In addition to Hong Kong, which was among the most severely hit, GDP growth rates in Taiwan, Singapore, and Thailand were also lower in 2003. Nowhere was SARS having more impact than on mainland China, where the disease started.

22. With regard to the FSU's relatively weakness of the market economy, Mikhail Gorbachev's speech on September 11 1990 might be revealing: "Our brains just could not handle this idea of a market." Cited in Hwang (1993, p. 147).

23. This assumption is based simply on the fact that all radicals have a CCP background and do not want any reforms that could lead to the collapse of the CCP-dominated nation.

24. We borrow this term from Bates *et al.* (1998, p. 31).

25. Note that if the expected length of time for the reforms is TBB for the radicals and TGR for the conservatives, we have TBB $\leq$ T* $\leq$ TGR.

26. Note that in Conditions 1 and 2 the optimal reform strategies have nothing to do with open-door policies.

6 Economic Growth and Income Distribution

1. All data are estimated according to the World Bank Atlas method of converting national currency to current US dollars.

2. The World Bank (1996, pp. 394-5) defined low-income economies, lower-middle-income economies, upper-middle-income economies and high-income economies with per capita GNPs of US$725 or less, US$726-2,895, US$2,896-8,955 and US$8,956 or more, respectively.

3. For example, related stories can also be found in *The Economist* (November 28 1992). Subsequent reports appeared in, among others, *Financial Times* (April 26 1993) and *The Economist* (May 15 1993).

4. As a matter of fact, the reason why the Chinese government repeatedly rejected the PPP-enlarged GDP may arise from, among others, the fears that it could have affected China as a less-developed country to obtain favorable loans and economic assistance from rich nations and international organizations (Zheng, 1996, p. 1).

5. See Box 6.1 for more details about "underground economic activities".

6. Examples of literature for the application in the Chinese economic analyses would include Lardy (1980, pp. 153–90), Lyons (1992), Denny (1991, pp. 186–208), Tsui (1991) and Yang (1992a).

7. Literature of the multidimensional measurement of regional inequalities would include Atkinson (1970), Atkinson and Bourguigon (1992), Maasoumi (1986) and Kolm (1976a, 1976b and 1977). In addition, as a demonstration in which two indices (per capita GDP and per capita hospital beds) are considered, Tsui (1994) applies the multidimensional GE method to calculate China's regional disparities between 1978 and 1989.

8. Recent surveys of the theories on the economic effects of income inequality would include Benabou (1996), Aghion *et al.* (1999) and Barro (2000).

9. See Perotti (1993), Alesina and Rodrik (1994), Persson and Tabellini (1994) and Benabou (1996) for detailed analyses.

10. This effect arises if the economy is partly closed, so that domestic investment depends, to some extent, on desired national saving (Barro, 2000, p. 8).

11. There is an indication in Barro's (2000) study that growth tends to fall with greater inequality when per capita GDP is below around $2,000 (1985 US dollars) and to rise with inequality when per capita GDP is above $2,000.

12. Source: www.fubusi.com/2006/3-14/142426956.html.

13. A longer version of this research has been published in Chinese (Guo, Li and Xing, 2003).

14. The team members involved in the two field surveys are Zhao Renwei, Li Shi, He Dingchao, Zhao Gongzheng, Zhang Yong, Zhu Shumiao, Xing Youqiang, Wang Xiaoping, Xie Yanhong and myself.

15. Since "share bonus" has nothing to do with workers' performances, we will not test the regression in which the dependent variable is represented by either "share bonus" or "total earning".

16. For example, the estimated ratios of return to education are 0.038 for urban China and 0.020 for rural China in 1988 (Li and Li, 1994, p. 445) and 0.042 for SOEs, and 0.032 for collectively-owned enterprises and 0.0791 for foreign-invested enterprises in 1996 (Zhao, 2001).

7 A Multiregional Economic Comparison

1. It is worth noting that the SNA has some shortcomings and is not a complete measure of economic welfare from which humankind may benefit. In fact, as illustrated in the United Nations (1990a, b), the SNA-based GNP (or GDP) indicator ignores the costs of both the depletion and degradation of natural and environmental resources.

2. More evidence may be found in Tsui (1993, pp. 30–1).
3. See, for example, Guo and Han (1991, pp. 10–21) for a more detailed explanation and the critical evaluation on the quality of Chinese GDP data.
4. Therefore, national income equals GVSP minus all material costs including depreciation of capital.
5. For example, according to a survey conducted by JPSB (1990, pp. 27–8), the rural GVIO data reported to the SSB might have been 21.8 percent higher than the real data in Jilin province in 1989.
6. For more evidence of the overstatement on China's GNP for the post-1992 period, one may also refer to Ling *et al.* (1995, pp. 18–19), *China Youth* (1995, p. 2), *The Economist* (1995, p. 19), *People's Daily* (1995, p. 2), Huang (1996, pp. 157–62), and so on.
7. See, for example, Guo and Wang (1988), Yang (1990), Denny (1991, pp. 186–208), Dong (1992), Lyons (1992), Tsui (1991), Wei (1992), Yang (1992a; 1992b), Zhang (1994, pp. 296–312), Wei and Liu (1994) and Song (1996).
8. See, for example, Yang (1991, pp. 504–9, and 1993, pp. 129–45), Liu *et al.* (1994, pp. 141–66) and Tsui (1993).
9. Data sources: Ottolenghi and Steinherr (1993, p. 29), Savoie (1992, p. 191), Smith (1987, p. 41), Higgins (1981, pp. 69–70), Nair (1985, p. 9), Hill and Weidemann (1989, pp. 6–7), Kim and Mills (1990, p. 415), and Hu *et al.* (1995, p. 92).
10. Data sources: *Yearbook of Provincial Statistics* (Guangdong and Hunan), related issues.

8 Spatial Economics and Development Strategy

1. Since this book covers only the economy of mainland China, in what follows in this section, we will only analyze the mainland part of the PRD area.
2. Examples of literature would include *Economic News* (1987, p. 1; 1988, p. 1), Hu (1992, p. 1), and Guo (1993, pp. 118–23; 1996, pp. 70–1).
3. See *Beijing Youth*, December 2 2002 (available at www.sina.com.cn).
4. The total disputed areas (about 140,000 km^2) include grassland (about 96,000 km^2), mining areas (about 5000 km^2), water (about 1000 km^2) and mixed grass-mining-forestland (about 30,000 km^2) and are distributed unevenly in the Western belt (about 130,000 km^2), the Central belt (about 17,000 km^2) and the Eastern belt (about 700 km^2). See *Baokan Wenzhai* (1989, p. 4).
5. This phenomenon has been described as Zhuhou Jingji (feudal prince economy) or Duli Wangguo (independent kingdom). See, for example, Shen and Dai (1990, p. 12), Li (1993, pp. 23–36) and Wedeman (1993, pp. 1–2) for more detailed analyses.
6. More detailed evidence may be found in Sun (1993, pp. 95–104), Feng (1993, pp. 87–94), Guo (1993, pp. 201–5), and Goodman (1994, pp. 1–20).
7. The largest ethnic minorities include Zhuang (15.6 million people), Manchu (9.8 million), Hui (8.6 million), Miao (7.4 million), Uygur (7.2 million) and Yi (6.6 million) (SSB, 1996, p. 56).
8. More detailed evidence may be found in Sun (1993, pp. 95–104), Feng (1993, pp. 87–94) and Goodman (1994, pp. 1–20).

9. Examples of the literature would include CASS (1992) and Guo (1993, pp. 189–95; 1996, pp. 146–50).
10. For details about China's regional development strategies and policies during the pre-reform period, viz., from the 1950s to the 1970s, see Chapter 9.
11. http://www.westchina.gov.cn/english/asp/showinfo.asp?name=2.11.11. 2003.
12. On this basis, three methods were developed: (i) spraying water into warm clouds; (ii) dropping dry ice into cold clouds (where the dry ice freezes some water into ice crystals that act as natural nuclei for snow); and (iii) wafting silver iodide crystals or other similar crystals into a cold cloud from the ground or from an airplane over the cloud (UWRL, 1971).
13. Cited from *Washington Post* (2004, p. A12).

9 Industrialization and Technological Progress

1. Examples of literature on the third-front area would include Lardy (1978), Leung (1980), Maruyama (1982, pp. 437–71), Liu (1983), Riskin (1987), Naughton (1988, pp. 227–304), Bo (1991, pp. 1202–3 and 1209), and Chen (1994, pp. 329–42).
2. Cited from Liang (1982, pp. 61–2). This clearly went far beyond the real capacities of this country.
3. Rural workers are classified by main activity. For example, those engaged primarily in agriculture and secondly in commerce are classified under the broad category of agriculture.
4. More details may be found in He *et al.* (1991, pp. 124–41).
5. The unemployment rates for some Western countries were 6.6 percent (USA), 9.4 percent (France), 10.9 percent (Italy), 15.2 percent (Spain) and 8.1 percent (UK) (ILO, 1993). However, the definition of "unemployment" differs from country to country, so it is difficult to conduct meaningful international comparisons.
6. There has been a saying that without rural workers Beijing would stop running.
7. The units used are yuan for Y and K and person for L.
8. Regarding the causes of China's backward state in technological innovation, Lu Xun, a well-known writer, noted ironically that while Western nations used powder to make firearms and the compass for navigation, China used powder to make firecrackers for entertainment and the compass to align the spiritual location within the landscape (*fengshui*).
9. The expenditure on research R&D refers to all actual expenditure made for R&D (fundamental research, applied research, and experimental development).
10. Data sources: (1) SSB (1996, p. 661) for the data of 1995; (2) SSTC (1988, p. 267) for the data of 1986; (3) As Ma and Sun (1981, p. 614) estimate that China's R&D expenses were 0.54 percent of GVIAO in 1979, using the estimated GVIAO/GNP ratio (0.5799) in Equation 7.3 of Chapter 7, we can obtain an approximation of R&D/GNP ratio ($0.54/0.5799 \approx 0.93$).

11. Examples would include Brezis *et al.* (1993), Jovanovic and Nyakro (1994) and Barro and Sala-i-Martin (1995, ch. 8).

10 The Quest for Sustainable Development

1. The exception that proves the rule is aluminum, for which China is a net exporter and produces about 25 percent of the world total. Compared with price increases of 379 percent for copper from January 2002 to June 2006, aluminum prices have increased modestly – up only 80 percent (Streifel, 2006).

2. Other sources suggest different estimates. For instance, after summing up the official data from the provincial statistics, the total cultivated land area is no more than 100,000,000 ha, while other figures (such as 120,000,000 ha, 133,333,000 ha, and 146,667,000 ha) have been estimated based on satellite photographs and sample surveys (Cheng, 1990, pp. 1–18). In 1979, Chinese official statistics defined the forestland area at 1,220,000 square kilometers, while the World Bank (1992) puts the figure at 1,150,000 square kilometers for the year 1980. According to Vaclav (1992, p. 434), China's forestland area was estimated as 124,650,000 ha in the third national survey (1984–88) and was reported by the State Statistical Bureau and the Ministry of Forestry as 1,246,000 square kilometers and 1,092,000 square kilometers, respectively, for the year 1989. For 1992 and 1993, NEPA (1993, p. 4; 1994, p. 5) evaluates it at 1,309,000 square kilometers and 1,337,000 square kilometers, respectively.

3. *Source*: CISNR (1990, p. 644) and the author's judgment.

4. Notice that the monetary values of the mineral resources might have been underestimated due to the use of low and officially fixed prices for the mineral products before the 1990s.

5. pH values below 5.6 are indicative of acid rain.

6. *Beijing Evening News*, May 25 2004.

7. As oxygen is required to aerobically decompose biologically degradable compounds, the higher the level of BOD, the poorer the water quality.

8. In 1979, for example, Chinese official statistics defined the forestland area at 1.22 million square kilometers, while the World Bank (1992) puts the figure at 1.15 million square kilometers for the year 1980. According to Vaclav (1992, p. 434), China's forestland area was estimated as 124,650,000 ha in the third national survey (1984–88) and was reported by the SSB and Ministry of Forestry of China as 1,246,000 square kilometers and 1,092,000 square kilometers in 1989, respectively. NEPA (1993, p. 4; 1994, p. 5) estimated it at 1,309,000 square kilometers in 1992 and 1,337,000 square kilometers in 1993, respectively.

9. Sheehy (1992, p. 303) estimates that the desertified grazingland has increased at a rate of over 10,000 square kilometers per annum.

10. These laws, regulations, and other relevant official documents have covered a broader range from air, inland water pollution control, protection of endangered wildlife, to the control of domestic marine pollution from offshore oil drilling and waste release into territorial seas (ACCA21, 1994, p. 1-1A-1).

11. This agreement is available at www.americansovereign.com/articles/weather.htm.

11 International Economic Influences

1. To be continued at the end of this chapter.
2. *Bulletins of the State Council, People's Republic of China*, various issues.
3. Based on Yin (1998) and Wan *et al.* (2004).
4. In this section, only FDI inflows are discussed. China's FDI outflows, though small amounts at present, are growing larger at an annual rate of US$5.5 billion (Winters and Yusuf, 2007, p. 23), mostly in Asia (especially Hong Kong), Latin America and Africa. In fact, the net wealth of Chinese affiliates abroad can be measured in hundreds of billion dollars. Officially, the Chinese SOEs had as many as 5666 affiliates abroad at the end of 1998 with a combined FDI of US$6.33 billion (Chandra, 1999).
5. Calculated by the author based on SSB (1996) and NBS (2006).
6. According to Qian (2002), the role of FDI in China is vastly overstated in the press. For the entire 1980s, the level of FDI in China was tiny. FDI only started to increase substantially in 1993, and at its peak it accounted for about 10 percent of the total investment. On a per capita basis, China's FDI was not high by international standards. The direct contribution of foreign trade and investment to large countries cannot be quantitatively as important as it is to those small countries. Like FDI, China's exports were concentrated in the coastal provinces. However, contrary to a popular perception, China's growth was not just a phenomenon of coastal provinces – it is across-board, both coastal and inland. Inland provinces grow fast while coastal provinces just faster.
7. There have been some remarkable differences in estimating China's imports and exports due to differing statistical systems. For instance, statistics from the US Department of Commerce indicated that Sino-US trade had been in favour of the US side during the 1979–82 period, but the USA began to register a deficit in 1983, with the figure rising to US$39.5 billion in 1996. Chinese statistics from the Customs of the PRC, however, suggested that China had recorded deficits in bilateral trade between 1979 and 1992. A surplus first appeared in 1993, and rose to US$10.5 billion in 1996. Cited from State Council Information Office (1996, p. 21).
8. Linnemann (1966) and Frankel *et al.* (1997a) have estimated the effects of both GDP and GNP on trade, but no significant difference is found.
9. Frankel *et al.*'s (1997b, p. 66) estimated coefficients on "adjacency" range between 0.5 and 0.7. Because trade is specified in natural logarithmic form in their estimates, the way to interpret the coefficients on adjacency is to take the exponent: that is to say, two countries that share a common border will, *ceteris paribus*, increase their trade by about 65–101 percent compared with two otherwise countries.
10. See, for example, Leontief (1956), Kravis (1956a and 1956b), Keesing (1966), Kenen (1965), Baldwin (1971), Branson and Monoyios (1977), Leamer (1980; 1984; and 1993), Stern and Maskus (1981), Bowen *et al.* (1987), and Salvatore and Barazesh (1990).

11. There is an exception in which Boisso and Ferrantino (1997) construct a measure of linguistic distance that is a continuous scalar.
12. This section is based on the first part of my paper ("Linguistic and Religious Influences on Foreign Trade: Evidence from East Asia") published by *Asian Economic Journal*, vol. 21, pp. 100–21.
13. The earliest application of the gravity model can be traced back to the 1940s (see, e.g., Zipf, 1946; Stewart, 1948).
14. Note that if there are a significant number of zero values in the pair-wise trade, then Tobit regressions techniques should be used. In this research, the number of observations identified by TRADE=0 is quite small.
15. For example, there are five main phylums in East Asia: the Sino-Tibetan phylum, the Ural-Altaic phylum (such as Mongolian and Manchu-Tungas), the Dravidian phylum (such as Telugu and Malay), the Austronesian phylum, and the Austro-Asiatic phylum (such as Khmer, Mon and Vietnamese). There are also some other phylums (such as Japanese, Korean and Papuan).
16. This formula has been used in Guo (2004, 2006) and Noland (2005). Several other methods can also be used to comprehensively measure linguistic and religious similarity indexes.
17. Boisso and Ferrantino (1997), for example, use $\sum x_i y_i$ as the construct of similarity index. However, using Equation (11.3) can prevent the index from further reduction when the values of x_i and y_i are small.

12 The Greater China Area: Retrospect and Prospect

1. There have been different names for the greater China area, such as "the Chinese circle" (Wen, 1987), "the Chinese community' (Zhou, 1989; and Hwang, 1988, p. 924), "the greater China community" (Zheng, 1988), "China economic circle" (Feng, 1992, pp. 6–9; Fei, 1993, p. 54), "Chinese economic area" (Segal, 1994, p. 44), "China economic zone" (Zhou, 1992, pp. 18–21; Yang, 1992), and so on. In addition, Dong and Xu (1992, pp. 10–13) and Wei and Frankel (1994, pp. 179–90) add Singapore, Malaysia, Indonesia, Thailand and the Philippines to this area.
2. See "Joint Declaration of the Government of the United Kingdom of Great Britain and Northern Ireland and the Government of the People's Republic of China on the Question of Hong Kong," Beijing, December 19 1984.
3. See "Basic Law of the Hong Kong Special Administrative Region of the People's Republic of China," Article 5, the Third Session of the Seventh NPC, April 4 1990.
4. For example, the Mainland Commission has been established by the Taiwanese government in order to officially manage its "mainland affairs," while in mainland China, the Office for Taiwan Affairs is also authorized by the State Council to deal with "Taiwan affairs."
5. During the early 1990s, average labor cost in Hong Kong, Macau, and Taiwan is 10–20 times that in mainland China (Yang, 1992, p. 3).
6. The PRC's attitude toward the Taiwan's position in the international community may be briefly summarized by Jiang (1995, p. 2) as that "... Under the principle of one China and in accordance with the charters of the relevant international organizations, Taiwan has become a member of the

Asian Development Bank, the Asian-Pacific Economic Cooperation Forum and other international economic organizations in the name of "Chinese Taipei."

7. In 1985, Chen Guoshun, a Taiwanese businessman, was sentenced in Taipei to 12 years in prison for "rebellious" activities. The prosecutor charged Chen with illegally entering mainland China in 1984, signing a contract, and engaging in direct investment in the mainland. Chen's sentence sent a shock wave to those who had engaged or intended to conduct direct business activities (*Pai Shing Semimonthly*, March 1 1986, p. 52).

8. According to CEC (1996), the direct cross-Taiwan Strait links would have resulted in a net saving of US$731.5 million per annum for postal, remittance, air and shipping services between the two sides of the Strait, including: (1) US$248.0 million for the shipping service; (2) US$437.5 million (6.95 million hours) for the air service; (3) US$24.0 million for the postal service; and (4) US$22.0 million or more for the remittance service. Cited from *Cankao Xiaoxi* (1996, p. 8).

9. Source: www.cnnb.com.cn, December 15 2008.

10. Kan (1994, pp. 172–3) maps out seven assumptions for the triangle relationships between Taiwan, Hong Kong and mainland China and argues that the successful transition of Hong Kong is believed to be the critical factor on which the future reunification of the greater China area will depend.

Bibliography

(*Note*: the titles of Chinese references are listed in English translations followed by *pinyin* forms in parentheses.)

Abramovitz, M. (1986) "Catching up, Forging Ahead, and Falling Behind", *Journal of Economic History*, vol. 56 (June), 23–34.

ACCA21 (1994) *Priority Programs for China's Agenda 21*, First Tranche, Beijing: Administrative Committee of China Agenda 21 (ACCA21) of State Planning Commission and State Science and Technology Commission.

Agarwala, R. (1992) "China: Reforming Intergovernmental Fiscal Relations", *World Bank Discussion Papers*, no. 178, Washington DC: World Bank.

Aghion, P. and O. Blanchard (1994) "On the Speed of Transition in Central Europe", *National Bureau for Economic Research Macroeconomics Annual*, Cambridge, MA: NBER, pp. 283–319.

Aghion, P., E. Caroli, and C. Garcia-Penalosa (1999) "Inequality and Economic Growth: The Perspective of the New Growth Theories", *Journal of Economic Literature*, vol. 37(4), 1615–60.

Alesina, A. and D. Rodrik. (1994) "Distribution Politics and Economic Growth", *The Quarterly Journal of Economics*, vol. 109, 465–90.

Alesina, A. and R. Perotti (1996) "Income Distribution, Political Instability and Investment", *European Economic Review*, vol. 81, 1170–89.

Anderson, D. (1987) *The Economics of Afforestation*, Baltimore: Johns Hopkins University Press.

Asian Development Bank (1996) *Key Indicators of Developing and Asian Countries 1996*, vol. XXVII, Economics and Development Resource Center, Asian Development Bank (ABD), Manila, published by Oxford University Press.

Asian Development Bank (2002) "Research on Poverty in Urban China", unpublished report, Manila: Asian Development Bank.

Asia-Pacific Economic Times, October 22 1996.

Åslund, A. (1991) "Principles of Privatization", in L. Csaba (ed.), *Systemic Change and Stabilization in Eastern Europe*, Aldershot: Dartmouth, pp. 17–31.

Atkinson, A.B. (1970) "On the Measurement of Inequality", *Journal of Economic Theory*, vol. 2, 244–63.

Atkinson, A.B. and F. Bourguignon (1982) "The Comparison of Multidimensional Distributions of Economic Status", *Review of Economic Studies*, vol. 49, 183–201.

Baldwin, R.E. (1971) "Determinants of the Commodity Structure of US Trade", *American Economic Review*, vol. 61 (Mar.), 126–46.

Baokan Wenzhai (1989) "The Armed Disputes in China's Internal Borders" (zhongguo bianjie da xiedou), *The Digest of Newspapers and Magazines*, June 13, p. 4.

Barro, R.J. (2000) "Inequality and Growth in a Panel of Countries", *Journal of Economic Growth*, vol. 5, 5–32.

Barro, R.J., and X. Sala-i-Martin (1995) *Economic Growth*, New York: McGraw-Hill.

Bates, R., A. Greif, M. Levi, J.-L. Rosenthal, and B. Weingast (1998) *Analytic Narratives*, Princeton, NJ: Princeton University Press.

Battan, Louis J. (1962) *Cloud Physics and Cloud Seeding*, San Francisco: Doubleday.

Baum, R. (1994) *Burying Mao: Chinese Politics in the Age of Deng Xiaoping*, Princeton: Princeton University Press.

Benabou, R. (1996) "Inequality and Growth", *NBER Macroeconomics Annual*, Cambridge, MA: NBER, pp. 11–73.

Berg, A. and J. Sachs (1992) "Structural Adjustment and International Trade in Eastern Europe: The Case of Poland", *Economic Policy*, vol. 14, 117–74.

Berthelemy, J.-C. and S. Demurger (2000) "Foreign Direct Investment and Economic Growth: Theoretical Issues and Empirical Application to China", *Review of Development Economics*, vol. 4(2), 140–55.

Bo, Y. (1991) *A Retrospect of Some Key Decisions and Incidents of China* (ruogan zongda juece yu shijian de huigu), vol. I, Beijing: The CCPCC Literature Press.

Boisso, D. and M. Ferrantino (1997) "Economic Distance, Cultural Distance and Openness in International Trade: Empirical Puzzles", *Journal of Economic Integration*, vol. 12, 456–84.

Bowen, H.P., E.E. Leamer, and L. Sveikauskas (1987) "Multicountry, Multifactor Tests of the Factor Abundance Theory", *American Economic Review*, vol. 77 (December), 791–809.

Boycko, M. (1992) "When Higher Incomes Reduce Welfare: Queues, Labor Supply, and Macroeconomic Equilibrium in Socialist Economies", *Quarterly Journal of Economics*, vol. 107, 907–20.

Branson, W.H., and N. Monoyios (1977): "Factor Inputs in US Trade", *Journal of International Economics*, vol. 20, 111–31.

Braudel, F. (1981) *The Structure of Everyday Life, Civilization and Capitalism 15–18th Century*, vol. 1, New York: Harper and Row.

Brezis, E., P. Krugman, and D. Tsiddon (1993) "Leapfrogging in International Competition: A Theory of Cycles in National Technological Leadership", *American Economic Review*, vol. 83(3), 1211–19.

Brun, J.F., J.L. Combes, and M.F. Renard (2002) "Are There Spillover Effects between the Coastal and No-coastal Regions in China?", *China Economic Review*, vol. 13, 161–9.

Burnaux, J.M., J.P. Martin, G. Nicoletti, and J.O. Martins (1992) "The Costs of Reducing CO_2 Emissions: Evidence from GREEN", OECD Economics Department Working Paper no. 115, Paris.

Byrd, W.A. (1987) "The Impact of the Two-Tier Plan/Market System in Chinese Industry", *Journal of Comparative Economics*, September, vol. 11, 295–308.

Cai, F., D. Wang, and M. Wang (2002) "China's Regional Specialization in the Course of Gradual Reform", *The Economic Research* (in Chinese), no. 9, 24–30.

Campos, N.F., and F. Coricelli (2002) "Growth in Transition: What We Know, What We Don't and What Should", *Journal of Economic Literature*, vol. XL (September), 793–836.

Cankao Xiaoxi (1996) "Reference News–Taiwan", October 16, p. 8, Beijing.

Carbon Dioxide Information Analysis Center (1990) *Trends '90*, Oak Ridge, TN: Oak Ridge National Laboratory.

CCPCC (1984) "Decision of the CCPCC Concerning the Reform of Economic Structure", Beijing: the Third Plenum of the 12th CCPCC, Beijing, October 21.

CCPCC Party School (ed.) (1988) *The Basic Plans for China's Economic Reform, 1979–87* (zhongguo jingji tizhi gaige guihuaji, 1979–87), Beijing: CCPCC Party School Press.

Chan, J. (2002) "Chinese Communist Party to Declare Itself Open to the Capital-ist Elite", available at: http://www.wsws.org/articles/2002/nov2002/chin-n13.shtml.

Chandra, N.K. (1999) "FDI and Domestic Economy: Neoliberalism in China", EPW Special Articles (www.epw.org.in/34-45/sa3.htm).

Chao, Y.R. (1970) *A Grammar of Spoken Chinese*, Berkeley, CA: University of California Press.

Chen, C. (1992) "Modernization in Mainland China", *American Journal of Economics and Sociology*, vol. 51(1), 57–68.

Chen, G. (1994) *China's Regional Economic Development: A Comparative Study of the East, Central, and West Belts* (zhongguo quyu jingji fazhan: dongbu zhongbu he xibu de bijiao yanjiu), Beijing: Beijing University of Technology Press.

Chen, L., Y. Yee, and R. Shu (1993) "A Study of the Feasibility of Opening the Indirect Commercial Funds Sent to the Mainland Area" (kaifang dui dalu diqu shangye xing jianjie huikuan kexing zhi yanjiu), Research Project prepared to the Mainland Commission, Taipei.

Chen, M. and Z. Cai (2000) *Groundwater Resources and the Related Environ-Hydrogeologic Problems in China* (in Chinese), Beijing: Seismological Press.

Chen, R. (1993) *The Craze of Xiahai* (xiahai kuangchao), Beijing: Tuanjie Chubanshe.

Chen, Y., Q. Cai, and H. Tang (2003) "Dust Storm as an Environmental Problem in North China", *Environmental Management*, vol. 33, 413–17.

Chen, Z. (1994) "An Analysis of the Industrial Development in the Third-front Area", in S. Liu, Q. Li, and T. Hsueh (eds), *Studies on China's Regional Economic Development* (zhongguo diqu jingji yanjiu), Beijing: China Statistics Publishing House, 1994, pp. 329–42.

Chen, Z. and F. Chen (2001) "Probing into Taiwan's Development in Democratic Elections from Its Political Characteristics", *Asian Studies* (Hong Kong), No. 41, 82–97.

Chenery, H. and M. Syrquin (1975) *Patterns of Development, 1950–1970*, published for the World Bank, New York: Oxford University Press.

Cheng, H. (1990) "A Brief Introduction to China's Natural Resources" (zhong-guo zhiran zhiyuan gaishu), in Commission of Integrated Survey on Natural Resources (ed.), *Handbook of Natural Resources in China* (zhongguo zhiran zhiyuan shouce), Chinese Academy of Sciences, Beijing: Science Press, 1990, pp. 1–20.

Cheng, Y.-S. (1996) "A Decomposition Analysis of Income Inequality of Chinese Rural Households", *China Economic Review*, vol. 7(2), 155–67.

Chi, F. (2000) "The WTO Accession and the Second Reform in China", *Business Management*, no. 11, 11–12.

China Daily, November 17 1993.

China Daily (2004) "Hey, You! Get Off of My Cloud", July 14, Beijing: China Daily.

China Enterprise Evaluation Center (1990) *China's Top 500 Enterprises*, published by *Management World* magazine for the Development Research Center of the State Council, Beijing.

China Meteorological Bureau (2002; 2004) *China Meteorological Report* (in Chinese), Beijing: China Meteorological Bureau.

China Youth, January 3 1995.

Chinese Academy of Sciences (1989) *Ecological Deficit: The Biggest Crisis of the Nation's Survival in the Future*, Beijing: Chinese Academy of Sciences, and State Science and Technology Commission.

Chinese Academy of Social Sciences (CASS) (1992) *China's Yearbook for Horizontal Economy* (zhongguo hengxiang jingji nianjian), Beijing: China Social Sciences Press.

CIA (2008) *World Factbook 2007*, Washington, DC: Central Intelligence Agency.

CISNR (ed.) (1990), *Handbook of Natural Resources in China* (zhongguo zhiran zhiyuan shouce), Commission of Integrated Survey on Natural Resources (CISNR) of Chinese Academy of Sciences, Beijing: Science Press.

Coase, R. (1992) "The Institutional Structure of Production", *American Economic Review*, vol. 82 (September), 713–19.

Combes, P.-P., M. Lafourcade, and T. Mayer (2005) "The Trade-Creating Effects of Business and Social Networks: Evidence from France", *Journal of International Economics*, vol. 66, no. 1, 1–29.

Commission of Economic Construction (1996) "The Opening of the Three Direct Links of the Special Economic and Trade Zones May Save US$700 million" (kaitong jingmao tequ santong, niansheng qiyi meiyuan), Taipei, *Central Daily*, October 14.

Corbet, H. (1996) "Issues in the Accession of China to the WTO System", *Journal of Northeast Asian Studies*, vol. 15(3).

Cremer, R.D. (1989) "The Industrialization of Macau", in Y.C. Jao, V. Mok, and L.S. Ho (eds), *Economic Development in Chinese Societies: Models and Experiences*, Hong Kong: Hong Kong University Press, 1989, pp. 18–32.

Crook, F.W. and X. Diao (2000) "Water Pressure in China: Growth Strains Resources", *Agricultural Outlook*, January–February, 25–9.

Cui, M. (2007; ed.), *China Energy Development Report – 2007*, Beijing: Social Sciences Literature Press, in Chinese.

Dasgupta, P. (1982) *The Control of Resources*, Oxford: Basil Blackwell.

Dasgupta, P, and Mäler, K.-G. (1995), "Poverty, Institutions, and the Environmental Resource-Base", in J. Behrman and T.N. Srinivasan (eds), *Handbook of Development Economics*, vol. III, Amsterdam: Elsevier Science BV, pp. 2331–463.

De Melo, M., C. Denizer, A. Gleb, and S. Tenev (1997) "Circumstances and Choice: the Role of Initial Condition and Politics in Transition Economies", *Policy Research Working Paper* No. 1866, Washington, DC: The World Bank.

Deardorff, A. (1997) "Determinants of Bilateral Trade: Does Gravity Work in a Classical World?", in J. Frankel (ed.), *The Regionalization of the World Economy*, Chicago: University of Chicago Press, pp. 110–30.

Deininger, K. and L. Squire (1998) "New Ways of Looking at Old Issues: Inequality and Growth", *Journal of Development Economics*, vol. 57, 259–87

Demurger, S. (2000) *Economic Opening and Growth in China*, Paris: OECD Development Center.

Demurger, S., J.D. Sachs, W.T. Woo, S. Bao, G. Cheng, and A. Mellinger (2002) "Geography, Economic Policy, and Regional Development in China", NBER Working Paper 8897.

Deng, X. (1992) "The Key Points of the Speeches in Wuchang, Shenzhen, Zhuhai, Shanghai, etc." (zai wuchang, shenzhen, zhuhai, shanghai deng di de jianghua yiaodian), in Literature Editing Committee of CCPCC (ed.), *Selected*

Works of Deng Xiaoping (Deng Xiaoping wenxue), Beijing: The People's Press, 1993, pp. 370–83.

Denniston, D. (1993) "Plunder Behind the Bamboo Curtain", *World Watch*, May–June, 9–36.

Denny, D.L. (1991) "Provincial Economic Differences Diminished in the Decade of Reform", in US Congress Joint Economic Committee (ed.), *China's Economic Dilemmas in the 1990s: the Problems of Reforms, Modernization, and Interdependence*, vol. 1, Washington DC: US Government Printing Office, pp. 186–208.

Dewatripont, M. and G. Roland (1992a) "Economic Reform and Dynamic Political Constraints", *Review of Economic Studies*, vol. 59, 703–30.

Dewatripont, M. and G. Roland (1992b) "The Virtues of Gradualism and Legitimacy in the Transition to a Market Economy", *Economic Journal*, vol. 102, 291–300.

Dewatripont, M. and G. Roland (1995) "The Design of Reform Packages under Uncertainty", *American Economic Review*, vol. 85, 1207–23.

Dittmer, L. and Y. Wu (1993) "The Political Economy of Reform Leadership in China: Macro and Micro Informal Politics Linkages", paper presented to the Annual Meeting of the Association of Asian Studies, Los Angeles.

Dodsworth, J. and D. Mihaljek (1997) "Hong Kong, China: Growth, Structural Change, and Economic Stability During the Transition', International Monetary Fund Occasional Paper No. 152, Washington, DC: IMF.

Dong, F. (1982) "Relationship between Accumulation and Consumption", in D. Xu *et al.* (eds), *China's Search for Economic Growth: The Chinese Economy Since 1949*, Beijing: New World Press, 1982, pp. 79–101.

Dong, F. (1992) "Some Comments on Analyses of Interregional income Gaps" (guanyu diqu jian shouru chaju biandong fenxi de jidian shangque yijian", *The Economic Research* (jingji yanjiu), no. 7, 63–4.

Dong, S. and C. Xu (1992) "Some Issues Relating to the Greater China Economic Cooperation" (da zhongguo jingji xiezuo de jige wenti), in Youths Committee of China Society of Natural Resources (ed.), *The Cross-Taiwan Strait: Sustainable Development of the Issues of Resources and Environment*, Beijing: China Science and Technology Press, 1992, pp. 10–13.

Donnithrone, A. (1976) "Centralization and Decentralization in China's Fiscal Management", *China Quarterly*, vol. 66, 328–54.

Du, P. (1994) *A Study of the Process of Population Aging in China* (zhongguo renkou laohua yanjiu), Beijing: The People's University of China Press.

Eaton, J., and A. Tamura (1994) "Bilateralism and Regionalism in Japanese and US Trade and Direct Foreign Investment Patterns", *Journal of the Japanese and International Economics*, vol. 8, 478–510.

Economic News, February 11 1987; December 21 1988.

EIA (2006) *International Energy Outlook 2006*, London: Economist Intelligence Agency.

Eichengreen, B., and D. Irwin (1995) "Trade Blocs, Currency Blocs and the Reorientation of Trade in the 1930s", *Journal of International Economics*, vol. 38(2), 89–106.

Eichera, T.S. and C. Garcia-Penalosab (2001) "Inequality and Growth: the Dual Role of Human Capital in Development", *Journal of Development Economics*, vol. 66, 173–97.

Fairbank, J.K. (1980) *The United States and China: Policies in Chinese–American Relations*, Cambridge, MA; Harvard University Press.

Fei, W. (1993) "Economic Analysis of China Economic Area" (dui zhongguo jingji quan de fenxi), *Asia-Pacific Economic Review*, no. 2, 54–9.

Feng, L. (1993) "On the 'Wars' over the Purchase of Farm and Subsidiary Products", *Chinese Economic Studies*, vol. 26, no. 5, 87–94.

Feng, Y. (1992) "The Trends of Asian–Pacific Regional Cooperation and the Formation and Development of the Chinese Economic Circle", in Youths Committee of China Society of Natural Resources (ed.), *The Cross-Taiwan Strait: Sustainable Development of the Issues of Resources and Environment*, Beijing: China Science and Technology Press, 1992, pp. 6–9.

Fewsmith, J. (1999) *China Since Tian'anmen: The Politics of Transition*, Cambridge: Cambridge University Press.

Fidrmuc, J. and A. G. Noury (2003) "Interest Groups, Stakeholders, and the Distribution of Benefits and Costs of Reform", Thematic Paper, Washington DC: GDN.

Financial Times, April 26 1993.

Fischer, S. and A. Gelb (1991) "The Process of Socialist Economic Transformation", *Journal of Economic Perspectives*, vol. 5, 91–105.

Food and Agricultural Organization (1987) *FAO Production Yearbook 1987*, Rome: FAO.

Forbes, K. (1997) "A Reassessment of the Relationship Between Inequality and Growth", Unpublished paper, MIT.

Foroutan, F., and L. Pritchett (1993) "Intra-Sub-Saharan African Trade: Is It Too Little?", *Journal of African Economics*, vol. 2 (May), 74–105.

Forrester, J.W. (1959) "Advertising: A Problem in Industrial Dynamics", *Harvard Business Review*, March–April, vol. 37(2), 100–10.

Frankel, J., and S. Wei (1995) "European Integration and the Regionalization of World Trade and Currencies: The Economics and the Politics", in B. Eichengreen, F. Frieden, and J. von Hagen (eds), *Monetary and Fiscal Policy in an Integrated Europe*, New York: Springer-Verlag.

Frankel, J., D. Romer, and T. Cyrus (1995) "Trade and Growth in East Asian Countries: Cause and Effect?" Pacific Basin Working Paper Series No. 95-03, San Francisco: Federal Reserve Bank of San Francisco.

Frankel, J., E. Stein, and S. Wei (1994) "Trading Blocs: The Natural, the Unnatural, and the Super-natural", Center for International and Development Economics Research (CIDER) Working Paper No. C94-034, University of California, Berkeley, April.

Frankel, J.A., E. Stein, and S.-J. Wei (1997a) *Regional Trading Blocs in the World Economic System*, Washington, DC: Institute for International Economics.

Frankel, J.A., E. Stein, and S.-J. Wei (1997b) "Trading Blocs and the Americas: The Natural, the Unnatural, and the Super-natural", *Journal of Development Economics*, vol. 47(1), 61–95.

Frankel, J.A., and D. Romer (1996) "Trade and Growth", NBER Working Paper No. 5476, Cambridge, MA: National Bureau of Economic Research.

Frydman, R. and A. Rapaczynski (1994) *Privatization in Eastern Europe: Is the State Withering Away?*, London: Central European University Press.

Fullen, M.A. and D.J. Mitchell (1994) "Desertification and Reclamation in North-Central China", *Ambio*, vol. 23(2), March, 131–5.

Garnaut, R. (1999) "Introduction", in R. Garnaut and L. Song (eds), *China: Twenty Years of Reform*, Canberra: Asia Pacific Press, pp. 1–20.

Garnaut, R. and Y. Huang (1995) "China and the Future International Trading Systems", in *China and East Asia Trade Policy*, Pacific Economic Papers, No. 250, Australia–Japan Research Center, Australian National University.

Ge, Y. (2000) "Probe into Countermeasures: A Path to Reducing the Unequal Distribution of Incomes" (duice yanjiu: huanjie shouru fenpei maodun de silu), Development and Research Center of the State Council, Beijing.

Gilley, B. (2004) "The 'End of Politics' in Beijing", *The China Journal*, no. 51, 115–35.

Goodman, D.S.G. (1994) "The Politics of Regionalism: Economic Development Conflicts and Negotiation", in D.S.G. Goodman and G. Segal (eds), *China Deconstructs: Politics, Trade, and Regionalism*, London and New York: Routledge, 1994, pp. 1–20.

Goodman, D.S.G. (1997) "China in Reform: The View from the Provinces", in D.S.G. Goodman (ed.), *China's Provinces in Reform – Class, Community and Political Culture*, London: Routledge.

Gottmann, J. (1973) *The Significance of Territory*, Charlottesville: University of Virginia Press.

Goulet, D. (1980; 1995) *Development Ethics: A Guide to Theory and Practice*, New York: Apex Press.

Greene, W.H. (2002) *Econometric Analysis*, 5th edn, Upper Saddle River, NJ: Prentice-Hall.

Groeneworld, N., A. Chen and G. Lee (2008) *Linkages between China's Regions: Measurement and Policy*, Cheltenham: Edward Elgar.

Grossman, G. M. and A.B. Krueger (1991), "Environmental Impacts of a North American Free Trade Agreement", *NBER Working Paper* No. 3914, Cambridge, MA: National Bureau for Economic Research (NBER).

Grossman, G. M. and A.B. Krueger (1995) "Economic Growth and the Environment", *Quarterly Journal of Economics*, vol. 110, 353–7.

Groves, T., Y. Hong, J. McMillan, and B. Naughton (1994) "Autonomy and Incentives in Chinese State Enterprises", *Quarterly Journal of Economics*, vol. 109(1), 183–209.

Gruver, G. W. (1976) "Optimal Investment in Pollution Control Capital in a Neoclassical Growth Context", *Journal of Environmental Economics and Management*, vol. 5, 165–77.

Gu, J. (1995) "Analyses on the Causes of Income Variable among Regions in China", Proceedings of the Fifth Annual Meeting of the Congress of Political Economists (COPE), International, Seoul, South Korea, January 5–10, pp. 45–51.

Guiso, L., P. Sapienza, and L. Zingales (2004) "Cultural Biases in Economic Exchange", NBER Working Paper Series 11005, Cambridge, MA: National Bureau of Economic Research, December.

Guo, F. and W. Wang (1988) *Poverty and Development* (pinkun yu fazhan), Hangzhou: Zhejiang People's Press.

Guo, R. (1991) "A Preliminary Study of Border-Regional Economics: Theory and Practice of China" (bianjie diqu jingji xue cutan: lilun yu zhongguo shijian), PhD thesis, CUMT.

Guo, R. (1993) *Economic Analysis of Border-Regions: Theory and Practice of China* (zhongguo shengji bianjie diqu jingji fazhan yanjiu), Beijing: China Ocean Press.

Guo, R. (1996) *Border-Regional Economics*, Berlin and New York: Springer.

Guo, R. (2004) "How Culture Influences Foreign Trade: Evidence from the US and China", *The Journal of Socio-Economics*, vol. 33, 785–812.

Guo, R. (2005) *Cross-Border Resource Management — Theory and Practice*, Amsterdam and Boston: Elsevier.

Guo, R. (2006) *Cultural Influences on Economic Analysis — Theory and Empirical Evidence*, London and New York: Palgrave Macmillan.

Guo, R. (2007) "Linguistic and Religious Influences on Foreign Trade: Evidence from East Asia", *Asian Economic Journal*, vol. 21(1), 101–21.

Guo, R., S. Li, and Y. Xing (2003) "Ownership Reform and Income Distribution in China's State-Owned Enterprises: The Case Study of Guangzheng and Chuangda" (zhongguo guoyou qiye gaizhi yu zhigong sgouru fenpei: guangzheng gongsi yu chuangda gongsi de anli yanjiu), *Management World*, No. 4, 103–11.

Guo, S. and W. Han (1991) *The Distribution and Utilization of China's GNP* (zhongguo GNP de fenpei he shiyong), Beijing: The People's University of China Press.

Gupta, D. (1990) *The Economics of Political Violence*, New York: Praeger.

Gustafsson, B. and S. Li (2000) "Economic Transformation in Urban China and the Gender Earnings Gap", *Journal of Population Economics*, July, vol. 13(2), 305–29.

Gustafsson, B. and S. Li (2001) "The Anatomy of Rising Earnings Inequality in Urban China", *Journal of Comparative Economics*, vol. 29(1), 118–35.

Gustafsson, B. and Z. Wei (2000) "How and Why Has Poverty in China Changed? A Study Based on Microdata for 1988 and 1995", *The China Quarterly*, no. 164, 983–1006.

Gustafsson, B., S. Li, and T. Sicular (eds) (2008) *Inequality and Public Policy in China*, Cambridge: Cambridge University Press.

Haggard, S. and S. Webb (1994) "What Do We Know About the Political Economy of Economic Policy Reform?", *The World Bank Research Observer*, vol. 8(2), 143–68.

Hammer, J.S. (1995) "Public Expenditure and Health Status in China", Policy Research Department, The World Bank, Washington, DC.

Havrylyshyn, O. and L. Pritchett (1991) "European Trade Patterns after the Transition", Policy, Research and External Affairs Working Paper Series No. 74, Washington, DC: World Bank.

He, B., R. Gu, Y. Yan, and Z. Bao (1991) *Studies on the Non-agricultural Development in Jiangsu"s Rural Area* (jiangsu nongcun feinonghua yanjiu), Shanghai: Shanghai People's Press.

He, J., Z. Zhu, and J. Liao (1960) "Criticizing Ma Yinchu's Reactionary 'New Population Theory'" (pipan Ma Yinchu fandong de "xin renkou lun"), *The Economic Research* (jingji janjiu), no. 4, 20–5.

Heckscher, E.F. (1919) "The Effect of Foreign Trade on the Distribution of Income", *Ekonomisk Tidskirift*, vol. 21, 497–512.

Helpman, E. (1987) "Imperfect Competition and International Trade: Evidence from Fourteen Industrial Countries", *Journal of the Japanese and International Economies*, vol. 1 (March), 62–81.

Heston, A., R. Summers, and B. Aten (2006) "Penn World Table Version 6.2", Center for International Comparisons of Production, Income and Prices at the University of Pennsylvania, September.

Hettige, H., M. Mani, and D. Wheeler (1997) "Industrial Pollution in Economic Development: Kuznets Revisited", Washington DC: Development Research Group, the World Bank, December.

Hibbs, D. (1973) *Mass Political Violence: A Cross-Sectional Analysis*, New York: Wiley.

Higgins, B. (1981) "Economic Development and Regional Disparities: A Comparative Study of Four Federations", in R.L. Mathews (ed.), *Regional Disparities and Economic Development*, Canberra: The Australian National University Press, pp. 69–70.

Hill, H. and A. Weidemann (1989) "Regional Development in Indonesia: Patterns and Issues", in H. Hill (ed.), *Unity and Diversity: Regional Economic Development in Indonesia Since 1970*, Singapore: Oxford University Press, 1989, pp. 1–7.

Hong, F. (1945a) "On the New Provincial Regions" (xin shengqu lun), *Dagong pao*, October 2.

Hong, F. (1945b) "Reconstruring Provincial Regions: A Preliminary Discussion" (chonghua shengqu fang'an chuyi), *Oriental Journal*, vol. 43(6).

Hsueh, T. (1994a) "A Synthesized Development Index System for China's Regions" (zhongguo diqu zhonghe fazhai zhibiao tixi), in S. Liu, Q. Li, and T. Hsueh (eds), *Studies on China's Regional Economic Development* (zhongguo diqu jingji yanjiu), Beijing: China Statistics Publishing House, pp. 22–56.

Hsueh, T. (1994b) "The Regional Economic Development Pattern in China and Its International Comparison" (zhongguo diqu jingji fazhan de xingtai, jianyu guoji jian de biaojiao), in S. Liu, Q. Li, and T. Hsueh (eds), *Studies on China's Regional Economic Development* (zhongguo diqu jingji yanjiu), Beijing: China Statistics Publishing House, 1994, pp. 74–99.

Hsueh, T., Q. Li and S. Liu (1993) *China's Provincial Statistics*, Boulder: Westview Press.

Hu, A. (2002) "Some Opinions Concerning the Employment Situation in China" (guanyu woguo jiuye wenti de ruogan kanfa), draft, available at www.cpric.org.cn.

Hu, A., S. Wang, and X. Kang (1995) *Regional Disparities in China* (zhonguo diqu chayi baogao), Shenyang: Liaoning People's Press.

Hu, H. (1991) "The Past, Present, and Future Administrative Divisions in China" (zhongguo xingzheng qu de guoqu, xianzai he weilai), in Chinese Society for Administrative Divisions (ed.), *Studies of China's Administrative Divisions* (zhonguo xingzheng quhua yanjiu), Beijing: China Social Press, 1991, pp. 144–67.

Hu, H. and J. Ding (1990) "The Past, Present, and Future of China's Administrative Divisions" (woguo xingzhengqu de guoqu, xianzhai he jianglai), *Journal of East China Normal University*, no. 2, 10–17.

Hu, X. (1993) "On the Typology and Organization of Economic Regions in China" (lun zhongguo jingjiqu de leixing yu zhuzhi), *ACTA Geographica Sinica*, vol. 48(3), 193–202.

Hu, X. and G. Yang (eds) (1990) *China's Coastal Port Cities* (zhongguo yanhai gangkou chengshi), Beijing: Science Press.

Hu, X., X. Shao, and F. Li (1988) *Chinese Economic Geography* (zhonguo jingji dili), Lixin Financial Economics Series, Shanghai: Lixin Accounting Books Press.

Hu, Y. (1992) "Guizhou Recovers its Broken Roads with the Neighbouring Provinces" (Guizhou yu linsheng xiutong duantou lu), *People's Daily*, September 20, p. 1.

Huang, W. (1996) *The Hidden Economy in China* (zhongguo de yinxing jingji), Beijing: China Commercial Press, the second edition.

Huang, Y. (1990) "Developing the Energy Industry and Protecting the Environment", International Conference on the Integration of the Economic Development and Environment in China, Hainan, China.

Huang, Y. (1999) "State-Owned Enterprise Reform", in R. Garnaut and L. Song (eds), *China: Twenty Years of Reform*, Canberra: Asia Pacific Press, pp. 95–116.

Huntington, S.P. (1996) *The Clash of Civilizations and the Remaking of the World Order*, New York: Simon & Schuster.

Hwang, E.-G. (1993) *The Korean Economies: A Comparison of North and South*, Oxford: Clarendon Press.

Hwang, Q. and W. Cheng (1994) *400 Years of the Macau Economy* (aomen jingji sibai nian), Macau: The Macau Foundation.

Hwang, Z. (1988) *The United States' 203 Years: An Analysis of the History and Future for the "American System"* (meiguo 203 nian: dui "meiguo tixi" de lishi yu weilai xue de fenxi), Hong Kong: Zhongliu Press.

Institute of Industrial Economics (1996) *China's Industrial Development Report* (zhongguo gongye fazhan baogao), Beijing: The Economics and Management Press.

International Labor Office (1993) *Statistical Yearbook*, Washington DC.

Jao, J.C. and C.K. Leung (eds) (1986) *China's Special Economic Zones: Policies, Problems and Prospects*, Oxford: Oxford University Press.

Jian, T. (1996) "The Disequilibrated of Regional Economic Development and the Reform of Fiscal System in China" (zhongguo quyu jingji bu pingheng fazhan yu shuizhi gaige), *Economic Highlights* (jingjixue xiaoxi bao), October 18, no. 198, p. 2.

Jian, T., J.D. Sachs, and A.M. Warner (1996) "Trends in Regional Inequality in China", *China Economic Review*, vol. 7(1), 1–22.

Jiang, Z. (1995) "Continue to Promote the Reunification of the Motherland", *China Daily*, February 2, pp. 1 and 2.

Jiang, Z. (1998) "Speech Commemorating the 20th Anniversary of the Party's Third Plenum of the 11th Party Congress", December 19, Beijing: the Great Hall of the People.

Jiang, Z. (2002) "Report to the 16th National Congress of the Communist Party of China", November 8, Beijing: the Great Hall of the People.

Jiao, J.J. and D. Wen (2004) "Perspectives on Chinese Ground Water Resources", *Ground Water*, vol. 42(4), 488–90.

Jin, G. and Q. Liu (1984), *Prosperity and Crises – On the Ultrstable Structure of the Federal System in China* (xingsheng yu weiji–lun zhongguo fengjian shehui de chao wending jiegou), Changsha: Hunan People's Press.

Jin, H., Y. Qian, and B.R. Weingast (2001) "Regional Decentralization and Fiscal Incentives: Federalism, Chinese Style", mimeo, Stanford University.

John, A. and R. Pecchenino (1992) "An Overlapping Generations Model of Growth and the Environment", mimeo, Department of Economics, Michigan State University, Ann Arbor, MI.

Jovanovic, B. and Y. Nyakro (1994) "The Bayesian Foundations of Learning by Doing", unpublished paper, New York University.

JPSB (1990) "Please Read the Results of An Investigation to Evaluate the Quality of Data for the Three Indices" (sanxiang zhibiao shuju zhiliang ruhe, qingkan diaocha pinggu jieguo), by Jilin Provincial Statistical Bureau, *China Statistics* (zhongguo tongji), no. 2, 27–8.

Kan, C.-Y. (1994) *The Emergency of the Golden Economic Triangle – Mainland China, Hong Kong and Taiwan*, Taipei: Lifework Press.

Kang, X. (2002) "An Analysis of Mainland China's Political Stability in the Coming 3–5 Years", *Strategy and Management* (in Chinese), No. 3, 1–15.

Kao, C. and E. Shong (1992) "A Positive Analysis of the Indirect Trade between the Two Sides of the Taiwan Strait via Third Areas", Chunghua Institution for Economic Research, Taipei, September.

Kaufmann, D., A. Kraay, and M. Mastruzzi (2008) "Governance Matters VII: Aggregate and Individual Governance Indicators, 1996–2007", *World Bank Policy Research Working Paper* No. 4654, Washington, DC: World Bank.

Keesing, D.B. (1966) "Labor Skills and Comparative Advantage", *American Economic Review*, vol. 56 (May), 249–58.

Keidel, A. (1995) "China's Regional Disparities", Washington, DC: World Bank.

Kenen, P. (1965) "Nature, Capital and Trade", *Journal of Political Economy*, vol. 73 (Oct.), 437–60.

Khan, A.R., K. Griffin, C. Riskin and R. Zhao (1993) "Household Income and its Distribution in China", in K. Griffin and R. Zhao (eds), *The Distribution of Income in China*, New York: St Martin's Press, 1993, pp. 25–73.

Khan, A.R. and C. Riskin (2001) *Inequality and Poverty in China in the Age of Globalization*, New York: Oxford University Press.

Khan, A.R., K. Griffin, and C. Riskin (2001) "Income Distribution in Urban China during the Period of Economic Reform and Globalization", in C. Riskin, R. Zhao, and Li Shi (eds), *China's Retreat from Equality: Income Distribution and Economic Transition*, New York: M.E. Sharpe, pp. 125–32.

Kim, K.-H. and E.S. Mills (1990) "Urbanization and Regional Development in Korea", in J.K. Kwon (ed.), *Korean Development*, New York: Green Press.

Knight, J. and L. Song (1993) "Why Urban Wages Differ in China", in K. Griffin and Zhao Renwei (eds), *The Distribution of Income in China*. London: Macmillan.

Knight, J. and S. Li (1993) "The Determinants of Educational Attainment in China", in K. Griffin and R. Zhao (eds), *The Distribution of Income in China*, New York: St Martin's Press, pp. 285–330.

Knight, J. and S. Li (1995) "Fiscal Decentralization, Redistribution and Reform in China", *Working Paper*, no. 168, Institute of Economics and Statistics, Oxford University.

Kolm, S.-C. (1976a) "Unequal Inequalities I", *Journal of Economic Theory*, vol. 12, 416–42.

Kolm, S.-C. (1976b) "Unequal Inequalities II", *Journal of Economic Theory*, vol. 13, 82–111.

Kolm, S.-C. (1977) "Multidimensional Equaliterianisms", *Quarterly Journal of Economics*, vol. 91, 1–13.

Kornai, J. (1992) *The Socialist System*, Princeton, NJ: Princeton University Press.

Kotlikoff, L. and J. Gokhale (1992) "Estimating a Firm's Age-Productivity Profile Using the Present Value of a Worker's Earnings", *Quarterly Journal of Economics*, vol. 107, 1215–42.

Kravis, I.B. (1956a) "Wages and Foreign Trade", *Review of Economics and Statistics*, vol. 38 (February), 14–30.

Kravis, I.B. (1956b) "Availability and Other Influences on the Commodity Composition of Trade", *Journal of Political Economy*, vol. 73 (April), 143–55.

Krugman, P.R. (1995) "Growing World Trade: Causes and Consequences", *Brookings Papers on Economic Activity*, no. 1, 327–62.

Kuznets, S. (1955) "Economic Growth and Income Inequality", *American Economic Review*, vol. 45, 1–28.

Lai, D. (1999), "Education, Labor and Income Distribution" (jiaoyu, laodongli yu shouru fenpei), in Zhao *et al.* (eds, 1999), pp. 451–74.

Lam, W.W. (1999) *The Era of Jiang Zemin*, Singapore: Prentice-Hall.

Landes, D. (1966) "Technological Change and Development in Western Europe, 1750–1914", in H. Habakkuk and M. Posten (eds), *The Cambridge Economic History of Europe*, vol. VI, Cambridge: Cambridge University Press.

Lardy, N.R. (1975) "Centralization and Decentralization in China's Fiscal Management", *China Quarterly*, vol. 61, 25–60.

Lardy, N.R. (1978) *Economic Growth and Income Distribution in the People's Republic of China*, New York: Cambridge University Press.

Lardy, N.R. (1980) "Regional Growth and Income Distribution in China", in R.F. Denberger (ed.), *China's Development Experience in Comparative Perspective*, Cambridge: Harvard University Press.

Lau, L., Y. Qian, and G. Roland (2000) "Reform without Losers: An Interpretation of China's Dual-Track Approach to Reforms", *Journal of Political Economy*, vol. 108, 120–63.

Leamer, E.E. (1980) "The Leontef Paradox Reconsidered", *Journal of Political Economy*, vol. 88 (June), 495–503.

Leamer, E.E. (1984) *Sources for International Comparative Advantage*, Cambridge, MA: The MIT Press.

Leamer, E.E. (1993) "Factor-Supply Differences as a Source of Comparative Advantage", *American Economic Review*, vol. 83 (May), 436–44.

Lee, F. (1995) "The Development of the Cross-Taiwan Strait Trade Relations: Present Situation, Issues, and Measures", *Taiwan Studies*, no. 2.

Lemione, F. (2000) *FDI and the Opening Up of China's Economy*, Paris: Centre d'Etudes Prospectives et d'Informations Internationales (CEP II).

Lenssen, N. (1993) "All the Coal in China", *World Watch*, March–April, 22–30.

Leontief, W. (1954) "Domestic Production and Foreign Trade: The American Capital Position Re-examined", *Economia Internationale*, February, 2–32.

Leontief, W. (1956) "Factor Proportions and the Structure of American Trade; Further Theoretical and Empirical Analysis", *Review of Economics and Statistics*, vol. 38 (November), 386–407.

Leung, C.K. (1980) *China: Railway Patterns and National Goals*, Department of Geography, The University of Chicago, Research Paper no. 195.

Lewis, R.D. (2003) *The Cultural Imperative*, Yarmounth, ME: Intercultural Press.

Li, D. (1998) "Changing Incentives of the Chinese Bureaucracy", *American Economic Review*, vol. 88(2), 393–7.

Li, H. and H. Zou (1998) "Income Inequality is not Harmful for Growth: Theory and Evidence", *Review of Development Economics*, vol. 2, 318–34.

Li, J. and M. Fan (1994) "A Comparison of the Regional Structures for the Economic Development in China During Pre- and Post-reform Periods" (gaige kaifang qianhou zhongguo jingji fazhan quyu jiegou de bijiao), in S. Liu, Q. Li, and T. Hsueh (eds), *Studies on China's Regional Economic Development* (zhongguo diqu jingji yanjiu), Beijing: China Statistics Publishing House, pp. 57–73.

Li, N. (1997) "Pearl River Delta Heading Towards Modernization", *Beijing Review*, vol. 40(4), 12–13.

Li, S. (2004) "China's Urban and Rural Income Surveys", *Journal of Financial Economics* (caijing zazhi), no. 3.

Li, S. and W. Li (1994) "Estimating the Ratios of Return to Investment in Education in China" (zhongguo jiaoyu touzi de geren shouyilv de guji), in Zhao *et al.* (eds, 1999), pp. 442–56.

Li, S. and F. Zhai (2000) "Access to the WTO and Its Influences on the Chinese Economy" (jiaru shijie maoyi zuzhi dui zhongguo jingji de yingxiang), *Yuce* (forecasting), no. 3, 12–21.

Li, S., R. Zhao, and P. Zhang (1997) "The Changes of China's Income Distribution during the Transition", Dissertation for the International Workshop, Institute of Economics, Chinese Academy of Social Sciences, Beijing, August.

Li, S., Z. Wu, and C. Wu (1994) "A Quantitative Analysis of the Inter-Regional Linkages in China" (zhongguo quji lianxi de shuliang fenxi), in Development Research Center of the State Council (ed.), *The Regional Coordinate Development Strategy in China* (zhonguo quyu xietiao fazhan zhanlue), Beijing: China Economy Press, 1994, pp. 139–75.

Li, W. (1997) "The Impact of the Chinese Reform on the Performance of Chinese State-Owned Enterprises, 1980–89", *Journal of Political Economy*, vol. 105, 1080–106.

Li, X., W. Zhang, and J. Zhong (1989) "Set-up the Wage System Oriented at Improving Efficiency" (jianli yi tigao xiaolu wei daoxiang de gongzhi zhidu), *The Economic Research*, no. 2, 34–40.

Li, Y. (1996) "Taiwan to Enhance the 'South-Oriented Policy' and Enlarge the Investment Area" (Taiwan kuoda "nanxia zhengce" touzi fanwei), *International Trade News*, 16 May, p. 2.

Li, Z. (1988) "Influences, Disadvantages and Suggestions", in P. Zhang (ed.), *Studies in the Economic Relations between Hunan and Guangdong Provinces*, Changsha: Hunan People's Press, in Chinese.

Li, Z. (1993) "In-Depth Exploration of the Question of Regional Blockades", *Chinese Economic Studies*, vol. 26, no. 5, 23–36.

Liang, W. (1982) "Balanced Development of Industry and Agriculture", in D. Xu *et al.* (eds), *China's Search for Economic Growth: The Chinese Economy Since 1949*, Beijing: New World Press, 1982, pp. 152–78.

Liang, Z. (1978) "The Political Corruption and Social Uprisings in the Late Qing Dynasty: A Quantitative Analysis" (wanqing zhi zhengzhi yu shehui shaoluan), *Journal of the Research Institute for Chinese Culture*, vol. 9, Chinese University of Hong Kong.

Liao, J. (1982) "Size of Industrial Enterprises Operation and Choice of Technology", in D.Xu *et al.* (eds), *China's Search for Economic Growth: The Chinese Economy Since 1949*, Beijing: New World Press, 1982, pp. 130–44.

Liew, L. (1999) "The Impact of the Asian Financial Crisis on China: the Macro-economy and State-Owned Enterprise Reform", *International Management Review*, vol. 39(4), 85–104.

Liew, L. (2000) "China's Economic Reform Experience: the End of a Pareto-Improving Strategy", *China Information*, vol. 14(2), 129–68.

Liew, L., L. Bruszt, and L. He (2003) "Causes, National Costs, and Timing of Reform", Thematic Paper, Washington DC: GDN.

Lin, C. (1995) "The Reform of State-owned Enterprises in China", unpublished draft, University of Oxford, Oxford.

Lin, F. and J. Liu (1996) "Towards the 21st Century: the Regional Disparities of China's Population" (maixiang 21 shiji: zhongguo renkou de diqu chayi), *Population Studies* (renkou yanjiu), no. 2, 10–14.

Lin, J. (1992) "Rural Reforms and Agricultural Growth in China", *American Economic Review*, vol. 82, 34–51.

Linder, S.B. (1961) *An Essay on Trade and Transformation*, New York: John Wiley and Sons.

Ling, Y., F. Xu and J. Chen (1995) "Be Attention to the Overstatement Wind!" (jingti! fukua feng), *Economic Tribune* (jingji luntan), no. 7, 18–19.

Linnemann, H. (1966) *An Econometric Study of International Trade Theory*, Amsterdam: North-Holland.

Lipton, D. and J. Sachs (1990) "Creating a Market Economy in Eastern Europe: The Case of Poland", *Brookings Papers on Economic Activity*, vol. 1, 75–133.

Litwack, J. and Y. Qian (1998) "Balanced or Unbalanced Development: Special Economic Zones as Catalysts for Transition", *Journal of Comparative Economics*, vol. 26, 117–41.

Liu, B. and J. Liao (eds) (1993) *China's Frontier Opening and the Neighbouring Countries* (zhongguo yanian kaifang yu zhoubian guojia shichang), Beijing: The Legal Press.

Liu, G. (1984) *A Study of China's Economic Development Strategy Issues* (zhonguo jingji fazhan zhanlue wenti yanjiu), Shanghai: Shanghai People's Press.

Liu, G. (1994) "China's Regional Economic Development Strategy – An Evaluation and Prospect" (zhongguo diqu jingji fazhan zhanlue de pinggu yu zhaiwang), in S. Liu, Q. Li, and T. Hsueh (eds), *Studies on China's Regional Economic Development* (zhongguo diqu jingji yanjiu), Beijing: China Statistics Publishing House, 1994, pp. 1–13.

Liu, G. (2004) "A Legal Blank Results from the Competition of Rainmaking by Five Cities and Prefectures in Henan province" (in Chinese), *Dahe Bao* (The Big River News), July 12, Zhengzhou, Henan Province, also cited by *China Daily* (2004).

Liu, J. (1996) *China's Administrative Divisions: Theory and Practice* (zhongguo xingzheng quhua de lilun yu shijian), Shanghai: East China Normal University Press.

Liu, S. (1982) "Economic Planning", in D. Xu *et al.* (eds), *China's Search for Economic Growth: The Chinese Economy Since 1949*, Beijing: New World Press, pp. 28–51.

Liu, S., Y. Gong, Q. Li, and Y. Wu (1994) "The Regional Income Disparity in China: Measurement, Analysis, and Policy Suggestions" (zhongguo ge diqu shouru chayi de jishuan, fenxi yu zhengze jianyi), in S. Liu, Q. Li, and T. Hsueh (eds), *Studies on China's Regional Economic Development* (zhongguo diqu jingji yanjiu), Beijing: China Statistics Publishing House, 1994, pp. 142–3.

Liu, T. (1995) "Changes to China's Economic System Structure" (zhongguo jingji tizhi jiegou de yanbain), *Management World*, no. 3, 51–6.

Liu, Z. (1983) "On the Construction of the Third-front Area" (lun shanxian jianshe), Department of Planning and Statistics, The People's University of China, Beijing.

Liu, Z. (1994) "The Overall Production Allocation and the Regional Coordinate Development" (zhongti shengchanli peizhi he quyu xietiao fazhan), in Development Research Center of the State Council (ed.), *The Regional Coordinate Development Strategy in China* (zhonguo quyu xietiao fazhan zhanlue), Beijing: China Economy Press, pp. 15–63.

Liu, Z. (1998) "Earnings, Education, and Economic Reform in Urban China", *Economic Development and Cultural Change*, vol. 46(4), 697–725.

Lo, C. (2004) "Bank Reform: How Much Time Does China Have?", *The China Business Review*, available at: http://www.chinabusinessreview.com/public/0403/chilo.html.

Lucas, R.E.B., D. Wheeler, and H. Hettige (1992) "Economic Development, Environmental Regulation and International Migration of Toxic Industrial Pollution: 1960–1988", in P. Low (ed.), *International Trade and the Environment*, Washington, DC: the World Bank, pp. 67–86.

Lyons, T. (1992) "Interprovincial Disparities in China: Output and Consumption, 1952–1957", *Economic Development and Cultural Change*, vol. 39, 471–506.

Ma, H. and S. Sun (eds) (1981) *A Study of the Economic Structure of China – Part 2* (zhongguo jingji jiegou yanjiu, xia), Beijing: The People's Press.

Ma, L. (2008), "A 'Happiness Curve' is Drawn by Ten Pieces of Pay-notes" (shizhang gongzitiao huichu shenghuo "xingfu quxian"), *Changping Weekly*, September 2, p. 5 (in Chinese).

Maasoumi, E. (1986) "The Measurement and Decomposition of Multidimensional Inequality", *Econometrica*, vol. 54, 771–9.

Machin, S. (1996) "Wage Inequality in the UK", *Oxford Review of Economic Policy*, vol. 12, 47–64.

Maddison, A. (1996) *A Retrospect for the 200 Years of the World Economy, 1820–1992*, Paris: OECD Development Center.

Maddison, A. (2001) *The World Economy: A Millennial Perspective*, Paris: OECD Development Center.

Magrath, W. and P. Arens (1989) "The Costs of Soil Erosion in Java: A Natural Resource Accounting approach", World Bank Environmental Department Working Paper no. 18.

Mäler, K.-G. (1974) *Environmental Economics: A Theoretical Enquiry*, Baltimore: Johns Hopkins University Press.

Mansfield, E., and R. Bronson (1997) "The Political Economy of Major-Power Trade Flows", in Edward Mansfield and Helen Milner (eds), *The Political Economy of Regionalism*, New York: Columbia University Press.

Mao, Z. (1949) "The Bankrupt of the Idealist Conception of History", in *Selected Works of Mao Tse-tung*, vol. IV, Beijing: Foreign Languages Press, 1975, pp. 451–9.

Mao, Z. (1956) "On the Ten Major Relations", in *Selected Works of Mao Tse-tung*, vol. V, Beijing: Foreign Languages Press, 1975.

Mao, Z. (1957) "Be Activists in Promoting the Revolution", in *Selected Works of Mao Tse-tung*, vol. V, Beijing: Foreign Languages Press, 1975, pp. 483–97.

Marea, P. (1985) *Dollar GNPs of the USSR and Eastern Europe*, Baltimore: Johns Hopkins University Press.

Markusen, J. (1986) "Explaining the Volume of Trade: An Eclectic Approach", *American Economic Review*, vol. 76 (Dec.), 1002–11.

Maruyama, N. (1982) "The Mechanism of China's Industrial Development: Background to the Shift in Development Strategy", *The Developing Economies*, vol. 20, 437–71.

Massahiko, A. and Y. Qian (eds) (1995) *Corporation Management Structure in the Transitional Economy*, Beijing: China Economics Press.

Mastel, G. (1996) "Beijing at Bay", *Foreign Policy*, vol. 104(Fall), 27–34.

Mastel, G. (1998) "The WTO and Nonmarket Economies", *The Washington Quarterly*, vol. 21(3), 5–9.

MCI (1997) "Several Opinions Concerning the Developments of Shareholding and Partnership Enterprises in the Coal Industry", Beijing: Minstry of Coal Industry (MCI), Meibanzi No. 245.

McKinnon, R. (1991a) "Financial Control in the Transition from Classical Socialism to a Market Economy", *Journal of Economic Perspectives* vol. 5, 107–22.

McKinnon, R. (1991b) *The Order of Economic Liberalization*, Baltimore: John Hopkins University Press.

McMillan, J. and B. Naughton (1992) "How to Reform a Planned Economy: Lessons from China", *Oxford Review of Economic Policy*, vol. 8, 130–43.

Meadows, D.H., D.I. Meadows, and J. Randers (1972) *Limits to Growth: A Report of the Club of Rome's Project on the Predicament of Mankind*, Rome: the Club of Rome.

Meadows, D.H., D.I. Meadows and J. Randers (1992) *Beyond the Limits: Confronting Global Collapse, Envisioning a Sustainable Future*, Post Hills, VT: Chelsea Green Publishing Company.

Minami, R. (1994) *The Economic Development of China: A Comparison with the Japanese Experience*, English edition, London: The Macmillan Press.

Ministry of Energy (1991) *Energy in China*, Beijing: Ministry of Energy.

Mizoguchi, T., H. Wang, and Y. Matsuda (1989) "A Comparison of Real Consumption Level Between Japan and the People's Republic of China: The First Approach to the Application of the ICP Method to Chinese Data", *Hitotsubashi Journal of Economics*, June.

Montinola, G., Y. Qian and B. Weingast (1995) "Federalism, Chinese Style: the Political Basis for Economic Success in China", *World Politics*, vol. 48, 50–81.

Morici, P. (1997) "Barring Entry? China and the WTO", *Current History*, September, vol. 96, 274–7.

Murphy, K., A. Shleifer, and R. Vishny (1992) "The Transition to a Market Economy: Pitfalls of Partial Reform", *Quarterly Journal of Economics*, vol. 107, 889–906.

Murrell, P. (1992) "Evolution in Economics and in the Economic Reform of the Centrally Planned Economies", in C. Clague and G. Raisser (eds), *The Emergence of Market Economies in Eastern Europe*, Cambridge: Blackwell, pp. 35–53.

Nair, K.R.G. (1985) "Inter-State Income Differentials in India, 1970–71 to 1979–80", in G.P. Mishra (ed.), *Regional Structure of Development and Growth in India*, New Delhi: Ashish Publishing House.

Naughton, B. (1988) "The Third Front: Defense Industrialization in the Chinese Interior", *China Quarterly*, vol. 115, 227–304.

Naughton, B. (2007) *The Chinese Economy: Transitions and Growth*, Cambridge, MA: The MIT Press.

NBS (various years) *China Statistical Yearbook*, various issues, Beijing: China Statistics Publishing House.

NEAA (2007) "China Now No. 1 in CO_2 Emissions; USA in Second Position", Netherlands Environmental Assessment Agency (NEAA), available at www.mnp.nl.

NEPA (various years) *Report on the State of the Environment*, Beijing: National Environment Protection Agency.

Newcombe, K. (1984) "An Economic Justification of Rural Afforestation: The Case of Ethiopia", Energy Department Paper no. 16, World Bank, Washington, DC.

Nolan, P. and J. Sender (1992) "Death Rates, Life Expectancy and China's Economic Reforms: A Critique of A. A. Sen", *World Development*, vol. 20, 1279–303.

Noland, M. (1994) "Implications of Asian Growth", Washington: Institute for International Economics, mimeo.

Noland, M. (1995) "The United States and APEC", in W.S. Kee, I.-T. Hyun and K. Kim (eds), *APEC and A New Pacific Community: Issues and Prospects*, Seoul: The Sejong Institute, pp. 69–99.

Noland, M. (2005) "Affinity and International Trade", Institute for International Economics, Washington DC, Working Paper Series No. WP 05–3, June.

North, D. (1997) "The Contribution of the New Institutional Economics to an Understanding of the Transition Problem", *WIDER Annual Lectures*, March.

North, D.C. (1981) *Structure and Change in Economic History*, New York: Norton.

North, D.C. (1990) *Institutions, Institutional Change and Economic Performance*, Cambridge: Cambridge University Press.

North, D.C. and R.P. Thomas (1973) *The Rise of the Western World*, Cambridge: Cambridge University Press.

NPC (1979) "Law of the People's Republic of China on the Joint Ventures with Chinese and Foreign Investment" (zhonghua renmin gongheguo zhongwai hezi qiye fa), Beijing: National People's Congress of China.

NPC (1980) "The Regulations Concerning the Special Economic Zones of Guangdong Province, the People's Republic of China" (zhonghua renmin gongheguo guangdong sheng jingji tequ de youguan tiaoli), Beijing: National People's Congress of China, August 26.

NPC (1993) "Anti-unfair Competition Law" (fan bu zhengdang jingzhen fa), Beijing: National People's Congress of China.

NPC (1994) "Law of Protecting the Taiwanese Compatriots' Investment" (baohu Taiwan tongbao tuzhi fa), Beijing: National People's Congress of China, March.

NPC (1997) "Criminal Law of the People's Republic of China", amended version, Beijing: Fifth Session of the Eighth National People's Congress, March 14.

NPC (2000) "Meteorological Law of the People's Republic of China", Beijing: the 12th Meeting of the Standing Committee of the Ninth National People's Congress of the People's Republic of China, October 31.

OECD (2000) "Main Developments and Impacts of Foreign Direct Investment on China's Economy", Directorate for Financial, Fiscal and Enterprise Affairs Working Papers on International Investment, No. 2000/4, Paris: OECD, December.

Oguledo, V., and C. MacPhee (1994) "Gravity Models: A Reformulation and an Application to Discriminatory Trade Arrangement", *Applied Economics*, vol. 26, 107–20.

Ohlin, B. (1933) *Interregional and International Trade*, Cambridge, MA: Harvard University Press.

Oi, J. (1992) "Fiscal Reform and the Economic Foundations of Local State Corporatism in China", *World Politics*, vol. 45 (Oct.), 99–129.

Oksenberg, M. and J. Tong (1991) "The Evolution of Central–Provincial Fiscal Relations in China, 1971–1984: the Formal System", *The China Quarterly*, March, 1–32.

Ottolenghi, D. and A. Steinherr (1993) "Yugoslavia: Was It A Winner's Curse?", *Economies of Transition*, vol. 1(2), 209–43.

Oxford Advanced Learner's Dictionary, 1974, 3rd edn, Oxford: Oxford University Press.

Pai Shing Semimonthly, March 1 1986.

Pan, G. (2006) "Synergy of East and West for Greater Creativity" (paper in both Chinese and in English), The Tan Kah Kee Young People's Invention Award Committee, Singapore, September 25.

Pearce, D., E. Barbier and A. Markandya (1988) "Sustainable Development and Cost–Benefit Analysis", Paper Presented at the Canadian Assessment Workshop on Integrating Economic and Environment Chinese Economic Sustainability Assessment.

People's Daily (1992) "On Regional Economy" (lun quyu jingji) (editorial), November 5, Beijing.

People's Daily (2004) "A Reflection on the Competition of Rainmaking by Five Cities and Prefectures" (in Chinese), Beijing: People's Daily, July 22, p. 16.

People's Daily, January 18 1995.

People's Daily, November 26 1989, Beijing.

Perlack, R.D., M. Russell and Z. Shen (1993) "Reducing Greenhouse Gas Emissions in China: International Legal and Cultural Constraints and Opportunities", *Global Environmental Change*, March.

Perotti, R. (1993) "Political Equilibrium, Income Distribution and Growth", *Review of Economic Studies*, vol. 60, 755–76.

Perotti, R. (1996) "Growth, Income Distribution, and Democracy: What the Data Say", *Journal of Economic Growth*, vol. 1, 149–87.

Persson, T. and G. Tabellini (1994) "Is Inequality Harmful for Growth? Theory and Evidence", *American Economic Review*, vol. 84, 600–21.

Portes, R. (1990) "Introduction to Economic Transformation of Hungary and Poland", *European Economy*, vol. 43, 11–18.

Pöyhönen, P. (1963) "A Tentative Model for the Volume of Trade Between Countries", *Weltwirtschaftliches Archiv*, vol. 90(1), 93–9.

Prendergast, C. (1999) "The Provision of Incentives in Firms", *Journal of Economic Literature*, vol. XXXVII (March), 7–63.

Price Yearbook of China, 1995, Beijing: China Price Press.

Qian, W. and Y. Zhu (2001) "Climate Change in China from 1880 to 1998 and its Impact on the Environmental Condition", *Climate Change*, vol. 50, 419–44.

Qian, Y. (2002) "How Reform Worked in China", draft, also in D. Rodrik (ed.), *In Search of Prosperity: Analytic Narratives on Economic Growth*, Princeton, NJ: Princeton University Press, 2007, pp. 297–333.

Qian, Z. and G. Zhang (2001) "Comprehensive Report on the Sustainable Development of China's Water Resources", *Research Report on Sustainable Development on China's Water Resources*, vol. 1, 3–32.

Qu, G. (1990) "Thoughts about the Policies for the Coordinated Development of China's Economy and Environment", presented at the International Conference on the Integration of Economic Development and Environment in China, Beijing, September, pp. 1–15.

Quah, D. (2002) "One Third of the World's Growth and Inequality", LSE Economics Department, CEPR Discussion Paper 2002:3316.

Ramsey, S.R. (1989) *The Languages of China*, Princeton, NJ: Princeton University Press.

Rauch, J.E. (1999) "Networks versus Markets in International Trade", *Journal of International Economics*, vol. 48, 7–35.

Rauch, J.E. (2001) "Business and Social Networks in International Trade", *Journal of Economic Literature*, vol. 39(4), 1177–203.

Rauch, J.E. and V. Trindade (2002) "Ethnic Chinese Networks in International Trade", *Review of Economics and Statistics*, vol. 84(1), 116–30.

Ravallion, M. (1998) "Does Aggregation Hide the Harmful Effects of Inequality on Growth?", *Economics Letters*, vol. 61, 73–7.

Ravallion, M. (2001) "Growth, Inequality and Poverty: Looking beyond Averages", *World Development*, vol. 29, 173–97

Repetto, R., W. Magrath, M. Well, C. Beer, and F. Rossini. (1989) Wasting Assets: Natural Resources and the National Income Accounts, Washington, DC: World Resources Institute.

Reti, P. (2001) "China's Path toward a Market Economy: Interview with a Prominent Reformer", *Transition Newsletter*, Oct.–Nov.–Dec., 17–19.

Riskin, C. (1987) *China's Political Economy: The Quest for Development Since 1949*, Oxford: Oxford University Press.

Riskin, C. (1994) "The Distribution of Income and Poverty in Rural China" (zhonguo nongchun de shouru fenpei yu pingkun), in R. Zhao and K. Griffin (eds), *The Household Income Distribution in China* (zhongguo de jumin shouru fenpei), Beijing: China Social Science Press, pp. 313–51.

Riskin, C., R. Zhao and Li Shi (eds) (2001) *China's Retreat from Equality: Income Distribution and Economic Transition*, New York: M.E. Sharpe.

Rock, M.T. (1996) "Pollution Intensity of GDP and Trade Policy: Can the World Bank Be Wrong?", *World Development*, vol. 24, 471–9.

Rodrik, D. (1996) "Understanding Economic Policy Reform", *Journal of Economic Literature*, vol. XXXIV (March), 9–41.

Roland, G. (1991) "Political Economy of Sequencing Tactics in the Transition Period", in L. Csaba (ed.), *Systemic Change and Stabilization in Eastern Europe*, Aldershot: Dartmouth, pp. 47–64.

Rose, A.K. (2004) "Macroeconomic Determinants of International Trade", NBER working paper, Cambridge, MA: National Bureau of Economic Research.

Russell, M. (1990) "Energy in China", presented at the International Conference on the Integration of "China", *Ambio*, vol. 21(4), 303–7.

Ryan, B. F. and W. D. King (1997) "A Critical Review of the Australian Experience in Cloud Seeding", *Bulletin of the American Meteorological Society*, vol. 78, 239–54.

Sachs, J. (1993) *Poland's Jump to the Market Economy*, Lionel Robbins Lectures, London: MIT Press.

Sachs, J. and A. Warner (1995) "Economic Reform and the Process of Global Integration", *Brookings Papers on Economic Activity*, no. 1, 1–95.

Sachs, J. and W.T. Woo (1994) "Structural Factors in the Economic Reforms of China, Eastern Europe, and the Former Soviet Union", *Economic Policy*, vol. 18(1), 102–45.

Salvatore, D. and R. Barazesh (1990) "The Factor Content of US Foreign Trade and the Heckscher-Ohlin Theory", *International Trade Journal*, vol. 16(Winter), 149–81.

Samuelson, P.A. (1948) "International Trade and the Equalization of Factor Prices", *The Economic Journal*, vol. 58 (June), 165–84.

Samuelson, P.A. (1949) "International Factor-Price Equalization Once Again", *The Economic Journal*, vol. 59 (June), 181–97.

Savoie, D.J. (1992) *Regional Economic Development: Canada's Search for Solution*, 2nd edition, Toronto: University of Toronto Press

Schulz, T.W. (1961) "Investment in Human Capital", *American Economic Review*, vol. 51 (March), 213–26.

SCSR (1996) "The Environment of Changes in the Role of the Government in China: Analysis of a Survey", in State Commission of System Reform (ed.), *Chinese Economic Almanac 1996*, Beijing: China Statistical Press.

Segal, G. (1994) "China's Changing Shape", *Foreign Affairs*, vol. 73, 40–65.

Selden, T. and D. Song (1994) "Environmental Quality and Development: Is There a Kuznets Curve for Air Pollution Emissions?", *Journal of Environmental Economics and Management*, vol. 27, 147–62.

Seldon, T. and D. Song (1995) "Neoclassical Growth, the J Curve for Abatement, and the Inverted U Curve for Pollution", *Journal of Environmental Economics and Management*, vol. 29, 162–8.

Sen, A. (1992) "Life and Death in China", *World Development*, vol. 20(9), 1305–12.

Sen, A. (2004) "Remarks at the Inaugural Meeting of the GDN Conference on Understanding Reform", Global Development Conference, New Delhi, January 27.

Shafik, N. (1994) "Economic Development and Environmental Quality: An Economic Analysis", *Oxford Economic Papers*, vol. 46, 757–73.

Shafik, N., and S. Bandyopadhyay (1992) "Economic Growth and Environmental Quality: Time-Series and Cross-Section Evidence", Discussion Paper No. 158, Woodrow Wilson School, Princeton University, Princeton, NJ, USA.

Sheehy, D.P. (1992) "A Perspective on Desertification of Grazingland Ecosystems in North China", *Ambio*, vol. 21, 303–7.

Shen, L. and Y. Dai (1990) "Chinese Federal Economy: Mechanisms, Impacts, and Sources" (zhongguo de zhuhou jingji: jizhi, houguo he genyuan), *Jingji Yanjiu* (Economic Research Journal), no. 3, 10–13.

Shirk, S. (1990) "The Political Price of Reform Cycles: Elite Politics in Chinese-Style Economic Reforms", manuscript.

Shirk, S. (1993) *The Political Logic of Economic Reform in China*, Berkeley, CA: University of California Press.

Shirk, S. (1994) *How China Opened Its Door*, Washington, DC: Brookings Institution.

Shorrocks, A. (1980) "The Class of Additionally Decomposable Inequality Measures", *Econometrica*, vol. 48, 613–25.

Shorrocks, A. and J.E. Foster (1987) "Transfer Sensitive Inequality Measure", *Review of Economic Studies*, vol. 54, 485–97.

Si, T. (2008) "Coal Efficiency Set to Get Boost", *China Daily*, November 3 (Monday), p. 2.

Sigurdson, J. *et al.* (2005) *Technological Superpower China*, Cheltenham, UK: Edward Elgar.

Simon, J.L. (1981) *The Ultimate Resource*, Princeton, NJ: Princeton University Press.

Sloman, J. (1991) *Economics*, Hemel Hempstead: Harvester Wheatsheaf.

Smith, A.H. (1890) (1972), *Chinese Characteristics*, 5th edn, Shaunow, Ireland: Irish University Press.

Smith, D.M. (1987) *Geography, Inequality and Society*, Cambridge: Cambridge University Press.

Solow, R.M. (1991) "Sustainability – An Economist's Perspective", Department of Economics, Massachusetts Institute of Technology, Cambridge, MA.

Song, X. (1996) "China's Regional Economic Development and Its Convergence", *The Economic Research*, no. 9, 38–44.

South China Morning Post (2004) "Soldiers Could Shoot at Clouds to End Drought", Hong Kong: *South China Morning Post*, July.

SPC (1996) *China Price* (zhonguo wujia), Institute of Market and Prices, State Planning Commission, Beijing, January.

SSB (1987b) *Materials of the 1985 Industry Census in the People's Republic of China* (zhonghua renmin gonghe guo 1985 nian gongye pucha zhiliao), Beijing: China Statistics Publishing House.

SSB (1988b) *China Population Statistical Yearbook* (zhongguo renkou nianjian), Beijing: China Statistics Publishing House.

SSB (1989b) *China Yearbook for Price Statistics* (zhongguo jiage tongji nianjian), Beijing: China Statistics Publishing House.

SSB (1990b) *A Compilation of Historical Statistical Materials of China's Provinces, Autonomous Regions and Municipalities (1949–89)* (quanguo ge sheng, zhiziqu, zhixiashi lishi tongji zhiliao huibian 1949–1989), Beijing: China Statistics Publishing House.

SSB (1991b) *China Energy Statistical Yearbook* (zhongguo nengyuan tongji nian-jian), Beijing: China Statistics Publishing House.

SSB (1991c) *Some Statistical Materials of Social Development for the Major Countries and Regions 1990* (shijie zhuyao guojia he diqu shehui fazhan bijiao tongji zhiliao 1990), Beijing: China Statistics Publishing House.

SSB (1993b) *China Population Yearbook* (zhongguo renkou nianjian), Beijing: China Statistics Publishing House.

SSB (1994b) *The 1993 Abstracts of International Economic and Social Statistics* (guoji jingji he shehui tongji tiyao 1993), Beijing: China Statistics Publishing House.

SSB (1996b) *China Industrial Economic Statistical Yearbook 1995*, Beijing: China Statistics Publishing House.

SSB (1997) *Historical Data on China's Gross Domestic Product 1952–1995*, Dalian: Publishing House of Northeast China University of Finance and Economics, in Chinese.

SSB (various years) *China Statistical Yearbook*, various issues, Beijing: China Statistics Publishing House.

State Council (1980a) "Provisional Regulations Relating to the Development and Protection of Socialist Competition" (guanyu fazhan yu baohu shehui zhuyi jingzheng de zhanxing tiaoli), Beijing: State Council.

State Council (1980b) "Provisional Regulations Concerning the Promotion of Economic Unification", Beijing: State Council.

State Council (1981) "Regulations of the P. R. China Concerning the Resolutions of the Disputes on Borders of the Administrative Divisions" (zhonghua renmin gongheguo xingzhengqu bianjie zhengyi culi tiaoli), Beijing: State Council.

State Council (1982) "Notice Relating to the Prohibition of Blockades in the Sale of Industrial Products" (guanyu jinzhi gongye chanpin xiaoshou bilei de tongzhi), Beijing: State Council.

State Council (1984) "Provisional Regulations on the Enlargement of Autonomy of State Industrial Enterprises", May 10, Beijing: State Council.

State Council (1986) "Regulations on Some Issues Concerning the Further Promotion of Horizontal Economic Unification", Beijing: State Council, March 26.

State Council (1988a) "A Retrospect on the Reforms of the Economic System and the Prospects on the Basic Thought of the Future Reforms" (jingji tizhi gaige de huigu yu jinhou gaige de jiben shilu), in CCPCC Party School (ed.), *The Basic Plans for China's Economic Reform, 1979–87*, Beijing: the CCPCC Party School Press.

State Council (1988b) "Regulations of the P. R. China Concerning the Resolutions of the Disputes on Borders of the Administrative Divisions", Beijing: State Council, revised version.

State Council (1990) "An Administrative Order to Remove all Regional Blockades to Trade", Beijing: State Council.

State Council (1992) "Regulations on the Transformation of the Operating Mechanisms of State-owned Industrial Enterprises", Beijing: State Council, July 22.

State Council (1993) "Resolution Concerning the Promotion of the Development of the TVEs in the Central and Western Area", Beijing: State Council, December.

State Council (1996) "Decision of the State Council on Several Issues Relating to Environmental Protection", August 3, Beijing: State Council.

State Council (2002) "Regulations Concerning the Artificial Weather Modification", Rule of the State Council of the People's Republic of China, No. 248, March 19, Beijing: State Council.

State Council Information Office (1996) "On Sino-US Trade Balance", *Beijing Review*, vol. 40(14), 20–7.

State Economic and Trade Commission (1994) "China Energy Annual Review" (zhongguo nengyuan nianping), Department of Resources Conservation & Comprehensive Utilization, State Economic and Trade Commission, People's Republic of China.

State Economic and Trade Commission (1996) "China Energy Annual Review" (zhongguo nengyuan nianping), Department of Resources Conservation & Comprehensive Utilization, State Economic and Trade Commission and China Energy Society, Beijing.

State Industrial and Commercial Administration (1995) *A Compilation of Industrial and Commercial Statistics* (gongshang xingzheng guanli tongji huibian), Beijing: State Industrial and Commercial Administration.

State Science and Technology Commission (1988) *Guide to China's Science and Technology Policy* (zhongguo kexue jishu zhengce zhinan), Beijing: Science and Technology Compilation Press.

354 *Bibliography*

33ff

Statistical Division of Hong Kong Government (various exports) *Re-exports by All Countries of Origin by Importing Countries by Items.*

Stern, R.M. and K.E. Maskus (1981): "Determinants of the Structure of US Foreign Trade", *Journal of International Economics*, vol. 24, 207–24.

Stewart, J.Q. (1948) "Demographic Gravitation: Evidence and Applications", *Sociometry*, vol. 2, 31–58.

Stiglitz, J.E. (1999) "Whither Reform? – Ten Years of Transition", Keynote Address to the World Bank Annual Bank Conference on Development Economics, Washington, DC: World Bank.

Streifel, S. (2006) "Impact of China and India on Global Commodity Markets: Focus on Metals and Minerals and Petroleum", draft, Development Prospects Group, World Bank, Washington DC.

Study Group of CASS (1994) "Theoretical Thinking and Policy Choice on Chinese Economy Towards the 21st Century" (zhongguo jingji jinru 21 shiji de lilun shikao yu zhengce xuanzhe), *Economic Research Journal* (jingji yanjiu), no. 8, 1–14.

Summers, L. (1992) "The Rise of China", *Transition Newsletter*, vol. 3(6), Washington, DC: The World Bank.

Summers, R. and A. Heston (1991) "The Penn World Table (Mark 5): An Expended Set of International Comparisons, 1950–1988", *Quarterly Journal of Economics*, vol. 106(2), 327–68.

Sun, G., S.G. MacNulty, J. Moore, C. Bunch, and J. Ni (2002) "Potential Impacts of Climate Change on Rainfall Erosivity and Water Availability in China in the Next 100 Years", the 12th International Soil Conservation Conference, Beijing, China, May.

Sun, J. (1987) *Territory, Resources, and Regional Development* (guotu, zhiyuan kaifa he quyu fazhan), Beijing: People"s Education Press.

Sun, Z. (1993) "Causes of Trade Wars over Farm Products, Their Effects, and Suggested Solutions", *Chinese Economic Studies*, vol. 26(5), 95–104.

Sung, Y.-W. (2004) *Greater China: An Emerging Economic Reality*, New York: Palgrave Macmillan.

Svejnar, J. (1989) "A Framework for the Economic Transformation of Czechoslovakia", *Planning Economic Report*, vol. 5, 1–18.

Tang, T. (1982) "The Economic Responsibility System and Accounting in China's Enterprises", *Caiwu Yu Kuaiji* (property and accounting), January, 7–11.

Tang, W. and W. Parish (1998) *The Changing Social Contract: Chinese Urban Life Under Reform*, New York: Cambridge University Press.

Teng, W. (1982) "Socialist Modernization and the Pattern of Foreign Trade", in D. Xu *et al.* (eds), *China's Search for Economic Growth: The Chinese Economy Since 1949*, Beijing: New World Press, 1982, pp. 167–92.

The Economic Research Materials, no. 6, 1996, p. 62, in Chinese.

The Economist, various issues.

Tinbergen, J. (1962) "An Analysis of World Trade Flows, the Linder Hypothesis, and Exchange Risk", in Jan Tinbergen (ed.), *Shaping the World Economy*, New York: The Twentieth Century Fund.

Topping, A.R. (1995) "Ecological Roulette: Damming the Yangtze", *Foreign Affairs*, September/October, 132–46.

Toshiyuki, M., H. Wang, and Y. Matsuda (1989) "A Comparison of Real Consumption Level Between Japan and the People's Republic of China: The First

Approach to the Application of the ICP Method to Chinese Data", *Hitotsubashi Journal of Economics*, June.

Tsui, K. (1991) "China's Regional Inequality, 1952–1985", *Journal of Comparative Economics*, vol. 15, 1–21.

Tsui, K. (1993) "Economic Reform and Interprovincial Inequalities in China", *Working paper* no. 31, Economics Department, the Chinese University of Hong Kong, Hong Kong.

Tsui, K. (1994) "A Multiregional Measurement of China's Inequalities", in S. Liu, Q. Li, and T. Hsueh (eds), *Studies on China's Regional Economic Development* (zhongguo diqu jingji yanjiu), Beijing: China Statistics Publishing House, 1994, pp. 180–98.

UNDP (1994) *China Environment and Sustainable Development Resources Book: A Compendium of Donor Activities*, Beijing: UNDP, April.

UNDP (2005) *Human Development Report 2005: International Cooperation at a Crossroad*, New York: Oxford University Press.

UNDP and CDRF (2005) *China Human Development Report 2005*, Beijing: UNDP and China Development Research Foundation (CDRF).

UNESCO (various years) *Statistical Yearbook*, Paris: UNESCO.

UNFAO (1992) *Statistical Yearbook*, Rome: United Nations Food and Agriculture Organization (UNFAO).

United Nations (1988) *World Population Prospect*, New York: United Nations.

United Nations (1990a) *SNA Handbook on Integrated Environmental and Economic Accounting*, Part I ("General Concept"), New York: United Nations.

United Nations (1990b) *Revised System of National Accounts*, New York: United Nations.

UNPD (2007) *World Population Prospects: The 2006 Revised Population Data Sheet*, New York: United Nations Population Division (UNPD).

US Academy of Defense Agency (1993) "US Arm Control and Disarmament", Washington, DC: US Academy of Defense Agency.

Utah Water Research Laboratory (UWRL) (1971) "Development of Cold Cloud Seeding Technology for Use in Precipitation Management", Logon: Utah State University, available at: www.encyclopedia.com/html/r1/rainmaki.asp.

Vaclav, S. (1992) "China's Environment in the 1980s: Some Critical Changes", *Ambio*, vol. 21, no. 6, 431–6.

Venieris, Y. and D. Gupta (1986) "Income Distribution and Sociopolitical Instability as Determinants of Savings: A Cross-Sectional Model", *Journal of Political Economy*, vol. 94, 873–83.

Vermeer, E.B. (1984) "Agriculture in China – A Deteriorating Situation", *The Ecologist*, vol. 14, no. 1, 6–14.

Wakabayashi, K. (1989) *China's Population Problem*, Tokyo: University of Tokyo Press (in Japanese).

Wan, G., M. Lu, and C. Zhao (2004) "Globalization and Regional Income Inequality Evidence from within China", Discussion Paper No. 2004/10, UNU World Institute for Development Economics Research (UNU-WIDER), Helsinki, Finland, November.

Wang, J. and J. Li (1996), "China's Energy Development Strategy for the First Half of the 21st Century" (21 shiji qian banye zhongguo de nengyuan fazhan zhanlue), The Research of the Chinese Economic Development Strategy for the First Half of the 21st Century, Report Series no. 8,

Institute of Industrial and Tech-Economics, State Planning Commission (SPC), Beijing.

Wang, Q. (1995) "A Study of the Energy Strategy in China" (zhongguo nengyuan zhanlue yanjiu), Beijing: Academy of Coal Science and Ministry of Coal Industry.

Wang, S. (2003) "China's Public Health Care: Crisis and Transitions" (zhongguo gonggong weisheng de weiji yu zhuanji), *Comparative Analysis* (Bijiao), vol. 4, 52–88.

Wang, X. (2000) "Sustainability of China's Economic Growth and Institutional Changes", *Economic Research Journal*, no. 7, 1–12 (in Chinese).

Wang, Z. and Y. Dai (1958) "A Critique on the 'New Population theory" ("xin renkou lun" pipan), *The Economic Research* (jingji yanjiu), no. 2, 10–14.

Washington Post (2004) "Chinese Rainmakers Competing for Clouds: Widespread Drought Leads to Regional Rivalries" (by Edward Cody), Foreign Service, August 2, p. A12.

Watts, J. (2005) "Satellite Data Reveals Beijing as Air Pollution Capital of World", *The Guardian*, October 31, available at www.guardian.co.uk/news/2005/oct/31/china.pollution.

Weber, M. (1904; 1930) *The Protestant Ethic and the Spirit of Capitalism*, London: Allen & Unwin.

Wedeman, A.H. (1993) "Editor's Introduction to Chinese Economic Studies", *Chinese Economic Studies*, vol. 26, no. 5 (special issue on regional protection), 1–2.

Wei, H. (1992) "On the Changing Pattern of The Interregional Income Gaps in China" (lun woguo quji shouru chaju de biandong geju), *The Economic Research* (jingji yanjiu), no. 4, 61–5.

Wei, H. and K. Liu (1994) "The Analysis of the Regional Differences in China and the Forecast of Their Changing Trends" (woguo diqu chayi biandong qushi fenxi ji yuce), *China Industrial Economic Research*, no. 3, 29–36.

Wei, S. (1993) "Gradualism vs. Big Bang: Speed and Sustainability of Reforms", mimeo, Harvard University, Cambridge, MA.

Wei, S. (1994) "Comrade Deng Xiaoping"s Concept of 'One country, two systems" and its Practice", *Foreign Affairs Journal*, no. 33, September, 1–7.

Wei, S. and J. Frankel (1994) "A 'Greater China' Trade Block?", *China Economic Review*, vol. 5, no. 2, 179–90.

Wei, S., and Y. Wu (2003) "Globalization and Inequality: Evidence from Within China", NBER Working Paper No. 8611, Cambridge, MA: NBER.

Weingast, B.R. (1995) "The Economic Role of Political Institutions: Market-Preserving Federalism and Economic Growth", *Journal of Law, Economics, and Organization*, vol. 11, 1–31.

Wen, Y. (1987) "The Prospects of the Asia-Pacific Area and the Chinese Circle: An Interview with Chen Kunyao, Director of Asian Studies Center of Hong Kong University" (yatai diqu jingji qianjing he zhongguo: fang xianggang daxue yazhou yanjiu zhongxin zhuren Chen Kunyao), *Economic Review*, November 30.

Williamson, J. (1965) "Regional Inequality and the Process of National Development: A Description of the Patterns", *Economic Development and Cultural Change*, vol. 13(4), 165–204.

Williamson, J. (1994) "In Search of a Manual for Technopols", in J. Williamson (ed.), *The Political Economy of Policy Reform*, Washington DC: Institute for International Economics.

Williamson, J. (1995) "What Washington Means by Policy Reform", *The International Political Economy and the Developing Countries*, vol. 1, 514–28.

Winters, L.A. and S. Yusuf (2007) "Introduction: Dancing with Giants", in Winters and Yusuf (eds), *Dancing with Giants: China, India, and the Global Economy*, Washington, DC: World Bank Publications, pp. 1–34.

Wolf, T. (1985) "Exchange Rates, Foreign Trade Accounting and Purchasing Power Parity for Centrally Planned Economies", World Bank Staff Working Papers, no. 779.

Wong, C. (1992) "Fiscal Reform and Local Industrialization", *Modern China*, vol. 18 (April), 23–42.

Woo, W. (1994) "The Art of Reforming Centrally Planned Economies: Comparing China, Poland and Russia", *Journal of Comparative Economics*, vol. 21, 276–308.

Woo, W.-T. (1998) "Chinese Economic Growth: Sources and Prospects" (zhongguo quan yaosu shengchan lv: laizi nongye bumen laodongli aai peizhi de shouyao zuoyong), *Jingji Yanjiu*, vol. 3, 16–23.

World Bank (1981) *China: Development of a Socialist Economy* (zhonguo: shehui zhuyi jingji de fazhan), Beijing: World Bank.

World Bank (1983) *China: The Development of a Socialist Economy*, Washington DC: World Bank.

World Bank (1990) *China: Revenue Mobilization and Tax Policy*, Washington DC: World Bank.

World Bank (1992) *World Bank Development Report 1992*, New York: Oxford University Press.

World Bank (1996) *From Plan to Market: World Bank Development Report 1996*, New York: Oxford University Press.

World Bank (2008) *Doing Business in China 2008*, Beijing: Social Sciences Literature Press.

World Commission for Environment and Development (1987) *Our Common Future*, New York: Oxford University Press.

World Resources Institute (1985) *Tropical Forests – A Call for Action*, International Task Force Report convened by the World Resources Institute, the World Bank, and the United Nations Development Program, Washington, DC.

World Resources Institute (1992) *World Resources 1992–93*, Oxford: Oxford University Press.

World Resources Institute (2003) *Water Resources and Freshwater Ecosystems*, Washington, DC: World Resources Institute, available at: http://earthtrend.wri.org.

Wright, T. (1984) *Coal Mining in China's Economy and Society 1895–1937*, Cambridge: Cambridge University Press.

Wu, C. and F. Hou (1990) *Territorial Development and Planning* (guotu kaifa ahengzi yu guihua), Nanjing: Jiangsu Educational Press.

Wu, J. (2005) *Understanding and Interpreting Chinese Economic Reform*, Mason, OH: Thomson South-Western.

Wu, J. and R. Zhao (1987) "The Dual Pricing System in China's Industry", *Journal of Comparative Economics*, vol. 11(3), 309–18.

Wu, J. (2000) "Saving, Investment and Economic Growth", in X. Wang and G. Fan (eds), *Sustainability of China's Economic Growth*, Beijing: Economic Science Press.

Wu, R. and Y. Liang (1990) "Hong Kong – The First Financial and Trade Center in the Far East" (yuandong diyi jinrong maoyi zhongxin–xianggang), in N. Hu and R. Yang (eds), *Studies of the Disequilibrated Development Issues in the Chinese Economy* (zhongguo jingji feijunheng fazhan wenti yanjiu), Taiyuan: The United Press of Shanxi Universities, 1994, pp. 234–44.

Wu, R.-I. (1996) "Importance of Integrating China and Taiwan into the WTO System", *Journal of Northeast Asian Studies*, vol. 15(3).

Wu, Y. (2004) *China's Economic Growth: A Miracle with Chinese Characteristics*, London: Routledge Curzon.

Xiao, L. (1993) "China's Economic Internationalization: A Prospect", unpublished draft, Institute of American Studies, Chinese Academy of Social Sciences.

Xie, H. (1992) "The Industrial Development in Macau", in Youths Committee of China Society of Natural Resources (ed.), *The Cross-Taiwan Strait: Sustainable Development of the Issues of Resources and Environment*, Beijing: China Science and Technology Press, 1992, pp. 110–16.

Xu, D. (1995) "China: Contradictory Measures Frustrate Bank Reform", *Economic Reform Today* (Banking and Financial Reform), No. 1, Center for International Private Enterprise, Washington, http://www.cipe.org/publications/fs/ert/e15/china.htm.

Xu, L.C. and H.-F. Zou (2000) "Explaining the Changes of Income Distribution in China", *China Economic Review*, vol. 11, 149–70.

Xu, X. (2004) "China's Gross Domestic Product Estimation", *Chinese Economic Review*, vol. 15(3), 302–22.

Yang, D. (1990) "Patterns of China's Regional Development Strategy", *The China Quarterly*, no. 122, 230–57.

Yang, K. (1989) *A Study of Regional Development in China* (zhongguo quyu fazhan yanjiu), Beijing: China Ocean Press.

Yang, K. (1991) "The Theory and Application of Regional Structure – An Application of the Regional Structure in China" (quyu jiegou lilun yu yingyong – zhongguo quyu jiegou yanjiu), in S. Sun (ed.), *The Economic Structure: Theory, Application and Policy* (jingji jiegou de lilun, xingyong yu zhengce), Beijing: China Social Science Press.

Yang, K. (1993) *For a Spatial Integration: China's Market Economy and Regional Development Strategy* (maixiang kongjian yiti hua: zhongguo shichang jingji yu quyu fazhan zhanlue), "Across the Century Series", Chengdu: Sichuan People"s Press.

Yang, S. (1990) "The Issues of China's Economic Regions" (zhongguo jingji quyu wenti), in S. Yang, Liu Zhenya and Gao Lianqing (eds), *Studies of Chinese Economic Regionalization* (zhongguo jingji quhua yanjiu), Beijing: China Zhanwang Press, pp. 38–43.

Yang, W. (1989) *The Locational Principles – An Economic Analysis of Industrial, Urban, and Regional Locations* (quweilun yuanli: chanye, chengshi he quwei de jingji fenxi), Lanzhou: Gansu People's Press.

Yang, W. (1992a) "An Empirical Analysis of the Changes in Interregional Income Inequalities" (Diqu jian shouru chaju biandong de shizheng fenxi), *The Economic Research* (jingji yanjiu), no. 1, 70–4.

Yang, W. (1992b) "Answers to Comrade Dong Fan's Comments" (dui dong Fan tongzhi shangque de dafu), *The Economic Research* (jingji yanjiu), no. 7, 65–6.

Yang, X. (1992) "The Resource Exploitation and Economic Development in the Greater China Economic Circle" (da zhonguo jingji quan de ziyuan yu jingji fazhan), in Youth Committee of China Society of Natural Resources (ed.), *The Cross-Taiwan Strait: Sustainable Development of the Issues of Resources and Environment*, Beijing: China Science and Technology Press, 1992, pp. 1–5.

Yao, S. and Z. Zhang (2001a) "Regional Growth in China under Economic Reforms", *Journal of Development Economics*, vol. 38, 16–46.

Yao, S. and Z. Zhang (2001b) "On Regional Inequality and Divergence Clubs: A Case Study of Contemporary China", *Journal of Comparative Economics*, vol. 29, 466–84.

Yin, X. (1998) *The Procedure and Effects of China's Reform of International Trade* (in Chinese). Shanxi: Shanxi Economic Publishing House.

Young, A. (2000) "The Razor's Edge: Distortions and Incremental Reform in the People''s Republic of China", *Quarterly Journal of Economics*, vol. 115(4), 1091–136.

Young, J.C. and H.H. Ho (1993) "China Moves Against Unfair Competition", *East Asian Executive Report*, September.

Yu, J. (2004) "Why We Don't Believe Economists", *Sohu Online Paper* (in Chinese), September 15, available at: http://culture.news.sohu.com/20040915/n222055879.shtml.

Zhang, L. (1982) "A Review of the Discussions on Two Production Theories" (liangzhong shengchan lilun de taolun zhongshu), *Population Studies* (renkou yanjiu), no. 5, 12–14.

Zhang, P. (1994) "The Peasant Income Distribution among Rural Areas" (nongchun jian de shouru fenpei), in R. Zhao and K. Griffin (eds), *The Household Income Distribution in China* (zhongguo de jumin shouru fenpei), Beijing: China Social Science Press, pp. 296–312.

Zhang, W. (1990) "Reform Well China's Administrative Division for the Continuous Peace and Stability of the Nation" (chong guojia changzhi jiu"an chufa, gaohao xingzheng qu hua de gaige), *Journal of East China Normal University*, no. 2, 1–9.

Zhang, Z., A. Liu and S. Yao (2001) "Convergence of China's Regional Incomes, 1952–1997", *China Economic Review*, vol. 12(2/3), 243–58.

Zhao, J. and J. Tang (2002) "Explaining Growth: The Case of China", draft, Global Development Network (GDN), New Delhi.

Zhao, R. (1990) "Two Contrasting Phenomena in China's Income Distribution", *Cambridge Journal of Economics*, vol. 14, 345–9.

Zhao, R. (1993) "Three Features of the Distribution of Income during the Transition to Reform", in K. Griffin and R. Zhao (eds), *The Distribution of Income in China*, New York: St Martin's Press, 1993, pp. 74–94.

Zhao, R. (1998) "Professor Gu Zhun's Academic Career and Emotional Experience", draft, CASS, Beijing.

Zhao, R. (1999) "Review of Economic Reform in China: Features, Experiences and Challenges", in R. Garnaut and L. Song (eds), *China: Twenty Years of Reform*, Canberra: Asia Pacific Press, pp. 185–200.

Zhao, R. (2001) "Increasing Income Inequality and Its Causes in China", in C. Riskin, R. Zhao and Li Shi (eds), *China's Retreat from Equality: Income Distribution and Economic Transition*, New York: M.E. Sharpe, pp. 25–43.

Zhao, Y. (2001) 'Earnings Differentials between State and Non-State Enterprises in Urban China, Working paper series No. E2001001, Peking University, Beijing, China.

Zheng, J. (1996) "How Large is China's Per Capita GDP in US Dollars?" (zhongguo de renjun GDP wei duoshao meiyuan), *Economic Highlights* (jingjixue xiaoxi bao), September 13, no. 193, p. 1.

Zheng, Z. (1988) "A Framework of the Greater China Community" (da zhonghua gongtong ti shichang de gouxiang), *Economic Review*, June 13.

Zhou, B (1989) "The Chinese Community and Southeast China Free Trade Zone" (zhongguo ren gongtongti hua dongnan zhiyou maoyi qu), *Economic Review*, November 6.

Zhou, F. (1994) "Measuring the Interregional Inequalities in Terms of Single Index and Multiple Indices" (zhuhe zhibiao he danyi zhibiao de diqu jian bu ping-dengxing chedu), in S. Liu, Q. Li, and T. Hsueh (eds), *Studies on China's Regional Economic Development* (zhongguo diqu jingji yanjiu), Beijing: China Statistics Publishing House, 1994, pp. 193–200.

Zhou, J. (1992) "To Establish the Greater China Economic Area between Hong Kong, Macau, Taiwan and Mainland China: A Basic Framework" (zhongguo dalu yu gang ao tai goujian da zhonghua jingji quan de jiben gouxiang), in Youths Committee of China Society of Natural Resources (ed.), *The Cross-Taiwan Strait: Sustainable Development of the Issues of Resources and Environment*, Beijing: China Science and Technology Press, 1992, pp. 18–21.

Zhu, W. (1990) "A Brief Introduction to China's Mineral Resources" (zhongguo kuangchan zhiyuan gaishu), in CISNR (ed.), *Handbook of Natural Resources in China* (zhongguo zhiran zhiyuan shouce), Commission of Integrated Survey on Natural Resources (CISNR) of Chinese Academy of Sciences, Beijing: Science Press, pp. 627–36.

Zhuravskaya, E.V. (2000) "Incentives to Provide Local Public Goods: Fiscal Federalism, Russian Style", *Journal of Public Economics*, vol. 76(3), 337–68.

Zichuan Annuals (1990), compiled by the Office of Annuals of the government of Zichuan district, Shandong province.

Zipf, G.K. (1946) "The P^1P^2/D Hypothesis: On the Intercity Movement of Persons", *American Sociological Review*, vol. 11(6), 677–86.

Index